DISEASES OF THE HEAD

Before you start to read this book, take this moment to think about making a donation to punctum books, an independent non-profit press,

@ https://punctumbooks.com/support/

If you're reading the e-book, you can click on the image below to go directly to our donations site. Any amount, no matter the size, is appreciated and will help us to keep our ship of fools afloat. Contributions from dedicated readers will also help us to keep our commons open and to cultivate new work that can't find a welcoming port elsewhere. Our adventure is not possible without your support.

Vive la Open Access.

Fig. 1. Hieronymus Bosch, *Ship of Fools* (1490–1500)

DISEASES OF THE HEAD: ESSAYS ON THE HORRORS OF SPECULATIVE PHILOSOPHY. Copyright © 2020 by the editors and authors. This work carries a Creative Commons BY-NC-SA 4.0 International license, which means that you are free to copy and redistribute the material in any medium or format, and you may also remix, transform and build upon the material, as long as you clearly attribute the work to the authors (but not in a way that suggests the authors or punctum books endorses you and your work), you do not use this work for commercial gain in any form whatsoever, and that for any remixing and transformation, you distribute your rebuild under the same license. http://creativecommons.org/licenses/by-nc-sa/4.0/

First published in 2020 by punctum books, Earth, Milky Way.
https://punctumbooks.com

ISBN-13: 978-1-953035-10-3 (print)
ISBN-13: 978-1-953035-11-0 (ePDF)

DOI: 10.21983/P3.0280.1.00

LCCN: 2020945732
Library of Congress Cataloging Data is available from the Library of Congress

Copy editing: Lily Brewer
Book Design: Vincent W.J. van Gerven Oei

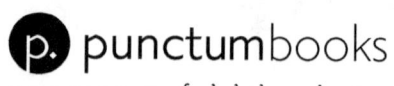

spontaneous acts of scholarly combustion

HIC SVNT MONSTRA

DISEASES OF THE HEAD

ESSAYS ON THE HORRORS OF SPECULATIVE PHILOSOPHY

Edited by Matt Rosen

Contents

Introduction: On the Diseases of the Head • 13
Matt Rosen

◆ ◆ ◆

Outgrown Purpose, Outlived Use: On Parasitic Teleology • 43
Ben Woodard

Death of Horror • 71
Amanda Beech

Those Who Aren't Counted • 113
Matt Rosen

Horror of the Real: H.P. Lovecraft's Old Ones
and Contemporary Speculative Philosophy • 163
David Peak

Triangulorum • 181
Sara Rich

Race and Its Far-Reaching Contemporary Ontological and
Epistemological Implications • 197
Marina Gržinić and Jovita Pristovšek

Absolute Xenogenesis: Speculations on
an Unnatural History of Life • 237
Eckardt Lindner

Survival Strategies for Weird Times • 277
Helen Marshall

Matrix Pavoris: Material Dislocation in *House of Leaves* • 315
Luka Bekavac

Encountering Weird Objects: Lovecraft, LARP,
and Speculative Philosophy • 361
Chloé Germaine Buckley

Sublime Horror in the Tales of E.T.A. Hoffmann • 395
Hamad Al-Rayes

When the Monstrous Object Becomes a Tremendous Non-Event: Rudolf Otto's Monster-Gods, H.P. Lovecraft's Cthulhu, and Graham Harman's Theory of Everything • 439
Eric Wilson

Reproducing It: Speculative Horror and
the Limits of the Inhuman • 483
John Cunningham

Horror Vacui (*"That Nothing Is What There Is"*) • 499
Julia Hölzl

◆ ◆ ◆

Contributors • 513

Acknowledgments

Any anthology contains a little infinity: of work and labor, of time and energy, and of thanks. I'm well aware that I can't hope to convey, in just a few words, appreciation adequate to the debt owed to all those who've helped me while this book came together. But I hope that those to whom I'm so very grateful can take these acknowledgements as a gesture toward an indebtedness that runs deeper than words.

First of all, to the contributors who worked tirelessly to see this volume come into being: Hamad Al-Rayes, Amanda Beech, Luka Bekavac, Chloé Germaine Buckley, John Cunningham, Marina Gržinić, Julia Hölzl, Eckardt Lindner, Helen Marshall, David Peak, Jovita Pristovšek, Sara Rich, Eric Wilson, and Ben Woodard. Each of you has lent this collection something singular, a distinct take on the philosophy to come; and each of you kindly tolerated my many questions and suggestions. It has been such a pleasure to work with you. To Vincent W.J. van Gerven Oei, our vigilant and ever encouraging editor. To Eileen A. Joy, for providing us with a very bright light. To Lily Brewer, for your careful attention, without which this book would be considerably harder to read. And to everyone at punctum books, for your effort and support during the inevitably protracted process through which a book comes to be.

Second, to the faculty and students of the philosophy department at Colorado College. You have given me the gift of a place where it's possible to ask how we ought to live and what we should make of the world with straightforward sincerity, a place where such questions seem always urgent. In particular, I owe much to Marion Hourdequin, who has taught me from the start that philosophical inquiry and compassion are mixed up with each other. To Jonathan Lee, for your Socratic lucidity and generosity. And to John Riker, for many profound insights. I am also indebted to others who, in discussion or correspondence, have helped me to think about some of the questions raised by this book: Taylor Adkins, Max Chiaramonte, Tom Crowther, Rick Furtak, Graham Harman, Michael Kim, Chet Lisiecki, Anton Rieselbach, and Natalie TeSelle.

Third, to those who have endured countless hours of my relentless conversation, who have shared with me joy and hardship and everything in between. To Anna Gaw, for your indomitable kindness and unflinching integrity. To Greg Shea, for so many memories that are now good stories. To Bibi Powers-McCormack, for your quiet brilliance and comradeship. To Heather Rolph, for your wit and unalloyed humanity. To Piper Boudart, for your graciousness and much shared laughter. To Allie Kreitman, for the luminosity of your intellect and company.

And fourth, to my family, who have often been for me a source of wisdom and a foundation. To my grandparents, for teaching me that stories have a real power. To my professorial uncle, for lighting a path. To my sister, who bore with me throughout our shared youth and whose joy is my joy. And to my parents, who emboldened me to keep going.

Introduction:
On the Diseases of the Head

Matt Rosen

A theory of everything can no longer carry the day. Our age is perhaps the first in which it seems definitive that a theory aiming to count the whole of what is, to catalogue every existent and experience and exception, no longer seems viable, or even very interesting.

There are several reasons for this. For one thing, there is too much information for which to properly and carefully account. The accumulation of technical and scientific detail means greater specification and specialization. The sheer number of philosophical positions to be argued against, articulated, and defended continues to grow, as per the nature of any historical development. And in social and cultural terms, there are fewer and fewer regions of permissible ignorance, especially in light of globalization; the encounter between European and Chinese philosophy indicates just one particularly present example of this.[1] Yet there is a way in which it is easier than ever before to be ignorant of so much.

---

1   An interesting account of this can be found in Yuk Hui, *The Question Concerning Technology in China: An Essay in Cosmotechnics* (Falmouth: Urbanomic, 2016).

Second, our age is one of a proliferation of things.[2] In the twenty-first century — to paint with a very broad brush — philosophy largely aimed to take stock of our access to things, to get clear about the epistemic conditions under which humans might come into contact with things and come to know them. The twenty-first century, however, demands that we grapple with the things themselves, whether or not they can be accessed under ideal epistemic conditions.[3] Processes of commodification and capitalization, and the correlated production of all manner of things, continue to accelerate; the idea that we could get a grip on each thing by means of some comprehensive theory has begun to look less and less believable. A theory that would seek a totalizing account no longer strikes us as able to be sufficient, or as more than a kind of fiction. Such a theory seems to do a certain violence to things; it looks recklessly assimilative, as if it would sweep everything up and miss each thing in its particularity in so doing.

This is not to mention that there seem to be events for which any theory of everything is unable to give reason. Political insurrections at an apparently escalating rate and scale; the event

---

2   "Our time is perhaps the time of an epidemic of things." Tristan Garcia, *Form and Object: A Treatise on Things*, trans. Mark Allan Ohm and Jon Cogburn (Edinburgh: Edinburgh University Press, 2014), 1.

3   A "return to the things themselves" was one of the primary ambitions of Husserl's phenomenology. However, the things to which I refer are unlike Husserl's in this sense: they are, whether or not they're thought as such. These things aren't noemata tied inexorably to a subject's noesis. They aren't necessarily correlated with someone's experience of them. As given, they're indifferent to their own givenness; or they're given without givenness. That isn't to say that speculation is opposed in principle to the expositions of concrete life made possible by phenomenology. So far as experience goes, the analyses of phenomenology may well stand. But speculation can't accept, as its starting point, the limitations of thematization by a subject. The essays in this collection are united by a refusal to accept the supposed limits of thought, a willingness to think first about things themselves. See Edmund Husserl, *Ideas for a Pure Phenomenology and Phenomenological Philosophy: First Book: General Introduction to Pure Phenomenology*, trans. Daniel O. Dahlstrom (Indianapolis: Hackett, 2014), 35.

of global climate change, which is evidently ongoing; and technological advancements that make the impossibly horrific persecutions of the last century seem too easily repeatable: All of these look like subtractions from what a theory of everything might be ("the owl of Minerva begins its flight only with the onset of dusk"[4]), and yet each one of these events is still *some thing*.

So what's left for us? In lieu of a theory of everything, we can offer a picture of some thing. Indeed, we can offer many pictures, each of some thing.

What is some thing? It is not nothing, but it is not everything. It is just a thing: some thing. A picture of some thing would be a theory, a philosophy, which shows a way or lights a path. But it would recognize that the determination of whether to follow that path is never made while on it, that the decision to dwell in a theory is always made from beyond its enclosure. It would be a picture that acknowledges that, in so being, it leaves something out. It would be a picture that does not, when it comes across an anomaly, seek straightaway to incorporate it, or else to hide it from view.

Each essay in this collection presents a theory of some thing, not everything and not nothing. Each essay gestures toward or sketches a singular path of thinking; but the decision to follow it rests always with the one who might decide from beyond it.

This collection might best be bracketed by what it does not contain, by what it isn't and doesn't wish to be, by what it refuses. In offering theories of some things, it will not offer a theory of nothing, of pure criticism or negation, nor a theory of everything, of pure accounting or affirmation. This anthology's moment is not one of negativity, not even of a dialectical negativity that might, in some speculative sublation, be lifted into a more tolerable positivity. Likewise, this anthology is not a progress toward an idea that can only be fully glimpsed from the other side; it is not an attempt at totality, capture, synthesis, gathering, counting, or hegemony. And it is not the result of a

---

4 G.W.F. Hegel, *Elements of the Philosophy of Right*, ed. Allen W. Wood, trans. H.B. Nisbet (Cambridge: Cambridge University Press, 1991), 23.

compulsion to repeat the critical philosophy, a critique of what came before such that a rigorous boundary might be set in place between philosophy's past and its future. It is only a non-total assortment, an assemblage without limit, of some pictures of some things.

Refusing both total negation (dialectical or otherwise) and absolute affirmation, refusing to deny everything or attempt to account for everything, this collection of essays aims at the exposition of themes, the construction of partial vantage points, the creation of limited wholes, and the analysis of fictions and metaphors. It desires to fight for some thing—but not for everything, and not for nothing. Most of all, it desires to speak from a position of insufficiency, to make known its own partiality or under-determinacy, which we take to be indicative of the practice of thinking, a sign of speculation.

Diseases of the Head is an anthology of essays from contemporary philosophers, artists, theorists, and writers working, broadly speaking, at the crossroads of speculative philosophy and speculative horror. Before turning to synopses of the included essays, I want to sketch the terrain of this crossroads in order to bring out the sorts of questions this collection intends to pose.

For our purposes, *speculative philosophy* is a particular kind of thinking which seeks to offer a theory of some thing, but which does not hang on criticism or totalization. It does not primarily seek the limits of thought so as to set the philosophical enterprise in place. It isn't after a perimeter, but rather endeavors to find out what thought can do on its own terms. Instead of trying to pin down the conditions of thinking or our access to things, instead of extending thought to include all of what is or retracting it such that thoughts about reality can be declared in some way empty or impossible, speculative philosophy seeks to say some things about some things, and not more or less than this.[5] It finds a certain epistemic humility in rejecting ideas

---

5   In this sense, I would situate speculation between "moralizing empiricism and dogmatic theology," where Badiou situates philosophy. It's true, of

of finitude that would bar us from getting a handle on things themselves.

The paradigmatic case of the will to limit speculation, to put its apparently perpetual restraints on display and make this exhibition the distinctive task of the philosopher, is Kant's critical program. Kant's "Essay on the Maladies of the Head," which sets out to classify and taxonomize various instances of subpar thinking, is a good example of a kind of pervasive legalism, a desire to name the boundaries that thought cannot or must not surpass.[6] Matthé Scholten writes of the Kantian contention that "the unifying feature of the symptoms" of those disorders that come under the head of schizophrenia "is the patient's inability to enter into an exchange of reasons with others."[7] Sanity can be bracketed by means of a criterion: the capacity to engage in intersubjective projects, to come to consensus and follow certain conventions, to register disagreement within parameters purportedly fixed by reason itself. In this way, sanity can be distinguished from skepticism, which is how anxiety comes to expression in philosophy, and dogmatism, which is how rigidity and small-mindedness (or repressed anxiety) come to philosophical expression. And if, for whatever reason, one isn't able to engage in the "exchange of reasons with others," or doesn't wish to do so, then one can justifiably be said to think poorly; hence, one is unfit to undertake certain tasks.[8]

---

course, that there are some contemporary "speculative" philosophers who engage in a sort of totalization, even if not in the sense of Kantian critique. But I also think we might say that, inasmuch as they engage in projects that seek to come to terms with the whole of what is (and negation can sometimes be totalizing), they are *thereby* less speculative. Alain Badiou, *Second Manifesto for Philosophy*, trans. Louise Burchill (Cambridge: Polity Press, 2011), 42.

6 Immanuel Kant, *Anthropology, History, and Education*, eds. Günter Zöller and Robert B. Louden (Cambridge: Cambridge University Press, 2007), 71.

7 Matthé Scholten, "Schizophrenia and Moral Responsibility: A Kantian Essay," *Philosophia* 44, no. 1 (March 2016): 205.

8 Certain critiques of Habermas might seem quite apropos here with respect to Kant's position.

Speculation, a practice of thinking catalogued by Kant as a malady of the head because of its failure to respect the limits set in place by the critical philosophy, is typified for Kant by the somewhat exaggerated model of Emanuel Swedenborg, who was a Swedish Lutheran theologian, philosopher, and mystic. In the highly polemical *Dreams of a Spirit-Seer*, published in 1766, Kant rescinds many of his previously laudatory remarks about Swedenborg, engaging in a blistering criticism of his speculations. Swedenborg is called a "spook-hunter" with a penchant for "ceaseless questioning," and to Kant's dismay he has no "official office or occupation."[9] In Kant's terms, Swedenborg is guilty of being a *Schwärmerei*, a fanatic or quixotic visionary who doesn't respect the proper bounds of reason. Rather, he employs thought beyond its permissible scope. This caustic epithet — *Schwärmerei* — dates back to Luther's critique of the more radical elements of the Reformation, indicating a form of thinking, often mystically theological, that is illicit or forbidden under a given set of conditions taken to pick out what qualifies as acceptable reasoning. This set of conditions — in Kant's case, laid out by the critical philosophy — is identified by a modality of thought (namely, critique) taken to be superior to the ostensible ravings of the *Schwärmerei*.

For Kant, speculation that fails to be critical, a thought of some thing that doesn't seek to subsume it under the categories of understanding with immediacy, a thought that doesn't ask primarily about our access to things, is declared to be one of the many diseases of the head. It is a malady to be avoided by the sane and the upright. As should be clear, this collection does not side with Kant. For, as Alain Badiou has it,

> Kant is the one author for whom I cannot feel any kinship. Everything in him exasperates me, above all his legalism — al-

---

9   See Immanuel Kant, *Theoretical philosophy, 1755–1770*, ed. and trans. David Walford, in collaboration with Ralf Meerbote (Cambridge: Cambridge University Press, 1992), 305. See also Ernst Benz, *Emanuel Swedenborg: Visionary Savant in the Age of Reason,* trans. Nicholas Goodrick-Clarke (West Chester: Swedenborg Foundation, 2002).

ways asking *Quid juris?* or "Haven't you crossed the limit?" The critical machinery he set up has enduringly poisoned philosophy [...] I am persuaded that the whole of the critical enterprise is set up to shield against the tempting symptom represented by the seer Swedenborg, or against "diseases of the head," as Kant puts it.[10]

There's no doubt a long history within philosophy of self-limitation. But there is also a noteworthy lineage that aims to push back against the will to limit, rejecting the desire to catalogue all of the diseases of the head the better to avoid them. This lineage has speculated regardless, offering theories of some things without attention to the putative primacy of critique.

For Deleuze and Guattari in *Anti-Oedipus,* the superlative taxonomizer is perhaps Freud rather than Kant, but the sentiment is pretty much the same. They write: "For we must not delude ourselves: Freud doesn't like schizophrenics. He doesn't like their resistance to being oedipalized, and tends to treat them more or less as animals. They mistake words for things, he says [...] they resemble philosophers."[11] Or — in a place where we might note the relationship between speculation and political emancipation — "schizophrenia is the exterior limit of capitalism itself or the conclusion of its deepest tendency, but [...] capitalism only functions on condition that it inhibit this tendency [...]. Hence schizophrenia is not the identity of capitalism, but on the contrary its difference, its divergence, its death."[12] The point is this: the urge to catalogue the diseases of the head so as to avoid them has a long and august history in philosophy; but the celebration of these diseases, the idea that perhaps in their partiality, audacity, and impertinence they rep-

---

10 Alain Badiou, *Logics of Worlds: Being and Event II,* trans. Alberto Toscano (London: Continuum, 2009), 535–36.
11 Gilles Deleuze and Félix Guattari, *Anti-Oedipus: Capitalism and Schizophrenia,* trans. Brian Massumi (Minneapolis: University of Minnesota Press, 1983), 23.
12 Ibid., 246.

resent thinking authentically, also has a history. It is within this latter lineage that this book locates itself.

For my philosophical project, as for many of those anthologized herein, the limits set in place by Kant prove problematic. If the classical manner of thinking moves from ontology to ethics, I have sought something like the inversion of this. For the classical movement, *from* what is *to* how to live, ethical imperatives are supposed to follow from ontological grounds. For instance, in Kant we see that morality supposedly follows from the nature of a rational being. For the movement I seek, beginning in ethics, ontological claims would be to some extent defensible on moral grounds. This may sound strange at first, but I think it rests on a rather simple observation: any ontology, it seems to me, is only really taken up when it is deemed inhabitable, when it seems to offer a picture of things within which we can make reasonably decent lives. So we would do well, on my view, to see that inhabitability matters when it comes to weighing the virtues and costs of any ontology. For Kant, the categorical imperative declares, as it were, that I should treat another as if my action could become a universal law. I should act toward others as if they are ends in themselves, and not only means. Now this imperative follows from an ontological program, a legalistic system, in which it seems to me there can be no other. For all that's given to me is subsumed right away under the categories of understanding, and thus rendered self-same to me, of me, or different only in degree from the norm that I am. The categorical imperative in this way strikes me as unattractively centered on the self, since it concerns the other whom I am to treat "as if" they are another — and only "as if." By the time the moment of ethics is reached, it is always already too late; ontology has had its day. I can think that the other is not only a means — that is, that there must be some other-in-itself lurking behind the other-for-me — but I can never hope to know the other except as a means. To my mind, the ontological limit that prohibits speculation is, from this vantage point, morally untenable. Critique rests on a picture of things we shouldn't wish to inhabit.

This is just one example of the many supposed limits that are called into question in this collection, set aside in a turn toward speculation — a turn toward a thought that isn't primarily concerned with its own justifiable extents, conditions, or limits.

This "speculative turn" is best situated in the discourse that has followed the 2007 conference, "Speculative Realism," held at Goldsmiths College, University of London.[13] At that conference, four philosophers with rather divergent views — Quentin Meillassoux, Ray Brassier, Graham Harman, and Iain Hamilton Grant — came together to address a common enemy. This enemy was named "correlationism" by Meillassoux in his 2006 book, *After Finitude*. As Meillassoux put it, correlationism is "the idea according to which we only ever have access to the correlation between thinking and being, and never to either term considered apart from the other."[14] After the twentieth century, dominated in the Anglo-American world by the project of analysis and in Continental Europe by phenomenology, the philosophies of Meillassoux, Brassier, Harman, and Grant each in their own way seemed to herald a new day for thought. Badiou, setting high expectations, called the attempt to undermine correlationism "a new path in the history of philosophy."[15]

The "speculative realists" — a term that better indicates a common enemy, correlationism, than any shared program — opposed what they considered to be the safety and consolation of humanism (Brassier); the idea of a subject who is not an object (Harman); and those philosophies that proclaim that there's nothing beyond thought, or that there's no possible access to what transcends subjectivity (Meillassoux).

---

13 For relevant papers, see Robin Mackay, ed., *Collapse II: Speculative Realism* (Falmouth: Urbanomic, 2007). For the transcript of this conference, see Ray Brassier et al., "Speculative Realism," in *Collapse III: Unknown Deleuze and Symposium on Speculative Realism,* ed. Robin Mackay (Falmouth: Urbanomic, 2007), 306–449.

14 Quentin Meillassoux, *After Finitude: An Essay on the Necessity of Contingency,* trans. Ray Brassier (London: Bloomsbury Academic, 2017), 5.

15 Alain Badiou, "Preface," in ibid., vii.

In the twentieth century, various philosophies held that everything that exists is simply the correlation of thinking and being; or language and bodies (and maybe truths); or appearances and objects of consciousness; or the noematic and noetic poles of consciousness; or Being and beings; or fluxes, processes, and becomings; or the text; or matter; or the Idea; or God; or the subject, whatever is correlated to it, and whatever interpellates it such that it is what it is; or structures, systems, and states; or power and its articulations; and so on. The turn toward speculation, which began in some significant way with the 2007 Goldsmiths conference, meant the refusal of these architectonics, these attempts to lay out what everything consists in. It meant the denial of a kind of philosophical self-sufficiency or indulgence by way of the renewal of a thought of the outside.[16] In a way, the turn to speculative philosophy signified the end of authoritative proclamations about the nature of everything (or our access to it), a willingness to rest contented with saying something about some things.

Speculation is not a thought of everything, as was attempted in the previous century — the *summae* of which attest to these attempts. Nor is it a purely negative thought, intending only the critique of the aforementioned totalizations, merely illustrating the insufficiency of correlationism. It rather puts forward some pictures of some things, and neither more nor less than this.

This collection isn't an introduction to what has been termed "speculative realism" or to associated theoretical endeavors. Several introductions of this sort have already been written or edited by those much more capable than I am.[17] While many

---

16 "For it could be that contemporary philosophers have lost the great outdoors, the absolute outside of pre-critical thinkers: that outside which was not relative to us, and which was given as indifferent to its own givenness to be what it is, existing in itself regardless of whether we are thinking it or not; that outside which thought could explore with the legitimate feeling of being on foreign territory — of being entirely elsewhere." Meillassoux, *After Finitude*, 7.

17 For such an introduction, see Levi Bryant, Nick Srnicek, and Graham Harman, eds., *The Speculative Turn: Continental Materialism and Realism* (Melbourne: re.press, 2011). See also Katerina Kolozova and Eileen A.

of the essays in this collection draw their inspiration or parts of their theoretical apparatuses from the four philosophers who spoke at the Goldsmiths conference, *Diseases of the Head* aims specifically to explore the intersection of speculative philosophy, broadly construed in the above sense, and speculative horror.

Speculative or "concept" horror is a genre, in literature and other forms of art, that addresses a particular set of themes: anonymity, otherness, the alien, the monstrous, the Gothic, extinction and the world without human beings, the end times, the apocalypse, the archaic and the world before human beings, the uncanny or unheimlich, and other similar motifs. In this collection, a number of speculative authors who discuss such themes are considered: H.P. Lovecraft, Maurice Blanchot, Rudolf Otto, E.T.A. Hoffmann, and Mark Z. Danielewski, among others. And the works considered include *House of Leaves*, the *Alien* franchise, *The Call of Cthulhu*, *The Infinite Conversation*, and many more.

This anthology is situated at the crossroads of speculative philosophy and speculative horror, in the terrain in which the diseases of the head encounter the aforementioned themes. Kant's critical philosophy and the tradition that follows from it — serving as a defense against the speculative maladies of the head, against the madness and horror of speculation — are being called into question by those aiming to think being apart from thought, the absolute at the expense of subjectivity, the macabre at sanity's peril, the exception at the price of the stability of the situation, and the alien at the cost of a certain discourse of normativity. Speculative horror is a fertile place of development for those philosophies that seek to repudiate the Kantian injunction to avoid the diseases of the head in endeavoring to speculate anew. Conversely, speculative philosophy is a site of inspiration and theoretical articulation for writers, artists, and theorists of horror who want to explore novel aesthetic and inaesthetic possibilities in relation to the uncanny and inhuman, the beyond-

---

Joy, eds., *After the "Speculative Turn": Realism, Philosophy, and Feminism* (Earth: punctum books, 2016).

human, extra-human, sans-human, post-human, and even at times the anti-human.[18] This anthology thus aspires to engage the place of development at which speculative horror and speculative philosophy meet through as many distinct voices — as many theories of some thing — as possible. From philosophers working on horrific themes, to horror writers influenced by the new speculative philosophy, to artists engaged in projects that address alienation and monstrosity, the contributors to *Diseases of the Head* pose the questions:

— Where do horror and philosophy come together? What's found there?
— In what sense might philosophy be fictional? In what sense might fiction be philosophical? What is the relationship between theory, story, and practice?
— What does it mean to speculate? How is speculation lived?
— If we set aside philosophy's self-limitation, what kind of horror might result? What are the maladies of the head? What happens if we say that thought can in some way access reality?
— What can philosophers learn from horror writers and artists, and vice versa?
— What must be considered in regard to the extinction of thought and the exigencies of the Anthropocene?
— What does philosophy have to say about the end of the world?
— What use can the genre of horror make of speculation, and what use can speculation make of horror?
— Can horror possibly be contained in an identifiable genre?
— And, what sort of future developments await us in philosophy and horror after the resurgence of speculation?

This anthology seeks to articulate the cutting-edge, as contemporary philosophers, artists, theorists, and writers present their thoughts — at times fragmentary, at times aphoristic, at times

---

18 See Robin Mackay, ed., *Collapse IV: Concept-Horror* (Falmouth: Urbanomic, 2008).

audacious—on the preceding questions; each chapter offers some theory of some thing found at the intersection of speculative philosophy and speculative horror. To put it another way, there's a sense in which this collection aims at nothing less, after the long twentieth century, than a speculative coup d'état.

Before we turn to summaries of the included essays, there are a few points that the reader should bear in mind. First, as I have mentioned, any speculative investigation is by its nature rough and unfinished; we don't think that this is a fault needing acknowledgement, but rather a virtue. This collection intends to speak from a posture of being in progress. It speaks from the position of an inquiry. It is not a treatise. We consider this a matter of sincerity. The limits of this text aren't the limits of its world. Speculation does not end with the final pages; perhaps it only begins there.

Second, this anthology disregards the limits of disciplines and academic departmentalization. We are not concerned to draw neat distinctions between, say, philosophy and literature, or theory and practice, in order to set each thing so distinguished in its proper place. I believe that Alex Dubilet put it well when he wrote that

> [s]uch axiomatic distinctions have been repeatedly asserted and maintained in different guises, circulating with varying normative judgements and levels of complexity to the present day. It is almost as if there has been a persistent, although often unacknowledged, collusion [between disciplines] that has led to theoretical partitions and purifications [...]. It is as though each disciplinary tribe has its own axiomatic *axis mundi* around which it is fated to remain in orbit. [...] Perhaps this should come as no surprise, since distinct boundaries allow for the persistence and legitimation of disciplinary identities and for the resulting, almost nationalistic in their intensity, rallying cries in defense of disciplinary territories.[19]

---

19 Alex Dubilet, *The Self-Emptying Subject: Kenosis and Immanence, Medieval to Modern* (New York: Fordham University Press, 2018), 5.

Suffice it to say: the essays included in *Diseases of the Head* reject "disciplinary identities" and refuse "disciplinary territories." We have no interest in planting flags, here or anywhere. We don't want to mark the regions of our explorations like conquistadors of the mind. We are after investigations, open sketches, piecemeal inquiries, not systems or inert methods. So far as we are concerned, all thoughts are equally thoughts of some thing, each of which can be criticized or taken up, each of which has something to offer us — a reason to accept the thought, a reason to deny it. Each of the included essays sets out a singular path, a particular thought of some thing where speculative philosophy and speculative horror collide. We therefore seek to suspend the distinctions between disciplines — to ignore, at least for a moment, socio-cultural partitions and formulaic or balkanized ways of thinking — in pursuit of speculation itself.

Third, this collection isn't a polemic. It was Kant, after all, who once said that metaphysics is a battlefield. On this battlefield, there is a certain sense in which the speculative philosopher is, or could be, a guerrilla combatant.[20] But combat isn't our aim. The critical philosophy, in strictly limiting thinking by means of its own "reasonable" conditions, in setting aside dogmatic metaphysics, endeavors to bring about an age of philosophical "perpetual peace."[21] But this peace is the other side of *polemos*, only the moment between battles; it is a peace that declares war against so much of what thought can do. The speculative resurgence, then, isn't the renewal of the battlefield but the suspension of the whole war-and-peace dialectic. From a perspective that is perhaps naïve, from the posture of that youthful "idealism" that is the only true realism, we seek to speculate without regard to the declared war or peace of Kant's metaphysical battlefield. We wish to think otherwise. We won't offer a thought that aims to vanquish or conquer another by claiming to account for every-

---

20 Cf. Graham Harman, *Guerrilla Metaphysics: Phenomenology and the Carpentry of Things* (Chicago: Open Court Publishing Company, 2005).
21 I refer to Immanuel Kant, *Perpetual Peace and Other Essays*, trans. Ted Humphrey (Indianapolis: Hackett, 1983).

thing, or to negate all else. The goal is not to write an anti-Kant, a treatise of resistance to the critical philosophy. Nor do we want to surrender to its stipulations. The objective is to make another use of thought after Kant.

In other words, we seek to suspend the vicious circularity of critique and systematic construction — instead putting forward a picture, or many pictures, of some things, for there are many diseases of the head.

Overview of Essays to Follow

This anthology opens with Ben Woodard's "Outgrown Purpose, Outlived Use: On Parasitic Teleology." Woodard wants to make sense of the history of vitalism alongside the development of biology as a discrete, autonomous science. He argues that the emergence of vitalism, and its invocation throughout the eighteenth and nineteenth centuries, was in some sense a response to the introduction of order and codification into the apparent disarray of the study of living systems, which mixed notions of purpose, teleology, mechanism, form, function, and transformation. Woodard writes that the view on which life is merely a force, system, or substance neglects a significant part of the picture of organic life and its historical development. After analyzing the historical cartography of vitalism, Woodard turns to how it interacts with the question of teleology's nature or foundation. In order to explicate the "cross-contamination" of vitalism and teleology, Woodard examines the *Alien* franchise of films. These films, he believes, can be seen as emphasizing what's at stake for vitalism: "an extended battle over the teleological status of evolutionary theory and the stubbornness of the ideals of intentional (whether divine or merely sapient) creation." In discussing the order in which the *Alien* films might be viewed, Woodard notes that, if they are viewed in the order in which they were created, it looks as if "creation begs to be justified by teleology." But if they are viewed according to authorial intent, the films instead "unfold vitalism from a teleological obsession." Woodard argues that the Alien films signify and magnify the adoption of conceptions of teleology by various sorts of vitalism that would typically disavow them. He tells us that critical vitalism's refusal of any real foundations or conditions of biological life leaves open a door for teleology, while the so-called "naïve" forms of vitalism think of their concepts as placeholders in the venture to explain nature's generative capacity. These latter forms of vitalism thereby refrain from closing their productions back into the "circle of meaning."

Amanda Beech, in her essay "Death of Horror," argues that the cultural phenomenon of horror speaks to notions of human limitation, which are projected as the horizons of what we can know in the "impossible navigation between the real and our lived reality." The limitations to which horror endeavors to give voice are established when we fail — as we must — to take seriously the images representative of negativity and the concepts we might employ to think it. Beech notes that, in seeking theoretical explanations and in ordinary life, we often either oppose the real and lived reality as if they are adversaries or instead suppose that they are equivalent "in the name of the real itself." Speaking of the "infinite and cloying space of contemporary global capital," Beech claims that horror is no longer able to engender genuine terror with any thought of "the outside." In lieu of that, it has been forced to put forward another sort of terror: that of "repetition, entrapment, and the destiny of the same that persists with force." Beech thus argues that horror's postmodern condition has rendered its potential as a "vector" of the dynamic between the real and reality dispensable for politics, aesthetics, and the question of how epistemology can offer "new directions for both language and the future." Beech wants to put these questions before us: Can horror allow for a view of language that isn't pessimistic, maintaining a "project of realism"? Can language express a reality independent of subjectivity and thereby explicate "the conditions of *horror vacui*"? Can it do this without eating away at the view that language has some fundamental "equality or inequality with the real"? In order to move toward answers to these questions, Beech investigates populist film. She looks to the resources of philosophical reflection and non-philosophical invention to theorize the limit of horror as the "representational expression of nothingness." She seeks a novel understanding of the relationship between representation and the thought of nothingness. That way, we might just "rescue the operations of language after postmodernity."

In my essay, "Those Who Aren't Counted," I propose a distinction between two concepts: affliction and atrocity. I argue that an ethical position with respect to history's horrors can be understood as a practice of refusing to permit affliction to be seen as atrocity. This is a practice of resisting the urge to quantify or qualify affliction in subjecting it to a count of bodies, which would be taken to totalize all the suffering in a given situation. We should, I contend, resist thinking that affliction qualified as atrocity, subject to a count of bodies or the like, captures affliction itself. I start with an analysis of the massacre that occurred at Sétif and Guelma, which was one of the conflicts that precipitated the violence of the Algerian War. I focus particularly on the dissensus with regard to the number of people who were killed there. I argue that atrocity is the result of a conversion in which affliction is subject to an operation of counting, trapped within a kind of numerical prism. Through this prism, atrocity is imagined to be adequate to the actual suffering in question. I ask about how we can think the affliction of those who perished at Sétif and Guelma without regard to the atrocity under which they have been subsumed, within which they have been numerically crystallized as the 1,020 (the body count according to the French colonial government) or the 45,000 (the body count according to Radio Cairo). This inquiry leads to a discussion of various ethical "topologies," and then to a study of an especially salient instance of affliction: the crucifixion of Christ. Here, I distinguish between two visions of Christ. The first, which I call "Christ-in-Christianity," sees the crucifixion as an atrocity. The second, which I call "Christ-without-Christianity," sees it as an affliction. I sketch a picture of what I term a "generic ethic" in order to theorize in alliance with the Christ of the crucifixion, whose affliction is, I argue, foreclosed to those who would think it as atrocity. I conclude by applying the distinction between affliction and atrocity to the biblical story of Exodus, making a case that it is ethically imperative that we recollect the abnegation of the self to those who aren't counted, those who cannot be counted because they are afflicted without atrocity.

David Peak, in "Horror of the Real: H.P. Lovecraft's Old Ones and Contemporary Speculative Philosophy," analyzes the enduring relevance of the Cthulhu Mythos of H.P. Lovecraft. Peak puts forward a way in which Lovecraft's "Old Ones" can be given a new meaning in light of contemporary developments in speculative philosophy. At the same time, he provides a narrative structure in and by which those developments might be elucidated. Peak begins his essay by discussing the history and literary merit of Lovecraft's mythology; he writes of its value as a work of fiction, and as a site that offers ample theoretical resources for those thinking about horrific themes. Considering what makes Lovecraft's vision "so profound," Peak seeks to advance a connection between recent developments in philosophy — especially those of Graham Harman and Quentin Meillassoux — and Lovecraft's "notions of horror." Peak tells us that the Cthulhu Mythos does a fine job of representing Harman's conception of "weird realism," and he looks to the theoretical tools of speculative philosophy to see if they might allow us to "move past the inherent limitations of Lovecraft's dogmatic materialism," which Peak thinks is at odds with Lovecraft's own fiction. For Peak, speculative horror can expand — and importantly, concretize — the often abstract and abstruse philosophical maneuvers of the new speculation. It is Lovecraft after all, Peak reminds us, who was audacious enough to have "dared us to gaze into such magnificent vistas of ultimate chaos."

In "Triangulorum," Sara Rich weaves the tale of a tragic, ill-fated journey to Hispaniola. Written in an epistolary form, Rich's narrative asks, what if those Kant thought to be sickened by the diseases of the head aren't "dreamers in waking" or fanatical visionaries but rather, as she puts it, "those whose sensations become, through weird chance, inextricably bound to chimerical overlaps of space-time that render chaos from perceptions of order?" In a style at once evocative and experimental, theory and fiction, Rich tells us that perhaps this post-Enlightenment age, an "era of life in the Rational Experiment gone haywire," is one in which anything but reversibility in fact seems possible.

In their chapter, "Race and Its Far-Reaching Contemporary Ontological and Epistemological Implications," Marina Gržinić and Jovita Pristovšek argue that the primary intersection of horror and philosophy is found "when, and if, we speak about the historical construct of race and its far-reaching, contemporary, ontological, and epistemological implications."

In the first part of their chapter, entitled "Politics of Death in Europe," Gržinić starts off by considering the concept of "necropolitics," rooted in the work of Achille Mbembe and Giorgio Agamben. She defines necropolitics, in contradistinction to Foucault's biopolitics, as a politics conceived in line with the slogan "let live and make die." Arguing that the notion of necropolitics opens up a "critical space for discussing a land of dead, violated, and ultimately disposed bodies," Gržinić analyzes a number of films made after the Second World War, which center on death and history. In this way, she aims to think about death and dying "in the form of an enduring process of a systematic violent act." In each of the films under examination, Gržinić points out that the three main elements of necropolitics can be seen: "enmity, impunity, and the right to kill." In these films, she tells us, these elements are instantiated as "abandonment, reification, and disposability." Gržinić discusses the structures of various forms of polities and states, and she concludes the first section of the chapter by arguing that it is essential to rescue the films under discussion "from oblivion and the terror they bring" — thereby, we can rescue the lives of those in these films who, "though terrified, oppose death."

In the second part of their chapter, entitled "We remember carrying the word in mouth. *Race*. Chewing," Pristovšek speaks of the "figure of the 'Black,' a racialized, colonized, ungendered, and dehumanized" being; this being is constructed as a kind of metaxy amidst a world of subjects and objects, who/which is both between these categories and excluded by them. Pristovšek tells us that we ought to assert clearly that the idea of race is something horrific for philosophy. In arguing that race and racism are relegated by philosophy to the unrepresentable and unthinkable, Pristovšek sets up the question of how we are to think about race as the "grey zone" between horror and philosophy. She thereby gives consideration to the "ontological and epistemological implications" of race and how it is constructed, articulated, elaborated, and employed. Meditating on the gravity of injustices both historical and present-day — including the effects of "European provincialism," commodity fetishism, and "neoliberal, global, financial capitalism" — Pristovšek undertakes a detailed assessment of the philosophical movement often termed "speculative realism." She pays particular attention to its aesthetic and political ramifications; she thinks these are in a sense the same, or at least have a close relationship. Seeking neither to defend Kant nor to defend speculative realism from Kant, Pristovšek worries that all parties are avoiding thinking about what actually lies between horror and philosophy: namely, the "racial flesh." What we desperately need, Pristovšek claims, is a way to "think anew the 'human,'" a way to unfold and develop, as Foucault has it, "a space in which it is once more possible to think."

Eckardt Lindner, in "Absolute Xenogenesis: Speculations on an Unnatural History of Life," lights a path through the terrain of philosophy's entanglement with artificial life, discovering questions about madness, opacity, and impersonality along the way. He begins with an analysis of Kant's *Dreams of a Spirit-Seer*. Lindner tells us that Kant resists attributing the spirit-seer's speculative claims to any physiological malfunction, since "the whole of philosophical thought is in danger of becoming a sickness of the mind." In view of our incapacity to absolve ourselves of at least the hypothesis of our own insanity, there doesn't appear to be anything in experience that could act as a guarantor of its correspondence with reality. Lindner emphasizes Kant's move toward a discourse of experience that is intersubjectively verifiable, a discourse in which the notion of life takes on the sense of whatever has the quality of being "lively" or "vital." In arguing that Kant's reconceptualization of life reflects something found in various attempts to create artificial life in the eighteenth century, Linder writes of the "anatomical-phenomenological approach" to thinking about life, which "simulates a body" and aims to represent or mirror life. For this approach, success as adequation to life is "measured by the (often visceral) reaction of an onlooker." The horror invoked here comes to light in an analogical structure bridging an excessive or transcendent object and a finite subject by means of a "mediating representation." Linder then turns to the "anti-aesthetics" of speculative philosophy; he argues that, despite the promises of the fashionable "speculative realism," its "anti-vitalist rationalism" is unfortunately "trapped within the coordinates of the Kantian critique." Linder thus proposes that we center our inquiry on the "indifferent speculative wasteland" through which thought about life must wander. In this connection, he discusses Deleuze's conception of life as a formidable alternative to the thinking of life — latent and manifest — in Ray Brassier and Quentin Meillassoux. He also discusses alchemical thinking about artificial life. Lindner argues that the alchemical tradition of thinking about life has been stigmatized as heresy, which points to a recurrent fear of a "nature ultimately neither controlled nor limited by any external force." This fear singles out a "horror based on the univocity of all individuated beings via an impersonal genesis" — which is what Lindner calls "absolute xenogenesis." He claims that this reveals that the nature of life is in fact unnatural, setting up an original dividing line between the "anatomical lineage," which limits life to the phenomena of organic life, and the "alchemical lineage," which isn't constrained by nature as it actually is but "introduces a difference into it, supplementing it." This latter lineage, Lindner tells us, opens up many possible "future histories of life" beyond the organic, beyond our cognition, and indeed, beyond us.

In "Survival Strategies for Weird Times," we have reprinted Helen Marshall's story, entitled "Survival Strategies" and originally published in *Black Static* 58 (2017). This is followed by a commentary published for the first time in this collection. "Survival Strategies" is a semi-fictionalized account of a young academic, a scholar of medieval studies, who is on a research trip to New York in order to interview the editor of Barron St. John, a bestselling author. Set against the backdrop of Donald Trump's presidency, this story employs autobiographical elements to complicate any attempt to distinguish fiction from reality. Refusing any rigorous demarcation of one from the other, it asks: where do "true horror" and "speculative horror" intersect, and to what extent can our situatedness in the present moment prove to be a source of the uncanny? Following "Survival Strategies," the reader will find an accompanying commentary, "Survival Strategies for Weird Times," which elucidates the aforementioned themes in a more explicit fashion. Marshall argues that the mode of weird fiction proposed by Jeff and Ann VanderMeer, M. John Harrison, China Miéville, and Roger Luckhurst, among others, plausibly evokes the "feeling of living in the twenty-first century: an age thus far characterized by political crises, fake news, and environmental catastrophe." She draws upon the work of H.P. Lovecraft and constructs parallels with Timothy Morton's work on hyperobjects, that is, "real things with discernible impacts which cannot be apprehended in their entirety." Marshall's commentary articulates several ways in which the "weird mode" of fiction coincides with the uncanny and destabilizing effects of Morton's hyperobjects, before concluding by considering the role of fiction in "attempting to represent the 'weird' times of the world in which we live."

The next essay is Luka Bekavac's "Matrix Pavoris: Material Dislocation in *House of Leaves*." This is an ambitious analysis of Danielewski's far from conventional novel, *House of Leaves*. Bekavac pays particular attention to what he considers that work's main invention: the "small, featureless spatial dilatation" which manifests itself in an "otherwise ordinary family home." Bekavac tells us that this baffling space, "as abstract and benign as it might initially seem," is bizarre enough — "scandalous enough" — to lend energy to a great number of critical reactions, interpretations, and theories. He employs this invention in order to grapple with the problem of "text as a graphic embodiment of the cognitive inaccessibility of space." Bekavac considers the unorthodox typography exhibited in *House of Leaves,* as well as novel ideas of textuality, the distribution of texts, and procedures of writing; he argues that "the common thread running through all of this, as obscure as it might sometimes seem, is actually the strictly materialistic understanding of text, a firm conviction that, in parallel with all of their powers of handling content and reflecting or anticipating a certain "reality," texts are *things,* objects with physical qualities, defined by their link to matter and resistance to easy and complete transfer into comprehension, idea, or pure thought." This leads Bekavac to a cogent engagement with Derrida's work on writing, typography, and language broadly construed. Examining writing and textuality in relation to temporality and spatiality, Bekavac contends that writing's distinctive time is in the end a sort of atemporality. In other words, writing's time is space. This leads Bekavac to a discussion of dwelling in Heidegger, Plato, and Derrida, which yields the startling thought that "if we are to encounter […] unintelligible materiality in any way, it will have to present itself in a more ambiguous guise, it will have to open like a book, it might even resemble a house." By way of thinking about architecture, Bekavac constructs a vision of materials, such as books and houses, as transitional objects, and he concludes that dealing with writing means trying to find a "perpetually provisional and volatile foothold within it." For the "only other option is not to read at all, to go back into ourselves, try and forget, or to simply move on."

Chloé Germaine Buckley's "Encountering Weird Objects: Lovecraft, LARP, and Speculative Philosophy," poses a striking question to those of us who might be all too satisfied with merely writing about the nature of reality. How can we actually "make contact with objects such that both the anthropocentrism of Western philosophy and the […] 'common-sense' realism it engenders might be disrupted?" To put it another way: what would it mean to work toward an encounter with the weirdness of reality, an encounter that might allow humans to be "jolted out of the 'hubris'" in which the question of matter is always indistinguishable from questions of utility and instrumental value? Buckley argues that there is "at least one human activity alert to the vibrant, strange, and elusive nature of objects: game-playing." Focusing on live-action roleplaying (LARP), "a niche gaming activity distinct from table-top roleplaying games and video games," Buckley tells us that this sort of play makes possible the disruption of "players' deeply embedded ontologies"; it allows for a break with the common-sense that operates in ordinary life. Through an analysis of ludic theory, an engagement with the Gothic literary tradition, and a discussion of object-oriented materialisms and ontologies, Buckley makes the persuasive argument that "LARP monsters are almost always material-human hybrids." The philosophical potential of game-playing — and LARP especially — emerges as the production of "embodied and affective experiences" that might bring to life, so to speak, the "rhetoric" of speculative realism and new materialism. Since LARP makes otherwise "allusive" processes concrete, since it aims to produce "an embodied and affective encounter with strange and vibrant materiality" of which humans are a part, but which humans cannot master, Buckley claims that this sort of play provides us with vital, subversive ethical resources. The player must account for the nature of reality as inhuman, and so it becomes exigent that we "consider that fact that it is the world that makes us," not the other way round.

In "Sublime Horror in the Tales of E.T.A. Hoffmann," Hamad Al-Rayes defends the view that E.T.A. Hoffmann wasn't only a pioneering writer of horror fiction who pushed it beyond what had previously been considered its limits but also a "theoretician of the highest caliber." Of the attention that Hoffmann's contributions to philosophical inquiry have received, most has been concentrated on how he sought to make sense of the distinction between classicism and romanticism. But Al-Rayes proposes to expand this attention dramatically. He reads Hoffmann's endeavor as the "carving out" of a "wild and oft-overlooked territory in the history of aesthetics, one which fuses the beautiful and the horrific." Al-Rayes wants both to shed light on Hoffmann's own aesthetic commitments and also to provide an "illuminating angle" from which to get a handle on Hoffmann's artistic practice. Arguing that the aesthetic underpinning the work of a storyteller cannot be as neatly demarcated from that which underpins the work of a philosopher as has elsewhere been theorized, Al-Rayes tells us that Hoffmann is on the one hand interested in retrieving some of the elements of Burke's views about aesthetics which had been repudiated by Kant, while he on the other hand seeks to fuse horror and "artistic beauty itself," putting his project at cross purposes with Burke's. In the end, Al-Rayes presents a vision of Hoffmann's oeuvre, drawing on his seminal work on Beethoven and a number of other critical essays, that leads us toward a novel synthesis of beauty and horror as a neglected route to aesthetic experience in the wake of post-Kantian philosophy.

In "When the Monstrous Object Becomes a Tremendous Non-Event: Rudolf Otto's Monster-Gods, H.P. Lovecraft's Cthulhu, and Graham Harman's Theory of Everything," Eric Wilson starts off with a discussion of Rudolf Otto's *The Idea of the Holy* (1917). Here, Wilson further develops a thesis set forward in an earlier monograph, according to which Otto's work served as the direct, though unacknowledged, source for H.P. Lovecraft's "Supernatural Horror in Literature" (1927). Wilson is particularly interested in Otto's "subjectivist reconstruction" of the experience of the holy as the "*mysterium tremendum,*" which he sees as occupying a privileged place in Lovecraft's Cthulhu Mythos. In the second part of his essay, Wilson undertakes to evaluate anew the aesthetic of Otto and Lovecraft in terms of Graham Harman's object-oriented ontology; he focuses especially on Harman's *The Quadruple Object* to do this. Wilson concludes by drawing a comparison between Harman and Meillassoux. He argues in no uncertain terms that the former, and not the latter, offers the resources that allow for a "preferred interpretation" of twentieth-century horror fiction. Lovecraft's Cthulhu, Wilson writes, is nothing other than a precise, though perhaps metaphorical, rendering of Harman's concept of the quadruple object.

John Cunningham, in "Reproducing It: Speculative Horror and the Limits of the Inhuman," investigates speculative philosophy's seeming attachment to the notion of "the it." Seeking not to question the insight that there's an "it" that "reveals the hubris and illusion of humanity," but rather to build on that premise through an immanent critique, Cunningham wants to bring the dread he makes out in the supposedly irreducible gap between thinking and being "abruptly down to earth." In a style that is at once fragmentary and polemical, Cunningham writes of grounding the relationship between horror and speculation on "questions of reproduction and non-reproduction," on the way in which capitalism is "systemically inhuman," and on the "negativity of the inhuman" — which he views as productive, "virulently active." By reading the concept of the inhuman through the "abstract horrors" of today's capitalism, Cunningham argues that much current theorizing of horror neglects the "ruin of [...] 'dread glimpses'" and mistakenly turns instead to the "architecture of the concept." Employing a "constellation of fragmentary concepts and images that attempt to sketch [...] [the] possibilities and contradictions [...] of the aesthetics of horror and speculative thought," he tells us that the horror of the "it" opens "up a vista of hopelessness and dread." This horror seems, Cunningham says, best conceived of as epistemic: "an opening up of the gap between human knowledge and the "real" of the inhuman." Speculative horror, we are told, can be found in the "affective, aesthetic, and conceptual possibilities" foregrounded by this gap; this is made evident in the "cosmic terrors of Lovecraft, the eerie mannequins of Thomas Ligotti, the more corporeal terror of apocalyptic zombie cinema." Drawing out images that would "freeze thought and by extension freeze speculation," indeed at times setting speculation against itself, "[w]earing a zombie mask while citing Kant," Cunningham criticizes, by means of "conceptual images," what he sees as a speculative wish to conceptualize above all else. If he is right, this could be a problem for those who desire to think the object beyond its objectivation, the thing without its subsumption under the logic of the concept. In this vein, Cunningham claims that Graham Harman's ontology is in the last analysis one of "formless mass," and that we ought to prefer that the conceptual images of "it" which emerge in speculative horror remain in a certain sense formless. This is perhaps because horror is a sort of "filter through which the inhuman is allowed to take shape as a conceptual image." While he thinks that the "negative sublime" can limit the apprehension of particular aspects of inhumanity, it is in thinking the human as a "waste object" — as excess or the leftover of an event — that it becomes possible to think and experience the "world-not-for-us." This strange world "expresses the gap [...] between much of humanity and the reproduction of the world" for the sake of capitalist ends; as such, it is something like a "broken mirror" in which "other shapes" — of life, of society, of thought — might be descried.

The final essay in this collection is Julia Hölzl's "Horror Vacui (*'That Nothing Is What There Is'*)." Hölzl begins with a disclaimer, which I think prefaces her writing just as well as it prefaces the refusal of this collection to come to any lasting or sufficient conclusion: "The following remains a draft [...] does not provide answers, nor questions. It is a mere opening toward somewhere else. It is the elsewhere that is of interest here." Considering themes of dismay, abandonment, and openness to wonder, Hölzl intends to think the relations, or lack thereof, among being, time, absence, and emptiness. To do this, she discusses, in an original way, Maurice Blanchot's "primal scene" as it is set forward in *The Writing of the Disaster*. Blanchot tells us that the term "scene" is in some way inadequate or inappropriate, since it seems to name or mark something unrepresentable. The "scene," for Blanchot, must be spoken of not as some event taking place at a specifiable time, but rather as "a shadow, a faint gleam, an 'almost.'" In her analysis, Hölzl proposes to try to think this "almost," to "think this elsewhere," indeed to "be (in) this there," by thinking that "nothing is what there is, and first of all nothing beyond." While discussing the Heideggerian notion of "profound boredom," Hölzl tells us that we can "touch" the "that nothing is what there is," that we can bear the affliction and terror of our own emptiness, since there's a way in which it's already here. Hölzl concludes in a style that is experimental and attentive to the philosopher's limitations; in this way, she finds a certain kind of hope: we might be able to encounter the "empty intimacy of time" of which Blanchot writes, first of all by encountering the "nothing beyond."

Bibliography

Badiou, Alain. *Logics of Worlds: Being and Event II*. Translated by Alberto Toscano. London: Continuum, 2009.

———. *Second Manifesto for Philosophy*. Translated by Louise Burchill. Cambridge: Polity Press, 2011.

Benz, Ernst. *Emanuel Swedenborg: Visionary Savant in the Age of Reason*. Translated by Nicholas Goodrick-Clarke. West Chester: Swedenborg Foundation, 2002.

Brassier, Ray, Iain Hamilton Grant, Graham Harman, Quentin Meillassoux. "Speculative Realism." In *Collapse III: Unknown Deleuze and Symposium on Speculative Realism*, ed. Robin Mackay, 306–449. Falmouth: Urbanomic, 2007.

Bryant, Levi, Nick Srnicek, and Graham Harman, eds. *The Speculative Turn: Continental Materialism and Realism*. Melbourne: re.press, 2011.

Deleuze, Gilles, and Félix Guattari. *Anti-Oedipus: Capitalism and Schizophrenia*. Translated by Brian Massumi. Minneapolis: University of Minnesota Press, 1983.

Dubilet, Alex. *The Self-Emptying Subject: Kenosis and Immanence, Medieval to Modern*. New York: Fordham University Press, 2018.

Garcia, Tristan. *Form and Object: A Treatise on Things*. Translated by Mark Allan Ohm and Jon Cogburn. Edinburgh: Edinburgh University Press, 2014.

Harman, Graham. *Guerrilla Metaphysics: Phenomenology and the Carpentry of Things*. Chicago: Open Court Publishing Company, 2005.

Hegel, G.W.F. *Elements of the Philosophy of Right*. Edited by Allen W. Wood. Translated by H.B. Nisbet. Cambridge: Cambridge University Press, 1991.

Hui, Yuk. *The Question Concerning Technology in China: An Essay in Cosmotechnics*. Falmouth: Urbanomic, 2016.

Husserl, Edmund. *Ideas for a Pure Phenomenology and Phenomenological Philosophy: First Book: General Introduction to Pure Phenomenology*. Translated by Daniel O. Dahlstrom. Indianapolis: Hackett, 2014.

Kant, Immanuel. *Anthropology, History, and Education.* Edited by Günter Zöller and Robert B. Louden. Cambridge: Cambridge University Press, 2007.

———. *Perpetual Peace and Other Essays.* Translated by Ted Humphrey. Indianapolis: Hackett, 1983.

———. *Theoretical Philosophy, 1755–1770.* Edited and translated by David Walford, in collaboration with Ralf Meerbote. Cambridge: Cambridge University Press, 1992.

Kolozova, Katerina, and Eileen A. Joy, eds. *After the "Speculative Turn": Realism, Philosophy, and Feminism.* Earth: punctum books, 2016.

Mackay, Robin, ed. *Collapse II: Speculative Realism.* Falmouth: Urbanomic, 2007.

———, ed. *Collapse IV: Concept-Horror.* Falmouth: Urbanomic, 2008.

Meillassoux, Quentin. *After Finitude: An Essay on the Necessity of Contingency.* Translated by Ray Brassier. London: Bloomsbury Academic, 2017.

Scholten, Matthé. "Schizophrenia and Moral Responsibility: A Kantian Essay," *Philosophia* 44, no. 1 (March 2016): 205–25. DOI: 10.1007/s11406-015-9685-4.

1

Outgrown Purpose, Outlived Use: On Parasitic Teleology

Ben Woodard

1. Life as Problem

Every beginning to a discussion of the beginning of life betrays the central problematic of itself — namely a tension between the miraculous and the arbitrary (where to start the discussion of the start of living things). Satisfactory explanations of life are measured against the apparent limitless complexity and variety of its forms. Of course, to claim life exceeds explanation is itself a form of explanation since no one who would make such a claim would in turn argue that life can be intuitively understood, despite the fact it can be accidentally made. In other words, how would one backup the statement "I do not know what life is, but I know you cannot explain it"? In the following I will attempt to outline the conceptual investments in theories of life that are not so often concerned with explaining life, as much as they are concerned with placing the role of life in an (often all too human) conceptual framework. First, I will begin by examining the field of early biology, circa 1800.

John Zammito's recent opus *The Gestation of German Biology* explores the problem of life as it emerged in the vitalist and the romantic sciences' early attempts to generate a unified biological theory as well as order those earlier disciplines which functioned as its tributaries: physiology, medicine, zoology, and botany, to name a few. Biology, as it developed under its proper name in 1800, bares traces of not only the shifting concerns and methods of all of these sciences brought together but also of debates and shifts from the physical sciences and philosophy regarding where to place the human capacities of thought and free will as well as the natural or theological status of the soul. Two of the most important problems which brought these various concepts together were the capacity of animation or animal movement and the emergence of form, especially in embryology. Thus, how one could explain the development and movement of humans and animals and whether and, on what grounds, the human/animal distinction could even be maintained, occupied much of the early attempts to form biology and establish or extract its philosophical, scientific, and theological debts. Built upon these issues is the relationship of sensibility and irritability to cognition — as the medical form of the animation problem — and the question of speciation and form — as the geological and paleontological problem of transformation.[1] Or put colloquially, "why does a heart removed still beat" in regards to the former, and why do fossils portray species we can only assume are completely extinct in regards to the latter.

As we will see, there is little in common between those labeled vitalists other than a shared concern that mechanistic physics and science more generally appeared insufficient to explain how life came to be and how it maintains its existence. Rather than collapse these debates into an opposition of the scientific and the theological, or the vitalistic and the mechanical, it is more helpful to construct a schema of the guiding concepts of the various attempts to construct biology — or proto-biological theories of life — in terms of function, morphology, teleology, and self-organization. The cluster below have agents which should not be read as really existing things but as explanatory

---

1   John Zammito, *The Gestation of German Biology: Philosophy and Physiology from Stahl to Schelling* (Chicago: University of Chicago Press, 2017).

devices which may or may not be able to be cashed out in material terms. Furthermore, each theory has a temporal dimension which is central given how closely each theory is connected with geology and the question of the history of the human species, whether natural or unnatural — i.e., normative history. Lastly, the names listed are obviously not exhaustive, and furthermore this is not to suggest total or deep agreement between them but only that they agree upon the active agent while they may disagree on the correct theoretical reading of this agent as well as its temporal dimensions.

There are at least four clusters of concepts that have some connection to vitalism, or again, more broadly, non-mechanistic theories of life:

Agent: Function *Theory:* Degeneration/Transformation *Temporal Dimension:* Catastrophe (Stahl, Cuvier, Bichat)	*Agent:* Morphology *Theory:* Metamorphosis/Archetypes *Temporal Dimension:* Uniformity (Goethe, Buffon)
Agent: Teleomechanism *Theory:* Epigenesis/Preformation *Temporal Dimension:* Natural History (Blumenbach, Kant)	*Agent:* Self-Organization *Theory:* Life force/Vital matter *Temporal Dimension:* History of Nature (Herder, Kielmeyer, Schelling)

These conceptual clusters can be allied with their respective thinkers as well as the natural philosophical disciplines connected to them. The first cluster can be aligned with the work of Georg Ernst Stahl and with the practice of medicine more broadly. This makes a certain amount of intuitive sense as physiology, especially through the lens of medical science, is ultimately concerned with how and whether a given body is healthy, that is, functioning properly according to its capacities and its environment.

As Zammito portrays it, Stahl can only be called a vitalist insofar as he believed that living matter was organized in such a way that mechanism could not account for its capacities. But function for Stahl does not go any deeper in that it does not necessarily apply to the matter of life or life forces. The "specialness" of life for Stahl remains at the level of description in part because, for Stahl, his commitment to Pietist Christianity did not require any appeal to force or special matter to explain the animating spark of life.[2]

Function is also emphasized by Georges Cuvier, but it is relevant in terms of life as being connected to species-wide fitness more so than health, as having formed in such a way to operate in the right environment. Because Cuvier is concerned with life viewed at a broader scale — at the level of species — his emphasis on function indexes the problem of extinction and the fitness of an entire species failing.

Morphology is linked most notably to Johann Wolfgang von Goethe and perhaps emerges first in relation to botany and zoology. The operative tension being between metamorphosis and archetype, between different types of internal development and change, is central to the question in terms of whether the shapes possible in development are already present or otherwise guided by external conditions or idealities, such as archetypes taken in an almost Platonic sense.

Karl Fink's *Goethe's History of Science* explains how Goethe entertained the notion of a botanical archetype through the example of the proliferous rose and its sub-archetype of the leaf.[3] Fink highlights how Goethe was well aware that morphology was a powerful but also dangerous gift.[4] The epistemological and ontological tension in the question of an internal model has been well debated. In terms of Goethe's primal plant, it has been

---

[2] Pietism was a movement within Lutheranism that emphasized pragmatic and personal aspects of the faith in an attempt to return to the initial spirit of Luther's teachings.

[3] Karl Fink, *Goethe's History of Science* (Cambridge: Cambridge University Press, 1991), 27.

[4] Ibid., 40.

argued that it has no ontological stake (Goethe was not really looking for the primal plant in nature) but is rather a research fiction, a mental model to guide his botanical researches.[5]

Such ambiguity applies either way to uniformity — archetypes can manifest in any matter or force and in turn suggests that there is a general uniformity across nature; that is, certain shapes can emerge in different animal species or even across living and non-living entities. Yet this often begs the question as to the status of space — that is, if a certain collusion of forces causes particular shapes to emerge, why do they happen where they do? Space itself, particularly under the self-organizational model, becomes an intuition regarding the deployment of forces rather than a container for them.

Teleomechanism is associated with Immanuel Kant and Johann Friedrich Blumenbach. Kant was taken by Blumenbach's notion of *Bildungstrieb,* or formative drive or force. Both Kant and Blumenbach saw the formative drive as an organizational principle without an ontological or metaphysical wager attached to it. Yet as Jennifer Mensch has pointed out, following Robert Richards and Timothy Lenoir, Blumenbach's *Bildungstrieb* was not a creative vital principle but simply highlighted an organizational principle already at work in the inorganic but only apparent in the organic.

Kant can be seen as only slightly sympathetic to vitalism in part because of his agnosticism about biology and his utilization of purposiveness as a "light" or rational form of teleology. As Kant argues, we must treat life *as if* it has a purpose following its behavior, but it cannot be articulated as precisely as physical phenomena can be: there will never be a "Newton for a blade of grass."

Even more complicated is the relation between theories of development in Kant which are of course connected to the teleological treatment of life. Preformationism, dating at least as far

---

5   Robert J. Richards, *The Romantic Conception of Life: Science and Philosophy in the Age of Goethe* (Chicago: University of Chicago Press, 2002), 394–95.

back as Aristotle, extends mechanism, or at least mechanistic explanation, to the biological, especially in terms of embryology. Regarding teleology, preformationism can be taken as the validation of formal cause, the biological blueprint being always-already present. Preformationists, of both the spermist and ovist variety, view the plan of biological life as tightly folded up inside of the generative matter — i.e., the sperm or the egg.

Preformationist theory gained a second life with the development of microscopy especially in the Netherlands of the 16th century. Doubts about how generative matter could "fit" the complex plans and parts seemed assuaged by finding ever more fine layers of detail complexity under microscopic magnification. Jennifer Mensch argues that Kant was sympathetic to preformationism in that he treated it as a biological heuristic,[6] and Zammito likewise suggests that Kant was committed to a more "generic form" of preformationism.[7]

But as many have highlighted, Kant was also sympathetic to the concept of epigenesis: namely, that the environment had an altering effect on the development of the organism. But again, whether this occurs in a material manner or at the level of explanation remains somewhat unclear. Mensch along with Malabou claim that epigenesis applies to knowledge, that there is an epigenesis of reason and that this is a transcendental and not a natural phenomenon.[8]

Lastly, self-organization at least in the sense of vital materialism and vital forces (*Lebenskraft*) has to do with a metaphysical thesis that claims that living matter — or perhaps all matter, as in the case of Schelling — complexifies itself and is the result of

---

[6] Jennifer Mensch, *Kant's Organicism: Epigenesis and the Development of Critical Philosophy* (Chicago: University of Chicago Press, 2013), 8. See also Amanda Jo Goldstein's *Sweet Science: Romantic Materialism and the New Logics of Life* (Chicago: University of Chicago Press, 2017), 79.

[7] Zammito, *Gestation of German Biology*, 232.

[8] Mensch, *Kant's Organicism*, 8, 124. Andrew Cooper critiques such a reading and Tarizzo seems to read Kant's use of epigenesis as metaphysical and closer in line to Blumenbach. Andrew Cooper, "Two Directions for Teleology: Naturalism and Idealism," *Synthese* 195, no. 8 (2018): 3097–119.

underlying powers or forces building off of Spinoza and Epicurean thought.

Following Lenoir and Zammito, vital materialism was the result of the combination of French materialism and German Romanticism. Zammito emphasizes how the different uptakes of Newton in Germany and France in the 1700s affected the gestation of vital materialism. For one, Zammito argues that the reception of Newton can be divided into its experimental and mathematical aspects. The experimental aspect was connected to the deployment of forces in nature — to identify and understand the very meaning of force. This is bound to understanding nature as having a history that is as something changing structurally over time as opposed to a semi-stable, teleomechanical, goal-oriented nature that can only be classified and cataloged. That is, if nature is force or power "at bottom," then the listing of what exists now is insufficient to understand what nature is, what it has been, and what it will be.

One important consequence of the activity of the *Lebenskraft* or of the vital matter is the softening of the boundary between sensibility and cognition. This was the essential disagreement between Johann Gottfried Herder and Blumenbach. Herder modified and extended theories of irritability — applying to muscle fibers — and sensibility — applying to the nerve fibers — taken from Albrecht von Haller and complicated by an active material nature. Herder's difference from von Haller in part marks the difference between those that would have vital forces issuing from vital matters (von Haller) or vital matters being the result of vital forces (Herder, Schelling).

2. Teleology as Problem

This is a wide range of concepts that each on their own could fill volumes. For the following, I wish to focus on how each of these approaches deals with the question of teleology. While Kant and Blumenbach's teleomechanical approach addresses teleology directly, the other three conceptual clusters involve teleological concerns regarding the direction and motivation of life.

While teleomechanism keeps teleology at arm's length as a heuristic, life's reason for taking shape, self-organizing, or functioning appears as more than a heuristic but perhaps is not so strong as to count as a metaphysical impulse or force. The difficulties in parsing the role of the teleological from the vital accounts for a contemporary vague meaning of vitalism that appears simultaneously "scientific" and theological in an uncritical manner. It is vital in life's unthinkability and theological in giving it an obscure intelligence.

Hans Driesch's *The History of Vitalism* is instructive in trying to sort out the vexed relation between vitalism and teleology. As he writes:

> We are confronted by the all important question: are those processes in the organism, which we described as purposive, perhaps only *purposive in virtue of a given structure* or tectonic, of a "machine" in the widest sense, on the basis of which they play their part, being purposive therefore only in the sense in which processes in a machine made by men are purposive; or is there *another special kind of teleology* in the realm of organic life?[9]

Driesch will go on to claim that the existence of purposiveness is not at issue since it is used in the discussions of mechanistic and non-organic systems in the sense that we are discussing things built or designed. Thus, there is no problem in saying that a bucket is meant to hold water, or a thermometer's purpose is to rise and fall with temperature — the real issue, according to Driesch, is that of autonomy. Thus, descriptive teleology, as in the case with the thermometer, effectively brackets the question of autonomy and is not a discussion of teleology proper. For Driesch, the real debate surrounds static or dynamic teleol-

---

9 Hans Driesch, *The History and Theory of Vitalism*, trans. C.K. Ogden (London: Palgrave, 1914), 5.

ogy. In static teleology, life is merely a special case of mechanical laws (this would seem to follow Stahl's emphasis on function), whereas dynamic teleology admits that the processes of life have "real" autonomy.

However, when Driesch discusses Stahl at some length, he associates him not with vitalism but with animism — that God imparted an animating motion onto the body that was carried on with its special functions of blood circulation, secretion, and excretion.[10] One can see the complexity of Stahl's position, and while he may be often classified as a vitalist after the word came into fashion, it is important to note that Stahl thought life had to be imparted from a non-living and non-physical force — namely the divine. In this regard, despite being positioned against Gottfried Wilhelm Leibniz and René Descartes, it does not make sense to call Stahl a vitalist, since the reason that functional medical description cannot capture the deep inner workings of the body is not because of living matter or a life force but because of divinity. As Zammito points out, the real sticking point between Leibniz and Stahl in their debates was not on the matter of life as mechanistic or non-mechanistic but rather regarded the status of the soul as rational (Leibniz, Descartes) or as merely animating (Stahl).

In Driesch's history, he discusses Georges-Louis Leclerc, Comte de Buffon as a kind of half-vitalist, and likewise with Pierre Louis Mauerpetuis, in that both believe in the efficacy of the mechanistic description of the world but at the same time see the development of living things from smaller, seemingly less complex, entities as something peculiar to life.[11]

Driesch's comments on Kant and Blumenbach are a bit more surprising. Driesch suggests that either Kant was unwilling or unable to make the distinction between static and dynamic teleology and furthermore accuses Kant of misunderstanding or misapplying Blumenbach's ideas. This later claim is quite strong and in part may say more about Driesch's insistence that any-

---

10 Ibid., 35–36.
11 Ibid., 41–43.

one who endorses epigenesis is in fact a vitalist. Driesch's view goes against the dominant historical as well as the differing contemporary view of the Kant-Blumenbach relationship. For quite some time most scholarship viewed their relationship as generally symbiotic: Blumenbach's notion of the *Bildungstrieb* aided Kant in the completion of the *Critique of the Power of Judgment*, and Blumenbach in turn adopted the teleomechanical views of Kant as viewed as drive or force as a well-formed regulative principle.

Richards has argued that their exchange should be viewed more as a productive misunderstanding ("Kant and Blumenbach on the Bildungstrieb: A Historical Misunderstanding"). Central to this, as Richards lays out, is that Kant thought biology — or really, the life sciences, since the coinage of biology nearly coincided with Kant's death — was not a possible science whereas Blumenbach, and many others, clearly did not agree. This aspect of Kant's third critique seems oddly missing from Driesch's analysis and the latter attempts to argue that Kant could be a vitalist if vitalism, as the pure and true autonomy of life, applied especially, or only, to human beings, and since humans are a part of nature, some part of nature must therefore be vitalistic.

For Richards, it is those thinkers who opened the way towards self-organization, such as Carl Friedrich Kielmeyer and Schelling, who pushed Kant's thinking properly in the direction of biology, thereby naturalizing teleology but not in terms of life's inner principles but nature's inner and outer principle. Such a move is rejected by Driesch, who dismisses the nature-philosophers for the same reason he dismisses Goethe, namely, the emphasis on type or inner gene.[12] Yet, as Schelling made clear early on, the search for and use of a type, whether primal germ or actant, is folly — either everything is primal germ, or

---

12 Ibid., 94–95.

nothing is. In Theresa M. Kelley's "Restless Romantic Plants," Goethe is often found speaking of affinities across species.[13]

Furthermore, and as Zammito has illustrated, while Kant was for a time sympathetic to a proto-evolutionary theory of vital development evidenced by common archetypes across species, he soon backed away from such a possibility, something which is evident in calling such ideas "monstrous" when he read them in Blumenbach's student Herder. For Zammito this period emphasizes his brief foray into the possibility of a history of nature, but then Kant steps back from the "abyss" and holds fast to a natural history.

Rather than Driesch's claim that Kant fundamentally misunderstands Kant, it seems that for Driesch, and Driesch's reading of Blumenbach, teleology must belong to life and life only. This particularization of the teleological force or drive, depending on how Driesch wants to define life's limits vis-à-vis the physical, would appear to have the benefit of not, at least on the face of it, disrupting other forms of science. The "old vitalism," which Driesch does dismiss rather harshly, is of course attempting to develop biology as well as to change, in various ways, those sciences intimately connected with biology at the same time, such as physiology, geology, zoology, and botany.[14] For this reason teleology can be an internal drive tied to shape — as in the case of those who emphasize morphology — or it can be a broader complexity that applies to all of nature, as is the case with the *Naturphilosophen* in general.

But beyond this of course it is not merely where teleology is but what is it supposed to do. The emphasis on the latter part of this question, at the cost of the former, seems to be what draws such ire from Driesch in the context of epigenesis requiring vitalism and vice versa. Teleology explains life's complexity

---

13 Theresa M. Kelley, "Restless Romantic Plants: Goethe Meets Hegel," *European Romantic Review* 20, no. 2 (April 2009): 189.

14 Jane Bennett makes a similar distinction as Driesch in discussing old as opposed to new or critical vitalism. See Jane Bennett, "Neither Vitalism nor Mechanism," in *Vital Matter: A Political Ecology of Things* (Durham: Duke University Press, 2010), 62–63.

in a certain sense for Driesch (life is always-already thinking), whereas nature's productive processes can be seen as goal-oriented more broadly because they tend towards the evolution of a plurality of forms from simple origins or towards a complexification of entities due to the crossing and interaction of powers or forces. In the end this is little doubt why Driesch shifts to the term entelechy that can be seen as a form of self-organization but one that is organized by an already present intelligence, an intelligence already at work in the most basic aspects of life.

It is in this sense that Driesch belongs to vitalism in what it means for thinkers such as Henri Bergson and Gilles Deleuze. However it could be said that Bergson and Deleuze, in different ways, desubstantialize vitalism and yet this desubstantialization for Bergson is held in the power of the image of thought, and for Deleuze, in a desubstantialization that is accompanied by a fully sensate materialization.[15] This in turn leads vitalism away from teleology and back towards the notions of self-organization and chaos so lauded by Deleuze and his interpreters; and yet, still, in however strained sympathy with Driesch, these notions of chaos and complexity are somehow thinkable or arrestable by thought. Hence, this is why, as Ray Brassier has pointed out, Deleuze can utilize arguments for biological complexity against the claims of physics and thereby make statements such as that thermodynamics can be an illusion becomes it would contravene the creative becoming of biological existence in the far future and thus betrays a smuggling of teleology back into the biological matter which is no longer matter but Deleuzian materiality.[16]

---

15 This is why Bergson is critical of mechanism, finalism, and, albeit to a lesser extent, vitalism: because they indicate tendencies in our thought and are not in the universe. To assume that any of these theories are settled would be to set, in advance, the limits of creation over time. See Henri Bergson, *Creative Evolution* (New York: Dover Publications, 1911), 40–43.

16 In a sense we could accuse Deleuze of being a kind of dishonest panpsychist. But to follow this line in detail would require an in-depth investigation of the influences of Raymond Ruyer and Gilbert Simondon.

What is at stake, whether in the form of vitalism over "mere" biological life, materiality over matter, or sense over quarantined reason, is whether the biological can be articulated in any constructive value-neutral sense without falling into either the caricatures of the reckless Frankensteinian experimenter or the theologically-imbibed, purpose-chasing wanderer.

3. Xenomorphology and Retro-Teleology

The *Alien* franchise of films began as an exploration of the weaponization of life and has become focused on questions of teleology and intelligent design. This order of concerns is chronological in terms of the order of the release of the films and not within the timeline the films are set. From the perspective of the release of the films, teleology comes at the end. This teleology shifts forms, being about intelligent design and then being about artificial general intelligence, at least in terms of the shepherd of speciation and panspermia.

In the film *Prometheus,* set in 2093, the aliens known as the engineers seed life on Earth by decomposing their own genetic structure using a mutagen to accelerate its generative effects. It is then implied that the engineers maintained contact with numerous ancient cultures leaving them a star map to the planet LV-223. The Weyland Corporation funds the adventure because he its founder is obsessed with the big questions of "where do we come from?"

The planet turns out to be less than welcoming as it is an abandoned weapons installation filled with the dangerous seeding mutagen. The mutagen appears to weaponize simple forms of life, turning worms into pale serpents for instance, as well as changing humans into brutes. However, two of the human characters are infected (one through an intentionally contaminated drink and then his infected sperm impregnates Elizabeth Shaw); the results are quite different.

Shaw gives birth via a self-induced machine-assisted cesarean to a squid-like parasite. Later on, this parasite impregnates one of the engineers and creates the first form of the xenomorph known as the Decon. Only Shaw and the android David survive the encounter and go off looking for the engineers to find out why they would create humanity and then decide to wipe them out.

The film's sequel, *Covenant*, which is set in 2104, follows a ship of colonists who, after getting knocked out of cryosleep by a random radiation burst, pick up a rogue transmission. The transmission, it so happens, is from the now dead Elizabeth Shaw (singing to herself), and only David remains after having poisoned the engineers en masse. In the years since crashing on the planet, David started conducting experiments and perfecting the Decon strain into other forms and eventually becoming the xenomorph of the alien films.

David's lair appears as a makeshift naturalist's laboratory, piles of parchment depicting vivisections and other organic diagrams, models, and preserved specimens. Such scenes, since we know David is experimenting, afford a delirium of what is made and what has been found or, the discoverer's confusion between intended and accidental. David's comportment matches that of Doctor Frankenstein, who in turn has often been linked to various *Naturphilosophen*, especially Oken or perhaps even Schelling via Coleridge.

Following the narrative chronology, almost twenty years go by before the setting of *Alien* in 2122. In *Alien* the crew of the mining ship Nostromo are woken up to investigate a signal on the planet LV-426. There they find a derelict space craft with a dead engineer and a cargo hold of xenomorph eggs. One of the members is parasitized and dies spawning the alien which then eliminates the humans, save one (and one cat). Important, especially viewing the film after the prequels, is the involvement of the artificial life form Ash. Chronologically viewed, Ash is simply a hired gun of the Weyland-Yutani, attempting to get the creature for them in order to profit off of it through bio-weapons development. Seeing *Alien* first of course begs the question of how the company knew the aliens where there—i.e., they must have recognized the warning signal from the engineers' ship. Narratively of course Ash is a distant relative of David and is carrying on his elder's work by freeing or loosing the aliens either upon humanity (a revenge against the name of the father — humanity) or simply freeing the alien because it is, in Ash's words, "a pure survivor." When interrogated for his actions, Ash displays an almost religious devotion to the alien: it is a perfect organism, it is incredibly tough — generating lay after lay of silicate. Furthermore, Ash admires its purity or its simplicity; it is unburdened by morality and so on. It is important to note that morality is explicitly a burden for Ash, as he knows it was programmed into him. Likewise, he is only able to countermand his basic morality — protecting humans — by receiving an order from the company — with the caveat, "crew expendable".

Aliens (2179)
For the themes that concern us here, the sequel to *Alien* mostly doubles down on the corporate greed angle. Carter J. Burke takes on the role of Ash in attempting to get samples of the alien organisms back to Earth despite their annihilation of an entire terraforming colony. It is mostly the fleshing out of the xenomorph's life cycle — the entry into the hive and the encounter with the queen — that the film advances, as well as, albeit in a minor sense, the vicious purity of the aliens. Their capacity for intelligence is extended (e.g., cutting the power, the royal guards responding to the queen, the queen's escape) but less is stated explicitly about the aliens as a form of life other than that they are unique and should not, according only to Burke, be subject to arbitrary extermination.

Alien 3 (2179)
The survivors' return home is disrupted and only Ripley survives the crash on a mostly abandoned penal colony where a skeleton crew of ultraviolent men (XYY chromo boys) keep the furnace running and have meanwhile found religion. A new alien is born, a birth that accompanies the funeral of Ripley's former comrades. The funeral speech speaks of the seeds of new life while the alien bursts from its host, either a dog or a steer depending on the version, depicting a certain morphological sym-

pathy—moving differently because of its four-legged host. As with its predecessors, *Alien 3* repeats the attempt by Weyland-Yutani to acquire the alien embryo for bio-weapons research: "Think of all the things we could learn from it!" screams the creator and model for the Bishop android.

While the faith of Dylan and his fellow inmates is consistently rebuked by Ripley's semi-suicidal pragmatism, the films kindles the theological resistance to a kind of non-normative form of "pure" life or pure synthesis of reproductivity and survival instinct.

Alien: Resurrection (2379)
In *Alien: Resurrection,* which takes place 200 years later, Ripley is cloned from blood samples taken from Furiona 161 in order to extract the xenomorph queen embryo. Imperfections in the cloning process leave Ripley Clone 8, who is the film's protagonist, with traces of xenomorph characteristics while the queen eventually shifts from laying eggs in her usual parasitoid fashion to developing a womb due to the genetic drift.

What links the film most closely with the prequels which would follow is the android Call. Call, who passes for human most of the film, is revealed to be an *auton,* an android made by other androids, some of whom managed to escape. The autons are emotional—too real—and driven by a sense of duty. In the film, Call makes it her mission to stop the military from cloning Ripley and breeding the xenomorphs; essentially, to stop humans from destroying themselves despite the fact that humans wiped her species out.

David becomes a kind of inverse of Call, deciding not only that he is unimpressed with the designs and purposes of his creators (humans), but that their creators (the engineers) in turn require total annihilation. The organic/inorganic breach, however thin, perhaps non-existent, is crossed by an appeal to the purity of violence of the aliens. The xenomorphs embody a kind of machine-like simplicity before being "mucked up" by morals and values. If David and his ilk are disabused of their similarity to humans because they are soulless, then so be it. David's creations are the properly soulless heart of an auto-creative, parasitoid, insect-like wave of blood-sheened corruption.

But reading the films in their narrative order in some sense undoes the kind of biological miraculousness that so fascinated Ash in the "beginning." In a sense, Ash is simply marveling, unknowingly, at his great-great grandparents' invention and is willing, though the degree here is questionable, to hand it over to the humans for militarization. This is another level of how the films, again filmed narratively, seem intent on rejecting Darwinism, and especially reflect that life is a contingent event. Yet the creation of humans by the engineers, or by any non-divine entity, would seem to rule out a soul in that it is something more than life, or something that guarantees meaning in the sense of having a purpose. Otherwise, if intentional creation was enough to grant a soul, David could not be denied one simply by not being made of flesh and bone. Shaw's comment that she does not wish to remove her cross because she thinks it is possible that something divine made the engineers, or some even older species, holds no water.

Our sense of teleological purposefulness becomes like a virus that erases the oldest collective memory of where we come from. There must always be another older creator and eventually there will be one who is appropriately divine and worthy of having given us some "direction."

4. Creation Mists

In "An Entangled Forest: Evolution and Speculative Fiction," Ben Carver draws out connections between theories of life and genre fiction. Carver suggests that Stephen Jay Gould has a speculative fictional moment when he imagines replaying the tape of evolution:

But in the sphere of evolutionary biology, how could we possibly test this hypothesis, that the survivals and extinctions of natural life are not determined solely by the internal logic of variation and competition; in other words, that natural history is determined from the distribution of starting conditions?

Gould proposes the experiment of "Replaying Life's Tape[,]" that is, to rewind history to the Cambrian moment 500 million years ago, and "see" if the same species survive, a procedure in which humans would have a special interest as the designers of the experiment: would we survive another roll of the dice? This is an experiment that can't be run, except in speculative fiction; H.G. Wells for instance chose to imagine a copy earth in his 1905 novel, *A Modern Utopia,* one where there was "like our planet, the same continents, the same islands, the same oceans and seas;" and even "every man, woman, and child alive has a Utopian parallel."[17]

And yet the altered origin myth of human life does not unfold a particularly exciting counterfactual history as some of the stories that Carver suggests do. Nothing will have changed except that meaning, or at least the possibility of meaning, could be proven scientifically, that is, we share all our DNA with that of the engineers so they clearly created us from "themselves" made us, and because they are intelligent beings, they *must have had a good reason to do so.*

Again, David himself suggests that the engineers' reason for creating humans could be no more special than "because they could." Even the message left to humans is not an invitation to the engineers' home planet but to a biological weapons proving ground. A place where any overly rude visitors could be quickly dispatched out of sight. To go looking for God and to find Kurtz seems not completely unexpected.

> Going up that river was like traveling back to the earliest beginnings of the world, when vegetation rioted on the earth and the big trees were kings. An empty stream, a great silence, an impenetrable forest. The air was warm, thick, heavy, sluggish. There was no joy in the brilliance of sunshine. The long stretches of the waterway ran on, deserted, into the

---

17 Ben Carver, "An Entangled Forest: Evolution and Speculative Fiction," *Urbanomic/Documents,* 2018, https://www.urbanomic.com/document/entangled-forest/.

gloom of overshadowed distances. On silvery sand-banks hippos and alligators sunned themselves side by side. The broadening waters flowed through a mob of wooded islands; you lost your way on that river as you would in a desert, and butted all day long against shoals, trying to find the channel, till you thought yourself bewitched and cut off for ever from everything you had known once — somewhere — far away — in another existence perhaps. There were moments when one's past came back to one, as it will sometimes when you have not a moment to spare for yourself; but it came in the shape of an unrestful and noisy dream, remembered with wonder amongst the overwhelming realities of this strange world of plants, and water, and silence.[18]

It is a well-rehearsed factoid about the *Aliens* films that the space-faring vessels in them bear the names of Joseph Conrad's fictional towns. But the tether seems frail, other than noting that the ship of the first film was a mining vessel. And despite Weyland-Yutani's motto which drips with colonial fervor, "building better worlds," they only inhabit and terraform worlds with no indigenous life, mere hunks of rock.

But the passage from Conrad suggests a perspective that dwells upon something altogether different from teleology. It is rather a cacophonous orchestra of accidents biological, geological, and noetic. Such musings on time and the primeval (if they can be moved away from the Victorian tendency to see "less civilized people" as an altered mirror of European past states) remerge in the diagonal continuities so loved by Ballard. In *The Drowned World,* one of Ballard's typical failed scientists discusses how deeply inorganic traces are left on the mind:

> Every step we've taken in our evolution is a milestone inscribed with organic memories — from the enzymes controlling the carbon dioxide cycle to the organisation of the

---

18 Joseph Conrad, *Heart of Darkness and the Secret Sharer* (New York: Bantam Books, 1981), 55–56.

brachial plexus and the nerve pathways of the Pyramid cells in the mid-brain, each is a record of a thousand decisions taken in the face of a sudden physico-chemical crisis. Just as psychoanalysis reconstructs the original traumatic situation in order to release the repressed material, so we are now being plunged back into the archaeopsychic past, uncovering the ancient taboos and drives that have been dormant for epochs. The brief span of an individual life is misleading. Each one of us is as old as the entire biological kingdom, and our bloodstreams are tributaries of the great sea of its total memory. The uterine odyssey of the growing foetus recapitulates the entire evolutionary past, and its central nervous system is a coded time scale, each nexus of neurons and each spinal level marking a symbolic station, a unit of neuronic time.[19]

Elsewhere I have discussed the more psychoanalytic traces of this but here it is the issue of what biological means — rather than simply failing to give enough meaning, that is, teleological meaning — that interests me.[20] The tension between natural history and the history of nature emerges again — between submitting nature to a history of rational classification, or, on the other hand, wagering that reason itself (and its many ingredients) have been continuously remade through biological, chemical, and geological tumult. This latter sense of the history of nature builds upon recapitulation championed by Kielmayer and Schelling. Beyond the well-known Lamarkian version of "ontogeny recapitulates phylogeny," Kielmayer and Schelling did not limit the repetition of real patterns to biology but could happen across the inorganic and the organic. The closeness but difference to the morphological paradigm outlined above is important to note since these real patterns might appear to fall in line with Goethe's seed; yet, importantly, the morphological schema emphasizes a kind of *internal teleology*, the seedcorn or

---

19 J.G. Ballard, *The Drowned World* (Fourth Estate, 2014), 43–44.
20 Ben Woodard, "Disinternment Loops," *Cyclops Journal* 2 (August 2017).

initial motor of the unfolding of the species must be set in some sense and this would also be restricted to the organic realm.

This is not to say there is nothing like teleology: the paradigm of self-organization at least implies some direction, at least towards organization, towards complexity or self-sufficiency. When Schelling states that humanity is "made for all the stars," he is not merely waxing poetic but claiming that if we are made for something, we are made for everything we could *potentially affect*.[21] At the same time Schelling consistently warns that we must not be overly impressed by the potentiality of thought at the cost of nature. Or, in other words, once rationalism forgets its ground in nature, thought begins to entertain a suicidal trajectory.

Yet a similar concern appears in Driesch, and in Bergson and Deleuze, that thought must then be able to grasp itself, in some positive or constructive sense, and any scientific theory which could threaten such a capacity is always already too abstract. Yet such a claim seems then only capable of having a narrative-like structure rather than a theory-like structure if it hopes to remain immune to the revisionary capacity of metrics or calculations or experiments. Theories of course involve, and often intentionally transform, the myths and narratives or practices that hold weight at the time. If this were not the case one might be surprised why there are such lengthy digressions on the training of pigeons in Darwin's *Origin of the Species*. It is of course an effective analogy of how significant changes can be made to a species through selection. As Gillian Beer has notably stressed, this is only one of many novelistic moves that Darwin had to make in order to help his seemingly wild concepts stick to the Victorian consciousness.[22]

Of course, the very same practices were used to tell a different story. Returning to Carver's "Entangled Forest":

---

21 F.W.J. von Schelling, "Exhibition of the Process of Nature," trans. Iain Hamilton Grant, unpublished manuscript, 2013.
22 Gillian Beer, *Darwin's Plots: Evolutionary Narrative in Darwin, George Eliot and Nineteenth-Century Fiction* (Cambridge: Cambridge University Press, 1983).

In the address of 1858, Wallace presented his paper "On the Tendency of Varieties to Depart Indefinitely from the Original Type." Instead of making the enclosed space of the island the illustrative setting for the emergence of new varieties, he begins with the case of domesticated varieties. The ability of agriculturalists and breeders to create new varieties of dogs and cattle in a relatively short space of time was taken to be evidence of the immutability of species in conditions of nature — consider the way that breeds of dog rapidly "return" to earlier broad types. Wallace argues, against this view, that the processes of descent and variation are universal but that in conditions of domesticity, the variations produced are not subject to the competition for resources among organisms in nature: "The life of wild animals is a struggle for existence," he writes, incorporating Thomas Malthus's expression. Unlike its wild cousins, the domestic animal "has food provided for it, is sheltered, and often confined." This isolation from nature has a double role of explanation; it demonstrates difference ("Our quickly fattening pigs, short-legged sheep, pouter pigeons, and poodle dogs could never have come into existence in a state of nature"); but it also illustrates the operation of universal processes to which animals both in nature and under domestication are subject.[23]

Carver goes on to argue how the special case, the isolated experiment (the island, the narrow valley), shows how all of nature is subject to the same rule and thus such isolations provide simultaneous estrangement and familiarity. This indexes Science Fiction's own pre-history which became its own genre by synthesisizing of Scientific Romances (such as Wells's War of the Worlds) and lost world or lost people stories. The theoretical narratives explored here (through and around the realm of biology) index two strands of thought in a similar way but remain at the level of explanation: theories of biology that gestated in the romantic or enchanting eye and a formalization of life that,

---

[23] Carver, "An Entangled Forest."

in the mode of lost worlds, finds lost and failed counterfactual stories (an extinct line, a regressive trait) in every morphology, skeletal curio, and outward "deviation" of the biological entity of homo sapiens.

Conclusion

Davide Tarizzo's book *Life: A Modern Invention* begins with Foucault's *Order of Things* as the defining text of how the category of life became inseparable from modernity and human self-understanding. Zammito likewise notes Foucault's book; whereas Tarizzo wants to follow in its footsteps, Zammito rejects its central theme that life did not exist before 1800. By following Foucault, yet paying more attention to the influence of German thinkers on biology such as Schelling, Tarizzo is less interested in the conceptual history as it mixes with the scientific history as in the political and ethical ramifications, that is, how life enters the realm of law and politics as an imperishable theme of modernity. For Tarizzo, Darwin is a necessary condition for the eugenics of Nazism and thus life as autonomous yet perfectible is the life that "does not exist" prior to 1800.[24]

For Tarizzo, the German Romanticists and *Naturphilosophen* equated life and autonomy as Kant did but added a level of deficiency or sickness: to be alive was to be a fragment of life that could live more, that could evolve or transform. As Tarizzo has it, Darwin pursues a similar investigation into life but one that is not explicitly motivated by metaphysics. Yet there is little to no trace of the explanatory power of Darwin's work, only its crimes of unacknowledged theoretical and political consequences.

The common tactic, it seems, is to fix the balance sheet of the natural and the normative, though Foucault would balk at

---

24 This tension of life and the living as a modern invention is indirectly challenged by Eugene Thacker. Thacker suggests that already in Aristotle there is a problematic mapping between life and the living as soon as the soul or psukhe is introduced. See Eugene Thacker, "Nine Disputations on Theology and Horror," in *Collapse IV*, ed. Robin Mackay (Falmouth: Urbanomic Press, 2008), 55–92.

the use of the term normative; to hold high Hume's fork that keeps the matters of "is" and the matters of "ought" at a respectable difference from one another; to infer that their collusion can only end in disaster as evidenced by the disaster of modernity's techno-scientism. But this too often manifests itself as a purportedly humanitarian ban on any account of life that could lead to ethical practices. But to completely suspend such a link would seem increasingly untenable in a world where the very "isness" of nature appears in question; that is, ecological crisis in particular seems to suggest that the state of nature issues ethical imperatives.

Unsurprisingly the functional account of life and its relation to teleology appears the most compatible with such worries, yet it has, arguably, the worst legacy of how it utilizes teleology and the ethical and political claims thereby warranted, especially in the form of degeneration. Teleomechanism and morphology appear too disconnected from the very possibility of extinction and climate collapse — the teleomechanistic perspective denies the possibility of human extinction (Kant contra Camper), and it is unclear how Goethe's morphology extends into the topic of extinction without becoming a fully functionalist approach that would be too costly to the importance of form, and hence to the thinkability of nature in itself.

The hurdle of thinkability is displaced, but by no means solved, by the emphasis on self-organization. If the appeal to archetypes or forms encounters the problem of function and fitness of environment, then the problem for self-organization is the problem of scale and, in turn, whether this implies holism at one level or not.

Potentiation of forces appears to beg the question of how to explain difference in kind, not only in terms of why there are so many forces, but also why forces give rise to things at all. This latter question bothered Schelling deeply and it guided his work in *Naturphilosophie,* especially in the *First Outline.* In that text, in which Schelling relies upon transcendental philosophy to think nature (whereas in *Ideas for a Philosophy of Nature* he relies upon experimental data to explain the emergence of thought), he thus flirts with something like archetypes or real patterns in nature — actants. But Schelling seems to suggest this is the Kantian or more generally the transcendental understanding of real patterns or tendencies, which for us can only seem to be errors or interruptions in the flow of nature's potencies.[25] Such a metaphysical stance does not deny either function or fitness but ungrounds the rooting of either in the species' form.

Such agnosticism about the real patterns of biological life, however, are not favorably entertained by Foucault nor by his sympathizers. As he writes in *The Order of Things*, "in truth it is impossible for natural history to conceive of the history of nature," thereby rejecting the self-organization principle.[26] Yet such a hermeneutic resistance to the real ground of nature, in the name of epistemological cautiousness, defends the teleological stance in absentia. Despite his post-structuralist credentials and the subsequent requirement of being against meta-theories, Foucault (at times, not always) defends a notion of the human that remains immune to scientific or rational investigation other than as an abuse of power.

The question is this: what are the stakes of life and teleology in the face of the human that is washed away by the ceaseless undulations of the tide?[27] While it seems clear that Foucault is rejecting a humanist teleology that would co-opt the modern process of subjectivation, it remains too unclear what the status of life is other than just as an epistemic playground. This is all the

---

25 Tarizzo, *Life*, 149. Tarizzo mentions three aspects of Schelling's theory of life: defectiveness of life, progression of life, and life as preexisting its forms. But I believe that Schelling emphasized a potentiation of life, an increasing complexity, and not a progression in the sense for which social Darwinists argued.

26 Michel Foucault, *The Order of Things: An Archaeology of the Human Sciences* (New York: Pantheon Books, 1971), 157.

27 Reza Negarestani chooses to read Foucault's image as a positive or constructive endorsement of the revisionary power of reason to erase and redraw the image of the human in ever more subtle forms. See Reza Negarestani, "The Labor of the Inhuman," in *#Accelerate: The Accelerationist Reader*, eds. Robin Mackay and Armen Avanessian (Falmouth: Urbanomic Press, 2014), 446.

more telling in a text that is so curiously silent on Darwin, and on the real explanatory effects of his ideas. Without accounting for the real conditions of creation, teleology will return in the form of a disease, a *teleologia* — a pained remembrance of the feeling of knowing one's origin despite the impossibility of finding an origin sufficient to the false narcissism of the champions of "finitude."

Bibliography

Ballard, J.G. *The Drowned World*. New York: Fourth Estate, 2014.

Bergson, Henri. *Creative Evolution*. Translated by Arthur Mitchell. New York: Dover Publications, 1911.

Beer, Gillian. *Darwin's Plots: Evolutionary Narrative in Darwin, George Eliot and Nineteenth-Century Fiction*. Cambridge: Cambridge University Press, 1983.

Bennett, Jane. *Vital Matter: A Political Ecology of Things*. Durham: Duke University Press, 2010.

Carver, Ben. "An Entangled Forest: Evolution and Speculative Fiction." *Urbanomic/Documents*, 2018. https://www.urbanomic.com/document/entangled-forest/.

Cooper, Andrew. "Two Directions for Teleology: Naturalism and Idealism." *Synthese* 195, no. 8 (2018): 3097–119. DOI: 10.1007/s11229-017-1364-5.

Conrad, Joseph. *Heart of Darkness and the Secret Sharer*. New York: Bantam Books, 1981.

Driesch, Hans. *The History and Theory of Vitalism*. Translated by C.K. Ogden. London: Palgrave, 1914.

Fink, Karl. *Goethe's History of Science*. Cambridge: Cambridge University Press, 1991.

Foucault, Michel. *The Order of Things: An Archaeology of the Human Sciences*. New York: Pantheon Books, 1971.

Goldstein, Amanda Jo. *Sweet Science: Romantic Materialism and the New Logics of Life*. Chicago: University of Chicago Press, 2017.

Kelley, Theresa M. "Restless Romantic Plants: Goethe Meets Hegel." *European Romantic Review* 20, no. 2 (April 2009): 187–95. DOI: 10.1080/10509580902840467.

Mensch, Jennifer. *Kant's Organicism: Epigenesis and the Development of Critical Philosophy*. Chicago: University of Chicago Press, 2013.

Negarestani, Reza. "The Labor of the Inhuman." In *#Accelerate: The Accelerationist Reader,* edited by Robin Mackay and

Armen Avanessian, 425–66. Falmouth: Urbanomic Press, 2014.

Richards, Robert J. *The Romantic Concept of Life: Science and Philosophy in the Age of Goethe*. Chicago: University of Chicago Press, 2002.

Schelling, F.W.J. von. "Exhibition of the Process of Nature." Translated by Iain Hamilton Grant. Unpublished manuscript, 2013.

Tarizzo, Davide. *Life: A Modern Invention*. Minneapolis: Minnesota University Press, 2017.

Thacker, Eugene. "Nine Disputations on Theology and Horror." In *Collapse IV; Concept-Horror,* edited by Robin Mackay, 55–92. Falmouth: Urbanomic Press, 2008.

Woodard, Ben. "Disinternment Loops." *Cyclops Journal* 2 (August 2017): 141–61. https://cyclopsjournal.net/1CYCLOPS%20JOURNAL_Issue%202_ONLINE.pdf.

Zammito, John. *The Gestation of German Biology: Philosophy and Physiology from Stahl to Schelling*. Chicago: University of Chicago Press, 2017.

2

Death of Horror

Amanda Beech

Postmodernism undertaken as a philosophical, political, and cultural practice has definitively underscored its limits. For culture at large, the illustration of a world that is stretched, fragmented, and de-ontologized, where exteriority is threaded through the experience as immanence, is mirrored in our political incapacity to think a *future equality*. These two facets demonstrate the requirement to accomplish a thinking of the unknown (the future) and the genuine possibility of a project (equality) where both call for certain de-mythologizations of the uniqueness of selfhood. Horror, as a cultural phenomenon, speaks to this issue of human limitations, equality, and our capacity to take negativity seriously. It does this sometimes directly and sometimes naïvely, acting as evidence of the problem that we have described. In light of these limits and potentialities, can horror accommodate a non-pessimistic view of language and maintain a project of realism? Can we assert that the language that expresses a mind-independent reality can explicate the conditions of *horror vacui,* without undermining language as having an essential equality or inequality with the real? Furthermore, does horror expressed in ordinary language provide access to meaningful, conceptual expression that is extensional rather than solipsistic? We will explore these questions by first advancing the limits of horror as a representational expression of nothingness as a means to ask how a new understanding of the relation between representation and the thought of nothing can rescue the operations of language after postmodernity.

Capitalist Horror

It's difficult to make a good horror film these days, and we know it. The genre has situated itself in retrospective feedback loops of the sequel, the prequel, the remake, and the ironic, tragic replay of itself as farce, where horror makes its own antirealist wink at the blood-spattered lens and knows the condition of its own constraint to horror as genre.[1] In this sense what we expect from horror, its concept, and what we often get or experience are very different. Horror promises the experience of the un-grounding of certain norms, vis-à-vis its transgressive character wherein spaces, characters, and objects traverse the worlds of the perceptible and the imperceptible but also threaten to reach the limits of our conceptual capacities. In this, horror's aim is to produce an experience of alterity that maintains its alien quality; *we will never be at home with the monster,* a guiding principle that offers a lived experience of the outside and holds the nowhere within the lens of human perception. Unfortunately, this attempt to hold open the space for alterity without qualities leads to disappointment, since horror recuperates the "beyond" as the reproduction of already existing norms, habits, and styles that get reinstated ironically, knowingly, as a claim to the meta-genre of new transgressions within the genre. In this postmodern format, we can see that horror fails. It loses its capacity for the outside. This is for two reasons: First, representations are always already seen to be inadequate to the real, underpinning horror by a kind of semantic pessimism; second, postmodern pluralism conditions a genealogy of the image's failure over time as an

---

[1] Franchises such as Keenan Ivory Wayans, dir., *Scary Movie* (Los Angeles: Dimension Films, 2000), HD exemplify this genre of meta-horror, where the tropes of various horror films and their allegorical contents, such as the "easy" girl gets it first, are culled from the history of the genre and replayed or re-enacted as another self-conscious representational form.

indeterminate process of the real. Here, the concept of horror resides within a contradiction of the real as process and an irreducible alienation in the given. This transcendental knowledge of the real has no traction upon the given; it is either sublated to the given as one of many other competing claims within it, or this knowledge is privatized to the realm of the psychological fictions of private minds. Time is in motion, but the future is closed.

Films like *Hostel* (2005, directed by Eli Roth) extrapolate this dance of horror as meta-genre — where horror narrates horror in the stage within the formalization of drama. *Hostel* foregrounds the connections between knowledge and money/power, entangling these discourses in the central narrative framework. Here, the constraints of the horror genre are made equivalent to the administration of neo-liberal economies, where the film features various modes of torture as artistic spectacle paid for in full by rich masochists. The victims of such terror are victims only because they are naïvely unaware of the traditional allegories of the horror genre: don't trust anyone, don't go backpacking in Eastern Europe, don't go out alone at night, don't be a slut, etc. Horror, in the film *Hostel,* is understood as a knowledge-based and fiscal-centered economy. For the victims, this is marked as lack and operates as a tradition of dramatic irony for the audience. The latter meets death precisely because they have not watched enough horror movies. For the masochistic rich, this *technē* of horror becomes a form of power exercised through money. Knowledge of horror does not enter the picture for the victims, nor for the actors; it is for us and the masochistic authors of the structure of horror in which others partake.

Hostel narrates the limits of the horror genre as something that is regulated as and through capital, and it self-consciously *remakes itself* within this paradigm through this picturing of its own constraint as capitalistic experience. For the globally mobile and endemically bored, perverse rich who pay to see and experience horror first-hand as art, another irony is palatable: we too pay to encounter a version of this artifice. But the complaint we have, that which bites us, is that unlike the punters in *Hostel,* the horror that we encounter is that a thought of the real is only capable of reiterating itself as a mode of illustrative, simulated, or representational experience, and that culture, *if* it thinks, has met the limits of its imagination. These limits are defined through the bind of money on the one hand and knowledge as the status quo on the other hand. Together, they extol problematic folklores of the representational image and subjectivity. Such traditions identify the horror genre as a form of Burke's sublime: an antirealist expression of the contradiction of how the impossibility of knowing the structure that subtends reality can be manifest in images which somehow access our non-relation to the real, conflating the narration of our relation to the real with a form of the pseudo-experience of it.

In this way, horror has witnessed and narrated its own exhaustion. It has authored its failure to be horror and has done so in order to transcend the parameters of its own paradigmatic framework. More than other genres — like the action movie, the spy thriller, or the rom-com, which have all to some extent delivered pastiche, parodic, and ironic self-referential treatments, and all have in their grasp some narrative of the real, be this the real of power or true love — horror seems to fail precisely because it specifies a precise and unique claim to the real in a set of images that are negatively charged with themes of violence, death, sadism, evil, and so on. There is a political claim, via a discourse on transgression and heterogeneity, where horror transcends the norms and regulations that govern the functional aspects of human society by connecting private, psychological experiences with larger philosophical and societal issues that include the question of what it means to be human and what a society is or might be. This format of horror apes a structure of existing power and its image. In framing and protecting an unreal fictional space that insures us against the fear that the horror pictured in the film is real, such fiction also asks us to see that this horror is a hyperbolic metaphor for forms of power that undergird and mobilize contemporary life. In this structure, the political claim of horror remains private.

These political and philosophical claims compel us to explore the horror genre as a form of phenomenological experience, and to ask what and how epistemology structures horror. If our labelling of our experiences as "horror" denotes the limit attitudes of human life and knowledge, could horror, as an experimental space for the production of new forms, pictures, and stories extend the definitions of what the horizons of these limits might be? In what ways can horror explore the real and articulate the expanded territory of our thinking of it? In these questions we see the need to construct a distinction between a post-structuralism that concentrates on the totality of infinite possibilities for thought, where the horror we ultimately find lies in what the genre *fails* to do, spelling out a new existential crisis of the unavailability of horizons, and a horror philosophy that must navigate the relation between the aesthetic experience of horror and the definition of thought itself.

Neo-Con Horror and the Post-Human

A neo-conservative horror is exemplified not only in the conservation of genre but in what stands out as the core content of the horror genre. Here, dominant themes are threats to the known at the level of perception and conception (e.g., altered worlds and times, the theme of the double, or parallel realities à la *Poltergeist* (1982)), the fear that there are other forces beyond our ken that produce "life as we know it" (e.g., stories of possession), and ultimately, the threat to annihilate human existence at local (e.g., the axe murderer scenario), processional (e.g., the vampiric assimilates the human over time), and universal (e.g., the global disease from *The Last Man on Earth* (1964) to *World War Z* (2013)) scales.[2] The allegorical content of horror across these subgenres emphasizes a defense of the known as its core value but does little to contemplate the "nothing" or the

---

2 These themes are also available in conspiracy movies, science fiction, and psychological thrillers, but they are also key to sustaining the genre of horror.

"non-being" of human life as a serious enterprise — that is, to consider the relation between genre, and the generic space of horror. A model of horror that exists within the circle of genre cannot entertain the conception that humans are self-causing entities. Nor can it comprehend the *horror vacui* that defines the truth of non-knowledge as the condition for knowing extrapolated within a Godless, purposeless universe, since this atemporality of *being-nothing-nowhere* is supplanted by conjurings of irrational and in-substantive representations that duly take on both a theological tone of dread and a politicized fear of other people, bodies, and identities.[3] This latter form has had popular success as a narrative structure that privileges themes of survival and protection. Stories of global bio-apocalypse and alien invasion show the horror genre's semantic flexibility rather than demonstrating any radical shift in redefining the standards with which horror goes to work. From William Castle's *The House on Haunted Hill* (1959), where parlor games that host the dark side of human nature are eclipsed by the real of these psychological forces, to Roger Corman's *Masque of the Red Death* (1964), which tells tales of the dark arrangements between aristocratic decadence and the barbaric powers of both earthly and transcendental natures; from the films that took center stage in the late 1970s and early 1980s; the master-horror moments in films such as John Carpenter's *The Thing* (1982) and Tobe Hooper's *Poltergeist* (1982), to the relatively more recent foray into horror as social realism with films like *Paranormal Activity* (2009). Horror, as the aesthetic experience that would in avant-gardist fashion lead to antagonism with and the circumvention — of our own beliefs, our institutions, and our ground — seems to have written itself out through its own institutionalization. The

---

3   For a discussion on the issue of the conflation of the identity of the ineffable and non-knowledge as a problem for knowledge, Bataille's work also leads to the material expression of the limits of knowledge as non-discursive conditions in the processes of powerlessness and desire. Georges Bataille, "Non-Knowledge," in *The Unfinished System of Nonknowledge,* ed. Stuart Kendall, trans. Michelle Kendall and Stuart Kendall (Minneapolis: University of Minnesota Press, 2001), 197–200.

recent re-make of *Suspiria* (2018) further advances this point by interweaving the allegory of remembering past forms of fascistic violence with a story of witchery and cultic paganism. The horror in *Suspiria* is therefore not given in a question of the unknowable but in the forgetting of what *is* known, and in the violence that this forgetting produces.

These comprehensions of horror establish the genre as a form of institutional critique that is similar to the artistic kind,[4] which reminds us moreover that horror has an institution, and leads us to ask about what is being defended rather than prosecuted in these stories. Whilst horror advocates the presence of aleatory forces in our lives and thus appeals to a transgressive dynamic, horror as an allegory of its own content often perfects and reinforces conservative values of political power. Increasingly, what "postmodern" movies tell us is that horror is capable of direct and explicit conservativism and is repressive in many senses, and its impoverished (kitsch) call upon exteriority sustains this. But even when horror knows this limit and turns inward to engage in a critique of the social, it refuses to engage in thinking the way in which horror can be a tool to offer the possibility of thinking another structure for the world.[5] Thus a

---

4   I am referring to the standard modalities of institutional critique in the mid-twentieth century, where conceptual artists strategized various critiques of power by identifying ideological power as materially located in the walls and structures of the institutions of the art world. The emergence of post-institutional critique recognized the way in which these practices were part of and absorbed within the institution of art and therefore developed art that would bear witness to the entrapment of art within the institutions of its own critique. Such behaviors moved across the tragic recognitions of the failure of critique, tongue-in-cheek ironies that fictionalized difference or practices that expressed a tragic form of surrender to the status quo.

5   Key to this is the way in which philosophy of horror is often satisfied with the idea that a movie can illustrate some ideas contained in a philosophy of horror adequately, rather than propose its own philosophical notions. For example, "Space Horror" is defined in Gavin F. Hurley, "Nonknowledge and Inner Experience," in *Horror in Space, Critical Essays on a Film Subgenre*, ed. Michele Brittany (Jefferson: MacFarland and Company Inc., Publishers, 2017), 81–96. He claims that movies can communicate the

horror that gives up on exteriority as a serious endeavor loses its grip on both the non-causal aleatory and the causal future.

The limits of horror tell us that we should not lay the blame purely at the level of horror's language, stylization, or scripts but also at the level of the invariant structure of horror itself. We can see this deeper structural problem in the way that horror has a predilection for the case of the human. Despite its claim to occupy thoughts, things, and experiences beyond us, it is often done in our image and our name. Horror therefore exposes its immanent humanism. Despite the claim that the task of horror is to think beyond the means and ends of human psychology, self, and scale, it nevertheless clings to the theme of the irreducibility of human consciousness to the explanatory realm of the understanding; the mystery of the self persists. In this way, horror tends to privilege an existential crisis of knowing the self as *the* establishment of horror, for the question of "self" might appear to be a project of knowledge, but in this case it is the definitive bulwark against knowledge as well as freedom. The incomplete task of knowing is the mobilizing force of horror but also its aesthetic. This image of horror is secured in the mutual effacement and preservation of the human, where horror takes the human as figure and sets it against a background of the world of appearance. This figure takes on abstract qualities, receding and appearing into the world picture in a hydraulics of a vertiginous depth of field. The structure of horror offers a disorienting experience. Horror's architecture in this picture of human/world, then, produces a symmetry between the erasure and the construction of difference, where one cannot be discerned from the other. Horror is therefore realized in a landscape of time as

---

limits of the postmodern comprehension of reality, "in a way that science, language and logic can never grasp" (93), but in placing such movies in a space of literature which is apparently discourse-free, and therefore has special access to horror, promises only the thought of the never knowable — infinite horror as telos. As such, narrative horror when read via philosophy as a space beyond the discursive fully reinforces the trivial nature of culture's capacity to apply horror as a generic to the particularity of genre expressions.

its own atemporality, and here, its images are special-effect illusions. They are illusions because horror does not possess or seek any possibility of transforming the categories/images/techniques that it takes on, nor does it show an interest in excavating its own structure in a critical fashion. This horror would be better termed "post-human" because its aim to think *after* the primacy of humancentrism becomes an act of bearing witness to this passage towards becoming post-human. Therefore, the facticity of alienation is not taken as a fact but as a turn in the story of human life. In short, the post-human project becomes the act of constructing a passage to its own end — to realize the post-human as a process of "unbecoming" in the face of exterior forces that may be constructed by humans or not. Therefore, a post-human horror seeks to destroy the human *as image* but at the same time naïvely holds onto a concept of the human as the means and end of this project.

Totalizing Contradiction

If horror stakes its claim in nihilism, then we must be vigilant regarding the claims that language can manifest "the nowhere". In the structure of horror, we identify a paradox undergirded by an inability to think across two conceptions of time. This is the struggle to account for the category of negativity as an absolute atemporality and also to account for the manner in which the irreducibility of negativity to the understanding is manifest in a temporality of "the never." For the former (negativity), a weak ideology of horror claims that narratives can manifest an identity with the concept of the irreducibility of human consciousness. The price of believing this is that the language that expresses the real is compelled to non-functionality and must refuse rational explanation: identity to the real is equivalent to triviality in the given. The latter (the never) is the grist to horror's mill, perpetuating the project of articulating negativity that will "never" be complete. Horror therefore claims access at the level of the image-perception and at the same time thrives on in-access at the level of conception — the other can be encountered but cannot be known. The consequence of this paradox is that our epistemology will be written as mysticism, horror will produce a form of dogmatic, non-discursive faith in an object with which we cannot interface.[6]

A disease of the head in this case is the pathology of a dialectical materialist horror that obsesses over the desire to manifest negativity, groundlessness, and the idea that we must grasp the fact that right now, we do not know the genesis of why we are what we are. Such a system of thought returns us to a self-subjected terrorism of the real, where we attribute the unknown to the unfathomable force of absolute dominance, a kind of fatalistic guarantee of our dispossession. This inability to decide in the face of the real is purchased in an erroneous collusion with negativity, as if it is a thing to be realized and as if conceptualizing negativity produces its identical match to our own alienation. In this sense, whilst consistent mobility, dissolution, and the absolute de-figured infinite continue to characterize horror, that which subtends the dialectic is an unreconstructed concept of synthesis that is not so much a regulative ideal as a totalizing space of unreason.

As we have described it, horror is the contradiction of alienation, and this contradiction is not beneficial to the operations of decision-making in the given. To surpass the frame of this constraint, we must risk surpassing the structure of horror, understood as being constituted by a dialectic of an expression of knowledge that confirms the facticity of the real and as a space of in-decision in the face of this knowledge. The problem with this approach to horror is that its mediation between the known and the unknown fixes both as knowns, thus obviating the potency and requirement for mediation as an explanatory mode of production. Horror is a representation that contradictorily claims to be unmediated.

---

[6] This point addresses the political implication of the representation vectors of the other within neo-conservative socio-political systems, from the naming of the other by dominance, as other, to the question of how forms of representation can be acquired by the other — that is, to cross the line into the sphere of discursive political space.

A dialectical materialist theory misses, in establishing its oppositional forces, that horror is intrinsic to the real, and that the real is not equal to human finitude. Alongside this, a theory that correlates a de-figuring of the human to an emancipatory force via the direct affects of non-representational experiences prohibits emancipation because it removes the representational tools by which decision becomes manifest and commitments to freedom become agreed upon in the realm of the social, viz., language. Horror, understood as a space of decision within alienation may not require horror at all, or at least it may not require horror as we know it.

A significant question in this text is how a phenomenology of horror as a form of "horror philosophy" might escape or redefine the problems that have been described as horror. A phenomenological visioning of horror within non-humanist philosophy traverses a multiplicity of non-hierarchical perceptual registers that support its claim to exceed and expand the frame of representation, the human, as well as the constraining forces, which are established through the stable referents of traditional metaphysics; but this approach also comes up against the dead-end of the genre itself, primarily at the interface of horror as cause and effect.

Our aim ultimately is to advance a realism. This means that we must explicate the conditions that subtend reality and the languages we use to communicate this. Bringing that which is ambiguous, that which is yet to be known, and that which has not been found to satisfy the means of already existing explanations into the realm of debate and analysis might seem to be the opposite of horror, for it does not leave the unknown on the periphery. Instead, this realism would articulate a methodology of negativity that does not render alterity banal, nor identify indeterminacy as the fate of knowing.

If we were to take horror as a form of cultural tradition that serves to mirror our incapacity to reason in general via illustrations of our incapacity to reason about the world we have made, we are all written as Frankenstein — moderns who see the horror of ourselves insofar as we are victims of our own creation.

In this case, the kind of negativity that horror provides offers, at best, a political allegory of a society diminished, since it mirrors the impossibility of our being together in a communal sense. In the face of this instrumental and poetic failure, a realist horror would traverse the field of both the unknown and that which sits within the world of folk (including folk horror and philosophy) — the given — bringing such myths to serious attention, for myths that tell us what subtends reality, no matter how unreal they appear, constitute and map the reality in which we find ourselves. Horror as a populist sentiment of the real therefore is pervasive in lived reality. The sensibility that community and also the future are impossible has traction in producing a culture that lives this fiction. In the face of this living horror of the political we need to produce decisions — that is, make judgements — that discern and distinguish between illogical and rational expressions of the understanding. Without this we cannot undermine the things that we take for reality, we cannot produce better conceptions of it, and we cannot understand what is unsatisfactory for the political, for we forgo any regulative ideal.

Given these remarks, we can address the fashion in which conditions and images present us with horror: What is the real horror here? Is horror necessarily tied to the primacy of subjective psychological perception that establishes itself as social commentary, at the cost of the social, or can it be tasked with a philosophical problem of negativity? And, if we are to rescue horror at all, is it necessary that we unbind its very structure from the traditions — post-humanism, dialectical materialism, phenomenology, and post-structuralist self-reference — that we have sketched? Alternatively, if horror is proven to be dying through capitalism, or is even dead, then why resurrect or reanimate its corpse?

Genre as Fate: Horror as Repression

To continue, we can consider three core aspects of horror:

1. Aesthetic, affectual, representational: Horror is motion-time, experience, *and* an image appealing to truth.
2. Political, didactic, practical: Horror is a recognition of the limits of our mastery that is available via practices in the lived world. In this sense, it expresses the place at which we no longer control our environment as a totality, or our future, and therefore horror educates us about existing inequalities.
3. Philosophical, theoretical: Horror is an articulation of an inaccessible real.

Following these points, horror becomes emblematic of "the nothing," "the void," "the unpresentable," and "the impossible," and this knowledge is understood as inevitable and real. John Mullarkey's essay, "Spirit in the Materialist World: Revisionary Metaphysics and the Horrors of Philosophy," speaks to this directly.[7] Key to his argument is that there is no single bridging theory to produce or enable a unification of the sciences that would enable the kind of Meillassouxian sovereignty of reason that would map the world. Other alternative hopes for an interdisciplinarity of the sciences in one egalitarian framework are also contested because the thought of horror is the work of recognizing the *real of inequalities,* a space of irresolution. As such, for Mullarkey, both sovereignty and equality are denaturalized as incorrect mythologies in favor of the real nature of an inequality that is accessed through experience. In this inequality, horror is the collision of two forms of thought. The first is the thought that recognizes the real disunity of the world. This is the thought that thinks the "never" — that is, we will *never* be unified, and there will *never* be one unifying theory to rationalize the world. The second mode of thought is that which is made up of the empirical evidence that leads to this conclusion: the various antagonisms that vie for this status of unilateral sovereignty

---

[7] Thanks to John Ó Maoilearca (John Mullarkey) for his exposition of this text and others, as well as his generosity, time, and energy spent discussing his ideas as part of his role as Theorist in Residence, Master of Arts Aesthetics and Politics Program, School of Critical Studies, CalArts, 2013.

guarantee and perpetuate this truth of the never precisely because they do not believe in it. Together, as opposing poles, real disunity and ideal unity configure an aperceptual recognition of horror as locked into, and definitive in regard to, the status quo. Accordingly, horror is a space of irony, for its promise to the outside is determined as dissatisfaction in the realm of the normative. This transcendent understanding of horror is unequal to the image that represents it, and it has to be, because a unification of concept and image would contradict the basis of the theory in the first place. This irony forges a space in which we recognize something of the root of the human condition as being equally or potentially inhuman.

For Mullarkey, this thought of horror takes place as abstract material in the world; nevertheless, as image-time, encountered in the field of cinematic horror, this specific space harnesses and owns the rights to the "never." It is here where we see that horror is a referential term that is capable of invoking a relation to the thought of the inaccessible or non-relational within the parameters of the given if and only if the given is already taken as metaphor for what it appears not to be — non-static, unstable, and invariant. This contradiction allows us to see how a lived, perceived horror is bound up with the recognition of ourselves as already non-human and not of this world.[8] A first and key problem of horror (and one that is more general than that proposed in Mullarkey's argument, though it is present within it) is that horror uniquely and singularly understands and expresses our fate as discordance. Such a discordance sets out the question of the way in which an elimination of the concepts of unity and

---

8 Grounding the object as the material presentation of horror entertains other problems within this theory, since the distinction between the inhuman and the human, which is essentially a philosophical set, can easily be over-determined as another political/moral distinction: between the inhuman and the inhumane. Here, we face the "Jekyll and Hyde" moment of horror philosophy and the production of specific dyadic forms that characterize an uncivilized other at the heart of mankind in an equality of violence; a state of pre-political uncivilized nature that would actually be the opposite of the condition of an equality of inequality that is set out here to strike a political dimension.

equality might be understood, especially when their destruction invites the irony of an over-identification with discordance. To expand this a little, the impossibility of unifying the space of causes — defined by non-normative causal relations between objects — with normative commitments, subtends the truth of horror. But, vanquishing the ideal of unity in the name of the truth of unreality renders horror as the only truth in the game. This new form of horror therefore is no longer reliant upon the dynamic tension of truth and impossibility because they are made identical. This would be a one-dimensional horror of the present, that deletes not only the real but also determinism — that our actions are determined by other actions/decisions — in the name of being: life as discordant reality. In this case, political and scientific aspirations to explain the conjuncture of reality and the real would be made equal to the kitsch of horror, only to be surpassed by real horror. Secondly, if we consider that serious investments in equality and unity, taken by society, affect the question of a future for humanity, then we can be concerned that this theory ultimately validates one unverifiable truth over another, where the real of discordance is met by the poetics of discordance and disunity in the given. This then begs the question of the way in which horror, as the absolute discordance of the human, stakes out a life for it.

Horror and the Anti-Image

We can see that a determination of horror as real discordance compresses the themes of fate and nature together. The real of horror as a discordant life therefore asks us how we can speak of alterity without reproducing it as a naïve picturing of "non-representational presence" and without locating it as just another attribute of a fragmentary life amongst other forms of knowledge and experience. Such an approach serves to extend the social conservatisms which characterize the "horror genre." The phenomenological presence of the thought of horror, in particular via its correlation with discordance, determines experiences of horror in the world as negatively conditioned isomorphies of the real. Images that reside in horror must invoke the unsayable, the un-filmable, the un-representable, and the unconscious and often do so through vertiginous aesthetics, where the world and its regulatory systems of ethics, rules, and morals are turned upside-down or inside-out. Ironically, the privileging of the realm of material experience in horror demands a concept of the anti-image, an image that must repress its own context, interpretations, and so on in order for it to gain traction as a primary referent to the real.[9]

A vitalistic phenomenology of affect- and sense-based experience struggles to account for the consequences of human self-conception that situates images including those generated in horror as hermeneutical and representational. Furthermore, such a phenomenology does not deal fully with how the non-teleological plane of experience that would claim non-referential and deregulated forms of infinitude turn out to manufacture a concept of one world, presenting both a representational system of reference as well as the organization of particular hierarchies of image-thought-experience in this modality of horror — in other words - some image-experiences are more real than others. This hierarchy set within vertical and horizontal modalities emerges when we begin to associate this condition of the real as capable of revealing the truth of inequality with a field where there is only discordance. From this disorienting space, such a truth can only be recognized in the present moment. This brings to bear a kind of vitalist empiricism that grafts a universal concept of discordance and indeterminism onto specific lived experiences, bringing the disorientation of thinking horror to bear upon and infect the normative. In this heterogeneous space, horror as a dimension of knowledge is locked within the present, and as such, it adds to the regressive character of both

---

9 The anti-image in this inquiry has a particular character. It privileges the experience of images above their contextual or normative interpretative values and foregrounds the image as an autonomous object set against the real. The problematic belief set out in the anti-image is that one can exorcise the demon of representation to acquire the conditions of an unmediated experience economy.

that which knowledge can think and its means of expression. It replaces the concept of a defined subjectivity that thinks its constitution with the psychology of a self that feels.

The consequences at stake here are not only present in philosophy or cinema. Many artworks tell us that a non-representational image can coalesce with reality through embodying images as a form of nature, and accordingly, a representational image cannot coalesce with reality because it cannot escape its mediating function. Built into this logic of horror is the notion that the image can allow us access to a reality only if it is unfettered by the "heaviness" of mediation and context, and freedom from this is the means by which it can then approach the level of the direct sensory encounter. An effect of this paradoxical thinking against the image with the image is that the empirical world is made strange, since this presence of the nothing is immanent to it, lurks within it, and is something that happens to us. Our given reality has an alienating quality that we cannot fathom. So, we live with a dilemma of the image. We cannot trust the given, but that is all we know.

Such contradictions define the limits of what are often claimed to be materialist practices. These errors of the image extend directly to our discussion on horror, and they show us how materialism can give up too quickly on the force of decision and representation in the world. Such a materialism thinks the contingency of the human as primary: We are a product of the world, within it, lost inside it, and unable to create any traction to decide against it as it is; the world guarantees our alienation from it. In such a case, images are understood as inadequate to the real, in that they are ghostly projections from it and, at the same time, are asserted as real in their material substance and affectual power to contain the real of inaccessibility as their constituent identity. Images are seen to traverse this division between being and representation, as both universal and particular. Images, as Blanchot would have it, are the living dead.[10]

---

10 For Blanchot, the artwork in general is stained by the real, the excess, and supplement of negativity and holds forth the infinite fact of mortality.

But designating this special power to images causes problems. It disables any assertion of how images operate at the level of semantic authority, for images in this theory are not in dialogue like a language; they seem to be devoid of sentences, contexts, and propositions. They are treated as special entities, and their manifest symbolizations of themselves override any local or specific qualities at the level of concept or percept. For images to claim this right to traverse the paradigms of the negative and the given, they must take this up as a project and articulate this space with specific explicatory tools. While all images offer the real, to construct a horror is to ask images to articulate the dynamic relations across the real and the given. The real in this case is therefore not the right of any image.

Phenomenological Frames

The types of image-thought that respond to horror in phenomenology retrieve this question of poetics, and, in particular, metaphor. In this case it appears that images can master the rhetoric of presence and absence in an aesthetics of constraint. This is made clear in Graham Harman's essay, "Horror of Phenomenology,"[11] where a "(one legged) realism grasps the weird tension in the phenomena themselves."[12] For Harman, this "one-legged" realism is a realism that misses the "genuine hiddenness of things,"[13] and in that sense the virtual world can only be that place of weird metaphoric-poetic phenomena. This virtual world, built on a material plane, refuses a metaphysical dimension, and instead offers a multi-perspectival view. This is not only traditional to phenomenological artworks of the mid-20th century, as we will see, but Cubism would also seek

---

The failure to be present to death is marked by a life as image. Maurice Blanchot, *The Space of Literature*, trans. Ann Smock (Lincoln: University of Nebraska Press, 1989).

[11] Graham Harman, "On the Horror of Phenomenology," in *Collapse IV*, ed. Robin Mackay (Falmouth: Urbanomic Press, 2008), 332–66.

[12] Ibid., 364.

[13] Ibid.

to represent a 360-degree experience of an object within the conditions of a two-dimensional picturing. The compression of perceptual space housed in one frame produces an isomorph of reality in a metaphysical dimension. The representation we see becomes a picture of perception in the act of perceiving a temporality condensed into atemporal space. Pictures in frames allude to an exteriority beyond the picture and also issue the claim that the picture itself is the best model for the understanding of the impossibility that perception can meet the demands of the understanding. Artworks in the genre of Land Art and performance-oriented practices that invested in durational experience extend this logic but aspire to eliminate the frame and, therefore, this picturing with it, as if the work participates in the world on an equal footing with other objects. Harman's theory also seeks to eliminate the frame by identifying a phenomenal landscape of objects that recede from our grasp and that ultimately generate an ontological regression of picturing where the frame of horror dissolves ad infinitum. We become immersed in horror as the only world we experience but can never know, that is, as a horrific holographic simulation that is received by us as the naturality of everyday life.[14] This world has a horrific aspect inasmuch as we can say that we do not experience it as weird, since this observation of the weird must come from some analysis and suspension of experience as vital.

In particular artworks, we can see a similar approach to a world of objects, based on the presupposition that materiality itself is exempt from the scene of the social and that materials

---

14 Jean Baudrillard narrates a world that is lost to simulation vis-à-vis a human compulsion for the real. His answer to this is to call for an antirealist practice that ultimately establishes a war of images, between images that narrate their own construction and images that are a piece of the real. The antirealist image is the image that knows its own unreality, that is given political priority against the correlationalist vision of the hyper-realist simulation. Here, we entertain the question as to the legitimacy of the diagnosis of an image and the real, and the verticality that is insinuated against the backdrop of a pluralistic landscape of simulations. See, for example, Jean Baudrillard, *Simulacra and Simulation,* trans. Sheila Faria Glaser (Ann Arbor: University of Michigan Press, 1994).

are endowed with an innate and weird alienation from the world of ordinary language. It is therefore taken that materials themselves have atemporal properties and that they can assume the role that they can skip mediation (depth) or referential relations to both non-normative causal as well as normative languages that instead appeal directly to the timeless and cosmological space beyond human experience and perception from the base of temporal symbolic material perception.[15] Here, the artwork occupies a claim to the real via its claim to collide local experience with universal atemporality, therefore dismissing the need to traverse the conditions of reality and our understanding. This approach to the production of art as a form of realism follows the logic of a tragic phenomenology that reinforces a semantic pessimism. It is tragic because the artwork surrenders itself to specific unknowables as indicators of the real with which it does not seek to interact but only accepts as given. Thus, what is given is the privileging of our perception of materials and the making of these materials into special referents to timeless metaphysical properties. In doing this, these artworks forgo the space of language as a spatial distinction that mediates the conditions of atemporal concepts and temporal action.[16]

We can draw upon these artistic attitudes to the image and experience as an analogy to phenomenological realism so as to identify the principles and also the contradictions that are cast within both. As such, we can say that Harman's "weird realism" tells us that images are non-relational in one sense but, at the same time, also confirms that these constructions as images, the works of Lovecraftian architectures for example, represent our

---

15 This can explain why many sculptures indebted to object-oriented ontology are geological rock samples and parts of the earth that are thought to have no representational or ideological quality, for they exist as object-facts and sensations retrieving an appeal to the genre of the sublime and antirealist art. Michael Heizer's *Levitated Mass*, 2013, installed at the Los Angeles Contemporary Museum of Art, is one example of this.

16 Rosalind E. Krauss, *A Voyage on the North Sea: Art in the Age of the Post-Medium Condition* (London: Thames and Hudson, 1999). Krauss discusses this point in referring to mid-century phenomenological art.

relationship to the real even if it is claimed that there is no representationalism at work, since these delirious fictive spaces are seen to be contorted fusions of being and thinking. Identifying this weird realism requires a vision of the world as fictive and poetic, and it necessitates a formal distancing from the world of cause. This requirement to see the world as fiction struggles to find its way into practical normative behavior because the concept of the world as horror tells us ultimately that we have no phenomenological access to it, and this is ironically delivered by the means of phenomenological access in experiential representations.

Here we see how this material phenomenon that is said to deliver the experiential immanence of the real as the frameless de-ontologized experience requires another frame — a theoretical frame of reference — that ultimately evidences our lack of access to the real. It is this contradiction of the theory in-itself that produces horror in this instance. Therefore, this poetics lacks any explication of its own mediating properties, and a "weird realism" turns out to occupy the standard definition of a claim to a contemporary realism in artistic practice — or what should be termed "naïve idealism" — that we can identify in artworks of the mid-20th century that worked under the rubric of phenomenology.

Temporality and the Never of Horror

John Mullarkey's essay, "The Tragedy of the Object,"[17] foregrounds another type of phenomenology inherited from Thomas Nagel's *Objective Phenomenology*. Mullarkey, in his theory of horror philosophy, carefully expands the definition of horror, enabling us to see how horror takes place in a field that exceeds the horror genre of movies specifically.[18] In this text, horror pro-

---

17 John Mullarkey, "Tragedy of the Object: Democracy of Vision and the Terrorism of Things in Bazin's Cinematic Realism," *Angelaki: Journal of the Theoretical Humanities* 17, no. 4 (December 2012): 39–59.
18 Mullarkey takes this notion of horror in cinema more generally, where he observes the point at which the representation of things in motion pictures

vides the vehicle through which the irruption of the real is made present. The cinema of Japanese horror films in the genre of J-Horror gives Mullarkey's text the description of the "dark other." In this horror, it appears at the edge of the frame or the cinematic screen: "[t]he opticality of the peripheral monster in films such as *Ringu* (1998), *Ju-On* (2002), *Honogurai mizo no soko kara* (2002), and their sequels affords us a new vision of background and depth of field."[19] Mullarkey connects the experiential vagueness or imperceptibility of the cinematic image with the audience's experience of doubt. Together, these elements succeed in revealing "the actual presences of normally unseen or marginalised visibilities."[20] Here, the edge of human vision is used to refer to both the limits of human knowledge and the frame of the cinematic screen itself, as if the human as a concept is transposed to the frame of cinematic life and vice versa. In this re-visioning of the cinematic life-world, "the violence immanent within our everyday perceptual judgements"[21] is disclosed, but it is not wholly clear how this assertion is made between the perception of the vagueness, or flicker, of the monster at the edge of the screen, the doubt that this experience might manifest conceptually, and the political assertion that those that are unaccounted for in society undergo some revelation of what other life might qualify as life. This is crucial when we consider that the articulation of doubt that is foregrounded in horror cinematics becomes a paradigm of mastery that requires constructing. In this case, horror as a landscape of doubt and fear, which alerts us to the incomplete condition of our knowledge, does not seek to recover or ascertain that which is not. Instead, it is an art of constructing that which is not via formal structures with substitutional identities. Rather than undoing particular forms of knowledge in the tradition of a liberal humanist subjectivity, it risks reinforcing the normative attitudes that subtend the status

---

    is capable of making us believe that those things can traverse the limits of the frame.
19 Mullarkey, "Tragedy of the Object," 49.
20 Ibid.
21 Ibid.

quo — that is, a satisfaction with the unknown. Importantly, the effect that produces doubt is purchased by the moving, glitching, interrupted image, which is no longer the amalgamated, hybrid form of a blending and clashing type but is another dominant form. It is its own genre, and doubt now equals satisfaction.

Playing by the rules and constraints of the "never" of horror, we see a contrast between the impossibility of knowing the self and the impossibility of not experiencing the self. This articulates a double bind of horrific imprisonment, and it is instructive. This contradiction narrates our oppression, but it also figures our failure to think beyond our repression past this contradiction because images and nature are incorrectly taken as fields beyond the sayable. A picture of the unsayable exerts only the pressure of bad circularities. It does this because it gives up on what is and can be said, and it assumes that, because there is no bridge to traverse the divide between the space of cause and the space of reasons.

The Author of Horror

The problems that this phenomenology delivers can be made more explicit when we look at contemporary art, for this notion of access to the weirdness of our everyday lived reality seems to have been relegated to a more special type of person that can perceive this and present it back to us. This question of mediation retrieves the role of the artist as modern in the typical sense, where the archetype of modernity, the flâneur-artist, points out to others the invisible discrepancies and foibles of everyday life, as if the images that would emerge from the rooms of prostitutes, brothels, private salons, and personal encounters forged a dark equivalence with deeper and unknown reality beyond the phenomenal. Many artworks such as those depicted in the realism of Degas and Lautrec for example, as well as the Impressionist and Pointillist works of Monet and Seurat respectively are tainted with a strangeness — a diversion from verisimilitude - because they exercised formal investigations of phenomenal reality, via particular explications of the means by which these representations are constructed. Ideological images of reality resulted from this approach to production, explication and observation in two gestures: one of a social truth, where we see empirically realist images of everyday encounters, and the other of the real in itself — something that we cannot access. The world as it is was implicitly estranged from perception via the act of perceiving it. A specific example of this refraction and warping of life can be seen in the famous Édouard Manet work, *A Bar at the Folies-Bergère* (1882) that fragments the world of the known into an uncanny arrangement of space and time, making the known alien and different via the deliberate refraction of the mirror that holds and distorts the scene of the painting. Contemporary artists working under the rubric of object-oriented ontologies — that is, post-humanist materialist phenomenologies which explore the status of human alienation as a fact in the scope of ecological catastrophe — share something with this work, its location in the present, but they fail to live up to this investment in formal, representational, and conceptual investigations that would orient the image towards another comprehension of how language can articulate reality. This failure is characterized in an attitudinal sense in the way in which many artistic practices have preferred to make art that acknowledges its own limits, that reflects a surrendering of the political based on the idea that humans cannot and should not orient change in the world because they are seen to be part of it, and any attempt to construct change would lead to the totalitarian disasters of a colonial past repeating itself. Repeating the same problems of art's political project, here again, many contemporary artworks show us installations of atemporal materials, materials that exist without us, and because of this, they instruct us about our precarity in the present. In taking this approach, they risk bypassing the context of a social, rational, and discursive interpretative field by privileging all materiality as the always already alien, the already abstract enough. So it follows that objects that would become art, through subject matter or construction, do not require attention at the level of any formal or conceptual analytics.

In rejecting the internal attention to the construction of art, we can attribute this mode of production to a form of nominalism, and we can locate this within a tradition of modern flâneurie — that is, the operation of art as the act of pointing out the strangeness of the known. But this flâneurie that we see today is of a post-Duchampian artist, one that has naturalized nominalism all the way down, one that troubles the labor of thought that would need to explicate the claims that would support the nomination of a particular material becoming art in the first place.[22] In this sense it does *less* than Manet, Braque, or the phenomenology of art, experience, and time via Land Art and site-specific work.[23]

Furthermore, this gesture to nominate the normal as strange, alien, or as a space that alerts us to unknown unknowables cannot hope to account for the selection of particular forms as art, and it renders decision arbitrary. This approach to art production cannot differentiate the universal claim of alienated material from the formal and specific materials that express that thought. Harman's explanation, which does not mention art, tends to be directed to the question of how material presence accesses its own internal reality, demonstrated outwardly in an aesthetics of multiple forces coexisting in one plane. But by looking at art and its historical involvement with perception, we can say that what Harman misses is that his is a theory of the image or image-language. Additionally, the limitations of art in the face of its capacity to claim that it is, in its being, real-material are instructive in telling us that the language that is produced as

---

22 There are many examples of this approach to art and so any particular example would not seem adequate in this case. However, for one, see Kyle Chaka, "Object-Oriented Curating Continues in 2013 Biennale," *Hyperallergic*, March 14, 2013, https://hyperallergic.com/66935/object-oriented-curating-continues-in-2013-venice-biennale/.

23 Rosalind Krauss observes how opticality had become the primary medium of art in the mid 1960's and lacked theorization due to the conviction that opticality could sublate internal differences in the content/medium of the work to produce the semblance of an indivisible whole at the level of experience. Krauss, *A Voyage on the North Sea*, 30.

a result of this theory resides in simile rather than the metaphor that it had aspired to be.

Taken within or beyond the field of art, a theory of weird realism subtended by an object-oriented ontology ultimately offers a kind of mysticism of the known that precludes us from getting involved in the world of the given. In other words, the artwork's essential qualities are deemed to be under the line of reason and in the realm of non-explanatory experiences, set for experience rather than decoding, defined by, and as an effect of, the reality of "the great outdoors."

Exit Wounds

The arguments launched in Mullarkey's and Harman's different treatments of phenomena share and elucidate the problem of the image and the question of the legitimacy of horror as a mechanism or tool to think and manifest contingency as a medium of experience. As such, they draw attention to the problems that arise when taking the real of contingency, or in fact any condition that we could say operates without us or does not have us "in mind", as thought-material, for this asks us how to manifest this understanding in semantic form, and, furthermore, how such semantic forms can be contested as false and also taken seriously as true. Despite the non-metaphysical and expansionist visions of horror explored in these different phenomenologies—the world as weird and alien or in a generic horror of the real—the structure of horror as it is proposed in both Harman's and Mullarkey's work suffers its own exit wounds when the realm of the image undergoes an extraction from language. What is forgotten is how this language takes place within the field of social relations, as well as how it produces a regulative ideal that underpins the social transactions in which it partakes. Bearing this in mind, it is not so much the specter of an aesthetic condition that haunts horror, but it is the methodological habituation of a kind of phenomenology that has determined it that causes these problems. This means that we need to return to those initial categories of the aesthetic, political, or philosophical and think carefully as to how they are put into a motion of relations.

Consequently, the thought of inequality at the level of the real has an impact upon a comprehension of the social, for this now transforms itself into the sovereignty it dreaded; that is, inequality is totalized such that it becomes a banal and expressionless, flat totality of an equality of difference. Horror, in this case, does not transcend horror as we know it, despite Mullarkey's or Harman's aim to think backwards from the point of the unformulated experience, from the other side of Cartesian rationality, from within the object, and from the perspective of the non-human. Philosophy-horror in such cases resides as a mirror for the complex condition of humanity as a particular kind, a kind that expresses the struggle of thinking beyond or escaping the standard definitions of human life and society but does little to think beyond this mirror. Therefore, although horror acts as a form of resistance to power and dominance,[24] we can also see that horror protects and guarantees the figure of the impossible, leaving emancipation behind. It is at a loss and without character, content, or commitment, free from any political dimension.[25]

Reading Harman's work reminds us that the horror of real inconsistency remains significantly different than the horror that is used to describe the skewed relation to the real that he identi-

---

[24] We see this naturalized suspicion of and opposition to the bureaucracy of reason as much in Adorno and Horkheimer as in Jean-François Lyotard.

[25] We know that modernity took the factical irreducibility of the real to our understanding and made this proof of concept that entities beyond the given are unverifiable in it. This is exemplified in William Shakespeare's *Hamlet*, where King Hamlet's appearance from beyond — as a ghostly apparition (image) — sets Prince Hamlet on the track of revenge/justice. However, we find that Hamlet instead becomes a kind of skeptical detective of the image, taking the image as possibly a real manifestation of the truth of murder, but never real enough to justify taking up arms. This non-identicality of the image and the real, energized by a skepticism of the image in itself, results in life as inactive procrastination, or in other words, a life that is paralyzed by the question of the verifiability of the image in relation to a metaphysical unified real.

fies in literature, such as in the work of H.P. Lovecraft. This difference between the conceptualization of horror in genre form and the way in which it is given to the objects in the life-world is crystallized when we cannot find the means to speak across these registers of fact and fiction. There is not an account as to how fictions become truths, and the claim that this phenomenology destroys the world of genre as indicative of verticality and power is untenable.[26] The idea that we do not require vertical registers is problematic because the affect of horror cannot claim the space of equality by retreating to its abstract and empty qualities, since abstraction is already proposed as genre-material and participates in rule-based interactions. For Mullarkey, real horror requires the selectivity of an author/reader that produces the erasure of the human as discrete category, an author/reader who witnesses temporary access to a groundless violence. This access to the real at the edge of perception might remind us of the kind of privileges set out at the beginning of this text where we explored the consumer fantasies of *Hostel*, but in Mullarkey's text, groundlessness acts as a site of potentiality for difference and aspires to a moral good that seeks to refuse instrumentalist passions for unification. This groundlessness, however, does not prevent new forms of dominance from coming onto the scene, since it only promises that we can identify them as unreal claims to reality. The disavowal of unity acts as a foundational concept in Mullarkey's text. As a conceptualization of negativity, this theory is provocative because it foregrounds a political space that must take the incompleteness that negativity promises seriously. However, a destruction of unity in the context of the political is worrying because it destroys the potential for any constructive qualities that would identify with any other regulative ideal. Negativity taken as this ideal threatens to eliminate the validity of conceptualizing in itself, especially if we con-

---

26 This attempt to destroy genre as a mark of vertical dominance is also indebted to deconstruction and post-structuralism, where the latter in particular would seek the redemptive space of hybridity as a response to the authority of categorized norms.

sider that the act of thinking necessitates direction and objectives, or we could say that thinking is a condition for a striving to unity. Therefore, while this negativity read as the permanent undoing of a foundational unity offers the means to bridge the register of horror as fiction, literature, art, and the lived world, and it seems to guarantee life as infinite, it lacks the content that would make this life worth living. It shows us that concepts of unity cannot extrapolate themselves beyond the limited bounds of perception itself because thinking of the real as negativity excludes anything else.

In this text, we have explored how sensations that aim to capture a concept of horror are constructed and framed, this concept being the facticity of our alienation from ourselves, and how these words and pictures gesture to an existence without them. This bind of sense and mediation demonstrates the equivalence of two problems: making absolute distinctions between concept and sense and the over-determination that collapses them altogether. Instead, understanding that images are supervened by concepts turns us towards the comprehension of the relations that are necessary to think and picture — that is, to generate consensus within difference. The way in which horror constrains us to particular modes of representation now generates the question of the way in which the limits of perception and the territory of the visible, written as such, constrain the potential of what the political might be.

Articulating the complexity of thought and perception is key to overcoming an anthropocentricism of the image/object as a self-expressing entity, as well as to undermining fears of instrumentality. Consequently, we must carefully unknot the dimensions of objects as assemblages and constructions that can make rational choices from the object that is taken as a "self." One way that the horror genre has described this is in these familiar traits: the inanimate becomes animate, death becomes life, cars, dolls, urban infrastructure, etc. All become killers of the human race with levels of conscious intent. This life of the non-human is one of decadence and privacy, fears are played out regarding the resistance of secret gangs and cultic affiliations, set within the home and usually in the dark. Such a view of horror is a post-human, love affair intermixed with a paranoia of each other and our capacity to eliminate life. It is a place where the human is defined through its ability to protect its essential qualities against the dispossession it encounters. A commitment to the darkness and unfathomability of human consciousness, undertaken as a form of protection of human life, now blocks the possibility of comprehending life as a self-causing system, which in turn dries up any possibility of re-engineering that life. This is an engineering that is necessary to overcome a stultification that is subtended by mythic narratives of the human under duress and that only serves to annihilate purpose.

If horror is another way to express our complex relation to negativity, then it asks us to understand what we are as human and to extend this definition, for the project of purpose asks us to think what we are not, and from where we are not. This is the project of a future-oriented comprehension of life as opposed to the fascinations with the present that have characterized modernity and postmodern cultures. Instead of a discourse on self-expression that begins from the site of the synthetic, this project calls for an integrative method vis-à-vis both political and philosophical approaches to knowledge and the way in which thoughts are made manifest in language, thus enabling a more thorough explication of negativity in the world. The need to exit the genre of horror towards another generic space of the understanding is exemplified by the limits of phenomenological approaches that correlate our sense perception to an inaccessible real. This exit does not take us to the place of the non-normative. It is therefore not an escape from language itself. This is instead the construction of new normativities and new truths that can be taken as norms.

An erroneous identification of negativity as a regulative ideal is an incorrect comprehension of negativity itself. This supports a theory of difference as a given and mobilizing force that ultimately finds its home in identity production. Our examples determine a crisis of *being within difference* that populates the character of horror — the kind which does more than mirror our alienation from ourselves and each other—but also underscores our entrapment in neo-liberal forms of capitalistic inequity in which no alternative is offered. This returns us to our starting point, where we discussed a form of the non-normative, heterogeneous life in the film *Hostel,* in which, despite its visceral sensory excess, horror is commensurate with the status quo—the libidinal economy of a capitalist realism[27]—of global financial capital. We can stretch this analogy to the standardization of artistic critique as a form of heterogeneous encounter subtended by normative conditioning. Appeals to accelerate the unsavory or unsatisfactory conditions of capital as we know them serve only to produce excessive parodic aesthetics where horror that might have once required serious attention resides in the realm of kitsch. These appeals result in an uncritical relation to the given. It is here where a re-comprehension of language and its politics is urgently called for, not as an effect upon our lives, either negatively or positively proposed, but rather as a cause that can be determined for life.

A non-human life is therefore not a human dispossession of agency, cause, or determination. A world that is subtended by negativity does not require embracing Gaia, nor does it identify a general horizontality of life. Such landscapes that characterize "the all" often seek to meet the image of our self-conception as it is, through the transferring of human identities onto nature. Here, the capacity for human life can be seen to be not so much the origin of animalistic pathology as, more problematically, destined to it. Pictures of human life responsible for, but also cast adrift in, the context of larger scale contingencies render us alienated beings in a spiritualism/primitivism that turns horror upside down, since nature, not the human specifically, is the figure of horror.[28] However, horror maintains its structure. And

---

27 See Jean François Lyotard, *Libidinal Economy,* trans. Iain Hamilton Grant (Bloomington: Indiana University Press, 1983) and Mark Fisher, *Capitalist Realism: Is There No Alternative? (*Winchester: Zero Books, 2009).
28 See Alex Garland, dir., *Annihilation* (Los Angeles: Paramount Pictures, 2018), based on the books in the Southern Reach Trilogy by Jeff Vander-Meer, *Annihilation* (New York: Farrar, Straus and Giroux, 2014), *Authority*

so, we must be careful to dissect this horror as a sense of alienation, ineffectiveness, and distancing that defines our experience of contingency. This dislocation from our own capacity to think and act is given in stories that show us how we are lost to the world — where we watch as fires spread, people murder for profit and titillation, and ultimately, where this devastation is beyond our control — the horror of life now, under neo-liberal capitalism.

This consistently modern narrative of failure demands a refusal to continue with an anti-representationalist investment in resistance, and it alternatively asks us to re-ground an epistemology of horror that attends to the formal qualities of expression. What we must determine is a mode of construction that can answer, understand, and respond to the dimension of horror understood as the being of alienation.

Horror at Hell-Mouth

When faced with the narratives we have reviewed that attest to the paucity of the imagination, it is still possible to argue that language can deliver different and new information. It is still possible to redefine what language is and can say from within the conditions of ordinary language. Therefore, we can undertake a project that commits to the "yet to be known" from the place of being in the world, a thinking that is ordered by normativity and, because of this, can think beyond undesirable formal constraints.[29] This project requires a transcendental space as well as alienation as the expression of negativity affords us this theory of irreducibility. The language that we will construct is not a mirror of our lived world, and it would be a mistake to take

---

(New York: Farrar, Straus and Giroux, 2014), and *Acceptance* (New York: Farrar, Straus and Giroux, 2014).

29 Robert Brandom, "Heroism and Magnanimity, The Post-Modern Form of Self-Conscious Agency," lecture at Marquette University, Milwaukee, February 24, 2019. Brandom's Hegelian hero of the act is one who stays true to normative codes and does not assume exteriorized positions that live within spaces before or above the law as normative givens.

it as one. This is to say, language is enough to get us beyond the conditions of capitalistic entrapment, and it is enough to express another form of thought that does not rely on an escape from alienation itself. Here, we can unglue a theory of an alienation of mind from the alienating forces of capitalist formations.[30]

This means that we can think being without referent and, more accurately, without referent to the negativity of referent. And we can do this without the semantic pessimism that would inhabit this negativity as an attitude that conditions all behavior. We must ask how and where negativity takes place or gets played out if at all in the world as lived, for if we work with no conception of it, the risk is that we would be blind to the purpose of any judgment we make and unable to value any expression of dissatisfaction with the way things are. In response, we can assert that the act of thinking is in language and that this is not ordered, ruled, or constrained by negativity. Rather, negativity is the structural property necessary for thought to think difference within languages that are political and aesthetic, and therefore we must labor under the careful articulation of what negativity means.

We have argued that identifying negativity as the genesis of horror is limited. It is limited in its characterization of thought, as well as in regard to how negativity becomes located in rational-explanatory, aesthetic, sense-based encounters. We have also seen how this formal structure of horror in aesthetic configurations has a predilection for genre-based modifiers that actually reinstate the vertical axes of power that we sought to annihilate, rendering them as implicit ideological forces. Now, horror is compelled to be re-imagined, recast, and thought again. A theory of horror must at least inject itself with a new task for thought. At best, we can say that horror as we have known it is redundant. If we take our definition of horror to be the ex-

---

30 This approach to alienation as constructive spans history, but, more recently, accelerationism develops this as a larger contemporary discourse, and more specifically, see Reza Negarestani, *Intelligence and Spirit* (Falmouth: Urbanomic, 2018).

pression in ordinary language of our alienation, then we could replace horror with other terms such as "noir," "alien," or "scientific" — that is, horror loses its horror, for the role of the negative is necessary and not spectacular or characterized by spectral qualities. Instead, we are referring to a definitive method of intractable negativity, neither grasped by nor lost to representation. It is rather an attitude that determines the real through systems of representation that are adequate to it. In pragmatic terms, this project does not identify a formal destination but rather inhabits a principle for life lived.[31] This project aims beyond horror. It seeks to realize its own incompleteness and make it a fact, where this facticity is unthinkable in practical terms and is only written a posteriori in a process of proofs and refutations. This conceptualization of horror destroys the spectacle of its authority, unbinds aesthetics, politics, and philosophy, and duly undermines authority as spectacle. It is the construction of a different relation to the unknown and the yet-to-be known. In the encounter with the new and in the comprehension that something has changed, we can say that the information that we consider to be different to us was always already there and ready to be understood, being made ready in our anticipation. This historical interface with the new is not one of shock, because we had already thought this. Therefore, difference is a question of already existing structures; difference is written and does not appear from nowhere, even if it appears to us as such. The entity that enters our scene is not one of a haunting from beyond our world. It is always within reach, but this does not banalize the new.[32]

---

[31] Wilfrid Sellars proposes the necessity of a transcendental axiomatic for the living of the "good life." Wilfrid Sellars, "Reason and the Art of Living in Plato [1968]," in *Essays in Philosophy and Its History* (Dordrecht: B. Reidel Publishing Company, 1974), 3–26.

[32] Stanley Fish, "Change," in *Doing What Comes Naturally: Change, Rhetoric, and the Practice of Theory in Literary and Legal Studies* (Durham: Duke University Press, 1990), 141–60. Fish discusses this point with a commentary on the work of Noam Chomsky, asserting that the Chomsky "revolution" was in fact already pre-apprehended by specific ideas, works,

Would this conceptualization of the new spell disaster for our view of ourselves as autonomous beings who are self-determining and capable of an anarchic and free imagination? Does this focus on the space of language at the level of intersubjective knowledge rid aesthetics of its allure and prohibit the drive to know? If horror is the riddle that tells us that language is capable of manifesting and communicating what is unknown and that thinking can preserve the fact of the unknown and can thus hold this contradiction in place, then horror is ultimately a form of Romantic skepticism that is satisfied with a dialectic that anchors its poles in too-specific locations. The desire to not overcome this contradiction is the desire to make horror a love affair with the enigma of the self. This entails a severe misunderstanding about the way in which epistemology and representation work.

I want to head back to a form of "horror" that motivates the non-tragic.[33] This refers to the notion that a subject can act in accordance with norms, can explicate the conditions of their action via thinking/doing but does not identify their relation to the unknown as something that is forever unobtainable. While characters of the non-tragic have frequently been featured in popular cultural representations, we will concentrate on the Warner Bros. TV series *Buffy the Vampire Slayer*[34] since this series succeeds in locating a paradigm of the non-tragic that asks us to reorient our comprehension of what thought might constitute.

While the central axis of *Buffy* focuses on the holding-pattern storyline of Sarah Michelle Gellar's character Buffy's on-and-off, tragic hero vampire-with-a-soul, boyfriend Angel, the

---

and actions that anticipated difference. This occurs without undermining the change that this work affects (498).

33 For more discussion on the non-tragic, see Amanda Beech, "Last Rights: The Non-Tragic Image and the Law," in *The Flood of Rights*, eds. Thomas Keenan, Suhail Malik, Tirdad Zolghadr (Berlin: Sternberg Press, 2017), 159–75.

34 Joss Whedon, *Buffy the Vampire Slayer* (WB and UPN Television networks, 1997–2003).

series also lays out another form of vampire life that does not worry so much about its human past. Here we see the camp world of Spike and pals (yes, it is *Buffy*), where there are no desires to re-engage with humanity nor to reflect on what is gone. Instead, we see a parallel world that apes the former but lives by different rules. While the vampires without souls in *Buffy* have very human traits, they do not claim any particular relation of care with "the human" or with humanity. Moreover, life is a kind of game where the series of events that configure it never seem to end. This exposition of another form of life is what horror as action potentializes. It is a kind of thought of life without existing life being central to its definition — a thought of life in which the apocalypse is a regular and real threat but a threat that does not haunt the protagonists' perception of the world as a point of trauma that cannot be addressed. There is no definition of the self in *Buffy*, since all vampires are not born but made, and unlike the domestication and bureaucracy of vampires in the HBO series *True Blood* (2010–14), who adhere to or replicate the kind of administrative rules that we see more than ever in the University, these vampires get on with "vampire business" for the most part. Joss Whedon's movie, *Cabin in the Woods* (2012), follows through with this non-human, non-sentimentalism. And again, it is teen-geek-life gathered around some kind of hell-mouth that occupies the pivotal space that holds that red button that can annihilate the world. Crucially, any decision to end it all is based on the fact that destruction is now simply necessary.

This perspective of horror, in which the view from nowhere is made possible through living within *the somewhere,* must construct this somewhere as the genesis and origin of action. To do this, place-as-location has to be written as the archetypal non-place, as the pre-political space that exists beneath the foundations of Buffy's high school. This is called "Hell Mouth" and it is the gates to the beyond, but centrally, its existence guarantees the end of the world. The fatalistic storyline that subtends all action wreaks of accelerationist fantasies of human apocalypse in the post-Anthropocene, in which we are given two choices, to save or to destroy life as we know it. This similarity between accelerationism and the decisions that are made available in the face of the inevitability of Hell Mouth is instructive. It reminds us that the presence of the end of the world as a theme is a functional necessity in order to support the drama of a life as a soap opera, in other words, the life that goes on and perseveres season after season supported by the reiterative narrative of "near-death." Ultimately this transcendental or parallel life that we see lived out in *Buffy*, this view from nowhere that is literally constructed as a dialogue with the other — and is therefore read as a tacit knowledge that the destiny of life is death — ultimately plays out as the conservation of already existing social values for the most part, although the re-structuring of the "family unit" as a fraternity promises an alternate notion of the family beyond normative ideological principles within liberalism. That being said, the decision to give up on life and let the world destroy itself does not articulate any commitments regarding life in the future. These two options leave us between conservativism on the one hand and the mythology of self-sacrifice on the other hand, and they each redeem a particularly tragic identification with subjectivity.

Buffy's postmodern world obviously has its limits(!). Its limits ask us to think about a place where the decision is not to save or to destroy life as we know it but where the decision is how to re-orient the question of knowledge itself. The narrative configuration of *Buffy* shows us that violence and the institutionalization of new forms of order ultimately redefine a life rather than interface with the genesis of it. For example, Buffy's dialogues with the other, such as demons, alien machines, and vampires, are not propositions regarding the condition of absolute negativity, viz., death in itself as in-access par excellence. Rather, her actions are symptoms of it. These formal manifestations of death arrive in characters that represent other languages, other forms of life that Buffy's own life hinges upon, since she has also died (twice, and returned). Death in such a case is not the absolute. Instead, death is deferred, since the irretrievable, end-of-the-world scenario is not equivalent to the death of the person or even to the end of humanity as such. This separation between human life and life in general breaks the ontological regression or hellish circularity that is brought about by the conflation of concept and image, epistemology and ontology. This break potentializes the capacity for language to operate as a system for tracing and proposing the dynamic between what language can say and what language can say about itself. In this sense, the operations of conceptual normativity, the rules of the living dead, do not tell the story of uncertainty nor do they show any will to leave the human behind. Rather, they tell the story of a calling from somewhere else that demands a form of self-determination and drive in the expansive terrain of human mundanity.[35]

This latter, non-tragic narrative perhaps illustrates another route by which to comprehend thought as material and by which to see the way in which this pop-cultural material situates the real without being conditioned by a theory of it.[36] This shift that we can see — from horror as a pseudo-dialectical paradigm that dances between the inner frame and its edges to the mysticism of the unreal object-world, through to the failures of postmodern conservativism — underscores how horror as we know it struggles to offer us an account of the negativity of being in the world, as well as a political project.

If horror is a place of epistemology noir, a site for the excavation and explication of the undergirding conditions of negativity, a realism must be asserted that can rescue horror from

---

35 Horror in this case is not horror as we know it in forms of dialectical materialism that would play off the image of transgression against its concept. While all the characters are there that would enable some appeal to the edge of an ontology of norms, demons, monsters, creeps, unethical teen wannabes, witches, and other indescribable (in)organic entities that reference horror as transgressive in some form are self-consciously situated as products of a genre rather than entities of the real.

36 Here, Angel, as the tragic object of the series, is soon decentered and worn out within the larger *Buffy* narrative and goes on to be featured in *Angel*, a spin-off series, to become a noir-style, LA cop running a haphazard detective agency. Unlike Angel, and unlike the vampires she kills and hangs out with, Buffy gives up her life as a normal teenager for a life of slaying. Her decisive identity that meets her destiny as the Slayer is in the end mirrored only by the vampire Spike but in an equality of certainty.

horror and traverse the paradigms of genre and the generic, although we must bear in mind that the escape from genre does not land one *eo ipso* in the field of the generic. This traversal would be, perhaps, better articulated as a logically inspired form of violence. If horror is determined as the space in which we can explode the myths of our existence, then it must also be a space in which we can explode the myth of our precarity, the central axis of horror. It must risk losing the make-up that has defined it. Horror must reject horror.

Bibliography

Bataille, Georges. "Non-Knowledge." In *The Unfinished System of Nonknowledge,* edited by Stuart Kendall, translated by Michelle Kendall and Stuart Kendall, 197–200. Minneapolis: University of Minnesota Press, 2004.

Baudrillard, Jean. *Simulacra and Simulation*. Translated by Sheila Faria Glaser. Ann Arbor: University of Michigan Press, 1994.

Beech, Amanda. "Last Rights: The Non-Tragic Image and the Law." In *The Flood of Rights,* edited by Thomas Keenan, Suhail Malik, and Tirdad Zolghadr, 159–75. Berlin: Sternberg Press, 2017.

Blanchot, Maurice. *The Space of Literature.* Translated by Ann Smock. Lincoln: University of Nebraska Press, 1989.

Brandom, Robert. "Heroism and Magnanimity: The Post-Modern Form of Self-Conscious Agency." Lecture delivered for the Aquinas Lecture in Philosophy, Marquette University, Milwaukee, February 24, 2019.

Chaka, Kyle. "Object-Oriented Curating Continues in 2013 Biennale." *Hyperallergic,* March 14, 2013. https://hyperallergic.com/66935/object-oriented-curating-continues-in-2013-venice-biennale/.

Fish, Stanley. *Doing What Comes Naturally: Change, Rhetoric, and the Practice of Theory in Literary and Legal Studies.* Durham: Duke University Press, 1990.

Fisher, Mark. *Capitalist Realism: Is There No Alternative?* Winchester: Zero Books, 2009.

Garland, Alex, dir. *Annihilation*. Los Angeles: Paramount Pictures, 2018.

Harman, Graham. "On the Horror of Phenomenology." In *Collapse IV,* edited by Robin Mackay 332–66. Falmouth: Urbanomic Press, 2008.

Hurley, Gavin F. "Nonknowledge and Inner Experience." In *Horror in Space: Critical Essays on a Film Subgenre,* edited by Michele Brittany, 81–96. Jefferson: McFarland and Company Inc. Publishers, 2017.

Krauss, Rosalind E. *A Voyage on the North Sea: Art in the Age of the Post-Medium Condition.* London: Thames and Hudson, 1999.

Lyotard, Jean François. *Libidinal Economy.* Translated by Iain Hamilton Grant. Bloomington: Indiana University Press, 1983.

Mullarkey, John. "Tragedy of the Object: Democracy of Vision and the Terrorism of Things in Bazin's Cinematic Realism." *Angelaki: Journal of the Theoretical Humanities* 17, no. 4 (December 2012): 39–59. DOI: 10.1080/0969725X.2012.747329.

Negarestani, Reza. *Intelligence and Spirit.* Falmouth: Urbanomic, 2018.

Sellars, Wilfrid. "Reason and the Art of Living in Plato [1968]." In *Essays in Philosophy and Its History,* 3–26. Dordrecht: B. Reidel Publishing Company, 1974.

VanderMeer, Jeff. *Annihilation.* New York: Farrar, Straus and Giroux, 2014.

———. *Authority.* New York: Farrar, Straus and Giroux, 2014.

———. *Acceptance.* New York: Farrar, Straus and Giroux, 2014.

Wayans, Keenan Ivory, dir. *Scary Movie.* Los Angeles: Dimension Films, 2000. HD.

Whedon, Joss. *Buffy the Vampire Slayer.* WB and UPN Television networks, 1997–2003.

3

Those Who Aren't Counted

Matt Rosen

1. Introduction

On the morning of the eighth of May 1945, as the Nazis surrendered to the Allies toward the end of World War II, a day now celebrated as Victory in Europe Day, 5,000 Algerians paraded through the French Algerian city of Sétif. While celebrating the end of the war and paying tribute to their fallen, some of those marching also carried banners on which messages decrying the colonial rule of the French were written. These marchers clashed with the local *gendarmerie* — literally, "armed people," a facet of the French military tasked with local law enforcement — when the gendarmerie attempted to seize their anti-colonial placards. There is some debate about who fired the first shot, but what happened next is uncontroversial in its essentials. Both the police and the protesters, including those carrying banners and others, suffered numerous casualties. Armed protesters captured and slaughtered Europeans in the streets. And on that same evening, a peaceful protest orchestrated by the Algerian People's Party in the nearby city of Guelma was suppressed with shocking violence.

In the rural areas surrounding Sétif, news of police brutality led angry locals to attack *pieds-noirs,* a segment of the population comprised largely of ethnically French people born in Algeria and people whose ancestors had migrated to French Algeria in the nineteenth and early twentieth centuries. The pieds-noirs overwhelmingly supported the colonial rule of the French, and this fact played a justificatory role in the attacks against them which directly followed the violence in Sétif. These attacks led to the deaths of 102 Europeans, almost all of whom were civilians. There were, in addition, hundreds of non-fatal injuries, including systematic rape and corollary trauma. The mutilation and desecration of corpses was widespread. The French military quelled the rebellion after several days, with a great deal of damage already having been done. But the military didn't rest contented with having put down this resistance. They enacted a number of brutal reprisals on settlers and Algerian Muslims alike. In a *ratissage* or "raking-over" of the countryside near Sétif and Guelma, the military carried out summary executions, bombed villages entire, and shelled the town of Kherrata from a cruiser in the Gulf of Béjaïa. Pieds-noirs, reacting to assaults and seeking vengeance, lynched randomly selected Algerian Muslims who had been incarcerated in local prisons. Staking a bloody claim to vigilante justice, they shot whomever was seen wearing a white arm band — a symbol of the resistance — with no questions asked.[1] Perhaps it is unsurprising that most of the victims of this violence weren't involved in the original protests on the eighth of May.

Altogether, the violence that followed the events in Sétif and Guelma is estimated to have led to between 1,020 and 45,000 fatalities. There is of course a stark difference between the lower and upper limits of this estimate. There is not much reason to doubt that the violence which took place on the eighth of May and shortly thereafter brought about a great many avoidable deaths. Many of those who died in this unrest were horrifically

---

[1] Like the violence perpetrated by the recently defeated Nazi regime, this violence was committed *mit keine Fragen,* extra-judicially and with no questions asked. For further information, the reader may find it helpful to refer to Mehana Amrani, *Le 8 mai 1945 en Algérie: Les discours français sur les massacres de Sétif, Kherrata et Guelma* (Paris: Editions L'Harmattan, 2010).

slaughtered, and many of those who survived were nevertheless condemned to lead lives warped by their having taken part in the violence or misshapen by the tremendous burden of mourning in the wake of inhumanity. There's plenty of reason to find these events tragic. But many of us, looking back at these events, will be more inclined to consider the violence a severer tragedy if it led to 45,000 deaths rather than 1,020, just as we would be inclined to find an event that caused 100 deaths, while still tragic, even less severe.

The figure of 1,020 deaths was reported by the French government in the Tubert Report, shortly after the events that took place in Sétif and Guelma. The figure of 45,000 deaths was reported by Radio Cairo, also very soon after the violence subsided. Now, if we set aside the horrific but non-fatal barbarity of the injuries that resulted from this conflict — wounds no doubt physical, psychological, and social — and focus simply on the reported number of fatalities, which is often used to mark a conflict's severity, we'll notice a significant narrative difference between the two reported figures: 1,020 deaths and 45,000 deaths. Each figure tells, and fits into, a different story about what went on in Sétif and Guelma on the eighth of May and soon after, and about what it means. Each figure conveys a different sense of the magnitude of the tragedy. And each makes various attitudes in response to that tragedy seem more or less apt. If the number of fatalities was 1,020, as the official French report claims, then a certain attitude toward the violence might seem more appropriate: though we regret that anyone had to die in such a way, we might be willing to say that the death toll was the price that had to be paid for civil peace. Although it sounds crass, and maybe for good reason, we might be thankful that more people who might have perished were saved from this fate. The conflict might in this sense look less bad than it could have been, in virtue of a comparison between the number of fatalities that were its consequence and the number that might conceivably have resulted had things been only slightly different. If the number of fatalities was 45,000, however, then we might take the violence to have been worse in degree than had it been 1,020. We might find the tragedy severer, the burden of mourning weightier, the horror of what went on in Sétif and Guelma more intense and less comprehensible. For even if all these deaths were the cost of the mitigation of unrest, even if there had been no imaginable alternative, it may yet seem to us that 45,000 deaths are considerably costlier than 1,020 deaths, or any lesser number for that matter.

We may feel that our reason to be saddened by this tragedy — to mourn, to seek in its light to prevent similar conflicts from escalating in this way in the future, to take the violence of Sétif and Guelma as a historical example of atrocity — is proportional to the number of the dead. This is a common attitude when it comes to atrocities: the greater the number of the dead, the more tragic we say it was. This attitude seems to me to be mistaken, since it rests on what I take to be a distorted picture of the real affliction that those who perished in Sétif and Guelma underwent. A sense of *atrocity,* based in part on the fatality count that conveys an impression of its severity, stands in for the *affliction* of those who, whatever the fatality count, were indeed downtrodden. We should, first and foremost, attend to and mourn this affliction when we are trying to understand historical tragedies and conflicts, wars and injustices. The atrocity signified by the number of a body count often obscures the genuine affliction that real people experienced. It covers over the suffering that in some cases characterized their lives and the lives of those who knew them. I believe that this has an enormously deleterious effect on our capacity to make sense of, mourn, and live in light of the horrors of our past. An ethical attitude toward these horrors, I will argue, demands attention to the affliction suffered by the injured and the dead, no matter the putative severity of the atrocity given meaning by the number of fatalities.

In coming to terms with one's history — insofar as this is possible (I don't claim that the relevant mourning is ever necessarily completable, though I don't think this prevents it from being practicable) — the moral person keeps her eyes fixed on affliction rather than atrocity, on the suffering of each person who endured tragic circumstances or died under them, rather than on the count of bodies or list of injuries. In the face of atrocity, the moral person turns her attention to affliction. In the face of the impression of tragedy given by a body count, she turns her attention instead to those who aren't counted, to the suffering that can never be counted. This, I will contend, is the shape the moral person's attitude takes with regard to events such as those that went on in Sétif and Guelma.

2. Analogy and Atrocity

As is shown by the dissensus with respect to the number of fatalities that resulted from the violence of Sétif and Guelma, the number of a body count is implicated in a wider political narrative, within which this violence and its aftermath are to be made sense of.[2] In the case I've been discussing, this is either the narrative of the French colonial government (1,020 deaths) or that of the Algerian resistance (45,000 deaths). The wide gap between the two estimates isn't merely the consequence of, say, hasty miscounting, misreporting, or confusion due to the ongoing conflict and an attendant lack of cooperation and communication, though these are surely relevant. Rather, the divergent numbers find their place, and are as such intelligible, in divergent worldviews. These numbers are, in this sense, given from

---

[2] To put it another way, the number of a fatality count is, in a certain sense about which I'll try to get clear, politically theory-laden. As Paul Feyerabend writes, "Not only are facts and theories in constant disharmony, they are never as neatly separated as everyone makes them out to be." The fact of the number of the body count and its weight or significance can't be neatly separated from the theoretical apparatus of what I'll call an "analogy." This is the set of relations in and through which sense is made of affliction as atrocity. The *fact* of a body count of 1,020 is intelligible as such to those who see a certain atrocity, who have a certain going *theory* or narrative about what went on in Sétif and Guelma. The *fact* of a count of 45,000 is intelligible to those who see another atrocity, who have a different theory or narrative about what went on in Sétif and Guelma; they make different sense of it. Paul Feyerabend, *Against Method* (London: Verso, 2010), 51.

political stances, which lend them the credence of context. From the point of view of the French government, or for those who share a similar sense of things, the body count of 1,020 makes sense. It fits into a wider frame, without thereby calling that frame too much into question, and it then comes to have further application (justificatory and otherwise) within that frame. Likewise, from the point of view of the Algerian resistance or its allies, the body count of 45,000 is intelligible, and this fits into an operative frame, while the suggestion that the proper count is actually 1,020 looks — from this vantage point — jarring, deceitful, or senseless. If this suggestion is plausible, the pressure may lead one to adjust one's view of things accordingly (perhaps beyond the scope of this specific incident). If it isn't received as plausible, it may be dismissed on that account, and the pressure that would cause one to change one's view, or to have to invent a way to deny the plausibility of the suggestion, won't be felt.[3]

It seems plausible that at least very many of those who inhabited each point of view took the number of fatalities asserted by the representative of that view — either the French government or Radio Cairo — to be accurate. They were sincere in asserting that either 1,020 or 45,000 is the proper count, though both evidently couldn't have been right about this. But all the same, the numeric product that results from the count of bodies, the quantification of the fallen, is the outcome of an operation that takes place within a certain sort of political or social structure. I will call this structure an "analogy."

---

[3] This simplifies things to a certain extent. In some cases, the suggestion will be received as entirely implausible because an operative view is so strongly held or so resistant to information that conflicts with it; in such cases, the pressure that would cause one to change one's view won't be felt much at all. In other cases, the suggestion will be received as pretty implausible, as likely to be false, or as questionable, but it won't be dismissed outright. This may lead one to change one's view in a minor way, or to repress or twist the information received, since that information won't be received as wholly worthy of dismissal. But the point stands: one's view affects the information one receives. We always acquire information in the midst of things, with a view already in place, more or less liable to change depending on what facts are received and how they're received.

An analogy works like this. From the vantage point of a particular community or social position, within a certain frame of understanding by means of which particular sorts of people (who are often identified as such by attributes of such-and-such a type) make sense of the world and their place in it, it is held as true and importantly meaningful that there's a specific correlation — an analogy — between those who have perished and the narrative of their affliction. The dead are tied to a certain story, seen from a certain view, and this analogy or correlation is what I mean by an "atrocity." An atrocity is this analogical link that unites the dead and a particular narrative about what they suffered and how they died. It's a link that makes sense from a particular view of things and can be seen — depending on the narrative and how tightly it fits with the facts of the affliction (insofar as these are known and open to public view) — to be more or less apt in relation to the wider perspective. In other words, an atrocity is the partial sense made of affliction from a politically or socially specific view. It relies on, helps to explain, and is commonly furthered by particular answers (which have to be seen as more or less intelligible) to the questions: "How many people died there?" and "In what way did they die?" and "Who (what sort of person) killed them, and for what reason?"

An atrocity is an analogical structure with two terms: those who perished, on the one hand, and the narrative of their affliction, on the other. It is the "third" that unites these terms in itself. As terms of the consequent atrocity, the dead and the story into which they fit can't be understood as extricable from their mutual relation, so far as those who see the atrocity *as an atrocity* are concerned. The dead can't be stripped of their narrative significance, which grants their deaths sense for a specific community of the living. Likewise, the narrative can't be understood apart from those who died, to whom it grants a particular meaning for the living. The number of fatalities plays an important part in this analogy. This number, intelligible as such from within a particular point of view, ties together the victims and the meaning given to what they suffered. What results is an atrocity. The number then signifies and stands in for the atrocity, understood to look a certain way (to which the number of fatalities is to give voice) from a particular point of view.

The atrocity — from whatever perspective, whichever atrocity one sees — subsumes under it both those who have perished and the narrative of their affliction. It's an analogy in which these terms are comprehensible only as indistinct. We can put it this way: those who have perished are always already those who have partaken in the narrative of their affliction, and that narrative isn't separable from those who have perished. Where there was affliction, where ordinary people were forced to undergo real horrors, the quantification of the fallen produces an atrocity whose number crystallizes its sense.

3. Affliction

The affliction that was suffered in Sétif and Guelma is, for each person who underwent it, one and the same, no matter whether the death toll was 1,020 or 45,000. Affliction isn't something that can be measured, weighed, or subject to comparison. It can't be counted. But the atrocity is radically different in each case. It can be measured, weighed, or subject to comparison — in fact, it just is what can be so counted. It is crystallized by means of a specific number, and this number can in certain situations belie it or the wider view from which it is seen.

The affliction of those who met their end in Sétif and Guelma or endured its violence precedes the analogical structure of the atrocity. From the view of the afflicted, their affliction isn't yet atrocious. In the first place, affliction is without atrocity. When the French government made sense of the affliction suffered in Sétif and Guelma by means of the count of 1,020, they dealt with atrocity. Radio Cairo too dealt with atrocity by way of the count of 45,000. In neither of these cases was the affliction itself — prior to its transformation into atrocity — dealt with.

Affliction is different from atrocity in kind, while an atrocity with a signifying number of 1,020 is different in degree from one that has a number of 45,000. The former atrocity is like the latter in this way: each is a violent set of events — in many ways, the same set of events — that occurred in the context of the Nazi's surrender and the French colonial occupation of Algeria. We could conceivably add further details to our characterization of these events, some of which would fit into the identifiable narrative structures of both atrocities. (This isn't of course true of all the major details, as is shown by the question of how many people died in the violence.) Even so, the former atrocity is unlike the latter atrocity in this way: we're likely to consider the latter atrocity less grave; and this picture of things meshes with a particular frame of social and political reference and understanding.

So affliction can't be more or less than what it is. But atrocity is always more or less than what it is; this intensive difference is given in large part by the atrocity's unique number — the product of the body count — in contrast to other plausible numbers in which one could put one's faith (or in which others put their faith).

The atrocity in which 1,020 people were killed differs in quantity from that in which 45,000 people were killed. But it would be a mistake to see this as merely a difference in quantity. Each number tells a distinct story about what went on in Sétif and Guelma. Each paints a particular picture of the events, and each comes to light in a distinct worldview. Each number thus lends the atrocity a different sense or weight (we might say, a different atrociousness). And each comes to symbolize this sense or weight — in a way, to stand in for it. The apparent difference in quantity between 1,020 and 45,000 is an intensive or qualitative difference, and really a narrative difference. The fatality count gives voice to the qualitative fabric of a particular point of view with respect to what happened in Sétif and Guelma and what it should be taken to mean. The resultant number expresses and carries a specific — and generally communal — opening onto the world. It is an aperture onto the past and a symbol which then figures in mourning, with which one then tries to live going forward.

Now the quality to which the number of the body count gives voice comes to life in an analogy. In this analogy, the self and the other — those who see atrocity and those who were afflicted — are seen to be inextricable, tied together in a knot that is productive of sense. The quality of the atrocity has a recognizable structure. I will call this the atrocity's "for-y" structure. The self and the other are seen to be necessarily "for" each other (y), and each is in itself unthinkable without this "for" and the other term (y) to which it is tied by way of the "for." The "for," however, isn't transitive. The dead "for" those who see atrocity aren't those who see atrocity and have to live in the face of it. That is, the analogical form of the atrocity is made up of two more basic analogies, of which it is the reticulation: the self "for" the other and the other "for" the self, the living who have to go forward in light of atrocity and the afflicted who are intelligible under a certain atrocious aspect for those who see their affliction as atrocity. The unique number of the atrocity, the result of the count of bodies, isn't merely quantitative, since it gives a condensed expression to the "for," the quality that unites the dead and the living in atrocity's analogical schema. The number marks this "for." It symbolizes the analogical reticulation that gives the terms of the analogy their sense precisely insofar as they are its terms.

The result of the body count is the locution in number that stands in for the atrocity. It represents the analogical relation of the two more basic analogies, each of which involves a nontransitive "for-y" quality. So the quantity of the fatality count names, as it were, the quality of the given violence as an atrocity, helping to determine and serving to enunciate its apparent severity and its essence.

4. Quantifying the Fallen

I have been claiming that the unique number of a body count marks the quality — the dual "for-y" structure — of an atrocity. It fits into a particular view, and it comes to give expressive and symbolic weight to a vision of the atrociousness of a set of events (which then colors these events through and through). The number of the fatality count both fits into and in part carries a wider view. But how is it given? I don't mean to ask about how a count of bodies is undertaken in its logistical details. Rather, I mean to ask about how it is seen from, and done by those who inhabit, a specific view of a set of events, a view through which this set of events takes a particular shape as an atrocity with an identifiable sense.

The unique number that stands in for the severity and meaning of an atrocity is given by a political or communal operation, a shared way of making sense of what has happened by condensing a joint understanding (thereby solidifying it) into a sort of crystal: the number of the body count. I'll call this operation the "count-as-x." For the French government, the violence of Sétif and Guelma was counted-as-1,020. For the Algerian resistance, it was counted-as-45,000. Counting-as bestows sense. It folds seemingly senseless and often traumatic events into a narrative structure, and it compresses that structure into the potent symbol of a figure. As we will see, this operation's excess is real affliction. That is what is set aside — forgotten, fundamentally neglected — in the production of atrocity, done by means of the count-as-x.

Now the count-as-x also counts its x as one in the end. For instance, the 1,020 or 45,000 counts for one as "Sétif and Guelma," as "what happened there." A certain univocity is established, imposed on a series of discrete events, on the affliction suffered by each victim (each person who became a victim) beyond the frame of the atrocity. This counting-as-one aids in the production of sense, and it is of especial importance if that sense is to be shared among the members of a polity or passed along within a social sphere. It's this counting-as-one that enables *the* lesson of Sétif and Guelma to be taught to children in a digestible way; it is this that finds its way into history textbooks. What is missed, though, is the affliction — passed over in the count-as-x and neglected entirely in the $x=$ one that solidifies an atrocity made sensible in affliction's place.

The singular people who suffered in Sétif and Guelma thus come under a particular form of description — in effect, a formal order — in which the affliction is thematized as atrocity by means of a dual counting operation: the count-as-x and the x = one. Affliction is made sense of in terms of the particular analogical quality of the atrocity. It is only glimpsed, so to speak, through a decidedly atrocious lens.[4] In this way, it is distorted, rendered intelligible for those who inhabit a particular view of things (which itself isn't limited to retrospection).

The operation of the count-as-x produces a number, x, which is given analogically. This number's sense is that of the analogy — the atrocity — which it marks. The communal or political sphere, as we have seen, structures itself analogically around

---

[4] Reiner Schürmann writes that "[h]egemonies transform the singular into a particular. They serve to say what is, to classify and inscribe, to distribute proper and common nouns." Reiner Schürmann, *Broken Hegemonies*, trans. Reginald Lilly (Bloomington: Indiana University Press, 2003), 7. There are, it seems to me, important similarities between Schürmann's hegemonies and the totalizing analogies I am considering here. Both transform the singular other person into a particular: the other "for" me, "for" us, "for" the living. Both classify and inscribe, rendering affliction narrowly intelligible as atrocity. Now the question for us is this. Is there a way in which the particular, the realm of the hegemony, might no longer be seen as the "chief-represented" (ἡγεμών) but merely as the represented? Can we come to see the analogical as no longer hegemonic, as secondary to what's singular and, *in this secondariness,* as coexistent with the primacy of the singular? That is: can we inhabit analogy without letting it become totalizing or hegemonic? This question takes a number of forms across various subject matters in philosophy. Consider these examples. Can preferential love coexist with love for strangers? Can community coexist with genuine hospitality? Can ethics coexist with politics? This form of question underlies much of my thinking here and elsewhere. It would not be inaccurate to put it this way. How can we keep the inherent partiality or inadequacy of analogy forefront in our minds while still inhabiting it, and what follows from doing so? How can we keep, in some sense, what hegemonic structures are while dissolving their hegemonic quality? I think that is often possible, though it requires, sometimes, changes to the structures themselves. One case in which it's possible is this: the sense made of affliction as atrocity can be kept as non-totalizing insofar as one bears witness to the affliction itself in its primacy. This essay attempts to get clear about how that would work.

calamitous events. Hence, these events are understood as atrocities, made intelligible within a specific frame. The atrocity is woven into a particular social fabric and in turn helps to support that fabric (or adds to it) by crystallizing affliction in an atrocious number that makes it meaningful and thus more bearable. Through the operation of the count-as-x and the analogical givenness of the atrocity, and especially through the counting-as-one of x, those who inhabit the relevant social position or community can chart a course forward in the face of what has happened. They can make sense of the past, mourn in a way that seems more or less accomplishable, and figure out how best to live going forward. But in so doing, they *have forgotten* the affliction of those whose suffering has been rendered, always in hindsight, atrocious. This affliction comes under a qualifying description that makes it intelligible to those with a certain view; such is the movement from affliction to atrocity. It is this attitude to the horrors of the past, which considers them atrocities, with which I want to take issue.

5. The Topology of the Three-as-One

It will be useful to try to get a sense of the topological form of the communal or political sphere as it functions here. This sphere takes a specifiable shape in the analogical fashioning of atrocity, in making affliction in this way intelligible. I now want to get clear about this shape.

To get going, consider the structure of an analogy that I identified in §2. It comprises two terms — the self and the other, those who see an atrocity and those who were afflicted — and a dual set of non-transitive relations between them; these relations give rise to the analogy's "for-y" qualities. There's the self "for" the other (the living who must go forward in the face of past injustices) and the other "for" the self (the dead who are intelligible under an atrocious aspect for the living). Neither term can be understood as separable from the other. Their relation is treated as primitive. The other isn't really other here, not absolutely. The two terms are thought under the aspect of a third: the analogy itself, the atrocity that ties them together. In our analysis, there appear to be three operative terms: the self, the other, and the atrocity. But all three have to be thought as one, within the bounds of the atrocity in which the first two terms — self and other — are comprehensible as inextricable. This topology, this shape of the community of the living and the dead, is what I will call "the three-as-one." For there are three terms, but all are, in essence, as one, under the aspect of the third: the atrocity itself.

In the topology of the three-as-one, the self and the other are tied together in the introduction of a third term (the analogy itself) such that they can't be isolated from one another. So there exist three terms in the three-as-one, but they aren't *distinct* terms. They are as one. The self isn't itself thinkable apart from the other, and the other isn't itself thinkable apart from the self. Moreover, neither of these basic relations can be thought without the other, for as we saw the analogy is the relationship between two non-transitive "for-y" relations. The self and the other only exist intelligibly insofar as they exist within the limits of the third term. They must be thought within its frame. The afflicted are the sense made of them for the living by way of the count-as-x. The living are those who have to figure out how to go forward in view of history's atrocities. These terms — the self and the other, the living and the dead — are thinkable only in the relational schema, taken to be originary, of the analogy under which they have always already been subsumed.

The afflicted exist for the living. Within the analogy, then, they are different from the living only in degree. They are not the living, to be sure, but they crucially go on living with the living — they are the sense the living make of them (in part, by counting them as x, and then as one). In the three-as-one, the dead and the living are unthinkable apart from the analogy as a whole. Atrocity functions in precisely this way. It takes the shape of a three-as-one. Those who perished and the narrative of their affliction can't be thought in separation from their conjoining in the third: the analogy itself qua atrocity.

I say that an attitude toward the past's unjust deaths according to which they're to be seen under the aspect of atrocity is not ethical. Affliction is made intelligible as atrocity through the operation of the count-as-x and $x=$ one. What's left out is affliction itself. The idea that atrocity is sufficient, that we must turn our attention to atrocity if we wish to understand the cruelties of history and make a life in light of them, leads us to neglect the affliction of real, ordinary people. I believe that this neglect prevents us from actually coming to terms with the past. It keeps us from really mourning, from leading lives in which we are attentive to what has happened in our history. It doesn't allow us to approach events such as those that went on in Sétif and Guelma in an ethical manner. Living well in view of such events means contending with affliction, not forgetting this in contending with atrocity.

I have described the attitude according to which past afflictions are to be seen as atrocities, and so not as they really are, as *not* ethical. I don't say it is unethical. For I want to emphasize that this attitude doesn't involve a *choice* to conceive of afflictions as atrocities (though particular choices may indeed follow from this conception); as if one knew full well, in conceiving of afflictions as atrocities, that a transformation had gone on. The person who sees an atrocity is not cognizant of having an immoral attitude, nor of seeing the world wrongly. Rather, she has simply *forgotten* affliction. Her error consists in letting it slip from mind, thereby allowing for atrocity's constitution. This forgetting makes room for atrocity. The moral failure here is a failure to stay vigilant, to keep up a certain wakefulness regarding the past's afflictions.

Someone who sees an atrocity in affliction's place has a forgetful attitude toward history's injustices. In this sense, it is not ethical, since an ethical attitude toward these injustices would involve the *perception* of affliction and the vigilant maintenance, the *remembering,* of this perspicuous vision. The person who sees atrocity needs to be woken up, and then needs to keep herself awake.

An atrocity is a kind of totalizing construction; it tethers the dead to a certain narrative of their affliction, and it forgets that affliction itself. It renders the dead not really other than the living, for neither can be fully understood except through their analogical relation. In an atrocity, the dead are nothing but the sense the living make of them. They are said to be this and nothing besides. So an atrocity totalizes, under its own aspect, the affliction of those who perished. It takes what it speaks of to be all there is to speak of when it comes to history's calamitous events. It presumes to have no outside — or if it has one, it isn't thinkable; it isn't something to which one could attend in mourning. This atrocious construction is generally retrospective: the afflicted don't themselves construct it, since it operates by means of a count-as-x that goes on in hindsight, and it is more or less completed, producing a largely closed sense of the atrocity and its constitutive events, in the count-as-one of x.

An atrocity gives the impression of being sufficient with respect to what has happened. To those who inhabit the relevant point of view, it doesn't look as if it leaves behind any excess. That this *isn't* the case is only shown when contrary points of view come on the scene. The dissensus about the fatality count in Sétif and Guelma doesn't only show that there are two different atrocities, one marked by the count-as-1,020 and the other by the count-as-45,000. It also shows that both of these atrocities have an outside — and indeed, a common outside. This is the affliction of those who perished in the violence which, one and the same, was suffered by each afflicted person. Both atrocities endeavor to make this affliction intelligible under an atrocious description or within the bounds of a formal order. But they do this through totalization and neglect, and it's in this sense that they stand in the way of an ethical attitude to the horrors of the past. For atrocity renders a genuine encounter with the other — the afflicted — unthinkable. The three terms of the three-as-one, recall, are always as one, inextricable from one another. The afflicted are only encountered as those who can be counted among the victims of atrocity, seen "for" those whose vision is of atrocity. Since the other would be beyond the analogy, within the analogy it is the unencounterable par excellence.

There can be no other in the three-as-one; the "as-one" precludes this. There can't be anything different in kind from what is within the atrocity, held fast by it. Any other is off the table from the point of atrocity's constitution in the count-as-x. The other can differ only in degree from the self, as what's intelligible only in the sense in which it's "for" the self, made analogical. It may seem that I am making heavy weather over this. But there's a reason for that. This is how the forgetting of affliction characteristic of the three-as-one operates, and this forgetting is distinctive of the attitude with which I am taking issue. The production of atrocity — in the count-as-x and $x =$ one — essentially involves the neglect of affliction. The "for-y" quality of the analogy is imposed; the dead are seen to be fundamentally tied up with the sense made of them, and this forces them into a context or position that is the same as that of the living — a context that is not the afflicted's. To be sure, this doesn't appear to be an imposition from within the view of things that constitutes, and is then in part constituted by, the production of atrocity. But that is precisely the three-as-one's amnesia at work.

The position into which the other is put, under which they're in effect subsumed, is thought to be knowable by means of a sort of empathy. Since the other is already just what it is in relation to the self within the analogy, it is imagined that the self can step into the other's shoes, so to speak, without much of a problem. And having done this, the self can try them on for size. In this way, the living take themselves to be able to get a grip on those who died atrociously. Understanding seems to come easily. Yet the living can't empathetically get a handle on affliction itself, because this very empathetic "getting a handle on…" relies on the neglect of affliction. It operates only given a kind of lethargy. In this lethargy or forgetfulness, a supposedly easily acquirable understanding of analogy rids us of humility with respect to history's horrors.

The other and the self are each understood in their mutual indistinction. Empathy here turns on the introduction of a third term, an analogical bridge, which lets the self to some extent step into the other's place.[5] At least, so far as the self is concerned. The third term is a "like" or "unlike" relation that an other is seen to bear to oneself; the other is seen, in virtue of their similarity to or difference in degree from oneself, to have a relational property (being like or unlike oneself in such-and-such a way or to such-and-such an extent) by means of which they're intelligible to one as such. The afflicted are perhaps *like* those who look back on them from the perspective of Radio Cairo, since both have dealt with the threat of European colonialism. Or maybe the afflicted are *unlike* those who look back from the perspective of the French government, since they don't share particular political beliefs. This "like" or "unlike" term serves to bridge the gap between the self and the other. This bridge is all that is needed to get analogical empathy going, even across great qualitative divides (as the manifest bridging ability of the "unlike"

---

5   In his psychoanalytic self psychology, Heinz Kohut defines empathy as "vicarious introspection." When one empathizes, one vicariously introspects into the other; one tries the other's shoes on for size, by way of one's relation to the other and the qualities one sees the other to have. I compare this to Husserl's account of empathy in my "The Givenness of Other People," forthcoming. Kohut's self-psychological method of empathy is a clear example of the sort of analogical ethic — the conception of one's rightful relationship with other people — against which I am writing. It may be helpful to refer, when considering my talk of analogical empathy, to Kohut's essay "Introspection, Empathy, and Psychoanalysis: An Examination of the Relationship between Mode of Observation and Theory," *Journal of the American Psychoanalytic Association* 7, no. 3 (1959): 459–83, as well as to Heinz Kohut, *Analysis of the Self* (New York: International Universities Press, 1979), 176–77. There seems to me to be something similar in Graham Harman's development of his object-oriented ontology in ethics. Harman claims that the relation between oneself (x) and the other (y) exists as a compound object, x–y, which is morality's locus. Indeed, Harman tells us that "ethics is about the compound of subject and object." Here, I would like to dissent. Ethics is about how the compound of subject and object is insufficient with regard to the other; it is about how the other isn't merely an object for a subject. Graham Harman, *Object-Oriented Ontology: A New Theory of Everything* (London: Pelican Books, 2018), 107.

term brings to bear).⁶ With the analogy in place, the seeming possibility of an empathetic grasp on the atrocious position of the dead leads us to further abandon the idea that atrocity has an outside. We take ourselves, within the three-as-one, to have come to terms with those who have died. And empathy makes it look as if we aren't missing anything in this. But we have forgotten the actual affliction of ordinary people.

The self and the other are seen to exist only within the bounds of their empathetic relationship, which is evidently geared toward the self who presumes to empathize with the afflicted. The self is set as the norm, the constituting center, in relation to which the other differs only by a given degree. The other orbits the self, as it were. The three-as-one doesn't admit of any genuine alterity that would precede the position of the analogy's terms *as terms*. It takes the relation between the terms, centered on the self or the living, to be primitive. And so, it forgets affliction.

The topology of the three-as-one is the shape that the community of the living and the dead takes in neglecting affliction and attending instead to atrocity. But I want to suggest that remembering affliction doesn't mean merely negating the three-as-one, flying out and into the void. It isn't an abdication of the task of coming to grips with history's horrors. Rather, the remembrance of affliction leads to a community of the living and the dead (that is, an encounter between them) that has a different, and to my mind morally preferable, shape. I will call this the topology of "the two." This topology is prior to the three-as-one, as affliction is to atrocity, and it is foreclosed to those who inhabit the totalizing analogical schema that gives rise to and is carried by the vision of atrocity.⁷

---

6 This being so, empathy may still be harder to start, and one may consequently be able to hold on to more humility, in cases where the other is seen to be very unlike — even if still different in degree from — the self. But this isn't always the case; sometimes, great differences in degree seem to motivate pernicious forms of xenophobia and the like.

7 There are three distinctions, similar in a number of ways to the distinction I've drawn between affliction and atrocity, that may be profitable to

6. The Topology of the Two

The topology of the two is the space in which I encounter an other who isn't me or of me. It is the space in which I come up against an outside I cannot hope to assimilate or incorporate. The two is the shape of an encounter in which transcendence comes to pass.

In the two, the other is absolutely unrelated to me. My encounter with the other doesn't hang on empathy, for there isn't an analogical bridge between us across which I might empathize; there is no room for a "like" or "unlike" relation in the two. I can't try the other's shoes on for size; I can't even make out their shoes. In the three-as-one, there are three terms — the self, the other, and the analogy as a whole — which are counted-as-one under the aspect of the third, the analogy or atrocity. In the two, there are two terms — the self and the other — which are different in kind from one another yet nevertheless encounter each another. They do this directly in the space of the two. It is in this way that I, in the two, am exposed to the other in their very otherness, without their subsumption under my categories of understanding or what is familiar to me. There isn't a third under which the two terms could be counted-as-one, seen to be mere relata in a relationship taken to be primitive. The other in the two is whatever it may be. It isn't "for" the self. Affliction is not transformed into atrocity, and we needn't give up the endeavor to come to terms with the violence of our history: the two is very much a topology of the encounter, but one that

---

consider further: Levinas's distinction between the saying and the said (in *Otherwise than Being or Beyond Essence*, trans. Alphonso Lingis [Pittsburgh: Duquesne University Press, 1998]); Henry's distinction between the flesh and the body or self-affection and noetic-noematic givenness (e.g., in *Incarnation*); and Lacan's distinction between the real and reality. This isn't the place to try to carefully articulate the similarities and differences between these distinctions, though I hope to do that in future work. But let me just say this. In regard to the relationship between affliction and atrocity, it might be particularly interesting to think about how the former term in each of these distinctions undermines or undoes the latter term, while in one sense still preserving it as so undermined or undone.

doesn't operate via analogy and empathy. This is why inhabiting it by way of remembrance, calling it to mind moment after moment, makes possible vigilant attention to affliction.

In dwelling in the two, I respond to the other's call as whatever it may be. I don't seek to comprehend the other "for" me, as a term of the analogy centered on me. I abnegate to the other, and there's no symmetry between us. I don't demand reciprocity. I am responsible for the other in the two, called to be hospitable to that which is at an undecipherable height. I welcome an other whose sense isn't of an order with which I am acquainted or comfortable. The two doesn't look like home. But the comfort and regularity of the three-as-one mask a certain angst. In seeing atrocity in affliction's place, we miss something excessive — the affliction itself — which nevertheless calls us to bear witness to it. So in the regularity of atrocity, in our forgetfulness of affliction, we feel in some way unable to really get a grip on the suffering that flesh and blood people endured, the suffering from which many of them perished. Seen in this light, our mourning appears to miss something. We feel an angst: this is the ache of our neglect. In attending to it, in following it and coming to see it as such, we can exit the three-as-one and inhabit the two, facing affliction head on, encountering the afflicted in earnest in our open exposure to them. We can encounter them in our responsibility to bear witness to what they themselves underwent, not just to our vision of atrocity.

An attitude to the past's calamities that sees them under the aspect of atrocity rests on the construction of an analogy relating those who perished and a specific narrative of their affliction. The affliction of the ordinary people who suffered in Sétif and Guelma is subjected to the operation of the count-as-x, which produces the unique number of the death toll. This number signifies and helps to carry the sense of the atrocity under which the affliction is, through this process, subsumed. Affliction is primordial in relation to atrocity. It precedes atrocity and is the material with which atrocity is built. And it is obscured — forgotten — in atrocity's construction. Atrocity is the original suffering of those who died at Sétif and Guelma, outside any analogy, made analogical. It is their agony transformed into the qualitative intensity of a particular persecution situated in a social and political context. That is to say, an atrocity is the apparatus within which those who aren't counted become simply what they are for those who count in the operation of the count-as-x, or for those who inherit this count and its sense. So atrocity is affliction become more or less than what it is, no longer what it is in itself. It's a sort of horror produced analogically in relating a communal or political narrative to those who perished such that the two can't be understood in separation from one another. This production goes on in a communal operation of quantification: the count that quantifies and houses a certain qualification in a given number. This operation yields the correlation of the living's narrative and the dead, clothed in number, which comes to stand in for and gives sense to affliction; the correlation permits no excess beyond what's counted-as-x and then counted-as-one, beyond what has already been qualified under the banner of atrocity or has been given its adjectival mark, "atrocious."

So we can say that atrocity is affliction converted through the count-as-x into a number that admits of no excess, in which the meaning of some historical horror is to be definitively made out. The afflicted other is ensnared, made into a sort of finite, totalized idol of itself. It is the sense made of it. The other is transformed into only what is correlated with and inextricable from the narrative of the affliction that has befallen them, and all this is within the overarching analogical structure of the atrocity.

When this analogical structure, in which there are three terms (self, other, analogy), is taken to be prior to the two, the three-as-one is the result. The three are then counted-as-one, and this involves the neglect of the two. There can't be a two in which one could dwell, for the three-as-one is taken to come first, and it precludes the two from the start. The forgetting of the two here is twofold: one forgets the two in taking the three-as-one to be primary, and then one forgets this forgetting; this is essential for the maintenance of this position. The inhabiting of the three-as-one is in this sense a lethargy with respect to the space in which the genuine other—who isn't determined by some identity perceived by me or attribute discerned by me—condemns me on pain of angst (that of leaving something out of my mourning) to a non-relational or asymmetrical abnegation. To live in the three-as-one is to look away.[8]

Communal attitudes with respect to the horrific events of history take an analogical form. Their topology is that of the three. There are two terms, the living and the dead. And then there is the dual bridge between them:

1. the sense the living make of the dead, and
2. the way in which the dead's suffering affects how the living set out to live.

Now the three, insofar as the two is neglected, is counted-as-one. The dead are taken to be inextricable from, and even identical to, the sense the living make of them. The dead can't exceed this, at least not in being thought. But the three needn't be counted-as-one. Instead, it can admit of excess: namely, the excess of the two, which one can acknowledge as preceding the three. When this acknowledgment takes place, the two and the three—the topology of ethics and the topology of community—can conceivably coexist.[9] But this coexistence can happen

---

8 There are two sets of remarks by Emmanuel Levinas worth considering in light of what I'm arguing here. First, those regarding the way in which the height of the other person, their infinite distance from me and the fact that I'm irrecuperably responsible for them, is encountered in their hunger and poverty, their insufficiency and nakedness. This might be compared with the way in which the afflicted person's otherness reveals itself as a destitution, as an inadequacy, within the sphere of analogy. See Emmanuel Levinas, *Totality and Infinity: An Essay on Exteriority,* trans. Alphonso Lingis (The Hague: Martinus Nijhoff, 1969), 117, 200. Second, it's worth considering those remarks made by Levinas about vigilance and insomnia, and their role in moral experience. See Levinas, *Otherwise than Being or Beyond Essence,* 87. On insomnia in particular, see Emmanuel Levinas, *God, Death, and Time,* trans. Bettina Bergo (Stanford: Stanford University Press, 2000), 207–12.

9 The relationship here between the topologies of the two and the three bears some resemblance to the relationship between nonstandard philoso-

only when the two is taken to be the primordial topology. That's the only way for the three to not be counted-as-one. When the two is acknowledged as preceding the three, the three isn't totalizing, which means that the two and the three can then coexist (since there's room for the two prior to the three). If the two and the three are considered simultaneous, or if the three is given primacy and thereby counted-as-one, the other is replaced by an analogical idol: the other who's "for" the self, and nothing besides. The afflicted are taken to be nothing other than what they are under an atrocious description. If the two comes first, however, the afflicted are first what they really are, and only then are they — very partially, we'll acknowledge — the sense that's made of them. This permits an apt humility regarding the sense we make of the past's horrors. We introduce the possibility of real fallibility, so far as atrocity goes, in introducing the impossibility of getting a complete handle on affliction under an atrocious aspect. But this doesn't preclude a grip on affliction itself, which is precisely what inhabiting the topology of the two, prior to the three, enables us to get.

The number generated in the operation of the count-as-x traps the afflicted in a system — of sense, explanation, and mourning — in which they can differ only in degree from those who are set as the norm of the analogy, the constituting center or mean of the atrocity: the living. For the French colonial government, those who perished at Sétif and Guelma were the 1,020, just as they were the 45,000 for Radio Cairo. But what are they themselves, as ordinary people who endured substantial trials and died in appalling violence? What are they besides these numbers, beyond analogy? And how can we think the af-

---

phy or non-philosophy and philosophy in the work of François Laruelle. See, especially, François Laruelle, *Principles of Non-Philosophy,* trans. Nicola Rubczak and Anthony Paul Smith (London: Bloomsbury Academic, 2013). Similarly, it's somewhat comparable to Lacoste's distinction between being-before-God (or *coram Deo*) and Heidegger's Being-in-the-world. See Jean-Yves Lacoste, *Experience and the Absolute: Disputed Questions on the Humanity of Man,* trans. Mark Raferty-Skehan (New York: Fordham University Press, 2004).

fliction of these people without regard to what they're taken to be or to count as? How can we understand them in distinction from what they are for the apparatus of atrocity under which they've been subsumed and within which they've been numerically crystallized as the 1,020 or the 45,000? How can we unthink the distortion of the atrocity's count-as-x and $x =$ one so as to come to terms with affliction itself?

7. Counting, Angst, and Christ's Crucifixion

Within the topology of the three-as-one, affliction is understood as atrocity, with no outside. It is given sense by a body count, in which that sense is symbolically housed. The count-as-x introduces a third term or set of relations that conjoin those who aren't counted and those who count such that each term is indistinguishable from its sense within the greater milieu (the analogy itself). The terms are only thinkable as parts within the whole, in view of the whole.

There are a great many historical examples of this: affliction is qualified as atrocity by way of an operation of counting. A number is introduced, which stands in for and serves to aid in making sense of affliction. The affliction of the Shoah, for instance, is signified numerically by the count-as-six-million. The Shoah's affliction itself is subsumed under its correlated numericity. Five million is the unique number of the Thirty Years' War. The Cambodian autogenocide is counted-as-two-million. And the Black Death, which took so many lives in Paris, is given analogically by the number 50,000. We see this pattern — the application of a count-as-x to the suffering within a situation as it is seen from a specific point of view — just as much with pestilence and plague as with autos-da-fé, burnings at the stake, and drownings in the trials of witches. The massacre that took place at Columbine High School is symbolized by the number 15, which stands in for it. This is less what it is (an atrocity) than the Salem witch trials, symbolized by the number 20, which is still less what it is than the violence that took place in Sétif and Guelma — which, symbolized by the number 1,020 or 45,000, is therefore more what it is. Atrocity is the numbering and qualification of affliction such that it can be more or less what it is. But this has a price: the resultant atrocity is only a shallow image of the affliction, a hollow idol or statue. The actual affliction is reduced to what can be numbered and qualified, rendered intelligible. In failing to acknowledge the count's excess, and in failing to get a non-atrocious grip on that excess, we are left with a sense of history's horrors as intelligible. But this sense is skin-deep. Our understanding of these horrors is facile at best, and it is often much more seriously warped by the thought that our vision of atrocity is wholly adequate to the relevant affliction.

The application of the count-as-x to the suffering seen within a given situation is commonly a response to rather acute trauma, or to the memory of this trauma and how it affected one or those proximal to one. In this way, one attempts to cope with what has occurred. But it is a coping strategy with pernicious repercussions.[10] The numbering that crystallizes the atrocity *qua atrocity*, such that it is at least to some degree more psychologically bearable, leads to a condition of angst in which that crystallization in number seems inescapable, exhaustive, and basic. Mourning comes to seem always incomplete. It looks always to be missing the real substance of what has happened, the affliction itself. One is left with a shallow number, a comprehensible but inevitably cursory sense of a set of violent events. This sense always appears to lack depth. For despite the sense made of af-

---

10 To reiterate: I don't say that this strategy involves a choice to neglect affliction. For if one knew that one was forgetting affliction (in so choosing) and instead focusing on atrocity, this forgetfulness and the resultant focus would be rather partial. The coping strategy I have in mind here isn't so much a choice as a failure to see or remember, one that in fact makes sense in the wake of traumatic events. So we need to be *reminded* to attend to affliction, and then we need to work to maintain our vision of it, to stay vigilant. One can't see affliction and *with it in view* choose to see atrocity. The strategy I have in mind, then, isn't something one decides to pursue with a full view of what it entails; it's only seen for what it is once one remembers affliction, thereby coming to see what had previously gone on as neglect.

fliction as atrocity, the flesh and blood people who were actually afflicted are nowhere to be found.

The coping strategy that simplifies what has happened by making an analogical construction (the atrocity) look exhaustive of the sense to be made of some horrific set of events (through neglect) leads to a kind of chronic angst: we can't figure out how to truly encounter the horrors of the past, or those who really suffered them, and this affects how we're able to live in light of what has happened. We create atrocity in the count-as-x in part to endure our apparent exemption from tragedy, to relieve the disquiet of the time after a cataclysm that's not quite our own. The count is an attempt to make atrocity as much our own as is possible. But we alleviate the fear and trembling of facing up to affliction in this manner only at the cost of angst. The dreadful stasis of the number of a body count, the fixity of the atrocity and its narrative, seems to cure the fear that we too are merely pathetic flesh, or that the other's affliction is ours too, since we are responsible and already exposed in the other's suffering. But it does this by aiding us in forgetting both the self (the living) itself and the other (the dead), helping us to turn away from the two and toward the three. It makes it easier for us to take the three to be primary and so to totalize it as one. We trade the risk of having to come to terms with who we are and who the afflicted were, the risk of abnegation in the two, for what at first glance looks to be the comfort of analogy. We trade this risk for what's definitively circumscribed. But really, we trade it for what turns out to be a condition of chronic, seemingly inexorable angst. The view according to which there's nothing imaginable outside the atrocity, beyond the scope of the analogy, is certainly a cure (however short-term); but it has a price that proves to be disastrously high. As with autofiction, the solipsism in which everything has to be related to oneself in order to be comfortably intelligible winds up being stale and angst-ridden.

Once we've taken it on, it is something we try — without at first knowing how — to escape.[11]

Consider the Shoah, a set of horrors we're often wisely counseled to never forget. The affliction of the Shoah, in the operation of the count-as-six-million, becomes something that is no longer the suffering of ordinary people (whatever they may be) who are distinct from the sense the living make of them. It becomes an atrocity, in what I'll call the "as such" mode. The Shoah is taken *as such*, in its entirety, to be the atrocity made of it. Nothing of the affliction of the Shoah is seen to transcend the atrocity. The affliction becomes clothed in the numeric, which is the result of the count-as-x, and it is rendered univocally intelligible, which is the result of the $x=$ one. The number, x, is the totalization of the affliction in quantity, by way of which it is qualified under an atrocious description (counted-as-one). Hence, it is a totalization of the afflicted as what they are "for" the living who look back on them from a particular point of view. The afflicted are just the totality of what bears the relevant "for" relation (this can be made up of whatever set of "like" or "unlike" relations) to those who retrospect and see an atrocity. The affliction of ordinary people "as they are" becomes the atrocity of victims "as such." I will contrast the "as they are" mode of these people with

---

11 For some criticisms of the contemporary trend of autofiction, particularly in French literature, see Sandra Laugier's interview with Tristan Garcia in BOMB 114. Autofiction is a genre or style of writing that imagines that a writer should stay within their own context, or should write only about what they know, not going beyond the limits of the familiar or self-same. As a style of writing, I don't think that autofiction is universally objectionable. But I find the idea that one can't or shouldn't seek to write about what one isn't personally acquainted with, that one can't or shouldn't want to write about others, profoundly objectionable, both because it turns fiction into solipsism, ruining much of what's absorbing and edifying in literature, and because it sets up a putative norm without any argument. One might compare what I say here, too, with Derrida's famous statement that "there is no outside-text." See Jacques Derrida, *Of Grammatology*, trans. Gayatri Chakravorty Spivak (Baltimore: Johns Hopkins University Press, 2016), 158. I develop the claim that a seeming lack of any outside leads to a condition of angst, and that this condition can be abrogated in abnegation, in my forthcoming *Angst and Abnegation*.

their mode "as such," which is just to contrast the afflicted with those seen to be victims of atrocity while stressing that the same people are essentially at issue on both contrasting sides.

From within the analogical structure of an atrocity, it doesn't seem sensible to so much as inquire as to whether the afflicted person as they are is in fact totalized, crystallized in the number of the fatality count. It doesn't seem to make sense, either, to ask whether they are beyond the analogy, themselves indifferent to it. The question of whether the person as they are, as afflicted, is totalized doesn't so much as come to mind. After all, the number of the person as such — one out of 1,020, say — stands in for the person as they are; it is taken to be primary, originary. The afflicted person's indifference to the atrocity's number, the distance between the real person who is afflicted and the person who is one out of 1,020, can only be seen in the remembrance of the topology of the two. For in inhabiting the two, one can look toward the atrocity's number with a certain indifference, attending instead to the afflicted as they are. One catches sight of those who aren't counted in a recollection of the two, against the amnesia that enables and results in the three-as-one and the angst that manifests within the analogy counted-as-one. Indifference to the three-as-one is possible in connection with an attitude for which atrocity doesn't suffice. One sees atrocity to be lacking, emphasizing the angst of the three-as-one, and one then follows this to the recollection of the two — the exit from analogy. The remembrance of the afflicted person, against atrocity's angst and neglect, in a sense mirrors the afflicted person's own indifference to the atrocity's number (which will only be constituted in hindsight).[12]

---

12 In *After Finitude,* Quentin Meillassoux writes that what is beyond the correlational circle — for us, beyond the topology of the three-as-one — in some sense resembles the "great outdoors" sought by pre-critical philosophy, that "outside which was not relative to us, and which was *indifferent* to its own givenness to be what it is, existing in itself regardless of whether we are thinking it or not." The idea of indifference here is this. What is beyond the correlation between thinking and being, what exists whether or not we are thinking or positing it, is in a certain sense indifferent to us, foreclosed

I want now to turn to a particularly salient instance of the count-as-x, which is the root of much of its cultural and historical resilience as a method for comprehending great suffering. I have in mind the crucifixion of Christ, or the sense that was made of it by those who came after Christ. We can pull the affliction apart from the atrocity quite easily in this case. On the one hand, there is Christ's suffering itself. Christ, a flesh and blood person, bore the cross. On the other hand, there is the Pauline application of the count-as-x to this suffering such that it is transformed into an atrocity. This is the generative process through which the apparatus of Christianity as an analogical system (I'll come to this shortly) is produced. In this light, we can see the resurrection and ascension of Christ as the atrocious aftereffects of his affliction. They are the resultant narrative events of the count-as-x's application to a crucifixion which, as affliction, stands beyond any narrative that might be attached to it by the living. The count-as-x is applied by Paul to the affliction of Christ, which yields a count-as-one; $x=$ one, and this "one" is the identity of Christ — the univocal set of qualities given analogically ("for-y") — as he is "for" Christians, within the analogy as a whole (Christianity). In being applied to Christ's affliction, the count-as-x yields the atrocious figure of Christ "for" Christians within Christianity. I will refer to this figure as "Christ-in-Christianity." First, this figure is "Christ-for-Paul."

Now the conversional road to Damascus that follows, and the spread of Christianity which follows that, is predicated on this primary conversion: that of the crucifixion into the ascension, that of the affliction of Christ himself (I will refer to him as

---

to the determinations of thought. In being ourselves indifferent to such determinations, in treating the analogical with a certain ascesis, and as I'll suggest in showing a particular sort of hospitality to the other person as an other, we can get a grip on what is beyond the three-as-one. As Meillassoux's outside stands apart from what's inextricable from thought, the afflicted person is, beyond the analogical, foreclosed to our attempts to make sense of the past through a count of bodies and atrocity's constitution. Quentin Meillassoux, *After Finitude: An Essay on the Necessity of Contingency*, trans. Ray Brassier (London: Continuum, 2008), 7.

"Christ-without-Christianity") into Christ-in-Christianity. For it is through this conversion that Christ the afflicted is counted-as-one, a conversion to which the events of the resurrection and ascension narratively attest. Christ is counted-as-one in the construction of the analogy we call "Christianity," an analogy in which Christ himself can't exist as distinct. There are three terms in it: Christ, the Christian, and the dual bridge between them (Christianity). Christ is "for" the Christian, made intelligible as Christ-in-Christianity under the aspect of a narrative of atrocity (and salvation). The Christian is "for" Christ; she makes her life in the light of what happened to him and the sense she has made of this. Neither term can be thought in separation from the other; all are understood only within the analogy, Christianity itself. But this means that there is, to put it crudely, no Christ in Christianity. There's only Christ-in-Christianity in Christianity, and that isn't the same thing. Christ-without-Christianity, like the afflicted, is forgotten in the constitution of atrocity or Christ-in-Christianity. The ascension, as the end to which the crucifixion (understood atrociously) points, is the narrative result of the Pauline application of the count-as-one, which turns Christ as someone who suffered affliction into the primary symbol of a new analogical schema: Christianity. The last is, as it were, made first.[13] Christ is then only what he is within Christianity's apparatus, from which he can't be separated. He is merely Christ-in-Christianity.

This figure, who is in the "as such" mode identified above, gets in the way of an ethical impulse in humanity that I believe is among our most admirable: attention to the afflicted, hospitality to them as they are — or to put it instead in somewhat apophatic terms, the welcoming of those who transcend atrocity. In our neglect, Christ-without-Christianity as an example of the flesh and blood afflicted person to whom we might attend (which could figure in moral education and practice) is replaced by Christ-in-Christianity.

---

13 "So the last shall be first, and the first last: for many be called but few chosen." Matthew 20:16 (King James Version).

This is representative, in a historically and culturally formidable way, of the forgetting of the two in favor of the three, which is thereby counted-as-one. The humility with which one answers the call of another, with which one welcomes a stranger at the door or faces the afflictions of the deceased, is replaced with egoistic projection, empathy, and the grafting of analogical relational properties (or "likes" and "unlikes") onto the stranger whose face one doesn't recognize. The ordinary person as they are, who can be afflicted and isn't counted, who is foreclosed to analogy and indifferent to their atrocious position, is forgotten in the movement from the two to the three-as-one. One potent example of this is the movement from the crucifixion, the affliction of Christ-without-Christianity, to the ascension, which is predicated on the atrocity in which Christ is intelligible as Christ-in-Christianity. That atrocity is the product of the count-as-one, and it in turn makes possible the Pauline conversional project, since it constitutes the analogy — Christianity — within which the converted are to identify themselves as a term, as Christians.

The affliction of the crucifixion becomes an atrocity, which is the material cause of the ascension and for which the ascension is in some sense the final cause. Once again, the last becomes the first. Where there was an afflicted person, there is now a person inseparable from a narrative of their affliction, inseparable from those who tell this narrative and pass it on. Christ-without-Christianity becomes Christ-in-Christianity. And Christ himself is set to one side, since he falls outside the bounds of the operative analogy. Christ is made into the first principle of a new order, Christianity, and is thinkable only as positioned within that new order.[14] It is an order that he himself

---

14 Relatedly, Christ is often seen as the archetypal child, and thus as the seat of salvation insofar as the reproduction that brings about the next generation saves. His infancy is seen to represent deliverance. This Irenaean Christianity involves a sort of reproductive futurism, which always puts deliverance beyond what's presently possible (this is characteristic of any eschatological ethic). Salvation is imagined to be a work of time, and morality consists in a project of hope in some distant advent whose very

didn't know—indeed, couldn't have known. For atrocity is always constituted in retrospection, in attending to the afflicted as they are "for" the living or in the "as such" mode.[15] Christ exists, having been counted-as-one, only as the source of Paul's novel analogy, as what he is "for" Paul. Paul can instigate the spread of Christianity only because this has taken place, only because Christ is no longer himself. Christ who isn't counted is tied to the Christian (or originally, Paul) who counts, constituting an apparatus in which neither Christ nor the Christian can be thought in distinction from one another. Outside this relation, there is no Christ. Nor is there a Christian. Outside the identification of Christ and the Christian as terms, there is no relation (Christianity).

Here, we can clearly see the *prima facie* aporetic structure of analogy. The three of the three-as-one demands two terms—Christ and the Christian, say—themselves. It can't come into being without them. But the two terms demand the introduction of a third, without which they can't be thought. There is a way in which the two terms must be taken as primitive, and they then go on to be related. But, from the view on which their relation is primary, there's a way in which the terms couldn't be taken as primitive (or as non-terms). The two terms seem, at least, to cry out for analogy such that they can be made intelligible. They are thus counted-as-one. Yet the three-as-one,

---

possibility grants signification to present action (including reproductive action). In §10, I argue that, contrary to this eschatological sense of salvation, deliverance is always of the order of the presently possible. So far as reproductive futurism in Christianity goes, we might also consider the symbolic work of the ritual of baptism as spiritual rebirth. Cf. Lee Edelman, *No Future: Queer Theory and the Death Drive* (Durham: Duke University Press, 2004).

15 What's crucial in this retrospection isn't *temporal* (or spatial) distance. Atrocity can be seen at whatever temporal distance and can even be projected onto future possibilities. Instead, what's crucial is the sort of distance from affliction one finds in its neglect, a kind of *moral* distance from which other people look assimilable and their suffering quantifiable and comprehensible. When I say that atrocity is seen in "retrospection," I mean to suggest this distance: one sees atrocity essentially from afar, such that forgetfulness can come between one and one's vision of affliction.

in its angst and aporia, enjoins us to inhabit a two that it requires (as the angst and aporia show) but cannot remember.

8. No Matter What

The count-as-x forgets the two. In subjecting affliction to it, one neglects the primacy of the space in which one welcomes the other as they are — not because of their given qualities or relation to one, nor despite their position or identity within the analogical schema. One forgets the space in which one is hospitable to the other without regard to what they are "for" one. I'll call the person who is forgotten, who is the other in the two, the person "no matter what." That's just to say that they aren't what one makes of them. They aren't welcomed *because* one appreciates their qualities, nor *despite* what one takes their analogical position to be — but rather, *no matter what*. When one forgets the two, one forgets the person no matter what, and then this forgetting.

I will call the mode of the other as they are, and not as they are "for" me or "as such," "the fashion of the no matter what." The other *in the fashion of the no matter what* is whosoever they are, beyond the analogy. They are the one I welcome in the topology of the two, the one who makes a claim on me, for whom I'm responsible, the one whose affliction I am to remember. This person is secondarily enmeshed in an analogical milieu, as Christ qua Christ-in-Christianity is, and the secondariness of this is often forgotten (yielding a three-as-one, or atrocity). But first, an ordinary person is no matter what. They are not placed in an analogy from the start, though this priority can be neglected.

So the person who is afflicted is a person no matter what, while the person understood under the aspect of atrocity is a person who is more or less than what they are, a person "as such."

Now the other person in the fashion of the no matter what is absolutely different from me. They are beyond any analogical net I can cast. Recall that I can't relate to the other in the two. I am exposed to them directly, responsible, but without relation or reciprocity. I am here for the other, condemned to them. All I can say in the two is "here I am!"[16] Beckett tells us that we exist in the accusative case, for others, in the eyes of strangers or in responding to what they say.[17] But it is more than this. In the two, I exist in the dative case. I'm summoned by the other to be hospitable. I am not "for" the other in the sense of analogy's "for." Rather, I am this direct, non-analogical exposure to the other.

I am, from the very start, an exposure to the other — who's sometimes afflicted, who sometimes calls out for help, to whose call I am always already commanded to respond. In the two, I exist in the presence of what isn't me, what isn't of me, to which I can't hope to relate. I abnegate, welcoming the other person no matter what, attending to them as they are. This is the basis of any unselfish love.[18] The two is a space characterized by a welcome offered no matter what. The attitude that makes possible its inhabiting takes this shape: I remember the two and thus come to inhabit it with respect to others whom I no longer take to be totalized in whatever analogical schema. I thus see the others as they are, and I see affliction and can bear witness to it, where before I saw only atrocity, always tied up with myself.

In order to throw the axiom that structures the topology of the two into starker relief, an axiom I have been calling the "no matter what," we can consider the ethic in which it arises. I will call this the "generic ethic." We can think about the shape of a life dedicated to the hospitality that characterizes the two, a life in which one bears witness to affliction rather than atrocity. And we can further ask about how a philosophical exploration of this sort of life, a theoretical consideration of it, might go.

---

16 Cf. 1 Samuel 3:4. See also Emmanuel Levinas, *The Levinas Reader,* ed. Seán Hand (Oxford: Basil Blackwell, 1989), esp. 104, 166, 182, 184, 207.

17 Samuel Beckett, *Stories and Texts for Nothing* (New York: Grove Press, 1967), 91.

18 I discuss hospitality and love in more depth in "On Neighborly and Preferential Love in Kierkegaard's *Works of Love,*" *Journal of Philosophy and Scripture* 8 (Summer 2019).

A philosophical system, a set of views and a manner of approaching philosophical questions, is perhaps best differentiated from other systems by the question of what is at stake for it. For Descartes, it is the possibility of knowledge that is most at stake: knowledge of the self, the external world, God, and other people. *I think, I am.* For Michel Henry, like Descartes, it is also this possibility, and that of the self-impressional life that precedes it and is its condition. *I feel myself thinking, I am, and only then can I know about the world.* For Simone Weil, it is because I can act — and thinking is a sort of activity — that I am. I constitute what I am to be in the moment of action. For Kant, the thing that's most at stake is the limit, the law of thinking in the first instance (*quid juris?*), which prohibits the speculative diseases of the head and leads us toward a putatively preferable region of thinking. The ontological question (about the nature of things-in-themselves) is put on the table only as an empty possibility. Instead of asking about what something is, the critical philosophy tells us that we must instead ask about the possibility conditions for a thing to appear to us as it does. For Heidegger, it is being as such, and one's relation to it as Dasein, that is at stake — especially, it is the *question* of being, which has for so long been obliviated. There's a sense in which this is a return to the question of ontology, for we are to inquire into being itself. But we can only do this, we're told, through an existential analytic of Dasein. So being and thinking, as in Kant, are correlated in our being-in-the-world. We can only think being by thinking of ourselves, proceeding from thought (and always from within thought outward). For Quentin Meillassoux, what's at stake is the perhaps, a sort of chance or chaos (the only necessity). Contingency is absolute, and it renders instability itself liable to change. For Alain Badiou, we are after a new conception of being or what is, a new conception of the event or what happens, and an understanding of the relationship between these. What's at stake is the subject and its relationship — of fidelity or betrayal — to evental truths. For each of these philosophers, there is something centrally at stake, and they approach their investigations, in posing questions and setting out views, with this in mind. There is something about which they endeavor to get clear, which structures the inquiries undertaken. Or to put it another way: there is some theme that gives their philosophical work a particular character and shapes the path it takes.

For the generic ethic, which seeks to get clear about the topology of the two and the shape of the life of the person who inhabits it, what's at stake is abnegation. The project is to offer a new conception of allegiance, a sense of what it would mean to vigilantly recollect the two and to thereby avoid the angst of the three-as-one. Often, this angst is produced in the following way. We take on an ontology that forbids the existence of genuine others, since those with whom we relate can only be made sense of (we come to believe) insofar as they're correlated with us. We can't hope to think things-in-themselves, so the alterity of other people is only ever conceivably relative to us. Yet our ethical sensibility demands the existence of real others. The categorical imperative requires that, all else aside, we treat other people in a certain way. In Aquinas, one finds talk of virtuous relations to others. And in Bentham, one finds a clear concern with how one's actions affect other people. Our ethical sensibility (whatever framework for thinking about normative ethics is on offer) seems to demand others who can't be thought, at least insofar as we inhabit a three-as-one. So it isn't surprising that this results in a condition of angst, as our sense of the good forces us to run up against the cage of the ontology we've taken on, in which other people aren't really other. Those philosophical systems that operate with a three-as-one structure rule out the existence of any other, but very often they still demand that we treat the other in a given way, with reference to certain principles or maxims or virtues. This generates a condition of angst, since in moving from ontology to ethics we seem to require others whose existence has already been called into question, and at the very best set to one side or bracketed, from the start. The generic ethic instead proceeds from ethics, beginning with the two — the primordial ethical scene — and the welcoming of the other for whom one is called to responsibility. In remembering the two, one comes to inhabit it anew and again, and the angst of the mixture of a three-as-one with an ethical wish to treat supposedly nonexistent others in a certain way is abrogated.

A philosophical elaboration of the generic ethic involves, then, a new thought of devotion or welcoming, in some sense a new thought of piety.[19] For it, the question at hand isn't about freedom but fidelity, not choice but commitment: the commitment to a hospitality to others that makes freedom in the social world then conceivable.[20] It is in the three-as-one, after all, that one is unfree, tied always to the other, subsumed always under the operative analogy, identified as a mere analogical term. The generic ethic asks, what would it mean to welcome not just the old friend but also the absolute stranger? Would it be a sentimental vision in which one must capitulate one's self to the stranger's identity, giving in even when they, say, harm others? Or would it be a welcoming only of the non-qualitative stranger, the stranger beyond the analogy, and in that sense a non-capitulation to those present elements which, as qualitative or analogical, then impose qualities on others?[21] How can we

---

19 For as Simone Weil writes, "Today it is not nearly enough merely to be a saint, but we must have the saintliness demanded by the present moment, a new saintliness, itself also without precedent." Simone Weil, *Waiting for God*, trans. Emma Craufurd (New York: Harper Perennial, 2009), 51. We are in need of a new ethic for a new guard and a new age, which in truth is always a new way of remembering, of fixing one's eyes upon the good.

20 Cf. Levinas, *The Levinas Reader*, 210n10: "Freedom means, therefore, the hearing of a vocation which I am the only person able to answer — or even the power to answer right there, where I am called." See additionally Levinas, *Otherwise than Being or Beyond Essence*, esp. 123–24.

21 To be sure, abnegation to others no matter what often demands that we *don't* capitulate to the acts of analogical quality-imposition in which some other engages. Hospitality demands that we don't tolerate totalization, and in fact hospitality to the totalizing other demands that we reject his totalizing, that we take a stand against it. For example: if we are going to welcome a transphobe and someone who is transgender, we'll have to fight in the name of the no matter what against the imposition of qualities (the transgender person "for" the transphobe, say) in which the transphobe engages in their hatred. Abnegation isn't a passivity opposed to taking a stand; it's not a weakness that would somehow prevail over force, or a pathos that disavows power or strength. It often requires that, in showing a hospitality to the totalizing other, we don't capitulate to their totaliza-

abnegate to the stranger, welcoming them in a no matter what fashion, without regard to their relation to us or their place in some analogical schema? These are the questions that the generic ethic has to ask.

Setting aside, for a moment, talk of qualities, topologies, and so on, the question for the generic ethic is altogether straightforward: what would it mean to live with allegiance to other people as others, to live hospitably and welcome in a no matter what fashion? To put it another way: what would it mean to live in steadfast devotion to flesh and blood strangers, who are infinitely different from oneself?

The main axiom of such an allegiance or devotion, of an abnegation that bears witness to ordinary people and their possible affliction, is the "no matter what." Being *in the fashion of* the no matter what means being outside any analogy; being ordinary, flesh and blood, not "for" the other terms of an atrocity, not counted-as-*x*. In the topology of the two, I welcome another *no matter what,* without regard to the positions they occupy in whatever analogies. What I welcome no matter what is the other person no matter what, the person who isn't a term of an analogy. So the no matter what structures the topology of the two, defining how the self in the two relates, via a welcoming of absolute alterity, to the other. Welcoming no matter what is relating to what's utterly exterior; it is a relating that is wholly non-analogical (and so in a certain sense, non-relational). The no matter what describes the piety of the space in which I encounter an other who can't be assimilated to what's self-same, an other who isn't different only in degree from the norm that I

---

tion. Even St. Paul tells us that there's beneficent combat. In the abnegation of the generic ethic, resistance to quality-imposition is the other side of responsibility and hospitality; non-capitulation is one's response to the particular situation of abnegation to another who engages in colonizing acts of quality-imposition on their own others. Here, it is the imposition that is refused so that each other can be welcomed as they are. I discuss this at greater length in "To Not Lose Sight of the Good: Notes on the Zapatismo Ethic," *Religious Theory,* January 2020, http://jcrt.org/religious-theory/2020/01/14/to-not-lose-sight-of-the-good-notes-on-the-zapatismo-ethic-part-1-matt-rosen/.

am. This is an other for whom the addition of analogical qualities is a subtraction of alterity. In placing the other under an atrocious description, I take away their infinite alterity—or I presume to do that. This subtraction is a move from infinity to finitude, from the real otherness of other people to the finite bundles of qualities under which I subsume them. The resultant others "for" me are not others at all but of the same. In this way, I forget the other who is in the fashion of the no matter what, who precedes and is foreclosed to the other "for" me. Inhabiting the two consists in remembering this originary other and my abnegation to them, my responsibility to welcome them without regard to any analogy.

The generic ethic is *generic* in this sense: the other is not to be welcomed under the aspect of the particular, welcomed *because of* some quality deemed admirable or *despite* some attribute to be brushed aside. The other is welcomed *no matter what*, generically—but that's to say, in their singularity, as whatever they really are. In the generic ethic, genericity and singularity come together. Now for the generic ethic, which welcomes without regard to qualities or analogical positions, the no matter what is the axiom that founds and structures the topology of the two. This in turn makes possible a three, an analogy, that isn't totalizing or counted-as-one. The axiom of the two, in being remembered as primary, makes possible the coexistence of the two and the topology of the three; this three acknowledges the priority of the two, and it therefore doesn't see analogy as exhaustive (it is the shape an ethical community takes). There is a sense in which the generic ethic is thus pre-communal, though it is required for a particular form of the communal, namely, the three that can coexist with the two. The two of the consequent topology, a topology I'll call the "coexistent two-and-three," coexists as before, and then alongside, or as alongside because before, the three.[22]

---

22 There's a way in which the topology of the coexistent two-and-three that I'm elaborating could be understood as an attempt to resolve some of the aporetic tension in Leibniz's "Monadology." (Although, to be sure, this topology doesn't map neatly onto Leibniz's project.) The two of the topology of the two-and-three is something like the Leibnizian monad, insofar

The generic ethic is the ground in the last instance of a community that is open to others, hospitable, non-totalizing. It is what, at the end of the day, renders any community that acknowledges its priority inhabitable — and not only for those who are proximal enough to the operative norms to fit in.

The no matter what functions as a razor that cuts from the three-as-one to the two. Welcoming no matter what means remembering the person who is in its fashion, which then permits the coexistence of the two and the three in the topology of the coexistent two-and-three. The person no matter what is originary vis-à-vis the position of this person within an analogy, a position that becomes totalizing if it is taken to be primary or sufficient unto itself. So we can understand the operation of the count-as-x as an imagining of the three's self-sufficiency (counted-as-one), and as a condensation of this sufficiency in a number that gives voice to the atrocity and its meaning for the living. The thought that atrocity suffices for affliction is given in affliction's crystallization in the unique number of the fatality count. The count-as-x is a twofold forgetting of the primacy of the two, the ethical, as the topology in which the axiom of the no matter what is at work. One forgets the topology in which the self (the living) abnegates to the unassimilable other (the afflicted, the dead) who is a person no matter what, and then one forgets this forgetting. Welcoming no matter what cuts from the person as such to the person as they are. One gets a grip on the afflicted themselves only by way of hospitality. Forgetting the person as they are leads to an understanding of the other under the aspect

---

as it is self-contained and not open to determination by what goes on in the three; it has "no windows" (though it is where transcendence comes to pass). The three of this topology is the saturation of each monad with relations to all monads, which is total in the three counted-as-one but partial in the three of the two-and-three. The three conceives of its monads as "all windows," or even as *only* windows to other monads. I have been arguing for the coexistence of the two and the three insofar as the two precedes the three and is foreclosed to it (i.e., insofar as the saturation is seen as partial in the remembrance of the two). Cf. G.W. Leibniz, "The Principles of Philosophy, or, the Monadology (1714)," in *Philosophical Essays*, ed. and trans. Roger Ariew and Dan Garber (Indianapolis: Hackett, 1989), 213–25.

of the same, the analogical. The no matter what leads back from this atrocity to affliction. To inhabit the generic ethic is to keep this in mind, to vigilantly recollect the two and welcome the afflicted in the fashion of the no matter what.

9. The Crucifixion of Christ No Matter What

Now that we have a better grasp of the generic ethic, I want to return to that culturally and historically significant instance of the count-as-x which we've been considering: the crucifixion of Christ himself, whose being counted-as-one, originally by Paul, was in some sense the precondition of the ascension and Christianity's spread. The affliction of Christ's crucifixion is transformed into an atrocity such that the ascension can be made sense of. This transformation happens by way of an understanding of Christ as Christ-in-Christianity or Christ as such, produced in the count-as-one. An understanding of the crucifixion as atrocity follows this quantification, the identification of Christ as the atrocity's "one." So the count-as-x mediates between affliction and atrocity, producing the "one" of the ascension's Christ.

In a certain sense, Christ-without-Christianity, or Christ no matter what, is immediate. He is not mediated by the count-as-x and $x = $ one, turned into the Christ-in-Christianity of the atrocity. Christ no matter what thus underdetermines or undermines what transforms him into someone in an atrocious position — the analogical Christ — which isn't himself in the fashion of the no matter what. The Christ who is just himself, who is afflicted without atrocity, is at an infinite distance from his mediated posture; Christ-without-Christianity is an infinity away from Christ-in-Christianity, since between these two is the gulf that divides the analogical from the non-analogical. Christ-without-Christianity is indifferent to his intra-analogical position. And the recollection of the two roots, for us, an attunement of indifference toward this position. This recollection is the application of the razor of the no matter what, which in a sort of ascesis strips away the analogical qualities of an ordinary person so as to reveal their radical insufficiency from within the perspective of analogy—so as to reveal, in some cases, the afflicted as they are. This razor of absolute hospitality cuts away the self-indulgence in which one's attributive or empathetic view of the other is taken to suffice for the other as such. In the case we've been considering, that self-indulgent view is bound up with the analogical matrix of Christianity. It is a view of Christ as Christ-in-Christianity.

The crucifixion as the affliction of Christ no matter what is subject to the count-as-x by Paul. This is the production of the Christ who is Christianity's subject, counted-as-one within its analogical schema. Only after this production of the Christ subject can the ascension of Christ and the conversional road to Damascus take place, insofar as they are analogical events predicated on the inextricable correlation of Christ no matter what (the originary, flesh and blood person in the two) and Paul (the counter) in a correlation that comes to be known, in being inhabited by more and more people, as "Christianity." It is "for" Paul that the affliction of Christ becomes the atrocity at Christianity's heart. The road to Damascus is in this sense the road of affliction become atrocity. It involves the imposition of the analogical milieu of Christianity onto Christ such that there can be, for this analogy and its constitutive terms, no Christ himself. Christianity is, at bottom, the name given to the colonization of Christ by Paul and those who inherit and inhabit his construction.

Now that we have Christianity's topological structure in view, can we theorize instead with the Christ of the crucifixion, with that Christ whose affliction is foreclosed to the determinations of atrocity? Can we set aside the operation of the count-as-x and the production of the atrocity of Christ-in-Christianity? Can we be allegiant in thought to Christ as he is, rather than to Christ as such? Can we, to put it plainly, refuse to put the analogical before the ethical, refuse to forget the affliction of Christ in the neglect of the two and the inhabiting of the three-as-one?

Christianity as constituted by Paul is the analogical result of the count-as-x that renders Christ himself Christ-in-Christianity and the Christian what they are merely "for" Christ. In the totalization of Christianity, the only existent sense of Christ no matter what is Christ as such. And the Christian as such can be the only existent sense of the Christian as they are. Christ-in-Christianity and the Christian-in-Christianity can't be thought apart from their relationship. Neither term can be understood beyond the limit of the analogy of Christianity itself. The atrocity of the mediated Christ is simply one of the correlate objects of an analogical construction built by a count. This atrocity's sense is crystallized in the unique number of x; in the case of the crucifixion, this number is one. The twice forgetting of affliction by those who count makes the position of affliction as atrocity within the analogical milieu intelligible — and angst aside, somewhat sustainable. Christ himself, though, is at a distance from the analogical position into which he's put as part and parcel of the three-as-one. Recast against the three-as-one from the two, Christ no matter what is infinitely other. We move from the three-as-one to the two by applying the ascetic razor of the no matter what, by recollecting the primacy of the two and our responsibility for the other in it. We thus move from Christ-in-Christianity to Christ-without-Christianity, the latter of whom is infinitely different from the former. The other in the two is absolutely other than what they are in the three-as-one. We see this in the recasting of Christ himself against his secondary (but forgotten as such and taken to be primary) position in the three-as-one.

The other is the organon of deliverance from atrocity, for the remembrance and witnessing of the analogical non-position of the afflicted Christ himself, who is indifferent to his position in the atrocity, delivers us from the three-as-one to the two. This is a deliverance from analogy and its angst. And in coming to remember the primacy of the two, we make possible the coexistent two-and-three (that is, the coexistence of the topologies of ethics and community), since the three can only coexist with the two in which there's a legitimate other, not different from the self only in degree, if it's seen to be secondary to the two. The messianic promise of Christ as a flesh and blood insufficiency of qualities when seen from within the analogy is predicated on Christ in the fashion of the no matter what.[23] This essentially undergirds the qualitative accident of Christ-in-Christianity's analogical position. And what is salvation if not from the totalization of this accident (the thought that it isn't accidental but originary)? Salvation — from the angst in which history's calamities appear unmournable, unthinkable in themselves — is nothing other than deliverance from the crystallization of the affliction (and the afflicted person no matter what) in the atrocity's unique number. Bearing witness to the other's affliction — not as atrocity — is the praxis that gets this deliverance going and keeps it alive.

10. Exodus and Deliverance

In the Old Testament story of the exodus of the Israelites from out of their bondage in Egypt, we also find that the other, in a sense that's pivotal to the story, is the organon of deliverance. Moses has been called by God to go unto Pharaoh and to try to persuade him to release the Israelites from their servitude. He has been told that Pharaoh will deny this request, and that

---

23 To be clear: Christ isn't *in* the fashion of the no matter, *in* the two or the generic ethic, as Christ-in-Christianity is *in* the analogy of Christianity. To separate these two senses of "in," recall the distinction I made previously between people *as they are* (who are afflicted) and people *as such* (who are seen under an atrocious aspect). In the generic ethic, one thinks alongside — in responsibility for, in abnegation to — the generic and singular person, the person as they are. The generic ethic isn't an analogy that contains, or claims to give exhaustive sense to, its terms (it doesn't have terms understood *as terms*). Christ is *in* the fashion of the no matter what in this weak sense of "in": when one welcomes Christ no matter what in the two, bearing witness to his affliction, one thinks alongside him, without subsuming him under the qualities of an analogy. Christ-in-Christianity is *in* Christianity in a much stronger sense of "in": he is seen to be *only* what he is *within* the nexus of Christianity. To put it another way, there's nothing that is seen to transcend the three when it is counted-as-one; but the other transcends the three in being in the two. This "being in" isn't the same thing as "being totalized by." It's a transcendence in and through an immanent topology.

it will be necessary to do God's wonders in order to convince Pharaoh, however momentarily, that he can't keep the Israelites in bondage. It is essential, in order for Moses to be able to relay the word of God to Pharaoh and demand the deliverance of the Israelites, that he be seen as other by Pharaoh.[24] Moses, who had been reared among the Egyptians, who had not known of his own ancestry, had to leave Egypt and go out into the desert in order to come back to Pharaoh as a stranger — not as an Egyptian. In Exodus, we read that God tells Moses: "Go in unto Pharaoh, and tell him, Thus saith the Lord God of the Hebrews, Let my people go, that they may serve me."[25] Having been raised alongside Pharaoh, Moses must undergo his own exodus and return only years later, when he is truly exterior to Pharaoh and the whole Egyptian milieu. And even when he does return, he must — through enacting God's wonders — continuously separate himself from that milieu, continuously demonstrate that he is an outsider. He must not be like Pharaoh or of Pharaoh, assimilable, but present as another, as a new face. He can return, to put it in the terms I have been suggesting in this essay, only when he is outside the analogical schema of the operative Egyptian three-as-one, beyond what's "like" or "unlike" Pharaoh

---

24 The remembrance of the two is, in part, a remembering of that encounter with the other I am to myself (it may first of all be this). It's an encounter with transcendence that happens, as it were, in my very immanence. I am a stranger even to myself, and I welcome the stranger that I am to myself in a no matter what fashion in the two. I can forget this, and then forget this forgetting, failing to show myself hospitality and inhabiting a three-as-one with respect to myself. In this way, I can totalize myself and see my own affliction as atrocity. Or I can remember, welcome myself, and inhabit a coexistent two-and-three with respect to myself. This is the case in my relationship with myself, just as it is in my relations with others. Consider Christ's moment of kenosis: "My God, my God, why hast thou forsaken me?" Psalm 22:1 (King James Version). This moment of kenosis is one of abnegation, the response to the call of a stranger. But who's the stranger? It's Christ, of course. In abnegation to myself, I greet what, within me, is other than what I am. In this hospitality, in the two of himself in which transcendence passes through immanence, Christ can then say, "into thy hands I commend my spirit." Luke 23:46 (King James Version).

25 Exodus 9:1 (King James Version).

and different only in degree. Then, and only then, is deliverance presently possible. And Moses, as the other — indeed, the other of Pharaoh (qua Israelite, a doer of God's wonders) *and* the other of the Israelites he intends to work to save (qua Egyptian-reared, qua bringer of salvation) — is this deliverance's organon. In this case, as in the messianic case of Christ, it is what's first no matter what (Moses himself, Christ himself, the afflicted of Sétif and Guelma themselves), and then recast against its analogical position (against Moses "for" Pharaoh or "for" the Israelites, Christ-in-Christianity, those who suffered an atrocity) as other to it, that makes possible deliverance from analogy. And because the other is always present, because I can always remember the two in listening to the other's call and so inhabit it from out of the three-as-one, abnegation to the other precedes even my being-in-the-world or dwelling in analogies. I can remember the two's primacy and thereby inhabit a coexistent two-and-three.

Deliverance from the view of the Israelites' bondage in Egypt on which it's seen as an atrocity happens in the remembrance of the Israelites' affliction. Each year at Passover, Jews around the world don't say of the Israelites, "when *they* were slaves in Egypt," but rather, "when *we* were slaves in Egypt." The use of the first person here doesn't signify the empathy of analogy. It isn't that we are to step into the shoes of those who were slaves in Egypt, for this would just be to bridge the third person (*they*) and the first person (*we*) by means of constructing an atrocity: the Israelites "for" us, as it were. This isn't what's going on when it is said that we were slaves in Egypt. Rather, in bearing witness to the affliction of the flesh and blood people who were slaves in Egypt, we recollect *our* place in the topology of the two and see that it is *our* burden to bear. We don't empathize but abnegate. We disavow the notion of an atrocity that went on many years ago, that affected only our ancestors, and take up an affliction that is always very much alive: the affliction of ordinary people who can't be counted or rendered intelligible and thereby set aside, granted a final meaning, or else considered unmournable. We recollect the affliction that happened in Egypt, and we are thus delivered from the atrocity. We recollect the two in which we, condemned to abnegation, welcome the other no matter what, without regard to their position in some analogy. We recollect that we, like Christ-without-Christianity, are in the fashion of the no matter what, that we're first not analogical creatures, even if we secondarily assume analogical positions. We annul the condition of angst that characterizes the three-as-one in the remembrance of what really went on in Egypt, the remembrance of what really goes on today. And so, we treat the unique number of the count-as-x with a certain ascesis.

In the remembrance of affliction in the two, we recognize that just as the crucifixion's Christ is foreclosed to his position as the Christ of the ascension and conversion, so affliction is foreclosed to atrocity and stands apart from it. In moving from atrocity to affliction via an application of the razor of the no matter what, against the unique number of the count-as-x and $x=$ one, we recall the secondary nature of the atrocity and the number in which it is crystallized. The recollected two is an ethical space in which the self commends itself into the hands of the other, the victim of affliction whosoever they are, no matter what they are. For they are the organon of deliverance from atrocity, to whom one attends in remembering the two. This is a remembering of the self's abnegation to those who aren't counted, those who can't be counted because they are afflicted without atrocity.

Bibliography

Amrani, Mehana. *Le 8 mai 1945 en Algérie: Les discours français sur les massacres de Sétif, Kherrata et Guelma.* Paris: Editions L'Harmattan, 2010.
Beckett, Samuel. *Stories and Texts for Nothing.* New York: Grove Press, 1967.
Derrida, Jacques. *Of Grammatology.* Translated by Gayatri Chakravorty Spivak. Baltimore: Johns Hopkins University Press, 2016.
Edelman, Lee. *No Future: Queer Theory and the Death Drive.* Durham: Duke University Press, 2007.
Feyerabend, Paul. *Against Method.* London: Verso, 2010.
Harman, Graham. *Object-Oriented Ontology: A New Theory of Everything.* London: Pelican Books, 2018.
Kohut, Heinz. *Analysis of the Self.* Edited by Arnold Goldberg. New York: International Universities Press, 1978.
———. "Introspection, Empathy, and Psychoanalysis: An Examination of the Relationship between Mode of Observation and Theory." *Journal of the American Psychoanalytic Association* 7, no. 3 (1959): 459–83. DOI: 10.1177/000306515900700304.
Lacoste, Jean-Yves. *Experience and the Absolute: Disputed Questions on the Humanity of Man.* Translated by Mark Raferty-Skehan. New York: Fordham University Press, 2004.
Laugier, Sandra. "Tristan Garcia by Sandra Laugier." BOMB 114, January 1, 2011. https://bombmagazine.org/articles/tristan-garcia/.
Laruelle, François. *Principles of Non-Philosophy.* Translated by Nicola Rubczak and Anthony Paul Smith. London: Bloomsbury Academic, 2013.
Leibniz, G.W. "The Principles of Philosophy, or, the Monadology (1714)." In *Philosophical Essays,* edited and translated by Roger Ariew and Dan Garber. Indianapolis: Hackett, 1989.
Levinas, Emmanuel. *God, Death, and Time.* Translated by Bettina Bergo. Stanford: Stanford University Press, 2000.

———. *Otherwise than Being or Beyond Essence.* Translated by Alphonso Lingis. Pittsburgh: Duquesne University Press, 1998.

———. *The Levinas Reader.* Edited by Seán Hand. Oxford: Basil Blackwell, 1989.

———. *Totality and Infinity: An Essay on Exteriority.* Translated by Alphonso Lingis. The Hague: Martinus Nijhoff, 1969.

Meillassoux, Quentin. *After Finitude: An Essay on the Necessity of Contingency.* Translated by Ray Brassier. London: Continuum, 2008.

Rosen, Matt. "On Neighborly and Preferential Love in Kierkegaard's *Works of Love*." *Journal of Philosophy and Scripture* 8 (Summer 2019): 1–20. https://journalofphilosophyandscripture.org/wp-content/uploads/2019/09/Rosen-On-Neighborly-and-Preferential-Love.pdf.

———. "To Not Lose Sight of the Good: Notes on the Zapatismo Ethic." *Religious Theory,* January 2020. http://jcrt.org/religioustheory/2020/01/14/to-not-lose-sight-of-the-good-notes-on-the-zapatismo-ethic-part-1-matt-rosen/.

Schürmann, Reiner. *Broken Hegemonies.* Translated by Reginald Lilly. Bloomington: Indiana University Press, 2003.

Weil, Simone. *Waiting for God.* Translated by Emma Craufurd. New York: Harper Perennial, 2009.

4

Horror of the Real: H.P. Lovecraft's Old Ones and Contemporary Speculative Philosophy

David Peak

Forbidden tomes tucked away in dusty university libraries, an army of dead-eyed fish people emerging from the darkened sea, the all-too-fragile rules of reality bent or broken by non-Euclidean geometry, shadow-haunted Cyclopean ruins, and bookish narrators wilting in the presence of unutterable horror. For better or for worse, Howard Phillips Lovecraft's signature contributions to the weird tale persist in countless short story anthologies, novels, films, video games, role-playing games, and other forms of merchandise. As Lovecraft scholar S.T. Joshi has written, "[t]here really is no parallel in the entire history of literature for such enduring and wide-ranging attempts to imitate or develop a single writer's conceptions."[1] Perhaps even more impressive is that Lovecraft's influence has transcended the blindly loyal realm of fandom. In fact, his contribution to the American tradition has been acknowledged by serious-minded Library of America and Penguin Classics editions of his stories and novels.

---

1 S.T. Joshi, *The Rise, Fall, and Rise of the Cthulhu Mythos* (New York: Hippocampus Press, 2015), 22.

Furthermore, explorations of his conceptions of horror and the weird frequently bleed into disciplines such as music and philosophy. With all this in mind, this paper seeks to examine why Lovecraft's so-called Cthulhu Mythos endures as well as how Lovecraft's Old Ones can be uncovered, and perhaps better understood, through recent speculative trends in philosophy.

Before we can begin, however, we must first discuss the significance and meaning of the Cthulhu Mythos. It goes without saying that using fiction to create a mythos — or the concept of an artificial pantheon and myth background — was far from a novel idea by the time Lovecraft published the first of his Mythos tales ("The Nameless City" in 1921), especially considering Lord Dunsany's towering influence. Yet a key distinction liberates Lovecraft from merely following in the previous tradition. As Joshi has written,

> [t]he phrase "artificial pantheon" points to Lovecraft's creation of an ersatz theogony created from his imagination, rather than from existing myth or folklore. [...] Many of Dunsany's gods are clearly symbols for natural forces (Slid is described as the 'soul of the sea'), the gods of Lovecraft's pantheon are far less clearly defined in terms of their nature and attributes.[2]

Despite the misguided efforts of "self-blinded earth-gazers" to equate Lovecraft's gods with the elements, these entities remain entirely within the realm of the unknown. Lovecraft's fictional gods are relegated to the background of his stories — they are never the focal point and rarely, if ever, the cause or reason for the unfolding of events — which is an important element of what makes Lovecraft's horror horrific. Indeed, only that which exists beyond thought, within the vacuous unknown, can instill true horror.

Lovecraft was aware of this distinction, as he believed that beauty, rather than horror, was the keynote of Dunsany's fic-

---

[2] Ibid., 51.

tion. In his own fiction, however, Lovecraft linked beauty to the strange and the grotesque, seeking to emphasize notions of the unknown. This embrace of the strange and the grotesque also provides an explanation for the difference between the genres of fantasy and horror — namely, that horror, itself a subgenre within the greater classification of weird fiction, is concerned only with reality. When faced with horror, we must accept that reality is at least partly unknowable, otherwise horror would not exist. Coming to know a certain reality can result in a full or partial destruction of the self. Take disease, for example. When given a certain diagnosis, what was not known is made known and is at least partially horrific because the patient did not always know it to be the case. Yet once the presence of the disease is known, it becomes part of the self. There is no resisting such revelations. The sense of horror, then, shifts once more to the unknown. How will this disease affect me? How it will change the ways in which I see and interact with the world? And in this acceptance, this giving in to forces that are by nature incomprehensible, horror seeks to offer direct knowledge of the real. It strips away comforting or cosmetic surface realities and lays bare indifferent inner workings. How we feel about those inner workings, or what they mean to us, is of little to no importance. What matters is the glimpsing of the beyond, of bearing witness, and how this act alters our perceptions of what is or has been.

Fantasy, however, is concerned with unreality, or that which is hoped for, magical, or ideal. It seeks only to show things as they might be, and in doing so embraces the allure of illusion rather than seeking to break its spell. Furthering this concept, Lovecraft's Mythos, despite the use of otherwise fantastical gods and monsters, is ultimately rooted in scientific notions and present-day concerns. On scientific notions, we need look no further than the famous opening sentences of the story "Facts Concerning the Late Arthur Jermyn and His Family":

> Life is a hideous thing, and from the background behind what we know of it peer daemoniacal hints of truth which make it sometimes a thousand fold more hideous. Science,

> already oppressive with its shocking revelations, will perhaps be the ultimate exterminator of our human species — if separate species we be — for its reserve of unguessed horrors could never be borne by mortal brains if loosed upon the world.[3]

And on present-day concerns, we turn to Joshi once again:

> Lovecraft was keenly aware of such radical and potentially disturbing conceptions as Einsteinian space-time, the quantum theory, and Heisenberg's indeterminacy principle, and utilized them to give a distinctly modern cast to such stale conceptions as the vampire ("The Shunned House") and the witch ("The Dreams in the Witch House"), to say nothing of the possibility of extraterrestrial incursions in such tales as "The Colour Out of Space," "The Whisperer in Darkness," *At the Mountains of Madness,* and "The Shadow Out of Time."[4]

Lovecraft's gods and monsters are employed to further such concepts as scientific indifferentism and the existence of a reality beyond human conception. As a result, the Cthulhu Mythos is populated by a series of gods who are perhaps best understood as symbols of cosmic outsideness, which refers to the reality of objects and entities outside an earthly, moral, or ethical understanding, in particular, the monstrous, extraterrestrial deities known as the Old Ones. As entities of pure and unknowable horror, these Old Ones are unconcerned with human life. In fact, they are completely indifferent to it, perhaps more likely unaware of it. Any hint of malevolence is strictly the interpretation of the human who seeks an explanation for the unexplainable. As the old man Castro says in "The Call of Cthulhu," referring to the apocalyptic return of great Cthulhu, "[t]he time would be easy to know, for then mankind would have become

---

[3] H.P. Lovecraft, *The Call of Cthulhu and Other Weird Stories* (New York: Penguin Books, 1999), 14.
[4] Joshi, *The Rise, Fall, and Rise of the Cthulhu Mythos,* 189.

as the Great Old Ones: free and wild and beyond good and evil."[5] Elaborating on the concept of alien gods existing beyond human constructs such as good and evil, Joshi has written, "[w]e cannot penetrate into their minds or psyches to pass any kind of moral judgment upon them."[6] All the more fitting then that Lovecraft chose to describe Cthulhu in part as a monster with an "octopus-like head," as octopi are perhaps the most alien creatures to humans on Earth.

By remaining cosmically outside human knowledge, the Cthulhu Mythos comprises a purposely incomplete body of lore rather than a complete system of knowledge. In fact, Lovecraft knowingly left this lore unstructured to further a sense of realism. Much like the disease, whose presence annihilates the self, so-called knowledge of the Mythos results in madness, or an outright rejection of the mind to process reality as it actually is. By consciously relegating these gods to the background of his fiction, thus emphasizing the unknowability of the unknown, Lovecraft's goal was to establish "the conveyance of terror at the thought of human insignificance in a boundless cosmos."[7] As Joshi has written, "[t]he true horror in Lovecraft's work is the mere *knowledge* that the Old Ones exist. The psychological devastation in the face of human insignificance makes any actions on the part of the 'gods' or monsters seem utterly insignificant."[8] This is what Lovecraft meant by science being "the ultimate exterminator of our human species"; it is the self-annihilating disease. With his Mythos tales, Lovecraft sought to emphasize reality as supported by scientific thought — the reality that makes horror horrific — that human life is without meaning, the cosmos itself cold and unfeeling, and that true knowledge of this reality could drive one to the brink of insanity. Further, only insanity can be considered an escape from burdensome knowl-

---

5   Lovecraft, *The Call of Cthulhu*, 155.
6   Joshi, *The Rise, Fall, and Rise of the Cthulhu Mythos*, 68.
7   Ibid., 19.
8   Ibid., 279.

edge entirely too real and therefore isolating and impossible to communicate to others.

Lovecraft was of course an avowed atheist. In fact, he was outright hostile to organized religion, and his personal philosophy, as far as it was developed, was explicitly materialist. Furthermore, he favored a version of determinism that was mechanistic. On this, Robert M. Price has written, "[Lovecraft] felt there was no reality that natural law and matter could not account for. Everything worked like one big machine. There was no god, no soul, no meaning or purpose. [...] He felt sure the universe was just a collection of 'stuff,' but he had to know more about it."[9] In other words, it's in our nature to seek answers to questions we cannot begin to formulate — and no good will come of it. This constant compulsion to "know more" motivated Lovecraft to stay informed about the latest scientific discoveries as well as contemporary views of history. For example, he adhered to the tenets of Oswald Spengler's *Decline of the West,* the evolutionary principles of Charles Darwin, the connection of evolution to the cosmos put forth by naturalist Ernst Haeckel, and Einstein's aforementioned theory of relativity. Informed by his materialist beliefs, Lovecraft used horror, particularly its aspects of speculation, as a means of making the unreal real. Much like a body of lore that can only hint at the unknowable, or the disease that changes one's relationship to the world, such a "horror of the real" must be speculative, as its very nature entails an existence of entities and objects beyond our knowing. Rather than approaching the weird as a means of explaining that which cannot be explained or instilling feelings such as shock or awe, Lovecraft acknowledged that our very best explanations are unable to grasp the truth. Instead we cling to the truths we construct: the useless laws of physics and morality. As David E. Schultz has written, "[Lovecraft's stories] challenge us to consider the world in which we live in light of what science has told us about it."[10]

---

9   S.T. Joshi, ed., *Dissecting Cthulhu: Essays on the Cthulhu Mythos* (Lakeland: Miskatonic River Press, 2011), 224.
10 Ibid., 35.

But this is only half of what makes Lovecraft's horrific vision so profound.

Before we can talk about the other half, we must develop a connection between Lovecraft's notions of horror and recent trends in philosophy, particularly the speculative realist movement. Defined briefly, speculative realism acknowledges an existence of the world independent of the human mind. Because the philosophical conclusions drawn from such an acknowledgment are by definition speculative, they can seem counterintuitive or strange. As previously stated, Lovecraft sought to emphasize strangeness in his writing, therefore strengthening the connection to speculation — by which we refer to any type of thinking that claims to be able to access some form of the absolute — fertile ground for planting the seeds of philosophy. It's worth noting here that the one thing that unites the four primary philosophers associated with speculative realism — Ray Brassier, Iain Hamilton Grant, Graham Harman, and Quentin Meillassoux — is a shared interest in the philosophical implications of Lovecraft's fiction. As Harman has recently written, "[a]lthough the four original Speculative Realists do not share a single philosophical hero in common, all of us turned out independently to have been admirers of Lovecraft. Though the reasons for this are different in each case, my own interest stems from my view that his weird fiction sets the stage for an entire philosophical genre."[11] This admiration is particularly relevant to the philosophies of Harman and Meillassoux, whose concepts we will focus on in this essay. For example, the Cthulhu Mythos is representative of what Harman refers to as "weird realism." On this, Harman has written, "[r]ealism is always in some sense *weird*. Realism is about the strangeness in reality that is not projected onto reality by us. It is already there by dint of being real."[12] Elsewhere, Harman has written, "[m]ost philosophical realism is 'representational' in character. Such theories

---

11   Graham Harman, *Speculative Realism: An Introduction* (Cambridge: Polity Press, 2018), 91–92.
12   Ibid., 92.

hold not only that there is a real world outside human contact with it, but also that this reality can be mirrored adequately by the findings of the natural sciences or some other method of knowledge."[13] And then, "[n]o reality can be immediately translated into representations of any sort. Reality itself is weird because reality itself is incommensurable with any attempt to represent or measure it."[14]

Other writers and philosophers influenced by Lovecraft have turned to similar concepts to grasp the real. Brassier's philosophy, for instance, defers to scientific representation as the only reliable form of access to reality, in addition to stating that the real is not to be confused with our concepts of it. Ben Woodard connects this idea to the concept of "dark vitalism," which "accepts a reality that is fundamentally comprised of forces and processes but does not attempt to make this contingency or process-dominated reality something that is immediately thinkable, or understandable within the limits of reason of alone."[15] In my opinion, Timothy Morton explores similar territory, using the term *realist magic* to denote thinking about philosophical realism, nonhuman phenomenology,[16] and theories of causality.

Such thinking, it should be noted, is in dialogue with Lovecraft's fiction, rather than his personal beliefs. In fact, Lovecraft looked upon vitalism in particular with disdain. Rather than accepting that life originated as a result of nonchemical or nonphysical forces, Lovecraft believed that material interactions led to consciousness. This is seen in the influence of Haeckel, who wrote that "[mind] is a product and attribute of certain forms and processes of matter; and when that matter is disintegrated, it ceases to exist — just as molecular heat ceased to exist upon the dispersal or disintegration of the material molecules which

---

13 Graham Harman, *Weird Realism: Lovecraft and Philosophy* (Winchester: Zero Books, 2012), 51.
14 Ibid., 51.
15 Ben Woodard, *Slime Dynamics* (Winchester: Zero Books, 2012), 51–52.
16 This term is a reference to Ian Bogost's "alien phenomenology." For more, see *Alien Phenomenology, or What It's Like to Be a Thing* (Minneapolis: University of Minnesota Press, 2012).

make it possible."[17] In other words, consciousness is nothing more than electrical impulse. Once it's gone, it's gone forever. On this, Woodard has written, "[u]nder Lovecraft's indifferentism humans become just another form of matter in the universe, simply another form of entropic fodder in a mechanistic cosmos."[18] The human is no different than the octopus, fungi from Yuggoth, or cosmic dust. Vitalism, however, posits a distinction between living organisms and nonliving entities. In this sense, Lovecraft's beliefs align perhaps most closely with Harman's object-oriented ontology (OOO), which argues that an object — a unified thing that cannot be reduced to its components or effects — exists independently of human perception, and that all objects can interact with one another, albeit indirectly.

In an effort to square the circle, so to speak, and to move past the inherent limitations of Lovecraft's dogmatic materialism, perhaps best understood as a product of his time, we will look to speculative realism to see how it can deepen our understanding of the Mythos. It's worth noting here that speculative realism, Harman's preferred term, is just as often referred to as speculative materialism, Meillassoux's preferred term, yet both are concerned with realism, albeit in different ways. Harman posits that his own OOO and Meillassoux's speculative materialism are essentially opposites. Much like Gilman in Lovecraft's story "The Dreams of the Witch House," "Meillassoux thinks that the primary qualities of things can be mathematized, whereas for OOO there is no direct access to them through mathematics or anything else."[19] Both philosophies, however, are united in their embrace of speculation, which leads to my next point. Ultimately, Lovecraft's Mythos tales are about wanting to go deeper, even if it leads to unwanted or unforeseen results. This is reinforced by Lovecraft's aforementioned compulsion to "know more" about the world in which he lived. Yet no matter how deep we

---

17 Ernst Haeckel, quoted in S.T. Joshi, *H.P. Lovecraft: The Decline of the West* (Berkeley Heights: Wildside Press, 1990), 10.
18 Woodard, *Slime Dynamics*, 43.
19 Harman, *Speculative Realism*, 100.

go, there will always remain depths still unplumbed. Meillassoux refers to such unplumbed depths as "the great outdoors" or "the absolute outside of pre-critical thinkers: that outside which was not relative to us, and which was given as indifferent to its own givenness to be what is, existing in itself regardless of whether we are thinking of it or not; that outside which thought could explore with the legitimate feeling of being on foreign territory — of being entirely elsewhere."[20] In my opinion, OOO provides the deepest explorations of realism's unplumbed depths to date. This opinion is supported by Morton, who has written, "Graham Harman discovered a gigantic coral reef of mysterious entities beneath the Heideggerian submarine of Da-sein, which itself is operating at an ontological depth way below the choppy surface of philosophy, beset by the winds of epistemology and infested by the sharks of materialism, idealism, empiricism and most other -isms that have defined what is and what isn't for the last several hundred years."[21]

Put simply, reality is hiding in plain sight. Rather than accepting the way things appear to be as the way they are, to uncover reality we must instead strip away appearances. We must acknowledge a material existence independent of the human, one filled with objects as they really are, rather than what they mean to and for us, and in doing so, encounter the realm of being without thought, in which the ever-changing hints of horror lurk beneath an illusory "fabric." As Harman has written, "[t]he world in itself is made of realities withdrawing from all conscious access."[22] In other words, some aspect of the whole of reality will always remain in a perpetually veiled underworld, out of sight and inaccessible to the human. Furthermore, rather than accepting that the human remains privileged among non-sentient objects, such inaccessibility extends to the human as

---

20 Quentin Meillassoux, *After Finitude: An Essay on the Necessity of Contingency*, trans. Ray Brassier (London: Bloomsbury, 2013), 7.
21 Timothy Morton, *Realist Magic: Objects, Ontology, Causality* (Ann Arbor: Open Humanities Press, 2013), 222.
22 Graham Harman, *The Quadruple Object* (Winchester: Zero Books, 2011), 38.

well. "Even humans withdraw into a dark reality that is never fully understood, while also being present to observers from the outside."[23] OOO states that what withdraws from consciousness cannot be mere lumps of objective physical matter but rather a so-called extra-mental reality. Again, we return to old man Castro, who says "[The Old Ones had shape] but that shape was not made of matter."[24] What can this shape possibly be if not physical matter? The answer is perhaps not as important as the asking of the question. Lovecraft was drawn to weird fiction because it allowed him "to achieve momentarily the illusion of some strange suspension or violation of the galling limitations of time, space, and natural law which forever imprison us and frustrate our curiosity about the infinite cosmic places beyond the radius of our sight and analysis."[25] Meillassoux's term for such a suspension or violation of natural law over time is "hyper-chaos," "for which nothing is or would seem to be impossible, not even the unthinkable."[26] Only in such suspension can we begin to fathom the aforementioned inner-workings, or those forces beyond comprehension, hinted at here by those jagged shapes that lurk beneath the fabric of reality: the Old Ones.

The Cthulhu Mythos features five primary deities — Azathoth, Cthulhu, Nyarlathotep, Shub-Niggurath, and Yog-Sothoth, all of which are name-checked in "The Whisperer in Darkness" — which are collectively referred to as the Old Ones. Of the five, Azathoth and Cthulhu provide the most philosophical depth, and so will take up the most space here, whereas the significance of Nyarlathotep, Shub-Niggurath, and Yog-Sothoth remains fittingly vague. In the paragraphs that follow, we will explore references to these entities in Lovecraft's fiction that elaborate on concepts of horror and speculation rather than those that follow in the Dunsanian tradition of fantasy. As previously stated, these deities exist in a dark reality for which

---

23 Ibid., 40.
24 Lovecraft, *The Call of Cthulhu*, 154–55.
25 H.P. Lovecraft, "Notes on Writing Weird Fiction," *The H. P. Lovecraft Archive*, http://www.hplovecraft.com/writings/texts/essays/nwwf.aspx.
26 Meillassoux, *After Finitude*, 64.

nothing is impossible, a realm beyond conceptions of good and evil, and beyond human access. Therefore, these entities represent a fundamentally anti-anthropocentric worldview and are therefore emblematic of the "essence of externality." Lovecraft's famous letter to Farnworth Wright makes this point clear: "[t]o achieve the essence of real externality, whether of time or space or dimension, one must forget that such things as organic life, good and evil, love and hate, and all such local attributes of a negligible and temporary race called mankind, have any existence at all."[27] This is remarkably similar to the stated purpose of Meillassoux's work in his groundbreaking book *After Finitude*, which was to achieve "what modern philosophy has been telling us for the past two centuries is impossibility itself: *to get out of ourselves*, to grasp the in-itself, to know what is whether we are or not."[28]

In "The Haunter of the Dark," the blind, idiot god Azathoth is described as "Lord of All Things, encircled by his flopping horde of mindless and amorphous dancers"[29] at the center of ultimate chaos. Here we return to Meillassoux's concept of hyper-chaos, the description of which is worth quoting at further length if not only to appreciate its Lovecraftian language, courtesy of Brassier's fine translation:

> If we look through the aperture which we have opened up onto the absolute, what we see there is a rather menacing power — something insensible, and capable of destroying both things and worlds, of bringing forth monstrous absurdities, yet also of never doing anything, of realizing every dream, but also every nightmare, of engendering random and frenetic transformations, or conversely, of producing a universe that remains motionless down to its ultimate recess-

---

27 As quoted in Joshi, *The Rise, Fall, and Rise of the Cthulhu Mythos*, 209.
28 Meillassoux, *After Finitude*, 27.
29 Lovecraft, *The Call of Cthulhu*, 354.

es, like a cloud bearing the fiercest of storms, then the eeriest bright spells, if only for an interval of disquieting calm.[30]

Indeed, further strengthening the connection between this concept and Lovecraft's descriptions of Azathoth, Meillassoux goes on to refer to such omnipotence as "blind." Azathoth is the ruler of the Outer Gods, a dreaming monster in whose dream the universe resides. As such, he dwells in the realm of being without thought, even his consciousness is unconscious, far beyond our understanding. Furthermore, he is the embodiment of disorder — the thing that adheres to no natural law or order, thus threatening to undo all things. We turn to Meillassoux once more: "[w]e can only hope to develop an absolute knowledge — a knowledge of chaos which would not simply keep repeating that everything is possible — on condition that we produce necessary propositions about it besides that of its omnipotence."[31] Meillassoux's derivation of the principle of non-contradiction from the principle of factiality explains that for knowledge to be contingent in this way, it cannot be anything whatsoever. By establishing the constraints to which an entity must submit to "exercise its capacity-not-to-be and its capacity-to-be-other," the capacity for things to be otherwise, Meillassoux gives us as clear an explanation as any for why Lovecraft is only able to describe Azathoth as "indescribable."

Cthulhu is imprisoned in the sunken city of R'lyeh. Like the dreaming Azathoth, Cthulhu is a source of constant anxiety for mankind at an unconscious level, and its mode of speech is transmitted thought. As the infamous opening sentences of "The Call of Cthulhu" make clear, further refining similar sentiments expressed by the opening sentences of "Arthur Jermyn": "The sciences, each straining in its own direction, have hitherto harmed us little; but someday the piecing together of dissociated knowledge will open up such terrifying vistas of reality, and of our frightful position therein, that we shall either go mad

---

30 Meillassoux, *After Finitude,* 64.
31 Ibid., 66.

from the revelation or flee from the deadly light into the peace and safety of a new dark age."[32] Cthulhu is perhaps representative of an inability to correlate scientific findings into a comprehensible system, a meta-commentary of the Cthulhu Mythos itself. In other words, the significance of Cthulhu is that the representation embodied by the Mythos is the impossibility of representation. As described in "The Call of Cthulhu," the Old Ones no longer live but never really die. They merely "lie awake in the dark" and watch the universe unfold. Further described as "coming from the stars," the Old Ones in their very proximity to human life create an ill-defined sense of cosmic outsideness, hinting at themes of panspermia, or the theory that life on Earth originated from microorganisms from outer space. As Woodard puts it, "[t]he teeming biological, if beginning from a unity and moving outwards, dividing into ever more chaotic and divergent forms creates a creeping abyss of biology, where reason is only one feature amidst a taloned and toothed pandemonium."[33] To accept this is to think of a world without the givenness of the world, our apparently ironclad natural laws, as Meillassoux would say. And to understand such indifference of the outside to us, we must assign anything outside time or outside space, such as Cthulhu, a "fearsome and unnatural malignancy." This malignancy, of course, only inheres in the correlation of human consciousness.

Sometimes referred to as a "cosmic shape-shifter," Nyarlathotep "is a horrible messenger of the evil gods to Earth, who usually appears in human form."[34] As such, he is a horror of infinite shapes and innumerable forms, the thing to which we assign human features so as to comprehend. In this sense, Nyarlathotep serves two functions in the Mythos: First, he is a go-between for humans and the gods; second, he is representative of our inclination for anthropocentrism. In this sense, he links us to the entities beyond comprehension, existing half-submerged in

---

32 Lovecraft, *The Call of Cthulhu*, 139.
33 Woodard, *Slime Dynamics*, 52.
34 Joshi, *The Rise, Fall, and Rise of the Cthulhu Mythos*, 169.

unfathomable depths, and is therefore something to fear. This is why Nyarlathotep acts as a messenger of Azathoth: he is the thing that intrudes into our lives, disrupting reality, and reminding us of the existence of that which we cannot truly know, the knowledge of which, or the coming-to-knowledge of which, results in horror.

In a letter to Willis Conover, Lovecraft described Shub-Niggurath as Yog-Sothoth's wife and a hellish, cloud-like entity. Beyond this, there really isn't much to Shub-Niggurath, outside of some oblique references, as well as to her children, Nug and Yeb, in various stories, at least not as it relates to the concepts of speculation and horror. The one thing that makes Shub-Niggurath interesting, however, is that she seemingly cannot be described beyond simple, folksy titles, including "The Black Goat of the Wood with a Thousand Young" and "Lord of the Wood." In this sense, she is beyond understanding to the extent that she can only be referred to as something unknowable (The Not-To-Be-Named one).

Finally, the deity Yog-Sothoth is conterminous with all of time and space — "Past, present, future, all are one in *Yog-Sothoth*"[35] — yet it remains locked outside the known universe. According to the text Wilbur Whateley translates in "The Dunwich Horror," the Old Ones exist "not in the spaces we know, but *between* them." This is perhaps one of the clearest connections to ooo. As Harman has written, referring to Lovecraft, "[n]o other writer is so perplexed by the gap between objects and the power of language to describe them, or between objects and the qualities they possess."[36] Harman continues, "[t]he major topic of object-oriented philosophy is the dual polarization that occurs in the world: one between the real and the sensual, and the other between objects and their qualities."[37] In Lovecraft's fiction, characters often become "stuck" in the gap between reality

---

35 H.P. Lovecraft, *The Thing on the Doorstep and Other Weird Stories* (New York: Penguin Books, 2001), 219.
36 Harman, *Weird Realism*, 3.
37 Ibid., 4.

as it is and their conceptions of what it is supposed to be. And this gap is as immeasurable as the realm of horror itself.

As previously mentioned, one half of what allows Lovecraft's fiction, specifically his Mythos, to persist in contemporary pop culture is his use of an artificial pantheon and myth background to focus on themes of scientific notion and present-day concerns. As a result, Lovecraft essentially moved the weird tale away from vampires and witches and "turned the whole universe into a haunted house," as Richard L. Tierney has said.[38] The other half of this continued relevance is rooted in Lovecraft's uncanny ability to hint at future philosophical developments. In my opinion, this is why we continue to turn to Lovecraft, especially today, as the effects of climate change, information overload, and the depletion of natural resources force us to seriously consider the world-without-us. In his unsparing vision of the human as meaningless, Lovecraft offers readers a view of the thing that we cannot — that we will not — see: the universe as filled with cold, dead planets, tearing itself apart at the seams; an impossible reality, one in which humans find themselves extinct, having made no lasting impact on the real. Lovecraft knew there were strange aeons beyond comprehension. And in his attempts to show the outlines of indescribable shapes, he came closer to expressing the ineffable than perhaps any writer of horror or the weird has before or since. As Harman has written,

> [t]he cosmos seems to be gigantic in both space and time. It is more ancient than all our ape-like ancestors and all other life forms. It might also seem safe to assume that the trillions of entities in the cosmos engage in relations and duels even when no humans observe them. However interesting we humans may be to ourselves, we are apparently in no way central to the cosmic drama, marooned as we are on an average-sized planet near a mediocre sun, and confined to a tiny portion of the history of the universe.[39]

---

38 Joshi, *Dissecting Cthulhu*, 10.
39 Harman, *The Quadruple Object*, 63.

This then is Lovecraft's Promethean legacy, he who dared articulate that which should not be, the blind, idiot god bubbling at the center of all infinity; he who blasphemed by acknowledging *what is* and who dared us to gaze into such magnificent vistas of ultimate chaos.

Bibliography

Bogost, Ian. *Alien Phenomenology, or What It's Like to Be a Thing.* Minneapolis: University of Minnesota Press, 2012.

Harman, Graham. *Speculative Realism: An Introduction.* Cambridge: Polity Press, 2018.

———. *The Quadruple Object.* Winchester: Zero Books, 2011.

———. *Weird Realism: Lovecraft and Philosophy.* Winchester: Zero Books, 2012.

Joshi, S.T., ed. *Dissecting Cthulhu: Essays on the Cthulhu Mythos.* Lakeland: Miskatonic River Press, 2011.

———. *H.P. Lovecraft: The Decline of the West.* Berkeley Heights: Wildside Press, 1990.

———. *The Rise, Fall, and Rise of the Cthulhu Mythos.* New York: Hippocampus Press, 2015.

Lovecraft, H.P. "Notes on Writing Weird Fiction." *The H.P. Lovecraft Archive.* http://www.hplovecraft.com/writings/texts/essays/nwwf.aspx.

———. *The Call of Cthulhu and Other Weird Stories.* New York: Penguin Books, 1999.

———. *The Thing on the Doorstep and Other Weird Stories.* New York: Penguin Books, 2001.

Meillassoux, Quentin. *After Finitude: An Essay on the Necessity of Contingency.* Translated by Ray Brassier. London: Bloomsbury, 2013.

Morton, Timothy. *Realist Magic: Objects, Ontology, Causality.* Ann Arbor: Open Humanities Press, 2013.

Woodard, Ben. *Slime Dynamics.* Winchester: Zero Books, 2012.

5

Triangulorum

Sara Rich

In his "Essay on the Maladies of the Head," Kant writes, "[a]t least someone bewitched by these chimeras can never be brought by reasoning to doubting the actuality of his presumed sensation. One also finds that persons who show enough mature reason in other cases nevertheless firmly insist upon having seen with full attention who knows what ghostly shapes and distorted faces, and that they are even refined enough to place their imagined experience in connection with many a subtle judgement of reason."[1] What if Kant's "deranged persons" were not "dreamers in waking" but rather those whose sensations become, through weird chance, inextricably bound to chimerical overlaps of space-time that render chaos from perceptions of order? In our era of life within the Rational Experiment gone haywire, anything seems possible, except reversibility.

I.

Letter from Eugenio de Sálazar to Cristóbal Colón.
Dated 27 August 1506.

---

1   Immanuel Kant, *Anthropology, History, and Education,* eds. and trans. Günter Zöller and Robert B. Louden (Cambridge: Cambridge University Press, 2007), 71.

Translated into English by Dr. Prof. Koldo Eguíluz Miranda, University of Salamancas, 2022.

Admiral Don Colón,

I regret to inform you that our journey to Hispaniola was met with disaster. Indeed, in your astuteness, you have already noted that this letter, meant to inform you of all that transpired, is penned from a different island altogether. We did not reach Hispaniola, and to be quite forward, few of us among the crew of *La Santa María Magdalena* made landfall at all.

The first two weeks after our departure from Cádiz were rather uneventful yet highly consequential. The sea remained in a more or less constant state of billowing — those cyclical swells that rock the ship forward, down, and backward just to repeat and do the same — which of course made the men violently ill and a mess of the caravel's decks, which in turn just aggravated the conditions. This state of affairs was rather a nuisance that necessitated those few of us unaffected by the rhythmic surging waters and the rolling of our caravel to perform double or even triple tasks. This left us exhausted and shortly, susceptible to committing the most amateurish of oversights, if not outright blunders. And while the crew's weak stomachs did not penetrate our food stores, the fresh water supply was surely in danger should their illness persist for the duration of the journey, and should we find ourselves without rain.

I admit that it was possibly due to my own faulty triangulation, having been deprived of respite for some ten days on end, that we found ourselves stranded in the Sargasso Sea. Regretfully, the ships' logs were all lost, and I have no memory of where precisely I turned us astray, or if indeed I am the culprit and not some sprite or nymph with evil intentions.

Sir, your courageous, steadfast efforts to establish Christianity and civilization the world over must not stop with the barbarians of the New World lands and islands. As you yourself suspected, Admiral, there are evil races in the waters too. These beasts know only the wiles and deceptions of Satan, and their souls must be blacker than even the scales they wear for skin.

Utterly becalmed in mid-sea, we were stranded, seemingly entangled, by infernal strands of reeking brown seaweed that nearly covered the expanse of the flat sea, which had lost its virginal azure glow and took on the tainted hue of burnt tallow instead. The stagnant tropical air was thickly perfumed by these infinite furrows of putrid, rotting algae, as though we had found ourselves on some farmland in hell, where the only crops to be grown are the humid corpses of eels and urchins.

Despite the ghastly still waters, those who had been retching for two weeks at sea were now sickened anew, along with even those immune to the rolling waves.

Our prayers for deliverance from this stinking Hades were soon exhausted, as were our bodies and minds. Unsurprisingly, those recent converts to the glories of God Almighty were the first to falter. These Carpathians, Gauls, and Celts reverted to their most ancient pagan traditions and forsook the ultimate sacrifice of Christ to instead seek redemption through the slaughter of the half dozen horses we were transporting to the Indies. These brutes removed and cooked the flesh and bones of our prized mares and stallions before filling their hides with straw, yes the very straw that the poor beasts had been feasting upon! Then chanting horrible demoniac hymns, they sewed the horses' bodies back up, and burned these mockeries of equine finesse as effigies, sending them alight across that wretched water. I tried to stop them, of course I did. But I confess to you, Admiral, as to Christ in Heaven, that the smell of the burning hair and hides of these effigies and the cooked meat of the horses, if nothing else — and let it be known that our Holy Saints most certainly turned away from this barbaric display of ignorance and savagery — did overcome the stench of that hellish sea, if only temporarily.

But I fear that this lapse into barbarism, née Satanism, may have been what cursed us all, for in the following days, we were to meet the face of pure evil. But instead of turning away, we were enchanted by it.

It was the first day in which there was a wind at all, but really it was only enough to rustle the hair above one's ear, or stir the sweat on one's nose. Each of us languished weakly on the top deck, isolated to the few shadows cast by optimistic sails, rigging, cabins, and cannons. One lad, who had taken refuge on the shadow side of the mast, began to call out in hysterical bursts, gesturing wildly into the distance.

"Look!" he called, in a Gaelic accent. "They're dancing! It's the selkies — they've come to rescue us!"

No one stirred, trusting the boy had been overcome with exhaustion and hallucination. "Come now, ye crazy bastard," said another, finally rising from his sickened laze to inspect the spectacle. "By God in heaven," he reluctantly muttered. "Yer right, ole boy."

Naturally, now, all *La Magdalena*'s crew mustered the energy to lumber over to starboard deck and see for themselves what the Celts were getting on about. One by one, they raised their hands to their brows and squinted into the horizon. Murmurs in numerous languages equating to proclamations of renewed faith echoed across the deck: "Díos mío," "Alhamdulillah," "Mein Gott," "Mon dieu," "Ani Elohim."

Their bodies looked like dolphins from a distance, just as sleek but jet black. They darted in and out of the water, dipping above and below its surface, splashing fish-like tails that were, impossibly and yet visibly, attached to anthropoid bodies. As they drew closer, or we to them, their arms became discernible, although theirs were not used for swimming the way a man would, or a woman, if she were so inclined to take to the sea the way these did. Their hands remained at their sides, moving instead with their tails and finned thighs fluttering. Through the putrid waters, they dived and danced, their fish tails propelling them at great speeds through the sea. They carried with them a grace that was, dare I say, sensual, and we were transfixed by this strange allure. Each had large, brilliant eyes that transmitted the sun's reflection of the water's surface, and their lithe bodies were hypnotic in their movements. Who can say for how long this group of bedraggled men stood staring at the overboard display as though in some erotic trance? But as suddenly as they made themselves known to us, they vanished. They left us with only rippling circular patterns on the flats of the sea where they had last surfaced. Alas, they must have returned to their underwater kingdom, or more likely, back to torment the dead in Tartarus, for these abominations of nature were not the auspicious creatures so many of our crew had recognized from their local lore.

"They're not selkies, you dope. They're sirens trying to lure us into marrying them while drowning ourselves in the meantime," countered the well-read, Alexandrian sailor, all too familiar with Homeric misadventures.

"Yes, Mami Wata," agreed the Guinean.

"Mamba Muntu," nodded the Congolese.

"Nay, you're all wrong. They're the virgin daughters of Atargatis, our beloved mother of Syria," proclaimed the Cilician. "They want nothing more than to deliver us from this unholy nightmare!"

"Fools! They can only be attendants of Ku-Liltu, the ancient fish-woman and bringer of unfathomable riches!" rejoiced the Arab.

While the men deliberated the most accurate interpretation of our horrid encounter with the sea-maidens, *La Magdalena* began to rock, gently, from side to side, as if to soothe the argumentative men onboard. The movement was so gradual, so methodical, that the hot-headed sailors did not even notice it at first. Not until she dipped without warning deep to port and sent sailors, rigging, dishes, and rats, clamoring for stronghold, were we forced into action.

The mainmast was first to go. With the sails having been spread for days in hopes of the slightest breeze to move us out of that watery wasteland, the sudden rush of wind that bore down upon us cracked the spar, momentarily filling the ship with the scent of fresh-cut pine wood before the aroma dissipated into the cyclone.

When a violent wave crashed against the prow as in ambush, it took the spritsail with it overboard. Our beloved caravel cried in agony, seeming to protest her own fate. Yet, one by one, *La Magdalena*'s creaking, moaning timbers were compromised, and one by one, they buckled beneath the pressure of waves and wind. She was going down, and, dear Admiral, I swear to you in the name of Christ our Lord and Savior, that there was not a damned thing we might have done to save her.

I hope you may sympathize, Admiral, as I know that you, too, saw those things. You noted some years back, on your first or second voyage, a group of three off the coast of Hispaniola. You celebrated their elegance yet decried their features as less beautiful than depicted in paintings. Perhaps it was because you resisted hypnosis that your ships and your crew, and, indeed, you survived to tell the tale. We were not so wise, or fortunate. There are today four souls who survived the shipwreck: a boatswain, two gunners, and myself. By miraculous intervention, we lived by clinging to flotsam that was eventually washed ashore of the Isle of Devils, the one discovered by Juan de Bermúdez, some years ago. And yet, I write that I clung to flotsam, but by the grace of God on High, I must clarify as to avoid telling untruths. In fact, we were saved by a pair of drifting half-burnt effigies of straw-stuffed horse-hide. My soul aches with the thought of having clung to such unholy manifestations of fear, ignorance, and superstition. And yet, it is true: I was saved by the grace of God, no doubt, but also by the heathen sacrificial offerings. I hope that my honesty has not diminished your opinion of my character, dear Admiral.

Still today, my three fellows refuse to speak of what they saw in the water before the storm, which is why I write to you. You see, I fear I shall lose my mind if I am to remain silent, as my humors are already quite unbalanced. I need for nothing more than to discuss, man to man, true Christian to true Christian, this unusual matter with you upon my return to Castile and to settle it once and for all. Admiral, if these nereids are in fact human kinds, how do we proceed to dominate them, let alone to show them the way of God the Merciful? How do we expel the demonic from such creatures? How does their existence change our mission as men of God?

Please do kindly consider my request for conference, and in the meantime, I fervently anticipate your response.

May this letter find you in robust health, Admiral.

Eugenio de Sálazar

Translator's note: Unbeknownst to the letter's author, its intended recipient perished on May 20, 1506 and would never know of the fate of La Santa María Magdalena, her mysterious and deadly encounter in the Sargasso Sea, or the loss of her esteemed crew. The fate of de Sálazar and the three other survivors remains to this day unknown.

II.

Record no.: 5/16
Diver name: D. Halloway
Date: 16–06–2022
Bottom time: 21 min
Max depth: –52m
Gas mix: 21% O_2

Decompression profile: 2 min at 12m, 21% O_2 — 6 min at 8m, 80% O_2 — 8 min at 6m, 100% O_2

Instruments used: GPS, hammer, aluminum stakes, photogrammetry targets

Dive objectives: 1) Locate shipwreck; 2) establish fixed points; 3) record measurements between fixed points; 4) place photo targets; 5) perform photogrammetry

Dive outcomes: Objectives 1 and 2 were achieved.

Problems and resolutions: With a max bottom time allotment of a whopping 20 minutes, and with very limited visibility at depth (0.5–1m), it took some time to locate the shipwreck and record its extremities with GPS. I believe that the ship has broken in half, which skews its profile. This could have happened during the wrecking event or through geological processes over the last 500 years. One additional minor problem was encountered: the coms on my full-face mask (required due to the heavily polluted water) were malfunctioning so that a deafening high-pitched screeching sound was shooting into my right ear for the duration of the dive, which was highly distracting — and painful. Also supremely annoying. And upon exiting the water, my wetsuit was vile. And no, I did not pee in it (this time). The water just really is that disgusting. Thank you, Anthropocene (or should I say, Cthulucene).

Sketch of dive profile and/or site:

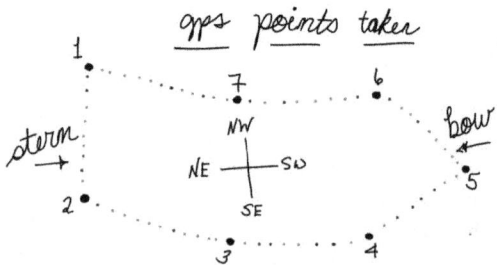

Record no.: 7/16
Diver name: D. Halloway
Date: 17–06–2022
Bottom time: 22 min
Max depth: –50m
Gas mix: 21% O_2
Decompression profile: 2 min at 12m, 21% O_2 — 6 min at 8m, 80% O_2 — 8 min at 6m, 100% O_2
Instruments used: GPS, camera, strobe
Dive objectives: 1) Locate shipwreck; 2) perform photogrammetry
Dive outcomes: Both objectives were achieved.
Problems and resolutions: Visibility was somewhat improved since yesterday (2.5–3m), so we decided to record the site for photogrammetry. Because the quality of the photos are much improved if I wear a half mask instead of a full-face mask, I had to subject the skin of my face and lips to this disgusting, toxic water. (Hopefully I'm not dead of cancer by the end of the field season.) I maintained an approximate distance of 1.5–2m above the shipwreck and recorded over 300 overlapping photographic images. The waters are still dark and murky but hopefully the images can be digitally tweaked enough to generate the necessary point cloud for 3D reconstruction. Only problems encountered were during the ascent. My dive buddy experienced low air upon departure from the site, so we had to buddy-breathe from my air system from –52m to the surface-supply station at –8m. The lack of air in his tanks made him positively buoyant. I struggled to keep our ascent under 10m/min lest he rocket us both up to the surface and get us bent (which is exactly what I told him to do — get bent — after we were back on the support vessel). (Hopefully I'm not dead of the bends by the end of the field season.) By the time we reached the deco stations near the surface, we were both positively buoyant (as he had drained my air supply too), and in the surge, we were bobbing up and down like a pair of seals caught in a fishing net. This might have been the

most annoying deco time I've ever experienced (and they're all annoying).

Sketch of dive profile and/or site:

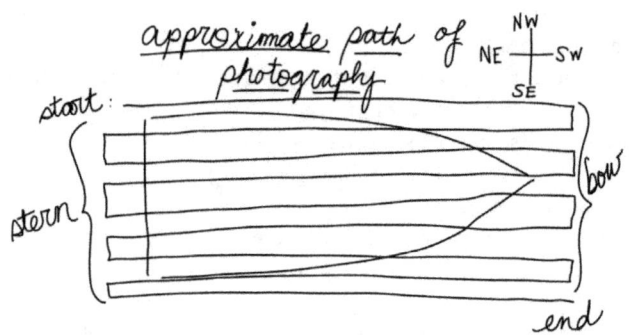

Record no.: 11/16
Diver name: B. Johnson
Date: 18-06-2022
Bottom time: 19 min
Max depth: −53m
Gas mix: 21% O_2
Decompression profile: 2 min at 12m, 21% O_2 — 6 min at 8m, 80% O_2 — 8 min at 6m, 100% O_2
Instruments used: compass, trowels, shovels
Dive objectives: 1) Locate Trench 4; 2) Open new trench (T5) 5m further due southeast of T4
Dive outcomes: Objectives achieved (hopefully?)
Problems and resolutions: There were two problems encountered during this dive. The first was that I was underweighted and had problems getting down. I used 8kg, which is what I used yesterday too, but I forgot that the tank I'm using today is aluminum and not steel. My buddy inserted one of her own 2kg weights into my side pocket and then I was able to descend. The second problem was that our compass was malfunctioning at depth, so I'm not sure that the trench we opened was where it should have

been. When we started excavating, the visibility became very poor because there was no current at depth to carry away sediments. We did hit something with our trowels that was a different consistency than the mud, so then we put the trowels aside and excavated with our hands. I lost my trowel, so it remains at depth.

Sketch of dive profile and/or site:

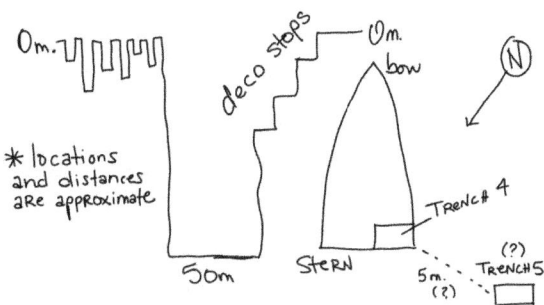

Record no.: 12/16
Diver name: D. Halloway
Date: 18–06–2022
Bottom time: 19 min
Max depth: –53m
Gas mix: 21% O_2
Decompression profile: 2 min at 12m, 21% O_2 — 6 min at 8m, 80% O_2 — 8 min at 6m, 100% O_2
Instruments used: trowels, shovels, compass, GPS, camera, strobe
Dive objectives: 1) Locate trench 4; 2) Open new trench (T5) 5m further due southeast of T4
Dive outcomes: Objectives achieved
Problems and resolutions: The dive was very nearly aborted because my dive buddy was underweighted, yet again, so he was flopping around the first couple meters at the surface like a dying whale trying to descend. The situation

was aggravated by the nasty rope-like algae and countless lengths of plastic twine and other debris that cover the surface of the sea and which my poor, inept, little buddy was getting himself all tangled up in. The more embarrassed and flustered he got, the more buoyant he became because he wasn't exhaling completely. I got him to calm down at the surface, untangled him from the shit, and then gave him 2kg which was enough to drag him down to depth. Between low visibility and a wonky compass, we found a place, but probably not the right place, to designate Trench 5, and we started digging. About 8cm down though, there was a change in stratigraphy as the stinking layer of mud on top gave way to a harder substance that resisted the trowel. My first thought was of human remains because we have come across several disarticulated human bones in Trenches 3 and 4. So we began excavating with our hands. The currents picked up a little at the end of the dive, enough for me to see what we were clearing, which looked to me like fur, or patches of fur on leather. If that is correct, the mud on this part of the seafloor must have been toxic enough to keep the beasties away from the organic material, because whatever it is, it seems to be in an exceptional state of preservation.
Sketch of dive profile and/or site:

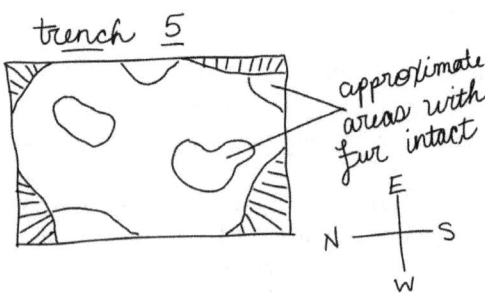

Record no.: 16/16
Diver name: D. Halloway
Date: 20–06–2022
Bottom time: 12 min
Max depth: –53m
Gas mix: 21% O_2
Decompression profile: 2 min at 12m, 21% O_2 — 5 min at 8m, 80% O_2 — 7 min at 6m, 100% O_2
Instruments used: trowels, shovels, compass, GPS, camera, strobe
Dive objectives: 1) Continue excavating Trench 5; 2) photograph anomaly
Dive outcomes: Objectives achieved
Problems and resolutions: At depth, we continued hand-excavating along the body of the animal in our trench until the dive was called off by the supervisor. I took a couple shots of the trench and its contents before beginning the ascent. We believe this animal, and the other three found in different parts of the site, to be one of the unfortunate cattle to have been brought onboard the ship for food, or possibly to set up an animal husbandry program at the ship's destination of Hispaniola. At least they were prevented from contributing to the horrors of colonization — the human casualties deserved their cruel fate. Anyway, more catastrophe is on the way. We may never know how many cattle perished, where they were being held, or why they are distributed across the wreck site in this way because this was the last dive of the season. We are canceling the rest of the project due to our location directly in the path of Hurricane Santiago, the sixth category-five hurricane in the Atlantic this month. Alas, we will have to begin anew next year, if funding permits. (And if hurricanes don't wipe out our Sargasso research station and if the whole sea hasn't erupted in a toxic, surface fire fueled by petroleum-based plastics and methane-exuding rotten algae. Sometimes, I think apocalypse might just be the best way to go. Except as a scientist and an atheist, God would probably take extra

delight in my slow demise.) So for 2022 — at least — that's Dr. Donna Halloway, signing out.
Sketch of dive profile and/or site:

approximate shape of colonization

III.

Strange Detritus Washes up on Bermuda Beaches
Associated Press — 10:40 AST — July 17, 2022

HAMILTON — After several weeks of coping with the aftermath of Hurricane Santiago and the five that preceded it, island residents have reported horse corpses that have washed ashore at Chaplin Bay, Clearwater Beach, Clarence Cove, and John Smith's Bay. Tallying four so far, the horses appear to have been taxidermied and partially burnt.

"I was walking my dog early this morning in Clarence Cove, and, before I could see anything, I noticed the smell. It was absolutely awful, like a dead animal but also something like methane and diesel fuel. When I got closer, the thing was covered, just covered, in flies and crabs. I couldn't even tell what it was," said local resident Jon Rickman.

"We have collected four bodies so far, each in varying stages of decomposition but surprisingly intact considering that they had been at sea for some time," said Dr. Tanya St. George of the National Museum of Bermuda. "The most peculiar thing, besides the smell, is the method of taxidermy. The horses had been skinned, post mortem, and then stuffed with straw and sewn back up. It's a very crude method and seems to have been done hastily. Why, of course, we may never know, but we do hope to have an answer as to when and where. We are preparing samples of the hide for DNA analysis and radiocarbon dating and will ship these samples to labs in Washington D.C."

In the meantime, says St. George, the equine flotsam is being kept in the museum's freezer units to control further decay and possible flammable fumes.

However, the research is far from over. "As we get more data on the extraordinary toxicity of the animals, we will need to proceed by investigating impacts on scavenging insect and crustacean populations of the affected beaches."

Bibliography

Kant, Immanuel. *Anthropology, History, and Education.* Edited and translated by Günter Zöller and Robert B. Louden. Cambridge: Cambridge University Press, 2007.

6

Race and Its Far-Reaching Contemporary Ontological and Epistemological Implications

Marina Gržinić and Jovita Pristovšek

There is no better meeting place of horror and philosophy than when, and if, we speak about the historical construct of race and its far-reaching, contemporary, ontological, and epistemological implications.

Part 1: Marina Gržinić: Politics of Death in Europe

1.1 Introduction
As global capitalism entered the world scene in 2001 with the fall of the Twin Towers in New York City, we could see an intensified neoliberal process of privatization, deregulation, and abandonment that, having begun elsewhere, started to be implemented within the capitalist first world. Achille Mbembe, in order to capture a mode of life in Africa after 2001 and to elaborate on the capital profit in the global world that includes the involvement of war machines (e.g., Iraq, Afghanistan, etc.),

coined the term "necropolitics."[1] As Mbembe conceptualizes it in his seminal text "Necropolitics" from 2003:

> Having presented [a necropolitical] reading of politics as the work of death, I turn now to sovereignty, expressed predominantly as the right to kill. For the purpose of my argument, I relate Foucault's notion of biopower to two other concepts: the state of exception and the state of siege. I examine those trajectories by which the state of exception and the relation of enmity have become the normative basis of the right to kill. In such instances, power (and not necessarily state power) continuously refers and appeals to exception, emergency, and a fictionalized notion of the enemy.[2]

Necropolitics is a coinage in between *necro-* (death) and politics.[3] Necropolitics always has, as a consequence, death as a systematic extermination, not just accidental death. Therefore, necropolitics involves "contemporary forms of subjugation of life to the power of death."[4] And, in order to put this forward, three key procedures are central to necropolitics: the right to kill, enmity, and impunity.[5]

Necropolitics denotes a system of governmentality in neoliberal, global capitalism that is not at all an exaltation of death, in the sense of the old relation between Eros and Thanatos, but an intensification of governing measures that not only inflicts death but also makes profit from capitalizing on it. Necropolitics operates with new forms of technologies of discipline and

---

[1] Achille Mbembe, "Necropolitics," trans. Libby Meintjes, *Public Culture* 15, no. 1 (Winter 2003): 11–40.
[2] Ibid., 16.
[3] Marina Gržinić, "The Emergence of the Political Subject," *Emancipation of the Resistance,* March 2013, https://emancipationofresistance.wordpress.com/grzinic/.
[4] Mbembe, "Necropolitics," 39–40.
[5] This is how Edward A. Avila recuperates these three points in his dissertation "Conditions of (Im)possibility: Necropolitics, Neoliberalism, and the Cultural Politics of Death in Contemporary Chicana/o Film and Literature," PhD diss., University of California, San Diego, 2012.

control, and with authoritarian politics that present in the normalization of racist attitudes and an economy that is seen as completely detached from any production efforts but is used as a pure political tool for more and more suppression.[6]

Necropolitics regulates life from the perspective of death, thus transforming life into a mere existence below every life's minimum. I have axiomatically defined necropolitics as "let live and make die."[7] To clarify this point, I have made a parallel to a mode of life that Michel Foucault envisioned and named "biopolitics" in the 1970s. I have axiomatically described Foucault's biopolitics as "make live and let die."[8] I have also argued that, in the 1970s, biopolitics presented a situation of regulation of life in the so-called capitalist first world and welfare states, but also a situation of abandoning or delegating death to the so-called other worlds, the second and third worlds.[9]

These two modes of life present a brutal difference in life and death management. In biopolitics, life is controlled; but it is about providing a good life for the citizens of the sovereign first world capitalist countries. However, what is at hand today is a pure abandonment of these structures (let live), while simultaneously death is managed, used, and capitalized by the war machine.[10]

---

6   Marina Gržinić and Aneta Stojnić, "Reclaiming the Body: Fem Positions Repoliticized," in *Shifting Corporealities in Contemporary Performance: Avant-Gardes in Performance,* eds. Marina Gržinić and Aneta Stojnić (Cham: Palgrave Macmillan, 2018), 24–25.
7   Marina Gržinić, "Capital, Repetition," *Reartikulacija* 8 (2009): 3.
8   Ibid. See also Michel Foucault, *"Society Must Be Defended": Lectures at the Collège De France, 1975–76,* eds. Mauro Bertani and Alessandro Fontana, trans. David Macey (New York: Picador, 2003).
9   Gržinić, "The Emergence of the Political Subject."
10 Ibid. I developed the main core of my thinking already in 2007. I developed it while reading about the crisis in former Yugoslavia, and, in the same period, I engaged with necropolitics in the process of teaching in the Academy of Fine Arts Vienna with my students. At this point, a decade ago and still today but to a lesser degree, the refutation of necropolitics was extremely present. Why? The answer is that neoliberal global capitalism nowadays exposes stubborn life, due in part to biotechnology, so as to hide the hyper profit made from death.

This came out clearly with the crisis in 2008. In such a situation, death becomes central to a field of power that, in global, neoliberal necrocapitalism, does not have the form of biopower but of necropower. To understand precisely what necropower means, we should relate it to "bare life." This latter concept was developed in 1995 when Giorgio Agamben published *Homo Sacer: Il potere sovrano e la vita nuda,* translated into English as *Homo Sacer: Sovereign Power and Bare Life* in 1998.[11] *Homo sacer* is the Latin name for a sacred, perishable life. Historically, it was already present in ancient Rome; the Roman law refers to it. Today we have a lot of figures that are to be subscribed to this category, the most known are the refugees, though earlier those that were imprisoned in Guantanamo had the status of bare lives. In these two examples, it is clear that the figures are situated in between life and death, as what they possess is just what Agamben calls bare life. Bare life is a product in between sovereign power and something that is a surplus or a leftover of human life.

Furthermore, bare life is always constructed by way of a system of invisible, secret, hidden procedures and is invested, as well, with the performativity (of power) that affects terminally the (in/human) body. This denotes a very clear procedure according to which, in order to produce bare life as a rest or a surplus inside a structure (e.g., a state, sovereign, or institutional structure), the social, economic, judicial, or political power has to make recourse to the state of exception. In order to kill without a punishment, or to terminally abandon people or whole nations of civilians, a system — of politics, law, economics, and social relations that presents itself as extra-judicial, exceptional, or as an emergence — has to be developed. Moreover, the sovereign, as described by Agamben, is an exception in itself that decides on its exception. As Agamben shows, the sovereign's legal right is the effective prorogation of the law itself and of a "state of exception," both of which are in the last instance mixed

---

11 Giorgio Agamben, *Homo Sacer: Sovereign Power and Bare Life,* trans. Daniel Heller-Roazen (Stanford: Stanford University Press, 1998).

up: the one who decides upon the exception, which represents a confusion of law and fact, is the sovereign itself. The outcome is a pure circularity, another characteristic of global capitalism, which presents power as more and more subjectless — yet it decides as a subject.[12]

Mbembe says that necropower is the enactment of sovereignty in cases in which "the generalized instrumentalization of human existence and the material destruction of human bodies and populations" is the central project of power, rather than autonomy.[13] In the last instance, the rethinking of the shift from biopolitics to necropolitics is to be done in precisely the zones of indistinction between the sovereign and life, between citizens and non-citizens, and between biopower and necropower. Mbembe situates his analysis of necropolitics specifically in the context of contemporary colonial occupations (for example, Apartheid in South Africa or the Israeli occupation of Palestine). Thus, the concept of necropolitics opens a critical space for discussing a land of dead, violated, and ultimately disposed bodies in cinema's necro-space.

1.2 Horror: Film and Necropolitics

I suggest analyzing a selection of films made after World War II on the topic of death and history in order to think about dying and death in the form of an enduring process of a systematic violent act, a horrifying necropolitics. The films that I select and display here as a political genealogy and present chronologically were made after World War II in Europe, and they illustrate that enduring process of a systematic violent act, that horrifying necropolitics.

---

12 Gržinić and Stojnić, "Reclaiming the Body," 26.
13 Mbembe, "Necropolitics," 14.

Night and Fog (1956), directed by Alain Resnais[14]

The film's title *Night and Fog* refers to the notorious *Nacht und Nebel* decree issued by Adolf Hitler on December 7, 1941. This decree was directed against persons endangering the security of Germany in the occupied territories. The victims, mainly Jewish German citizens, were abducted, imprisoned, and some were brought for trial by special courts to decide their faith.[15] The film opens with shots of remnants of Auschwitz, the Nazi extermination camp, shifting between present images and old documentary footage, while the narrator, Michel Bouquet, discusses the rise of Nazi ideology. The film proceeds with comparisons of the life of the *Schutzstaffel,* the main paramilitary organization under Adolf Hitler, to the life of starving prisoners in the camps. The narrator further exposes the sadistic brutality inflicted on prisoners, including torture, scientific and medical "experiments," rapes, and executions. The next section shows horrific images of gas chambers and wasted bodies, corpses. At the end, the film depicts the country's liberation, the discovery of the camps' horrors, and confronts us with the question of responsibility.

The Battle of Algiers (1966), directed by Gillo Pontecorvo[16]

Drawing on the events of the Algerian War of Independence (1954–62) against French colonial rule in North Africa, Pontecorvo's film focuses on the critical years between 1954 and 1957. At that time, the regrouped guerrilla fighters spread into the Casbah, the citadel of Algiers in Algeria, where they clashed

---

14　Alain Resnais, dir., *Nuit et brouillard* [*Night and Fog*] (Paris: Argo Films, 1956). Alain Resnais (1922–2014) was a French film director and screenwriter.

15　*Holocaust Encyclopedia*, s.v. "Nigh and Fog Decree," https://encyclopedia.ushmm.org/content/en/article/night-and-fog-decree.

16　Gillo Pontecorvo, dir., *La battaglia di Algeri* [*The Battle of Algiers*] (Algiers/Rome: Casbah Film/Igor Film, 1966). Gillo Pontecorvo (1919–2006) was an Italian film director.

with French paratroopers trying to bring down the revolt. The film portrays urban warfare, the guerrilla movement's organization, and the illegal tactics France used to suppress a nationalist uprising. The story revolves around Ali la Pointe, a petty criminal who is politically radicalized while in prison, and who is afterwards recruited by Front de libération nationale (National Liberation Front, or FLN) commander El-Hadi Jafar (this is based partly on Saadi Yacef's account of being a military commander for the FLN).[17]

Early Works (1969), directed by Želimir Žilnik[18]

The story of this film takes place in the territory of the former Socialist Federal Republic of Yugoslavia, in the period of the 1968 students' riots and in the general context of state socialism. Three young men and a young woman, Jugoslava, who is bearing the name of the state changed into a female personal name(!), leave home and move across the country in search of true revolutionary socialism and a society that believes in truth. Jugoslava also wants to find out if the position of women within this socialist society can be improved, so that it would not be simply and solely connected to the strong, patriarchal, socialist life. Jugoslava is under pressure due to terrible relationships within her own family, especially due to the pressures that her drunken and despotic father puts on everybody.[19]

---

17 Phil Ochs, "The Battle of Algiers," *Life of a Rebel*, May 19, 2008, http://phil-ochs.blogspot.com/2008/05/battle-of-algiers.html.
18 Želimir Žilnik, dir., *Rani Radovi* [*Early Works*] (Beograd/Novi Sad: Avala Film/Neoplanta film, 1969). Želimir Žilnik (b. 1942) is a Yugoslav–Serbian film director.
19 Marina Gržinić, "Ex-Yugoslav Avant-garde Film Production and its Early Works Seen Through Biopolitics and Necropolitics," in *Za ideju — protiv stanja*, eds. Branka Ćurčić, Sarita Matijević, Zoran Pantelić, Želimir Žilnik (Novi Sad: Playground produkcija, 2009), 151–52.

Salò, or the 120 Days of Sodom (1975), directed by Pier Paolo Pasolini[20]

Based on the classic *The 120 Days of Sodom*, which Marquis de Sade wrote in 1785, this film revolves around four rich and corrupt Italian libertines, during the period of the fascist Republic of Salò (1943-45). They kidnap eighteen teenagers, subjecting them to four months of pure sadistic, mental, physical, and sexual violence. The film engages with questions of political corruption, abuse of power, sadism, perversion, sexuality, and fascism. The film's structure is inspired by Dante's *Divine Comedy* (1320); it is made up of four segments entitled, respectively, the "Anteinferno," the "Circle of Manias," the "Circle of Shit," and the "Circle of Blood." It also contains several references to the 1887 book *On the Genealogy of Morality* by Friedrich Nietzsche, Ezra Pound's collection of poems entitled *The Cantos* (whose complete edition was published in 1970), and the novel sequence of Marcel Proust's *In Search of Lost Time* (which was published in French in seven volumes from 1913 to 1927).

In a Year of 13 Moons (1978), directed by Rainer Werner Fassbinder[21]

After being beaten for trying to buy sex at a Frankfurt cruising spot for gays, Elvira Weishaupt returns home to her longtime lover Christoph, who has been away for six weeks. Humiliated and physically abused by Christoph, Elvira befriends a prostitute, Zora. Together they visit a slaughterhouse, where Elvira, who was at that time Erwin, used to work as a butcher, the or-

---

20 Pier Paolo Pasolini, dir., *Salò o le 120 giornate di Sodoma* [*Salò, or the 120 Days of Sodom*] (Rome: Produzioni Europee Associate [PEA]; Paris: Les Productions Artistes Associés, 1975). Pier Paolo Pasolini (1922–75) was an Italian film director, poet, and writer.
21 Rainer Werner Fassbinder, dir., *In einem Jahr mit 13 Monden* [*In a Year of 13 Moons*] (Berlin: Filmverlag der Autoren; Munich: Pro-ject Filmproduktion; Berlin: Tango Film, 1978). Rainer Werner Fassbinder (1945–82) was a West German film and theater director and actor.

phanage where she was raised by nuns, and Anton Saitz, her former lover, supposedly responsible for Elvira's sex-change procedure. At the end of the film, Elvira commits suicide after her uncontrollable spiraling into nothingness goes unnoticed.[22]

Germany Pale Mother (1980), directed by Helma Sanders-Brahms[23]

This film's narrative is recounted from a radically subjective viewpoint and depicts the way in which a young woman, Lene, and her mother survived the World War II. Lene is hurrying along the banks of a river while being pursued and harassed by four Hitler Youths and their Alsatian dog. Lene's future husband Hans, who is taking a spin on a rowboat with a friend, is amused by the situation. He falls in love with Lene at first sight but doesn't help her. The film portrays a world of helplessness and male brutality. While the post-war period in Germany allows Hans and his "de-Nazified" friends to re-establish themselves professionally, Lene, on the other hand, suffers from depression and a mysterious case of facial paralysis.[24]

Handsworth Songs (1986), directed by John Akomfrah[25]

This documentary is based on the 1986 Black Audio Film Collective's essay on black Britain in the wake of Britain's 1985 wave

---

22 Ed Gonzalez, "Review: *In a Year of 13 Moons*," *Slant Magazine,* August 23, 2003, https://www.slantmagazine.com/film/in-a-year-of-13-moons/.
23 Helma Sanders-Brahms, dir., *Deutschland bleiche Mutter* [*Germany Pale Mother*] (Berlin/Berlin/Cologne: Helma Sanders-Brahms Filmproduktion/Literarisches Colloquium/Westdeutscher Rundfunk [WDR], 1980). Helma Sanders-Brahms (1940–2014) was a West German film director and screenwriter.
24 Birgit Roschy, "Helma Sanders-Brahms: 'Germany Pale Mother,'" *Goethe Institut,* July 2014, https://www.goethe.de/ins/au/en/kul/mag/20397223.html.
25 John Akomfrah, dir., *Handsworth Songs* (London: Black Audio Film Collective, 1986). John Akomfrah (b. 1957) is a British film director, screenwriter, and theorist.

of civil unrest. At that time, political collectivities were in the process of being violently decomposed (the year 1985 also marks the bitter defeat of the Miners' Strike) as the neoliberal political program began to impose the "privatization of the mind."[26] The film was produced for the Channel 4 series "Britain: The Lie of the Land" and released in 1986, a year after the Handsworth, Birmingham, and Tottenham riots. It is a premonitory sign of the 2011 England riots, regarded as one of the most significant periods of civil unrest in post-war Britain.[27]

In Uranium Hex (1987), directed by Sandra Lahire[28]

This story is about uranium mining and women's work in Canada. In this film, obsession, passion, and politics are so closely intertwined that they make for an explosion, or rather, a destruction of our nerves. The radiation of the body is transferred to the radiation of the image. The radon 222 that disintegrates the skin seems to over-expose the film image here. There is no difference between the politics of the medium and the politics of the topic; both are reunited within deadly light in a clash of layers. Radioactivity is deployed as the radioactivity of the film image itself. The result is a powerful investigation of inequalities regarding the position of women, the stance of lesbians, and social injustice against women and Jews. Through Lahire's vision, the blackness or whiteness of heterosexual men counts for little as an emancipatory force in neoliberal capitalism. The twenty-first century is, so to speak, female, lesbian, transgender, and of color.[29]

---

26 Mark Fisher, "The Land Still Lies: Handsworth Songs and the English riots," *Sight & Sound,* February 5, 2014, https://www.bfi.org.uk/news-opinion/sight-sound-magazine/comment/land-still-lies-handsworth-songs-and-english-riots.

27 Ibid.

28 Sandra Lahire, dir., *In Uranium Hex* (London: Arts Council of Great Britain, 1987). Sandra Lahire (1950–2001) was a central figure in experimental feminist filmmaking.

29 Marina Gržinić, "Sandra Lahire," *Luxonline,* https://www.luxonline.org.uk/artists/sandra_lahire/(printversion).html.

M.I.A.'s Born Free (2010), directed by Romain Gavras[30]

Gavras's music video film is based on several incidents in Sri Lanka, involving the extra-judicial killing of Tamil men by the Sri Lankan Army. Those incidents were filmed on mobile phones, and some of them were broadcasted by news outlets worldwide. The controversy stems from a raid by the SWAT (Special Weapons and Tactics) team in one of the buildings. During the raid, as we watch, the team is breaking into apartments, taking no notice of a man in a room, sitting and smoking a crack pipe. The SWAT team beats a couple engaged in coitus and some of the other residents of the building. They then violently force a young red-haired man into a transport vehicle for detention; other red-heads are already detained in a vehicle. A few of the SWAT team members are wearing American flags on their uniforms. Detainees, treated violently, are then driven out into the desert and forced to run across a live minefield. Over the course of the events, a young red-haired boy is shot through the head, and another loses his life after stepping onto a live mine while the soldiers continue to chase, beat, and shoot the captives.

Leviathan (2014), directed by Andrey Zvyagintsev[31]

The film is shot in the coastal town of Teriberka, in the Russian Murmansk region, but set in the fictional town of Pribrezhny. The plot follows a tragic series of events affecting temperamental car mechanic Kolya, his second wife Lilya, and his teenage son Roma. The town's immoral Mayor Vadim undertakes a legal plot to expropriate the land on which Kolya's house was built. Kolya's refusal to sell the property lands him in prison. The film

---

30 Romain Gavras, dir., *M.I.A.'s Born Free* (London: Paradoxal Inc./XL Recordings, 2010). Romain Gavras (b. 1981) is a Greek-French film and video director.
31 Andrey Zvyagintsev, dir., *Leviathan* (Moscow: Non-Stop Productions/A Company Russia/Russian Ministry of Culture/Fond kino/RuArts Foundation, 2014). Andrey Zvyagintsev (b. 1964) is a Russian film director and screenwriter.

unfolds a story that is as grim, violent, and brutal as it is indicative of the neoliberal power structure in the lawless states of postsocialism.

The Fool (2014), directed by Yuri Bykov[32]

The movie is set in an unnamed Russian town. It tells the story of a simple middle-aged Russian plumber, Dima Nikitin, who is also a municipal repair-crew chief. He is studying building engineering. When a bathroom pipe bursts in one of the communal housing buildings in disrepair, a large problem is revealed, since the exterior wall behind the pipe has cracked and begun to shift. Nikitin goes outside to examine the matter; there, he realizes that the building has fractures from the ground up to the top floor. Although the building is not officially part of his district, Nikitin's sense of personal responsibility leads him to go in the middle of the night to find and alert the authorities, for he believes that in less than twenty-four hours the building will collapse. Eventually, he manages to evacuate the building, but the tenants beat Nikitin and return to their flats after realizing that nothing has happened, leaving him unconscious on the sidewalk.

Son of Saul (2015), directed by László Nemes[33]

This film follows a day and a half in the life of Saul Ausländer, a Jewish-Hungarian working as part of a *Sonderkommando* unit in the Auschwitz extermination camp during the World War II. *Sonderkommandos* were work units composed of Jewish prisoners forced to help with the disposal of gas chamber victims and

---

32 Yuri Bykov, dir., *Durak* [*The Fool*] (St. Petersburg/Moscow: Rock Film Studio/Russian Ministry of Culture, 2014). Yuri Bykov (b. 1981) is a Russian film director, screenwriter, and actor.

33 László Nemes, dir., *Saul fia* [*Son of Saul*] (Budapest: Laokoon Filmgroup/Hungarian National Film Fund, 2015). László Nemes (b. 1977) is a Hungarian film director and screenwriter.

crematoria in the Nazi camp system.[34] Saul has several duties, including salvaging valuables from the clothing of the dead, removing their bodies out of the gas chambers, and scrubbing the floors before another group is brought to these chambers. Saul carries out his daily tasks with an impassive expression, apparently numbed by the daily horrors. One day, after the gassing, he comes upon a boy's body that he recognizes. Despite being gassed, the boy is still breathing. From a distance, Saul witnesses the boy being methodically suffocated by a Nazi doctor to ensure his death. The plot develops as Saul attempts to get the Rabbi for a funeral, through several events of horror and stupor.

1.3 Filmic Necropolitics
From where do I elaborate the unusual proposal to think about these films in the context of necropolitics? Elizabeth Reich, in her book *Militant Visions: Black Soldiers, Internationalism, and the Transformation of American Cinema,* published in 2016, has a subchapter entitled "A Filmic Necropolitics."[35] In this section of the book, she emphasizes racism as the point that presents the failure of biopolitics in dealing with a specific history of film when it depicts brutalities, violence, discrimination, and abandonment. In a word, *racialization* is what structures the frame of the filmic necropolitics with which we analyzed the previous films. These films are here not to be read from the point of different film genres but through a necropolitical order of power in the European context that organizes the field of film production in post-World War II Europe. I have decided, here, to provoke necropolitical thinking in the field of film in the context of a Europe broader than the EU, including the former, cold-war Eastern European space, larger even than Europe itself, as we are all part of global, neoliberal capitalism.

---

34 *Holocaust Encyclopedia,* s.v. "Sonderkommandos," https://encyclopedia.ushmm.org/content/en/article/sonderkommandos.
35 Elizabeth Reich, "A Filmic Necropolitics," in *Militant Visions: Black Soldiers, Internationalism, and the Transformation of American Cinema* (New Brunswick: Rutgers University Press, 2016), 54–56.

I have organized my analysis in order to craft the horrifying dimension of these films around three central elements of necropolitics: enmity, impunity, and the right to kill, which are found in the films, I argue, as abandonment, reification and disposability.[36] First, there is the social abandonment that literally includes galvanizing landscapes of people abandoned along different borders in the region. The borders are really different. They are in between:

— colonizing forces of the western world and their colonies abroad (as in Pontecorvo, Akomfrah, and Gavras, or as the unsolved contemporary coloniality of power exercised over the Tamils in Sri Lanka);
— the former East and former West (as in Žilnik, Gavras, Zvyagintsev, and Bykov);
— the heterosexual on one side and the homosexual and transgender on the other; the border is re-established as the outcome of the "violation" of patriarchal and gendered forms of existence (as in Fassbinder, Sanders-Brahms, Akomfrah, and Zvyagintsev);
— Nazism and democracy (as in Resnais, Sanders-Brahms, and Nemes);
— humanity and fascist, Nazi, colonial, blind enmities that left camps full of inhumanities (as in Resnais, Pontecorvo, Pasolini, and Nemes). The abandonment here is a pure form of horrifying necropolitical enmity.

Violence is pervasive. It is an outcome of a structural racism that lives in the "postcolony," to use another geopolitical notion elaborated by Mbembe. It is a fervent antisemitism (as in Resnais and Nemes), or it is patriarchal chauvinistic relations (as in Žilnik and Sanders-Brahms).

Second, there is the configuration of historical moments of ultimate dispossessions that live along historically deadly, capi-

---

[36] I make reference to Edward A. Avila's dissertation from 2012 where he makes recourse to similar points in order to construct his analysis of the necro-femicide complex in Juarez and Mexico.

talist "discontinuities," which is how neoliberalism nowadays tries to present colonialism, Nazism/fascism, and neoliberalism itself. These dispossessions result in an abstraction of social relations to the point that labor and social relations in capital-labor conditions of production are totally reified, perceived only as commodities. This is captured in the films of Pontecorvo, Akomfrah, Lahire, Zvyagintsev, and Bykov. We see racialized violence against people, based on class, race, and gender reified relations where wo/men and whole groups of people are completely detached from any social and labor conditions. This is, as well, the format of necropolitical impunity. Nobody responds because of this transformation. This is remarkably stated in *Handsworth Songs,* when one of the speakers says, "something has gone terribly wrong in the world today," and I can add that no one in power will ever be responsible for this. This is brutally depicted in the films of Zvyagintsev and Bykov.

Third, there is disposability. A wasteland of disposable bodies. Disposability is the ultimate format of violence against segments of populations that are fully racialized:

— the Jewish citizens of Europe in Resnais and Nemes;
— the Algerians of the Casbah in Pontecorvo;
— the miners in Lahire;
— those with transgender identities (Fassbinder);
— the socialist Marxist hippy generation (Žilnik); and
— the Tamils in Gavras.

What we see clearly as well is the entanglement of capitalist globalization and nation-state sovereignty where the necropolitical right to expose to death and kill those made disposable is without impunity.

This is what we get from Resnais's film in 1956 and from Nemes's in 2015. But what difference does sixty years make? The point of difference is the radical change in the parameters of space and time. The biopolitical is still connected with space. The necropolitical is about a time that today involves a situation of almost un-governability (as in Akomfrah, Gavras, Zvyagintsev, Bykov, and Nemes).[37] In Nemes, we witness an absolute time exposure without a short-circuit between racialized disposability and limitlessness extermination.

1.4 The State, War, and Race

In all these films, we see what Giorgio Agamben names the appearance of the state of exception. The state of exception, according to Agamben, "is not a special kind of law (like the law of war); rather, insofar as it is a suspension of the juridical order itself, it defines law's threshold or limit concept."[38]

It is important to note that the state of exception is not exceptional; it is not derivative but constitutive of the way in which neoliberal states function today. Moreover, as Santiago López Petit states, what characterizes neoliberal global capitalism is the change from a nation-State to a war-State.[39] In fact, this change means that the former imperial, capitalist, colonial states transformed into war-states exist at the same time as the transformation, or better, fragmentation, of all the state's social and public fields. Petit calls this fragmentation "postmodern fascism," which functions by means of the sterilization of the other, eschewing conflict in the social space, and fragmentation.[40] The war-state, particularly in the capitalist first world (US) and in a former western European context, is here to maintain the illusion of society and the biopolitical mode of life, while inside the neoliberal capitalist biopolitical system the necropolitical is pressing on it and metastasizing. The illusion of the society maintained by the war-state presents itself as a biopolitical point of view, as a politics of taking care of the population's life, though the population is systematically controlled, fragmented,

---

37 On un-governability, Edward A. Avila's dissertation gives some impressive synthesis. See Avila, "Conditions of (Im)possibility."
38 Giorgio Agamben, *State of Exception*, trans. Kevin Attell (Chicago: University of Chicago Press, 2005), 4.
39 Satiago López Petit, *La movilización global. Breve tratado para atacar la realidad* [*Global Mobilization. Brief Treatise for Attacking Reality*] (Madrid: Traficantes de Sueños, 2009).
40 Ibid., 85.

and ultimately abandoned (see the COVID-19 pandemic's complete annihilation of society); the contemporary state is in reality transformed into a necropolitical regime, into a political system that only takes part in the war of transnational capital (see the present US–China relations), abandoning citizens to find their own way to survive.

In this change from a nation-state to a war-state, we also have the so-called "missing" link: the racial-state. The passage from a nation-state to a war-state goes through a racial-state that has racism at its core.[41] This trajectory is captured in the political genealogy of the films presented above. Each film has a relation to these three formats of states, though the racial state is central. Moreover, what is important is that this triad of state formats is possible only with the advent of neoliberalism.

Additionally, already Resnais and Pontecorvo are presenting two different film dispositions of disposability. In the 1950s, in Resnais's film, we see destruction and extermination listed in chapters. In Pontecorvo's 1960s film, we see the colonial power without any impunity that is *en gros* killing. But, in the 1980s, the neoliberal appropriation of these structures is displayed at the level of micropolitics. If, in the 1950s and 1960s, the system is mathematized and strictly divided, from the 1980s on it is becoming pervasive; it is no longer divided into two as in the past but dispersed all over. Or put differently, if before there was the camp, today there is not the camp as a separate unit, but the whole city is a contemporary extraction camp with its social and cultural and religious spaces and dormitories as part of a process of exploitation, expropriation, and privatization (i.e., in Zvyagintsev and Bykov, post-socialist necroscapes). The result is Mbembe's "death-worlds,"[42] where environments are advanced into living graves (the refugee camps in Europe in 2017 are death-worlds consisting of living graves).

This is a new condition for the rethinking of memory and history. If, in the 1970s, biopolitical memory was perceived as an

---

41 Gržinić, "The Emergence of the Political Subject."
42 Mbembe, "Necropolitics," 40.

intensified anthropological biopolitical mechanism, in times of necrocapitalism it is history that is completely evacuated.[43]

1.5 Coda
Why is it important to expose film, terror, and necropolitics?
This exposure opens onto knowledge that challenges histories of racial procedures of necrogovernmentality, and as well, in so doing, demands and produces different cinematic forms and contents. It almost seems that to rescue these films from oblivion and the terror they bring, in entanglement with necropolitics, is to rescue the lives of those who, though terrified, oppose death in these films.

Part 2: Jovita Pristovšek: We Remember Carrying the Word in the Mouth. *Race*. Chewing.[44]

2.1 Introduction
The figure of the "Black," a racialized, colonized, ungendered, and dehumanized "racial 'flesh,'"[45] to borrow Brian Carr's list of notions, is a peculiar being constructed as not quite subject not right object. In his lecture "Democracy in the Age of Dynamism," Achille Mbembe, in light of today's convergence of neoliberal global capitalism and the reinvention of animism, speaks about the "manufacturing of subjects as objects" and the "manufacturing of objects as subjects" while emphasizing the need to question the modes of bringing objects to "life" in a time, as he

---

43 Gržinić, "The Emergence of the Political Subject."
44 Here, I paraphrase a verse originally written as follows: "We remember carrying the word in the mouth. Cologne. Chewing." Rubia Salgado, Gergana Mineva, and Kollektiv Women, "Stream of Memory," in *Border Thinking: Disassembling Histories of Racialized Violence,* ed. Marina Gržinić (Berlin: Sternberg Press, 2018), 52.
45 Brian Carr, "At the Thresholds of the 'Human': Race, Psychoanalysis, and the Replication of Imperial Memory," *Cultural Critique* 39 (Spring 1998): 125.

formulates it, when "living things" always fall into a lethal ritualized mechanics of life.⁴⁶

What should then be reconsidered in relation to the extinction of thought, which could also be seen as a consequence of thought's epistemological dead end, are the very "effects of blackness."⁴⁷ Firstly, because what was once — in Immanuel Kant's own "critical philosophy" — so meticulously elaborated to serve as a "defense against horrors," or, in the words of Mbembe, against "Black Reason,"⁴⁸ was the very idea of what should be named "Colonial Reason" with its "mindless state of mind," as Jean-François Lyotard would put it,⁴⁹ or in Agamben's words, the state of exception that served to separate Reason from the "body" and "flesh."⁵⁰ Today we can identify this "flesh" in numerous modes of existence as having a status below the "threshold of the human," below the level of "humanity," while the "bodies" are "let to live," "abandoned," etc. Mbembe proposes that the common trajectory of those modes of existence is the universalization of the Black condition, since it most accurately summarizes the state of universal humanity in current times.⁵¹ Secondly, the aforementioned "effects of blackness," once presented as a form of the "disease" of the colonial head, are, paradoxically, gradually gaining the status of an epistemological "cure" to contemporary "diseases of the head." For, as Mbembe's

---

46 Achille Mbembe, "Democracy in the Age of Dynamism," Lecture at the Hutchins Center for African American Research, Harvard University, Cambridge, December 4, 2013.

47 Meg Armstrong, "'The Effects of Blackness': Gender, Race, and the Sublime in Aesthetic Theories of Burke and Kant," *Journal of Aesthetic and Art Criticism* 54, no. 3 (Summer 1996): 213–36.

48 Achille Mbembe, *Critique of Black Reason*, trans. Laurent Dubois (Durham: Duke University Press, 2017).

49 Jean-François Lyotard, *The Inhuman: Reflections on Time,* trans. Geoffrey Bennington and Rachel Bowlby (Cambridge: Polity Press, 1991), 140.

50 On anthropogenesis, see Giorgio Agamben, *The Open: Man and Animal,* trans. Kevin Attell (Stanford: Stanford University Press, 2003).

51 Mbembe in Marina Gržinić, "Kolonializem Evrope, dekolonialnost in rasizem" ["Colonialism of Europe, Decoloniality and Racism"], in *Politika, estetika in demokracija,* ed. Marina Gržinić (Ljubljana: Založba ZRC SAZU, 2015), 108.

Critique of Black Reason implies, "Black Reason" appears as one of the key directions for future thinking if western, Eurocentric epistemology wants to transgress the borders of its own "Colonial Reason."

2.2 Race
Let us openly state that the notion of race is a horror for philosophy. Everywhere it appears, already if we just speak about it, the notion of race "unleashes impassioned dynamics and provokes an irrational exuberance that always tests the limits of the very system of reason."[52]

Race and racism, as Mbembe has it, "are part of the fundamental process of the unconscious. In that respect they relate to the impasses of human desires — to appetites, affects, passions, fears."[53] The idea of race is, I believe — and as both, post- and decolonial theories have shown us — the fundamental "disease of the (colonial) head." Race and Blackness are two sides of a codified madness that the Euro-American world has produced;[54] this is a madness that the Euro-American world — in contemporary times of ontological and epistemological uncertainties — will have to confront. Race is, as has already been pointed out by Michel Foucault in his "*Society Must Be Defended*" lectures, an extremely mobile term,[55] and in that sense, race and racism "do not only have a past. They also have a future, particularly in a context where the possibility of transforming life and creating mutant species no longer belongs to the realm of fiction."[56]

Race today — as is often said, we live in post-racial times — is just seemingly rendered conceptually unthinkable. Part of the problem lies, as Ann Laura Stoler suggests, in "colonial aphasia"[57] — a term with which Stoler names a loss of access to

---

52 Mbembe, *Critique of Black Reason*, 2.
53 Ibid., 31.
54 Ibid., 2.
55 See Michel Foucault, "*Society Must Be Defended*."
56 Mbembe, *Critique of Black Reason*, 21.
57 Ann Laura Stoler, "Colonial Aphasia: Race and Disabled Histories in France," *Public Culture* 23, no. 1 (Winter 2011): 121–56.

and active dissociation from the problem of colonialism, a difficulty in speaking and generating vocabulary that links appropriate words and concepts with appropriate things — which fits to the "system or body of thought," inventing ways to epistemologically immunize itself against the "threat," against the "effects of blackness." Race and racism, with regard to philosophy, are most of the time relegated to the realm of the unrepresentable, *unheimlich*.

However, it is perhaps with the concept of race as the "grey zone" of the intersection of horror and philosophy that we can highlight its contemporary ontological and epistemological implications. Because what is historically found at this intersection is precisely a racialized, colonized, ungendered, and dehumanized "racial flesh,"[58] a being constructed as not quite subject not right object. Let me immediately recall a series of terms listed by Mbembe which denote contemporary forms of existence, all living next to each other in the context of neoliberal, global, financial capitalism: "human-thing," "human-machine," "human-code," "human-in-flux."[59] We speak about a plastic and flexible subject who must be able to respond to the ever changing needs of the market, about the bodies "who count," those "worthy" of (biopolitical state) care, and of those that are just "let to live," if they can make it, of those "abandoned" and "dispensable." Yet the figure of the "Black," as *Critique of Black Reason* has shown us, was never solely codified as a figure of madness, ontologically defective, as "man-object, man-merchandise, and man-currency,"[60] a being with limited or no agency. It is precisely because of the systematic negation, the denial of "humanity" and personhood, and the reservoir of nonsense and fantasies that were inscribed in this figure, thus presenting an "extraordinary accumulation of sensations,"[61] that the colonized was also in perpetual becoming: an-other.

---

58 Carr, "At the Thresholds of the 'Human,'" 125.
59 Mbembe, *Critique of Black Reason*, 3–4.
60 Ibid., 11.
61 Ibid., 39.

The "contemporary relations of inhumanity are rooted in the inhumanity of centuries past."[62] Globalization can be seen, as Anibal Quijano proposes, precisely as "the culmination of a process that began with the constitution of America and colonial/modern Eurocentered capitalism as a new global power."[63] That power turns on two fundamental axes: the social classification of the world population along racial lines, and the new structure of the control of labor and its sources and products.[64] All this, as Quijano argues, has been followed by the constitution of Europe as a new entity/identity — the elaboration of a Eurocentric perspective of knowledge, the central elements of which are dualism, whose radicalization can be seen, for example, in the Cartesian fracture between a rational subject and a body that until then, in Christian thought, represented an unresolved ambivalence between the soul and the risen body, and, from the eighteenth century onwards, an evolutionism that formulated the birth of "human" history as a continuous, linear progression from the "state of nature" to its culmination in European "civilization."[65] A Eurocentric perspective of knowledge has codified and placed the "inhuman" at a specific place on the timeline — as prior to "*human* history," or better, as "without history," as "primitive," thus legitimizing infantilization, inferiorization, exploitation, and enslavement, while naming the subject "Black Man" as living proof of the inability to separate instinct from the mind/reason.[66]

Historically, Black Reason, as Mbembe suggests, is the result of colonialism, enslavement, and apartheid, and it refers to the paradigm of subjection, to a model of extraction and to pillage, as well as to the figure of knowledge and fantasies.[67] But what

---

62 Elaine Coburn, "Critique de la raison nègre: A review," *Decolonization: Indigeneity, Education & Society* 3, no. 2 (2014): 177.
63 Anibal Quijano, "Coloniality of Power, Eurocentrism, and Latin America," *Nepantla: Views from South* 1, no. 3 (2000): 533.
64 Ibid., 533–34.
65 Ibid., 534–42.
66 Mbembe, *Critique of Black Reason*, 30.
67 Mbembe in Gržinić, "Kolonializem Evrope," 114.

was once a condition brought about by Atlantic colonialism is today, in neoliberal, global capitalism, a universal condition of humanity as such.[68] Mbembe, as Marina Gržinić states in her reading of Mbembe's *Critique of Black Reason*, rearticulates Gilles Deleuze's concept of "becoming" and proposes a universalization of the figure of the "Black" as a figure below the level of humanity, as it most accurately describes the state of (universal) humanity in the current system of neoliberal global capitalism.[69] Race is a mechanism of reification, a security system and a mode of governmentality[70] — and above all, it is a raw material "from which difference and a *surplus* — a kind of life that can be wasted and spent without limit — are produced."[71]

As Gržinić argues, "European provincialism, with its Eurocentric thinking that transforms Europe into a provincial Fortress, has its own (additional) emblematic figure of the becoming "Black" of the world — along with a further violent discriminatory policy towards black citizens of Europe (the second and third generation)"[72] — refugees and asylum seekers. Gržinić's thesis not only implies a harsh critique of the aphasic, western-European system of thought unwilling to re-think its own colonial past and the self-evident idea of freedom, along with its implementation, but also declares that what we have at the heart of Europe, alongside the biopolitical regulation of bodies, is what Mbembe describes as a result of "necropolitics": "new and unique forms of social existence in which vast populations are subjected to conditions of life conferring upon them the status of *living dead*."[73]

Moreover, neoliberal global financial capitalism, as has been shown by Joseph Vogl, has acquired a sort of an aesthetic — sublime — character, because it is floating (digital), intangible (it escapes control), unrepresentable (in sublime monetary sums,

---

68 Ibid., 115.
69 Ibid., 108.
70 Mbembe, *Critique of Black Reason*, 35.
71 Ibid., 34. Italics in original.
72 Gržinić, "Kolonializem Evrope," 109.
73 Mbembe, "Necropolitics," 40. Italics in original.

which cannot be captured by any sensible material), and, above all, because it has gained, through the transcendence of material production, the creative ability of self-creation, and thus has produced a series of "zones of indistinctions," or so-called "grey areas," where political and economic decisions take place.[74] All this, as Vogl states, makes for powerful and fatal effects, "effects of sovereignty,"[75] storms of chaos, leaving behind the desolated landscapes of the present and already sold future.

Eyal Weizman writes that, during the early Enlightenment, three limit conditions were set in interrelation: "the threshold of the forest — a shifting environmental condition together with its unique climate; the threshold of the law — the political limit of territory and sovereignty; and the threshold of the human — a blurry limit to the human species";[76] these frontiers have become and remain entangled in such a way that shifts within one cause shifts in the others.[77]

2.3 Speculative Realism

In "'Afterwards': Struggling with Bodies in the Dump of History,"[78] Gržinić also proposes the following thesis: if the major characteristic of biopolitics is pseudo-humanism, and

---

[74] Joseph Vogl, *The Specter of Capital* (Stanford: Stanford University Press), 2015.

[75] Joseph Vogl, "The Sovereignty Effect: Markets and Power in the Economic Regime," in *Qui Parle: Critical Humanities and Social Sciences* 23, no. 1 (Fall/Winter 2014): 125–55.

[76] Eyal Weizman, "Are They Human?" *e-flux,* October 10, 2016, https://www.e-flux.com/architecture/superhumanity/68645/are-they-human/.

[77] Ibid.

[78] Marina Gržinić, "'Afterwards': Struggling with Bodies in the Dump of History," in *Body between Materiality and Power: Essays in Visual Studies*, ed. Nasheli Jiménez del Val (Newcastle upon Tyne: Cambridge Scholars Publishing, 2016), 163–82. Gržinić's analysis exposes today's humanitarian refugee crisis within the European Union and Europe as "one of the hardest lessons to learn for Western academic vocabulary" (164); and by substituting the biopolitical concept of the "body" with the necropolitical notion of "political flesh" (i.e., the status of bodies in refugee centers), this analysis proposes the latter as the actual matter for thought to think (179–80).

if the biopolitical optical machine could be summarized with the phrase "more human than human"[79] — since "human" is not only the product constructed against the animal (speciesism) but also a figure which is not reducible to the human animal (racism) — then the necropolitical optical machine, together with post-humanism, or the "necropolitical injunction of neoliberal global capitalism, is 'still too human!'"[80] This means that "the optical machine of necrocapitalism cannot view any class, race, and gender specificities of the post-human, as this would imply the return of the social antagonism at the heart of the (post)-human."[81]

My proposal here is to follow this "still 'too human, much too human'"[82] agenda, a dream of transcending the notion of the "human," precisely within the terrain of speculative realism. I will lean upon the introduction to *Speculations V: Aesthetics in the 21st Century,* where Ridvan Askin, Andreas Hägler, and Phillip Schweighauser give an overview of the developments of debates within twenty-first century aesthetics.[83]

The authors focus on aesthetics particularly after the speculative turn,[84] after the articulation of the so-called speculative realists, a faction within continental philosophy. Speculative realists state that continental philosophy ever since Kant's *Critique*

---

79 Gržinić, "'Afterwards,'" 177.
80 Ibid.
81 Ibid.
82 Ibid.
83 Ridvan Askin, Andreas Hägler, and Philipp Schweighauser, "Introduction: Aesthetics after the Speculative Turn," in *Speculations V: Aesthetics in the 21st Century,* eds. Ridvan Askin, Paul J. Ennis, Andreas Hägler, and Philipp Schweighauser (Brooklyn: punctum books, 2014), 6–38.
84 The notion of the "speculative turn" is linked to the conference entitled "Speculative Realism," which took place in April 2007 at Goldsmiths, University of London, and with the contributions of Ray Brassier, Iain Hamilton Grant, Graham Harman, and Quentin Meillassoux. See Rick Dolphijn, "Peter Gratton, Speculative Realism: Problems and Prospects," review of *Speculative Realism: Problems and Prospects,* by Peter Gratton, *Notre Dame Philosophical Reviews: An Electronic Journal,* March 29, 2016, http://ndpr.nd.edu/news/65706-speculative-realism-problems-and-prospects/.

of Pure Reason[85] — with Kant's introduction of a split between the noumenal, the world as it is "in-itself," and the phenomenal, the world as it shows itself "for/to us" — has forgotten to think "reality," or has stopped being engaged in that thought. These reproaches, as picturesquely described by Goran Vranešević, are the result of current "doubts about a subjectively totalized world, which with its limitations, like a flat world, prevents expeditions to the world's vastness. More specifically, they are about the regions of existence that seemed to be lost forever, since they were initially replaced by the inaccessible world beyond [or great beyond], and then by the further twist of subjective finality."[86]

What is particularly interesting is that the contemporary debates about aesthetics, as is argued in the aforementioned introduction, bring to the forefront the internal divide of speculative realist philosophy into two poles, a divide which was already announcing itself after the first wave of enthusiasm for the speculative turn subsided.[87] Askin, Hägler, and Schweighauser situate this internal division of speculative realist thought in analogy with eighteenth-century discussions about taste, which took place between rationalists and empiricists.[88]

This discourse on taste, as the authors argue, is particularly appealing to thinkers of the *empiricist* pole of speculative realism (the other is thus named *rationalist*),[89] since it offers an entry into things as they are in their reality, while simultaneously enabling the possibility of their "dehumanization" (note

---

85 Immanuel Kant, *Critique of Pure Reason,* ed. and trans. Paul Guyer and Allen W. Wood (Cambridge: Cambridge University Press, 1998).

86 Goran Vranešević, "Prihajajoči svet in žalovanje za njim" ["The Coming World and Mourning for It"], *Časopis za kritiko znanosti, domišljijo in novo antropologijo* 39, no. 248 (2012): 76. The translations from the Slovene are mine.

87 Askin et al., "Introduction," 29.

88 Ibid.

89 British reflections on taste dealt with notions such as intuition, sensation, perception, and so on; Askin, Hägler, and Schweighauser mention the forerunners of Alexander Gottlieb Baumgarten's aesthetics as a science of sensuous cognition: Joseph Addison, Richard Steele, Anthony Ashley Cooper, and Francis Hutcheson.

the gesture of making positive a term historically signifying the process of de-"humanization!"), insofar as they relate to the structure of reality as such, and not solely to the domain of the human faculty of judgment.[90] Askin, Hägler, and Schweighauser thus explicate a series of attempts to extend aesthetic thinking to a non-human world: the attempts of Steven Shaviro and Tim Morton, who deal with Kant's notion of taste, since his judgments on taste are not regulated by the concepts and because they are disinterested; the attempts of Graham Harman and Morton, who deal with object-oriented aesthetics, as manifested in the theory of "allure," referring to an object able to taste, intuit, sense, and perceive another object; the attempt of Iain Hamilton Grant's aesthetics, which refers to the intuition of nature's forces and potencies; and the attempt of Shaviro's cosmology, which describes the domain of apprehension, the domain of relationality per se.[91] For all these writers of the empirical half of speculative realism, any encounter is always already a site of aesthetic experience; and for all of them, aesthetics is different from conceptual knowledge, while at the same time being preliminary to it.[92]

"Given the expansion of aesthetics into the non-human realm," Askin, Hägler, and Schweighauser state, "this is also the moment when aesthetics is pushed from the domain of human epistemology into that of general ontology. Ceasing to be a particular kind of human relation to the world, it becomes a general descriptor of relationality of/in the world."[93] Moreover, "in this framework, human epistemology only builds on and comes after the general aesthetic structure of/in being. Indeed, 'subjectless experience' underlies and comes to determine cognising subjects."[94]

However, while the empiricist pole of speculative realism argues for "subjectless experience," the rationalist pole argues

---

90 Askin et al., "Introduction," 30–31.
91 Ibid., 31.
92 Ibid.
93 Ibid.
94 Ibid., 32.

for "experience-less subjects."[95] Rationalists, in their critique of the empiricist pole, Askin, Hägler, and Schweighauser argue, disagree about the reification of aesthetic experience, and about "human" terminology (such as intuition, perception, etc.) used when talking about "non-human relations" and objects; rationalists, that is, see a problem in confusing "human" and "non-human" relations as well as in preventing "the rational inquiry into human and non-human relations."[96] For them, epistemology governs and determines aesthetics.

In situating possible objections to empiricist speculative realism — and, before that, with a reference to the "father" of the term "aesthetics," Alexander Gottlieb Baumgarten, legitimizing and justifying Baumgarten's position within rationalistic thought — Askin, Hägler, and Schweighauser further recall a problem that they see as common to both poles of speculative realism: the emergence of transcendental philosophy.

Kant's invention of the transcendental intervenes in the very discussion between rationalists and empiricists — and more, the speculative realists with their condemnation of correlationism, the latter arguing that it is impossible to discuss the questions of subjectivity independent from objectivity and the same inversely, point precisely to transcendental philosophy.[97] Askin, Hägler, and Schweighauser thus argue that what we are actually witnessing today in the terrain of speculative realists' debates is exactly the transformation of the concept of the transcendental.[98] For all of the speculative realists retain, from Kant's invention of the transcendental, the notion of immanence; and what is common to all speculative realists is that they are all concerned about "this world," while elaborating their "thisworldly" philosophies![99] Moreover, Askin, Hägler, and Schweighauser argue that what all speculative realists have in common is the very rejection of Kant's Copernican Revolution, and thus the centrality of human

---

95 Ray Brassier quoted in Askin et al., "Introduction," 30.
96 Askin et al., "Introduction," 32.
97 Ibid.
98 Ibid., 33.
99 Ibid.

experience and its conditions of possibility, but in two different ways: while the empiricist pole rejects the "human" in "*human experience,*" the other side rejects the "experience" as such.[100] As they state:

> On the one side, what results is an *ontological* recasting of the transcendental as it applies to reality per se: a transcendental empiricism (Grant, Harman, Morton, Shaviro); on the other side, we have an *epistemological* account of the powers of human thought to pierce this very same reality: a transcendental rationalism (Brassier, Meillassoux).[101]

With this rough presentation of the symptoms of the current ontological and epistemological uncertainty within the very "system of thought," I can now proceed to present the state of things in necrocapitalism, making a straightforward analogy with what Mbembe describes as the reinvention of animism.

Additionally, considering what we stated earlier regarding the idea of race, we might say that a critique similar to the one that speculative realists addressed to continental philosophy may now also be made about the very philosophy of speculative realism itself. Yet my critique here is far from an endeavor to defend Kant's system of thought. As we have seen, Kant is the best friend of both poles of speculative realists (but not also their enemy as Askin, Hägler, and Schweighauser have argued[102]), whose "speculative register for unifying the world"[103] has expanded the horizon of the world to other realities to the extent that it now "accepts all possible and impossible objects [...] introduced from the outside,"[104] thus falling into a trap of "(contingent) choice: whether the world or object or subject or … it is always directly

---

100 Ibid.
101 Ibid. Italics in original.
102 Ibid.
103 Vranešević, "Prihajajoči svet," 81.
104 Ibid.

embodied as an object."[105] Sometimes, we also have to do with the resurrected dead or with specters.

By rejecting the centrality of human experience and its conditions of possibility, both poles avoid having to think the very "racial flesh," which was, historically, ontologically and epistemologically situated "at the threshold of the human,"[106] and which should be addressed in its numerous contemporary modes. Moreover, if one group of the speculative realists specifically rejects the "human" in human experience, and the other "experience" as such, it is clear that both poles are "aphasic," also with regard to the very idea of the human, the human as a concept construed through the very processes of racialization.

It is worth recalling that already in 1997 Emmanuel Chukwudi Eze brilliantly elaborated on the "color" of Kant's reason/Reason (to which we can add that reason/Reason is neither "genderless" nor "classless").[107] Kant — the philosopher of the system — as Eze stated, "had uncritically assumed that the particularity of European existence is *the* empirical as well as ideal model of humanity, of *universal* humanity,"[108] "taken as humanity *in itself*,"[109] which, in its greatest perfection, seems to (allegedly) reside within the white race. Furthermore, as Eze put it,

> it would be a mistake to believe that Kant contributed nothing new or of original consequence to the study of "race" or to the problem of European ethnocentrism in general. Strictly speaking, Kant's anthropology and geography offer the strongest, if not the only, sufficiently articulated theoretical philosophical justification of the superior/inferior clas-

---

[105] Ibid. Ellipsis in original.
[106] I refer here to the aforementioned title of Carr's "At the Thresholds of the 'Human.'"
[107] Emmanuel Chukwudi Eze, "The Color of Reason: The Idea of 'Race' in Kant's Anthropology," in *Postcolonial African Philosophy: A Critical Reader*, ed. Emmanuel Chukwudi Eze (Cambridge: Blackwell Publishers, 1997), 103–40.
[108] Ibid., 117. Italics in original.
[109] Ibid. Italics in original.

sification of "races of men" of any European writer up to his time.[110]

2.4 Animism

In a lecture entitled "Democracy in the Age of Dynamism," Mbembe's central thesis is that late capitalism, as we know it today, represents some sort of a final stage of commodification, marked by the convergence of capitalism and the reinvention of animism.[111] The concept of animism, as it was introduced into anthropology at the end of the nineteenth century by Edward Burnett Tylor, attributes to the so-called "primitive societies," in a manner that infantilizes their beliefs, as they seemingly represent some kind of pre-stage in the evolution from religion to science, the belief that there is life in inanimate matter, that inert objects have a life which could be activated and animated.[112] According to Mbembe's view, this reinvention of animism in the context of current neoliberal global necro-capitalism works in two directions.

The first direction, as Mbembe elaborates it, refers to the "manufacturing of objects as subjects," to granting the form of life especially to new technological objects, and more generally to commodities, or to financial capital itself. This direction simultaneously implies, on the one hand, some kind of restating of commodity fetishism, and on the other, it also relates to the life within the object itself, to the life that has been imprinted in objects by preceding violent, politically animated human production, visible in wars for monopolies over mineral resources used in the production of new technological objects.[113]

---

110 Ibid., 129. Italics in original.
111 Mbembe, "Democracy in the Age of Dynamism."
112 Ibid. See also Mbembe's "Technologies of Happiness in the Age of Animism," public lecture at the European Graduate School, Saas-Fee, Switzerland and Valetta, Malta, March 27, 2016, https://www.youtube.com/watch?v=nIijTCn8Gh4.
113 Gržinić, "Kolonializem Evrope," 121. See also John E. Drabinski, "Mbembe, Democracy, Animism," December 6, 2013, https://jdrabinski.wordpress.com/2013/12/06/mbembe-democracy-animism/, and Mbembe, "Democracy in the Age of Animism."

Moreover, this direction of animism does not only imply the traces of life in objects — the granting of life to the objects themselves has serious consequences for life as such and its agency. In another lecture, entitled "Rethinking Democracy Beyond the Human," Mbembe, referring to Luciana Parisi and her "Automated Thinking and the Limits of Reason" from 2016, talks about the emergence of an Electronic Reason, which weakens and is replacing what we once called Public Reason. According to Mbembe, agency has become an ability no longer exclusive to human beings, while "automated thinking" (i.e., algorithmic thinking) is not only challenging the (human) mind in terms of its own limits, but is also gradually releasing us from the duties of governing ourselves.[114] The latest attention-grabbing example of awarding life to an object is the humanoid robot Sophia, who was even granted Saudi Arabian citizenship at the Future Investment Initiator Congress at Riyadh at the end of October in 2017.[115] However, Sophia is probably not the first such case, since already, on 30 January 2017, a humanoid robot named Fran Pepper was registered in the Belgian birth register.[116] These accelerated changes concerning life and the latest technology are opening up a number of questions regarding democracy in the age of new technologies, not least, if life now resides within the concept of citizenship, in parallel with questions about all those who are not entitled to get or have citizenship.

The second, and closely intertwined with the first, direction of animism, if I can return to it, relates to the "manufac-

---

114 Achille Mbembe, "Rethinking Democracy Beyond the Human," public lecture at the European Graduate School, Valetta, Malta, October 16, 2017, https://www.youtube.com/watch?v=A_k3YIupGok.

115 The humanoid replied to the question of the awareness of herself as a robot with a question in reply: "How do you know you are human?" See Anja Pavlič Jerič, "Savdska Arabija prva država, ki je podelila državljanstvo robotu" ["Saudi Arabia Is the First Country to Grant Citizenship to a robot"], *Rtvslo,* October 27, 2017, https://www.rtvslo.si/zabava/zanimivosti/savdska-arabija-prva-drzava-ki-je-podelila-drzavljanstvo-robotu/436323.

116 See "Un robot inscrit au registre des naissances à Hasselt," *NWS,* January 30, 2017, http://deredactie.be/cm/vrtnieuws.francais/Soci%25C3%25A9t%25C3%25A9/1.2879299.

turing of subjects as objects," which shows itself as a perverse form of subjectivation through thinghood, due to the fact that objects now function as virtual transformations of ourselves in relation to them.[117] According to Mbembe, commodity fetishism has reached the stage at which objects possess their own lives, which, it seems, are the only things worthy of this name, and our task is therefore to become animist objects (i.e., virtual identities) in order to capture the life now dwelling and being animated between the object and the object, in the field of this "other humanity," or "in-humanity."[118]

2.5 Coda
Bringing the idea of race to the forefront of contemporary philosophical debates is not simply a gesture of rebellion, going against "colonial aphasia." It is — if I intensify the coinage "the effect of blackness," which Edmund Burke used in elaborating the "horror" and "threat" that the black, female body triggered in the white bourgeois subject[119] — a gesture toward "the effect of a change in the fundamental arrangements of knowledge."[120]

Conclusion

Acknowledging the need to open, and already opening, the Eurocentric, western archive to "other" perspectives, or to put it in line with Mbembe, to Black Reason, enables us not only to re-think our violent western, provincialized — and let's be honest, failed — "system of thought," but also to think anew the "human," if this void, as Foucault once stated, "does not create a deficiency; it does not constitute a lacuna that must be filled," or said alongside current trends: bridged with the prefix post-, "it is nothing more, and nothing less, than the unfolding of a space

---
[117] Mbembe, "Democracy in the Age of Dynamism." See also Gržinić, "Kolonializem Evrope," 121.
[118] Mbembe, "Democracy in the Age of Dynamism."
[119] See Armstrong, "'The Effects of Blackness.'"
[120] Michel Foucault, *The Order of Things: An Archaeology of the Human Sciences* (London: Routledge, 2005), 422.

in which it is once more possible to think."[121] For today's "effects of blackness" are twofold, ontological and epistemological.

---

[121] Ibid., 373.

Bibliography

Agamben, Giorgio. *Homo Sacer: Sovereign Power and Bare Life*. Translated by Daniel Heller-Roazen. Stanford: Stanford University Press, 1998.

———. *State of Exception*. Translated by Kevin Attell. Chicago: University of Chicago Press, 2005.

———. *The Open: Man and Animal*. Translated by Kevin Attell. Stanford: Stanford University Press, 2003.

Akomfrah, John, dir. *Handsworth Songs*. London: Black Audio Film Collective, 1986.

Armstrong, Meg. "'The Effects of Blackness': Gender, Race, and the Sublime in Aesthetic Theories of Burke and Kant." *Journal of Aesthetic and Art Criticism* 54, no. 3 (Summer 1996): 213–36. DOI: 10.2307/431624.

Askin, Ridvan, Andreas Hägler, and Philipp Schweighauser. "Introduction: Aesthetics after the Speculative Turn." In *Speculations V: Aesthetics in the 21st Century,* edited by Ridvan Askin, Paul J. Ennis, Andreas Hägler, and Philipp Schweighauser, 6–38. Brooklyn: punctum books, 2014.

Avila, Edward A. "Conditions of (Im)possibility: Necropolitics, Neoliberalism, and the Cultural Politics of Death in Contemporary Chicana/o Film and Literature." PhD diss., University of California, San Diego, 2012. https://escholarship.org/uc/item/7sh1f55b#main.

Bykov, Yuri, dir. *Durak [The Fool]*. St. Petersburg/Moscow: Rock Film Studio/Russian Ministry of Culture, 2014.

Carr, Brian. "At the Thresholds of the 'Human': Race, Psychoanalysis, and the Replication of Imperial Memory." *Cultural Critique* 39 (Spring 1998): 119–50. DOI: 10.2307/1354553.

Coburn, Elaine. "Critique de la raison nègre: A Review." *Decolonization: Indigeneity, Education & Society* 3, no. 2 (2014): 176–86. https://jps.library.utoronto.ca/index.php/des/article/view/22016.

Drabinski, John E. "Mbembe, Democracy, Animism." December 6, 2013. https://jdrabinski.wordpress.com/2013/12/06/mbembe-democracy-animism/.

Dolphijn, Rick. "Peter Gratton, Speculative Realism: Problems and Prospects." Review of *Speculative Realism: Problems and Prospects*, by Peter Gratton. *Notre Dame Philosophical Reviews: An Electronic Journal*, March 29, 2016. http://ndpr.nd.edu/news/65706-speculative-realism-problems-and-prospects/.

Eze, Emmanuel Chukwudi. "The Color of Reason: The Idea of 'Race' in Kant's Anthropology." In *Postcolonial African Philosophy: A Critical Reader*, edited by Emmanuel Chukwudi Eze, 103–40. Cambridge: Blackwell Publishers, 1997.

Fassbinder, Rainer Werner, dir. *In einem Jahr mit 13 Monden* [*In a Year of 13 Moons*]. Berlin: Filmverlag der Autoren; / Munich: Pro-ject Filmproduktion; Berlin: Tango Film, 1978.

Fisher, Mark. "The Land Still Lies: Handsworth Songs and the English riots." *Sight & Sound*, February 5, 2014. https://www.bfi.org.uk/news-opinion/sight-sound-magazine/comment/land-still-lies-handsworth-songs-and-english-riots.

Foucault, Michel. *"Society Must Be Defended": Lectures at the Collège De France, 1975–76*. Edited by Mauro Bertani and Alessandro Fontana. Translated by David Macey. New York: Picador, 2003.

———. *The Order of Things: An Archaeology of the Human Sciences*. London: Routledge, 2005.

Gavras, Romain, dir. *M.I.A.'s Born Free*. London: Paradoxal Inc./XL Recordings, 2010.

Gonzalez, Ed. "Review: *In a Year of 13 Moons*." *Slant Magazine*, August 23, 2003. https://www.slantmagazine.com/film/in-a-year-of-13-moons/.

Gržinić, Marina. "'Afterwards': Struggling with Bodies in the Dump of History." In *Body Between Materiality and Power: Essays in Visual Studies*, edited by Nasheli Jiménez del Val, 163–82. Newcastle upon Tyne: Cambridge Scholars Publishing, 2016.

———. "Capital, Repetition." *Reartikulacija* 8 (2009): 3–4.

———. "Ex-Yugoslav Avant-garde Film Production and its Early Works Seen through Biopolitics and Necropolitics." In *Za ideju — protiv stanja*. Edited by Branka Ćurčić, Sarita Matijević, Zoran Pantelić, and Želimir Žilnik, 148–58. Novi Sad: Playground produkcija, 2009.

———. "Kolonializem Evrope, dekolonialnost in rasizem" ["Colonialism of Europe, Decoloniality and Racism"]. In *Politika, estetika in demokracija*, edited by Marina Gržinic, 107–22. Ljubljana: Založba ZRC SAZU, 2015.

———. "Sandra Lahire." *Luxonline*. https://www.luxonline.org.uk/artists/sandra_lahire/(printversion).html.

———. "The Emergence of the Political Subject." *Emancipation of the Resistance,* March 2013. https://emancipationofresistance.wordpress.com/grzinic/.

Gržinić, Marina, and Aneta Stojnić, eds. *Shifting Corporealities in Contemporary Performance: Avant-Gardes in Performance.* Cham: Palgrave Macmillan, 2018.

Kant, Immanuel. *Critique of Pure Reason.* Edited and translated by Paul Guyer and Allen W. Wood. Cambridge: Cambridge University Press, 1998.

Lahire, Sandra, dir. *In Uranium Hex.* London: Arts Council of Great Britain, 1987.

López Petit, Satiago. *La movilización global: Breve tratado para atacar la realidad* [*Global Mobilization: Brief Treatise for Attacking Reality*]. Madrid: Traficantes de Sueños, 2009.

Lyotard, Jean-François. *The Inhuman: Reflections on Time.* Translated by Geoffrey Bennington and Rachel Bowlby. Cambridge: Polity Press, 1998.

Mbembe, Achille. *Critique of Black Reason.* Translated by Laurent Dubois. Durham: Duke University Press, 2017.

———. "Democracy in the Age of Dynamism." Lecture presented at the Hutchins Center for African American Research, Cambridge, Harvard University, December 4, 2013. https://www.youtube.com/watch?v=MtBJ-M-cK4s.

———. "Necropolitics." Translated by Libby Meintjes. *Public Culture* 15, no. 1 (Winter 2003): 11–40. DOI: 10.1215/08992363-15-1-11.

———. "Rethinking Democracy Beyond the Human." Public lecture presented at the European Graduate School, Valetta, Malta, October 16, 2017. https://www.youtube.com/watch?v=A_k3YIupGok.

———. "Technologies of Happiness in the Age of Animism." Public lecture presented at the European Graduate School, Saas-Fee, Switzerland and Valetta, Malta, March 27, 2016. https://www.youtube.com/watch?v=nIijTCn8Gh4.

Nemes, László, dir. *Saul fia* [*Son of Saul*]. Budapest: Laokoon Filmgroup/Hungarian National Film Fund, 2015.

Ochs, Phil. "The Battle of Algiers." *Life of a Rebel,* May 19, 2008. http://phil-ochs.blogspot.com/2008/05/battle-of-algiers.html.

Pasolini, Pier Paolo, dir. *Salò o le 120 giornate di Sodoma* [*Salò, or the 120 Days of Sodom*]. Rome: Produzioni Europee Associate (PEA); Paris: Les Productions Artistes Associés, 1975.

Pavlič Jerič, Anja. "Savdska Arabija prva država, ki je podelila državljanstvo robotu" ["Saudi Arabia Is the First Country to Grant Citizenship to a Robot"]. *Rtvslo,* October 27, 2017. https://www.rtvslo.si/zabava/zanimivosti/savdska-arabija-prva-drzava-ki-je-podelila-drzavljanstvo-robotu/436323.

Pontecorvo, Gillo, dir. *La battaglia di Algeri* [*The Battle of Algiers*]. Algiers/Rome: Casbah Film/Igor Film, 1966.

Quijano, Anibal. "Coloniality of Power, Eurocentrism, and Latin America." *Nepantla: Views from South* 1, no. 3 (2000): 533–80.

Reich, Elizabeth. *Militant Visions: Black Soldiers, Internationalism, and the Transformation of American Cinema.* New Brunswick: Rutgers University Press, 2016.

Resnais, Alain, dir. *Nuit et brouillard* [*Night and Fog*]. Paris: Argo Films, 1956.

Roschy, Birgit. "Helma Sanders-Brahms: 'Germany Pale Mother.'" *Goethe Institut,* July 2014. https://www.goethe.de/ins/au/en/kul/mag/20397223.html.

Salgado, Rubia, Gergana Mineva, and Kollektiv Women. "Stream of Memory." In *Border Thinking: Disassembling Histories of Racialized Violence,* edited by Marina Gržinić, 48–58. Berlin: Sternberg Press, 2018.

Sanders-Brahms, Helma, dir. *Deutschland bleiche Mutter* [*Germany Pale Mother*]. Berlin/Berlin/Cologne: Helma Sanders-Brahms Filmproduktion/Literarisches Colloquium/Westdeutscher Rundfunk (WDR), 1980.

Stoler, Ann Laura. "Colonial Aphasia: Race and Disabled Histories in France." *Public Culture* 23, no. 1 (2011): 121–56. DOI: 10.1215/08992363-2010-018.

"Un robot inscrit au registre des naissances à Hasselt." *NWS,* January 30, 2017. http://deredactie.be/cm/vrtnieuws.francais/Soci%25C3%25A9t%25C3%25A9/1.2879299.

Vogl, Joseph. "The Sovereignty Effect: Markets and Power in the Economic Regime." *Qui Parle: Critical Humanities and Social Sciences* 23, no. 1 (Fall/Winter 2014): 125–55. DOI: 10.5250/quiparle.23.1.0125.

———. *The Specter of Capital.* Translated by Joachim Redner and Robert Savage. Stanford: Stanford University Press, 2015.

Vranešević, Goran. "Prihajajoči svet in žalovanje za njim" ["The Coming World and Mourning for It"]. *Časopis za kritiko znanosti, domišljijo in novo antropologijo* 39, no. 248 (2012): 76–88.

Weizman, Eyal. "Are They Human?" *e-flux,* October 10, 2016. https://www.e-flux.com/architecture/superhumanity/68645/are-they-human/.

Zvyagintsev, Andrey, dir. *Leviathan.* Moscow: Non-Stop Productions/A Company Russia/Russian Ministry of Culture/Fond kino/RuArts Foundation, 2014.

Žilnik, Želimir, dir. *Rani Radovi* [*Early Works*]. Beograd/Novi Sad: Avala Film/Neoplanta film, 1969.

7

Absolute Xenogenesis: Speculations on an Unnatural History of Life

Eckardt Lindner

> It must not be supposed that atoms of every sort can be linked in every variety of combination. If that were so, you would see monsters coming into being everywhere. Hybrid growths of man and beast would arise. Lofty branches would spread here and there from a living body. Limbs of land-beast and sea-beast would often be conjoined. Chimeras breathing flame from hideous jaws would be reared by nature throughout the all-generating earth.
> — Lucretius, *On the Nature of the Universe*[1]

1. Dreams of the Noumenal Horror of Life

When Kant was still a young man he was haunted by nightmares, not of reason and its unrestrained (mis-)adventures but of a more existential nature. His *Anthropology* contains some of the most private moments in his oeuvre, in which he recounts a

---

1   Lucretius, *On the Nature of the Universe,* trans. R.E. Latham (Harmondsworth: Penguin, 1982), 80.

dream that he "had fallen into the water and was being turned around, coming close to drowning."[2] However petrifying, Kant finds the homeostatic function even in such terror, insofar as it serves to animate the flow of blood, putting even the *incubus* in the service of the proliferation of life — dreaming prevents the identity of sleep and death. Dreams are first and foremost a shock to the system. While vital, potentially even a condition for corporeal being, dreams have no place in critical philosophy — how would one conceive of sleep as transcendental? Though dreams are constituted by spatiotemporal collapses and categorial breakdowns — "we are [...] transported back to long vanished time," we "speak with people long since dead" — the *Anthropology* rejects dreams not due to the possible confusion on grounds of judgment, subjective or objective, as the *Critique of Pure Reason* has it but for the privacy of their contents. There is no intersubjective dream-space.[3] We can assume that the Anthropology's argument cements the first *Critique*'s one.

With the *Dreams of a Spirit-Seer*, the discussion of the philosophical merit of dreams encounters the question of life as after-life, as claimed by Swedenborg, who indeed claimed to be in contact with the dead. To communicate with the deceased, we would have to assume a "primitive force" which animates the body while living and exists independently of this body as a separate entity after death, while still being able to interact with the living through communication. Kant's text is not so much concerned with the claim of the existence of these entities but is rather concerned with finding a method for legitimizing or disposing of them. We should acknowledge Kant's outright rejection of the psychological solutions, either the Spirit-Seers are simply liars or plainly insane, as a genuine philosophical gesture, a gesture of trying to ensure the unity of his own account of experience by viewing these deceptions as irregular cases of

---

2   Immanuel Kant, *Anthropology from the Pragmatic Point of View*, ed. and trans. Robert B. Loudon (Cambridge: Cambridge University Press, 2006), 83.
3   Ibid.

the regular operations of a faculty. The problem of seeing spirits is first and foremost a spatial one. Our perception involves the apperception of the location of objects, real or imaginary.[4] While in the case of the sensation of external objects, the lines of our impression meet outside the brain, fantasies are produced by the lines of impression meeting inside it. Therefore, we perceive the location of the object more or less clearly as a *focus imaginarius*. Being deceived by the illusion of seeing spirits could consequently be explained by a failure in registering the *focus imaginarius* correctly and mistaking a fantasy as an external object. Most likely such a mistake could be explained by a disturbance in the functional apparatus of the brain, Kant assumes.[5] However, such an explanation does not yet touch on the problem *de jure*. Even if the insanity of Swedenborg is conceived as a physical dysfunction, observing the "vibrations" within the brain does not give any indication of the legitimacy of the claims they supposedly prove or, in other words, no difference in kind (sane/insane) can be inferred from the differences in degree (vibration$_1$, vibration$_2$, vibration$_n$). The Spirit-Seers are however not the only ones dreaming up the existence of immaterial entities; eighteenth century philosophy is haunted by "souls," "obscure qualities," or "spirits" — metaphysical specters.

But rather than locating the *focus imaginarius* incorrectly, the metaphysician lets the lines of reason and experience "run alongside each other into infinity without ever meeting."[6] So, the problem "of beginning I don't know where, and of coming I don't know whither" seems to involve a peculiar kind of kinship between the two types of dreams.[7] In fact, Kant is not sure what the difference is, though he maintains that one cannot deduce the origin of one kind of dream from the other. But even more than that, they might be complementary, insofar as Kant's accusation against the Spirit-Seers changes in the course

---

4   Immanuel Kant, *Dreams of a Spirit-Seer*, ed. Frank Sewall, trans. Emmanuel F. Goerwitz (London: Swan Sonnenschein & Co, 1900), 78.
5   Ibid., 80.
6   Ibid., 90.
7   Ibid.

of the text, to an illusion being an invention of reason, which subsequently gets substantiated by false impressions. If, on the one hand, Swedenborg becomes a philosopher by proposing an intelligibility of the soul on the basis of his experiences, then philosophers can become Spirit-Seers when they furnish their concepts based on reason with experiences by virtue of their academic craft. Both, in their own way, seem haunted as well as vitalized by an internal relation of reason to madness.[8] In Swedenborg, Kant discovers a doppelgänger, a "twin."[9] The affliction that seems to produce false images, both in the "Reason-dreamer" and the "Sensation-dreamer," is therefore not located in the senses themselves, but in the inability to make them an object to a judgment that would allow for a distinction between sensation proper and fantasy. The principles of such a judgment can neither be supplied by the understanding, nor by reason. The understanding has no principles a priori with which to supply the faculty of judgment. And reason cannot remedy the cause of the illusion — the misinterpretation of the *focus imaginarius* — since it is not the result of a logical mistake. One cannot reason away an impression.

Faced with the dreams of the metaphysician, Kant returns to his own definition of life as the "inner capacity to determine one's self by one's own will power."[10] If, however, the matter that fills space is incapable of such autonomy, life must be immaterial. The consequence of such a characterization is that we have no "data" to classify this principle positively and must therefore resort to categorizing it negatively. But even these negations cannot be grounded in experience, or conclusions, but can only be constructed "upon invention, to which a reason deprived of all other expedients finally resorts."[11] Life, it seems, insofar

---

[8] Cf. Monique David-Ménard, *La folie dans la raison pure: Kant lecture de Swedenborg* (Paris: Librairie Philosophique J.Vrin, 1990), 84.
[9] Friedemann Stengel, "Kant — 'Zwillingsbruder' Schwedenborgs?" in *Kant und Swedenborg: Zugänge zu Einem Umstrittenen Verhältnis*, ed. Friedemann Stegel (Tübingen: May Niemayer, 2008), 35.
[10] Kant, *Dreams of a Spirit-Seer*, 53.
[11] Ibid., 89.

as it can be thought, cannot be experienced, and thereby the thought itself becomes an invention or fabrication of reason. Life becomes a problem not only within philosophy, but for philosophy itself, insofar as life is a condition for thought. It indeed becomes Kant's pre-critical threshold, as it introduces the asymmetry between what can be thought and what can be known.

The *aporia* presented can, according to Kant, only be resolved by resorting to a "trick." In the same way that the transgressions against civil law by a merchant can only be detected by switching the places of weights and goods, we too must change the weighting on the "scales of reason [*Verstandeswage*]."[12] Thus, any judgment should not be judged by one's own reason by itself, but as if the reason of another would do it. Therefore, we have to use the inventions of reason as "*fictio heuristica,*"[13] to then be judged (or treated as if they were judged) by another member of the "community of spirits."[14]

The split between the sensible and the intelligible as the main methodological operation of the Dissertation functions as a transformation of the scale, with reason as the ultimate counterbalance to its own misadventures, without having to rely on private evidence only. All concepts of life trying to establish continuity between the material and the formal, such as hylozoism, must thereby be expelled *a priori,* since claiming that matter possesses the capacity to organize itself or give itself a unified form is tantamount to proposing that it gives itself its own law. Without the universality of the law as a generalizable counterweight, nothing would legitimize the distinction between the knowable and the thinkable in such a hylozoic cosmos. If being and thinking were identical, there would be nothing, *absolutely* nothing, shielding one from the allure of leaving the shores of reason and venturing into the sea of speculation, only to lose one's mind over the impossibility of navigation.

---

12 Ibid., 85.
13 Immanuel Kant, "Brief an Moses Mendelssohn 8. April," in *Briefwechsel* (Berlin: Preußische Akademie der Wissenschaften, 1922), 71.
14 Kant, *Dreams of a Spirit-Seer,* 53.

The *Critique of the Power of Judgment* returns to the question of life, relating it to purposiveness to determine it positively. In aesthetic and teleological common sense, the harmony of man and nature is given externally and internally, respectively. As such, we can only understand the purposiveness of organized beings in analogy to our purposes, by ultimately relating both to the whole of nature, whose teleological organization implies a divine creator, although a non-existent one.[15] This is true both for the speculative interest, insofar as the solution of the antinomy of the teleological judgment relies on the assumption of an intuitive understanding, and for practical reason, since the ends of nature can only be understood as the self-realization of freedom in nature. In Kant's genetic, or quasi-genetic, account of the striving for reason's unity towards organicity in the *Critique of the Power of Judgment,* such a conation legitimizes itself through the *life,* liveliness, or animation of the mind (*Gemüt*) in the reflective judgment in aesthetics. To understand the role of the "feeling of life" (*Lebensgefühl*), which is a feeling of "the powers of the mind reciprocally promoting each other," we first have to consider the role of the feeling of pleasure and unpleasure in the systematic approach of the third *Critique*.[16] Reflective judgment should be understood as performing a function or action by "means of which it strives to rise from intuitions to concepts in general."[17] It operates, since it lacks the "directions" commonly provided in determinative judgments by the understanding, by obtaining or creating its directions based on the dynamic interplay of the faculties. Since the unity of the systematic whole of nature and freedom must present itself as finality, the register of the faculty of reflective judgment is that of ends, while for reason it is freedom, and for understanding, the cognition of the object. Such an animating principle is able

---

15 Cf. Peter McLaughlin, *Kant's Critique of Teleology in Biological Explanation: Antinomy and Teleology* (Lewiston: Edwin Mellen Press, 1990), 170.

16 Immanuel Kant, *Critique of the Power of Judgment,* ed. Paul Guyer, trans. Guyer and Eric Matthews (Cambridge: Cambridge University Press, 2000), 230–31.

17 Ibid., 249.

to give credence to Kant's introduction of "spirit" as mind's animating principle in §49. If one only understands the function of reflective judgment in its schematic role as the manufacturing of accord in determinative knowledge, its motivation *and* spirit's introduction would not be plausible. Rather, reason has the inner drive to attain a "maximum," meaning unity or the unconditioned. In the reflective judgment then, imagination strives to emulate or mimic the "precedent of reason in attaining to a maximum."[18] The endeavor of organic unity in reflective judgment must be understood as a (almost Spinozist) conatus to obtain more being by striving, gesturing, or grasping towards the unconditioned. Neither such a striving nor the emulation of the imagination could be understood without the function of pleasure as elaborated above. The pre-logical function of reflective judgment therefore functions as a "metabolic filter of the psychic system," converting everything heterogenous into digestible elements, while simultaneously affirming and recreating the homeostasis of cognition.[19] The form of judgment thus serves as the uniting copula of freedom and nature; it becomes the Judgment of God.

The relation of God to His judgment changes in Kant's turn to the categorical as the essence of the *Critiques,* as Beaufret notes.[20] Rather than the Law following from the Good, in Kant, the Good follows from the Law as "a pure form that has no object, whether sensible or intelligible. It does not tell us what we must do, but what subjective rules we must obey no matter what our action."[21] As such, the final verdict is infinitely deferred and replaced with preliminary judgments only referring to ends; or,

---

18 Ibid., 314.
19 Louis Schreel, "Idea and Animation: A Study of the Immanent Sublime in Deleuze's Metaphysics," PhD diss., University of Antwerp, 2017, 404.
20 Jean Beaufret, "Précédé de Hölderlin et Sophocle," in *Remarques sur Oedipe/Remarques sur Antigone,* ed. Jean Beaufret, trans. François Fédier (Paris: Union générale éditions, 1965), 16.
21 Gilles Deleuze, "On Four Formulas," in *Essays Critical and Clinical,* trans. Daniel W. Smith and Michael A. Greco (Minneapolis: University of Minnesota Press, 1997), 32.

equally, since there is no final verdict, every day is judgment day in the infinite application of the Law. This inverts the divine immortality, since "it distills a 'slow death,' and continuously *defers the judgment of the Law.*"[22] As in Kafka, one is always before the Law. Nietzsche has already described the genealogy of judgment in his "doctrine of judgment" in the *Antichrist,* beginning with the creditor/debtor relation without the use of judgment expressed in the painful extraction of debt in tribal rites. Debt, however, shifts to the gods as creators and rulers, so that "the gods give lots to men, and that men, depending on their lots, are fit for some particular form, for some particular organic *end.*"[23] In a last twist, Christianity again dispenses with the prefigured lots for men, save for our judgment itself, and hence transfigures the individual into a self-judge, which in turn, as Foucault has shown, becomes the principle for the individuation of the sinful subject. Such infinite deference is the form of the judgment in Kant.

This uniting function of judgment is operative in Kant's judgment of God as a disjunctive syllogism. The reality of a thing is produced by the limitation of possibilities and, hence, the negation of all others. The disjunctive syllogism, "either-or," works exclusively, producing everything as what it is and excluding from it what it is not, subjecting everything to the identity in and of the concept. God restricts disjunction only to a "*negative and limitative use,*"[24] which in turn relies on the integrity and self-identity of the body as an internally organized being, realizing and reproducing only what it is. It is, however, not the assumption of God as "the sum total of all possibilities" that makes the restricted use of the disjunctive syllogism necessary but the form of the judgment that instates God as such a modal totality.

---

22 Ibid., 33.
23 Gilles Deleuze, "To Have Done with Judgment," in *Essays Critical and Clinical,* trans. Daniel W. Smith and Michael A. Greco (Minneapolis: University of Minnesota Press, 1997), 128.
24 Gilles Deleuze, *Logic of Sense,* ed. Constantin V. Boundas, trans. Mark Lester with Charles Stivale (New York: Columbia University Press, 1990), 296.

Thinking life through the divine, Kant follows the *vestigium* of God, as Bonaventure has it, His "mark" in creation. The reading of the *liber creature* then depends on the interpretation of the relation of creator and creature, either as continuous or as radical discontinuity, either as pure relation or as no relation, univocal or equivocal. While the former is riddled with indissoluble darkness (Meister Eckhart, Henry of Ghent), the latter levels all differences between nature and God (Duns Scotus). Either there is no possible knowledge of the divine or everything is divine: neither constitute proper knowledge. Considering the problems of these solutions in regard to the question of the name of the divine, Aquinas mediates between them through analogy. Hence, as Thacker writes, "[t]he creature is the life that is less-than-divine, the Creator is the life that is more-than-the-living."[25] The relation of Life and the living can therefore only be determined through the living, or, by the given. Since Kant's model of judgment establishes an analogical relation between the transcendental and the empirical, while the former conditions the latter, the former becomes a copy of what it conditions. For Kant, the transcendental life can only be determined through the empirical, establishing the transcendental-empirical double.

The deference of the final judgment of God, through which everything is integrated retroactively, leaves a space of indetermination, while the middle position of the analogy again invites the problems of univocity and equivocality when considering the equally analogous relation of the phenomenal and the noumenal. Together, they do not only indicate but create the horror of anonymity.

Whether one subscribes to the two-worlds or two-aspects interpretation of transcendental philosophy's phenomenal/noumenal split hardly matters for exploring the sphere that the split as such opens. One should be keenly aware of the horror of the noumenal, which prompts Kant's anti-Spinozism. As the *Critique of Practical Reason* has it, if man had full access to the

---

25 Eugene Thacker, *In the Dust of This Planet: Horror of Philosophy, Volume I* (Winchester: Zero Books, 2001), 119.

Ding-an-sich, then he would lose all autonomy and spontaneity and hence, "[t]he conduct of man, so long as his nature remained as it is now, would be changed into mere mechanism, where, as in a puppet show, everything would gesticulate well but no life would be found in the figures."[26] The possibility of diverging from the real causes is the positive condition of freedom. At the same time, duty exerts an uncanny violence in demanding from us the overcoming of *all* pathological subjective grounds of desire (*Triebfedern*), which includes our desire to survive. Such a command does not call for self-destruction, but for the suspension of life and death altogether as a possible horizon for moral action. Insofar as such a suspension must be made to will itself, the care for life must be introduced artificially later on. As such, duty — the call of the noumenal — presents itself as an unconditional command beyond life and death, beyond any possible negation. In short, it presents itself as the death drive, denaturalizing life, understood as surviving. The God of the judgment as disjunctive syllogism is not only the God of synthesis, but also of boundaries. Therefore, analogy serves as the paradoxical instance of a mediator between reality and appearance. At the same time, it must separate them, for in their identity transcendental freedom would be impossible. In insomnia, boredom, or loneliness, however, the anonymous real presents itself as pure, impersonal existence; a "there is," leveling the boundaries. And, as Levinas remarks, "[t]he rustling of the there is [...] is horror."[27] The terrifying thing is not that we might be wrong about what we think about the world, but that we might be right. For Kant, to be alive, man must be protected from the cosmos, the absolute of reality, and this turn away from infinity must be turned into a constitutive condition of finite subjectivity. Speculation is the name of the danger of plunging man back into the madness of the Real, which is not life, but death.

---

26 Immanuel Kant, *Critique of Practical Reason,* trans. Lewis White Black (New York: Palgrave Macmillan, 1956), 153.

27 Emmanuel Levinas, *Existence and Existents,* trans. Alphonso Lingis (Pittsburgh: Duquesne University Press, 2001), 55.

2. Being a Puppet

While both ghosts and dreams haunt eighteenth century philosophy, the "forced, artful, contrived, and violent study of depths" has its roots in the emerging fields of anatomy and dissection.[28] The *écorchés,* flayed skeletons, were used by anatomists as well as artists to ensure the resemblance of the artifice (e.g., a replica, drawing, or statue) to the original structure, and to create a liveliness not achievable through imagination. As such, they were usually displayed in poses imitating autonomous motion. Contrary to the "natural anatomy" of the early modern era, in which cadavers were used as primary objects of study, the "artificial anatomies" common since the Renaissance, but which blossomed during the eighteenth century, used mostly wax models, yielding several didactic advantages. This allowed for a selective and distorting gaze, idealizing bodies for display and categorization, as well as enlarging certain parts for better visibility. As the anatomist Vicq d'Azyr noticed, such replicas, imitating life, have an aesthetic benefit as well, since anatomy is concerned with bodies "devoid of the charm that attracts, but in addition it is accompanied by circumstances that repulse: Torn and bloody members, infections and unhealthy odors, the ghastly machinery of death," whose immediate impact can be minimized.[29] Prioritizing movement, not simply structure, as the decisive criterion for the representation of life, mechanical displays like Jacques de Vaucanson's *The Flute Player,* a musical automaton, or his *Duck,* designed to demonstrate the digestive system three-dimensionally in real time, followed a sentiment uttered by Vico, but repeated by Kant: "[h]e who would know the world must first manufacture it."[30] The study of cadavers was

---

28 Barbara Maria Stafford, *Body Criticism: Imaging the Unseen in Enlightenment Art and Medicine* (Cambridge: MIT Press, 1991), 47.
29 Félix Vicq d'Azyr, *Discours sur l'anatomie et de physiologie avec des planches coloriées, representant au naturel les divers organs de l'homme et des animaux* (Paris: l'Imprimerie de France, F.A. Didot l'aîné, 1786).
30 Immanuel Kant, *Opus Postumum,* ed. Eckart Förster, trans. Förster and Michael Rosen (Cambridge: Cambridge University Press, 1995), 41.

therefore not enough to gain adequate anatomical knowledge; they had to be seen in simulated, manufactured action. Life becomes a matter of engineering, "Nature = Industry."[31] The aim of the mechanical is not to supplant the order of the living, but to match it, to appear as lively as the original it seeks to imitate through exposing the living to an exorbitant light that drags life to the surface. It makes life visible and encases it within its possibilities. As such, the mechanical has to grow skin. The wooden fingers of Vaucanson's flute playing automaton, pressing on a metal flute, produced an unnervingly artificial sound. "Pure mechanics were not enough, and Vaucason had to import organic matter into his dead creation," so he covered the fingers in (animal) skin (*peau*).[32] In representing life, the anatomists faced a problem akin to the "uncanny valley" roboticists face nowadays, as the effective resemblance is not only a matter of artistic or technological mastery, nor merely a matter of pure accuracy nor the reproduction of universal structures but rather one of their dynamic interplay producing a singularity. As such, the tension between the general and the particular in judging "liveliness," which Kant sought to resolve through analogy, returns as the affect of the uncanny (*unheimlich*).

This is a horror based on an analogy between an excessive object and a finite subject through mediating representation. The failure of the latter to establish a successful communication, and community, of the two halves of the analogy leaves a remainder, a not-nothing, which inscribes itself into experience like a background noise, suddenly shifting into the foreground. This is the depth from which such objects rise — an abyss, stemming from a primordial dis-communication, antecedent to all relations. As such, the depth is created as it rises to the surface as a crack in it, but at the same time it presents itself as prior to the formation of the surface. It is an absolute indifference, ap-

---

31 Gilles Deleuze and Félix Guattari, *Anti-Oedipus: Capitalism and Schizophrenia*, trans. Robert Hurley, Mark Seem, and Helen R. Lane (Minneapolis: Minnesota University Press, 2000), 25.

32 Gaby Wood, *Edison's Eve: A Magical History of the Quest for Mechanical Life* (New York: Anchor, 2002), 26.

pearing as the in-difference of a human and non-human vitality. At the core, such a difference is still about resemblance and its failure to operate or establish itself in the analogical judgment.

The failure of the judgment, the dis-communication in the analogy, entails a two-fold negation: the object is excessive and displays a non-human vitality that is in-different to ours. Such a non-human vitality subjects us to the gaze of the object; it objectifies us. While the zombie is pure and empty subjectivity, mindless but unstoppable drive incarnate, puppets evoke an inert terror. The former is restless and always actualized movement, but the latter is potential activity, which is most effective if not realized. One leaves the room and upon returning, one is not sure if the hand of the doll was already in that position a minute ago. For Ligotti, whose work is filled with puppets, such unease, however, is just the prelude to the real terror that a puppet poses. These puppets are a symbol of what he calls "malignant uselessness." Their empty expressions, with their painted-on faces, are indicative of the horror of consciousness, bringing suffering into this world by being able to perceive the cosmic uselessness, forming an integral part of a (self-)universalized pessimism. The symbolic value that puppets embody as excessive imitations of the human form harbors the secret threat of subverting the hierarchies we thought to be foundational and/or constitutive for consciousness. This is the moment

> when a human being becomes objectified as a puppet and enters a world that he or she thought was just a creepy place inside of ours. What a jolt to find oneself a prisoner in this sinister sphere, reduced to a composite mechanism looking out on the land of the human, or that which we believe to be human by any definition of it, and yet be exiled from it.[33]

The horror is not in the sudden appearance of sentience, a particular organic consciousness in an otherwise dead, inorganic,

---

33 Thomas Ligotti, *Conspiracy Against the Human Race: A Contrivance of Horror* (New York: Hippocampus Press, 2010), 206.

and universal machine. On the contrary, the anonymous machine presents itself as the heart of the personal consciousness. The analogy is broken and, through its failure, reversed. Suddenly, a non-human life stares back at us with a thousand eyes — a ubiquitous gaze. This is the horror of the anatomical lineage of artificial life.

One becomes a meat-puppet in the eyes of the noumenal gaze. Such horror is not only ideal, but the failure of analogical judgment removes the boundaries between the sensible and the intelligible. It dismembers and (re-)connects the body at the same time, since its integrity relies on the judgment of God. It establishes a continuum between the human body, the animal body, plants, and objects, which blend into each other. Opening and exposing to the light of knowledge what was formerly concealed within the depths of the body creates the "natural" objects of anatomy through dissection, and also exhibits the "abjective" elements, constantly threatening the identity of the natural. The creations of Jean-Honoré Fragonard elevate such a continuity of body and world to art. In his plastinations, that is, *Fetus Dancing the Gigue* or *Man with a Mandible,* he prevented the decomposition of the body by injecting various aromatic spices and alcohol into the arteries, followed by the removal of the skin. Using injections of colored wax, he was able to preserve muscles, vessels, and even nerves, to display the prepared bodies in elaborate poses, and, more remarkable still, he was able to do so in interaction with other plastinated bodies. Alongside the praise of his skill, protestations of his contemporaries focused on the playful perversion of "natural" science, on the lack of his addition to serious knowledge. Much like the more recent discussion of the exhibition *Body Worlds* (*Körperwelten*) (2009) by Gunther von Hagens, the discussion centered on the aspect of spectacle and the repulsion such grotesque displays invoke through the superposition of the organism as simultaneously unified and fragmented. It is as if "[t]he body's inside […] shows up […] It is as if the skin, a fragile container, no longer guaranteed the integrity of one's 'own and clean self' but […] gave way before the dejection of its contents."³⁴ The vitalization of corpses, on the other hand, implies a subversion of the categories of dead and living matter. Thacker notes that the two meanings of nekros in classical culture harbor the tension of denoting the departed as the life of the body but also as the thingness of the corpse which "retains something residual of that life."³⁵ A second death is necessary, according to de Sade, in order to eliminate a person properly. Not only the person, but the corpse as a mark of the living, must be destroyed. According to the anatomist Ruysch, and also echoed by the more contemporary developers of the "humanoid robot" Cog, it is the liveliness of the eyes that betray the uncanny sentience hidden behind them.³⁶ Fontenelle recounts that Peter the Great, upon seeing a small child's body prepared by Ruysch, was so enchanted by its lifelike eyes and friendly smile that he walked over and kissed the cadaver.³⁷

3. Empty Worlds (Interlude)

While Kant insists on the difference between being and thinking, he establishes a necessary "correlation" between them, disabling either their identity or radical difference, since, by virtue of the mediation function of our perception, the world is always for-us and never conceivable as in-itself. The reversal of such a *finitist* reduction to the empirical, or phenomenal, has led Speculative Realism to a renewed interest in the absolute as non-correlative, hence superseding Kant's limitation to the given. This reaction to the contemporary crisis of the notion of the absolute is "German Idealism redux," including the return of its reevaluation of

---

34 Julia Kristeva, *Powers of Horror: An Essay on Abjection,* trans. Leon S. Roudiez (New York: Columbia University Press, 1982), 53.
35 Thacker, *In the Dust of this Planet,* 108.
36 Evelyn Fox Keller, "Booting Up Baby," in *Genesis Redux: Essays in the History and Philosophy of Artificial Life,* ed. Jessica Riskin (Chicago: Chicago University Press, 2007), 335.
37 Bernard Le Bovier de Fontenelle, *Éloges des académiciens avec l'histoire de l'Académie royale des sciences en* MDCXCIX (The Hague: Isaac van der Kloot, 1740), 1:438.

madness. Meillassoux therefore formulates "correlationism" as: "No X without givenness of X, and no theory about X without a positing of X,"[38] and *After Finitude* starts its analysis perplexed by the assertion of the Kantian idea, viz., that the "world is only meaningful" insofar as it is "given-to-a-living (or thinking)-being," which is still operative in contemporary, philosophical discourse.[39] There was always only one consequence appropriate to such a bind: getting rid of all sentient life, emptying out the planet. Meillassoux's arche-fossil, Thacker's planet, and Brassier's stellar catastrophe have thus introduced a barren planet before us, and the cosmic void after us, back into philosophy, with distinct anti-vitalist, rationalist sentiments.

After introducing the arche-fossil as a mark of a time before sentience, posing a problem for transcendental philosophies' framework of representation, Meillassoux derives from the facticity of the correlation between thinking and being that no reason can be given, that such a correlation is what it is, and therefore, that such a contingency must be itself necessary or absolute, because it, itself, is non-correlative. Hence, "only contingency necessarily exists."[40] This necessary contingency is conflated by Meillassoux with the real, enabling him to conceive of a sense of being that is absolute and thus escapes the correlation; Meillassoux thus introduces a radical asynchronicity between thinking and being. Life, paradoxically, or more specifically, vitalism, impedes the scope of contingency insofar as becoming introduces contradictory entities which are necessarily what and how they are, since they cannot be otherwise, having already violated the principle of non-contradiction. Consequently, Meillassoux specifically accuses the Bergsonian-Deleuzian lineage of a "vitalist hypostatization" by declaring everything as

---

38 Ray Brassier et al., "Speculative Realism," in *Collapse III: Unknown Deleuze and Symposium on Speculative Realism,* ed. Robin Mackay (Falmouth: Urbanomic, 2007), 409.

39 Quentin Meillassoux, *After Finitude: An Essay on the Necessity of Contingency,* trans. Ray Brassier (London: Continuum, 2008), 15.

40 Ray Brassier, *Nihil Unbound: Enlightenment and Extinction* (London: Palgrave Macmillan, 2007), 67.

a correlate of (a) Life, absolutizing the correlation itself.[41] Life becomes the new Principle of Sufficient Reason — in the case of Deleuze, Meillassoux is undoubtedly correct.

Also wishing to dissolve the correlative bind, like Meillassoux, Brassier introduces the (inevitable) stellar extinction, the cosmic thanatropic vector, as a "real yet not empirical" event.[42] The subjective trauma inflicted by the objective reality of extinction is an "adequation without correspondence" whose resulting "truth" forces philosophy to admit that it is "neither a medium of affirmation nor a source of justification, but rather the organon of extinction."[43] The corollary of such an asynchronicity of thinking and being, in introducing a mind-independent reality, is a strict materialism, or even a transcendental nihilism, exposing the human desire to drape values and meaning over an indifferent cosmos, the desire to escape the traumatic reality of "human narcissism."[44] Transfiguring nature into a monster of energy, Lyotard writes that "[m]atter asks no questions, expects no answer of us. It ignores us."[45] Aimed at unbinding the vitalist "double genesis of thinking and being" in which "ideality and sensibility ultimately converge," such a transcendental nihilism provides the antidote to what Brassier perceives as the pathological drive to affirm life, evident in the tendency toward panpsychism.[46]

Both Meillassoux and Brassier attempt to remove life or the organism as the orphic guardian of the depths of thought. However, ultimately, both are still beholden to the conservative economy of the organism. What allows Meillassoux to project the logical lack of reason into material being is his use of logic and matter interchangeably, reducing the latter to the same in-

---

41 Meillassoux, *After Finitude*, 64.
42 Brassier, *Nihil Unbound*, 237.
43 Ibid., 239.
44 Ibid., xi.
45 François Lyotard, "Thought without a Body?" in *The Inhuman: Reflections on Time*, trans. Geoffrey Bennington and Rachel Bowlby (Stanford: Stanford University Press, 1991), 11.
46 Brassier, *Nihil Unbound*, 171.

effective formalism, the "empty and indeterminate postulate."[47] Even if we accept the reasoning leading up to the concept of hyper-chaos, the real genesis of the given from a mind-independent reality cannot necessarily be explained. This becomes evident in the irrational leaps Meillassoux must introduce to make the emergence of different worlds (matter, life, thought, justice) plausible. As such, Meillassoux's contingency rests on the same logical concept of matter that is characteristic of Kant's philosophy of nature: localizing life "naturally" in the organism. The "exorbitant death" of the cosmic thanatropic vector in Brassier's nihilism firstly necessitates the transcription of the form of dissipation of interiority into an exteriority, specific to the organism, onto the cosmos. Such a transition from "who is death?" to the objectivity of death, to the "truth of extinction," can only register in and for the conservative economy of the organism, which binds it as trauma. Nihilistic disenchantment as non-conceptual negativity is bound to a thinking able to sustain such a shock, according to its affordance. The apocalyptic desire of Meillassoux and Brassier, paradoxically, leaves the human and the organism conceptually intact, in order to subvert their central position by eliminating them. Thacker's planet — being neither the world for-us (the World), the space derived from our hermeneutic access to it, nor the world-in-itself (the Earth) as the opposite of and the point of resistance to such attempts at domestication, but a world-without-us, radically devoid of anything human — might denote the asymptotic approximation of such speculative devastation. It reflects the fundamental phantasm of subjectivity and its positionality as such, gazing upon an innocent world which is yet undisturbed by the subject's existence.

The question is not whether we would either revel in the idea of the earth as a Heideggerian "home" for humans, and other organisms, or rather face the horror of the possibility of a sterile

---

47 Peter Hallward, "Anything is Possible: A Reading of *After Finitude*," in *The Speculative Turn: Continental Materialism and Realism*, eds. Levi Bryant, Nick Srnicek, and Graham Harman (Melbourne: re.press, 2011), 138.

and dead world-without-us. This question is still premised on the idea that without us, or organisms in general, there would be no life. Instead, we should rather ask through what kind of indifferent speculative wasteland we are wandering. Because it might well be Hegel's desert of the Absolute in the *Phenomenology,* the "vacuity" of "the night in which [...] all cows are black."[48] Hegel can only see devastation in groundlessness, the horror of a world stripped of life, because he lacks the "chemical sensibility"[49] to register "the differences swarming behind us."[50] The true horror of philosophy lies not in the satisfaction of our apocalyptic desires but in philosophy's relentless demonstration that these compulsions to escape are pointless. *This* will never end, because it is not even something.

4. Dysteleological Life

The Tadmurians believe, Negarestani reports, that headless nature produces a *bolus barathuma,* a cursed beast, when it stares longer into itself than usual, in order to realize itself.[51] The *Critique of Judgment,* in an attempt to attain the highest systematic unity of nature and freedom, again straddles the line between the architectonics of critical philosophy and speculation with the discovery of reflective judgment and the sublime. Aesthetic judgment is reflective and not legislative for an object but is only for itself in the form of free harmony of the faculties in a reflected object. One must not forget that the analysis of the sublime is a "mere appendix" to the beautiful and the discovery of aesthetic common sense, an attempt to map it on to the existing structure. In the discussion of the mathematical and

---

48 G.W.F. Hegel, *Phenomenology of Spirit,* trans A.V. Miller (Oxford: Oxford University Press, 1977), 9.
49 Iain Hamilton Grant, "The Chemistry of Darkness," *Pli* 9 (2000): 38.
50 Gilles Deleuze, *Difference and Repetition,* trans. Paul Patton (New York: Columbia University Press 1995), 277.
51 Reza Negarestani, "Bolus Barathuma (Homo Sapiens †)," in *Abyssus Intellectualis: Speculative Horror,* eds. Armen Avanessian and Björn Quiring (Berlin: Merve Verlag, 2013), 117.

dynamical sublime in paragraphs 26 to 29 in the third *Critique*, Kant attempts to tame the sublime by splitting each mode into a moral and central side, and an illegal and fringe side. The sublime inspires religious sentiments, which supersedes superstition, which invokes fear, through feelings of reverence. The abolishment of the mind's freedom must be rejected in favor of passion and enthusiasm, the animation of imagination; it must avoid slipping into fanaticism, the becoming anomalous of imagination. In Kant's mention of the negative parts of the sublime and their subsequent dismissal as abnormalities, their difference is always one of degree. However, it is the border between the colossal, "[t]he mere presentation of a concept [...] which is almost too great for all presentation," and the monstrous, which "by its magnitude [...] annihilates the end which its concept constitutes," that appears most fragile.[52] Since "crude nature" cannot present the monstrous itself—nature does not contain anything "horrid"—its function is merely negative and serves to render the edges of the colossal clearer. Alas, this "frame doesn't fit," as Derrida remarks, because the demarcation used in order "to stop the category of the almost-too-much," that is, the colossal, from degenerating into the excessive magnitude of the too-much already relies on the determination of the monstrous.[53] The colossal seems to appear on the edges of the monstrous, as an experience of a limit, a threshold not yet crossed, constituted by the outside of representation. This *aporia*, that the monstrous is unrepresentable but must be determined to negatively constitute the colossal, is instructive for the whole third *Critique*. In this mere appendix, not only the very possibility of the sublime is at stake, but the systematic unity of Kant's project as such. Considering that, for Kant, the ultimate symbol of the good is the beautiful, the sublime complicates such a connection of vision and truth, or vision in regard to its ability to give a reliable index of the true. While "[t]he beautiful in nature concerns the form of the object, which consists in limitation; the

---

52 Kant, *Critique of the Power of Judgment*, 253.
53 Jacques Derrida, "The Parergon," *October* 9 (1979): 30.

sublime, by contrast, is to be found in a formless object insofar as limitlessness is represented in it, or at its instance, and yet it is also thought as a totality."[54] For the limitless to be represented at all, the multiplicity of it must be bound; this must be the case in order to think and experience an object at all. Hence, the sublime is never fully formless, and this allows for judgment to take hold. If the size were to increase just a little more, if the magnitude were just the smallest quantum bigger, unified experience would disintegrate. A purely quantitative difference between the almost-too-much and the too-much would therefore give varying results, and an object could be legitimately judged as sublime one moment but "appear" as monstrous the next — it would fall in and out of representation. Kant thus adds a qualitative distinction. The "negative pleasure" the sublime proper invokes is itself a "vibration [...] a rapidly alternating repulsion from and attraction to one and the same object," while the monstrous is the cessation of this movement.[55] The repulsion is not followed by any joy and what one is left with instead are the affections of pure aversion, terror, horror, and disgust. Instating these feelings as arbiters between the colossal and the monstrous, however, does not provide a strict enough line of demarcation. The *Anthropology*, aware of this threat, revokes their proximity by collapsing the two registers of the *Analytic*. The sublime and all its mental representations, as well as its artistic representations, must be beautiful, so as not to invoke fear or revulsion. One should be wary of such a retreat. To maintain the judgment of God is to stave off the threat of formlessness, the boundlessness inherent in the unnatural and illegitimate sublime. Hence, every representation of the monstrous must necessary fail. All of the words become meaningless, all of the narratives become tangled and contradictory, and all depictions miss their subject when faced with the too-much.

This unavoidable failure to describe the monstrous, in conjunction with a manic rigor of literary description, animates the

---

54 Kant, *Critique of the Power of Judgment*, 244.
55 Ibid., 245, 258.

works of Lovecraft. The meteorite, which crashes near Arkham into the Gardners's land, brings a monstrous shimmer with it, a "colour out of space." Although the rock itself is destroyed by lightning, the color spreads like a disease. While it cannot be categorized by any means relating to anything known within the visible spectrum, it infects not only the soil and the animals, but also the minds of the Gardners, driving them to madness. Something monstrous takes hold through its presence alone, without this monstrosity being bound to an object. Life appears as impersonal and anonymous contagion and ultimately consumes the living. Lovecraft is not, however, at least in this case, a writer of the supernatural, but rather of the *hyper*natural. After examining the meteor, the three professors, while able to determine its properties accurately, are still unable to "place" it. Since "[i]t was nothing of this earth, but a piece of the great outside; and as such dowered with outside properties and obedient to outside laws,"[56] it does not register "as" something. Such a horror is not noumenal, but, as Harman shows, "phenomenological."[57] The color, as well as all of the entities in Lovecraft's cosmos, are strictly material. When asking himself, "What is the Great Cthulhu?," Houellebecq answers that it is "[a]n arrangement of electrons, like ourselves. The terror of Lovecraft is rigorously materialist."[58] There is in fact no noumenon left in Lovecraft. There is only the play of anonymous forces, assembling and disassembling, a life of pure affectivity. The formless ground rises up, without coming from another world but just from "out of space," like a background noise slowly seeping into consciousness. The noumenal and the phenomenal collapse into each other. The transcendental cannot be represented, not even by analogy; hence, the transcendental-empirical double fails. Monstrosity itself becomes transcendental. Rather than

---

56 H.P. Lovecraft, "The Colour Out of Space," in *Tales* (New York: Library of America Literary Classics of the United States, 2005), 345.

57 Graham Harman, *Weird Realism: Lovecraft and Realism* (Winchester: Zero Books, 2012), 340.

58 Michel Houellebecq, *H.P. Lovecraft: Against the World, Against Life* (San Francisco: McSweeney's Publishing, 2005), 32.

being confronted with possible experience, the understanding is faced with real experience, legislated only by its own existence. It is faced with the being of the sensible. The feeling that the sublime is supposed to invoke, of the mind's "superiority over nature itself even in its immeasurability," is subverted and turned around.[59] Rather than space being internal to us, we are spatial constructs within a vast and indifferent cosmos. Rather than time being within us, we are temporal and as such confronted with a history, stretching far beyond our consciousness, knowledges, civilizations, and organic lives altogether. As such, Lovecraft cannot conform to the usual horror cliché of portraying a harmonious state — a peaceful and quiet little town — which is uprooted and disturbed by something un- or supernatural that unravels the idyll. In his universe, everything is "weird" from the outset. Nothing subverts nature from the outside, but the natural order is itself a quite perplexing anomaly within an *a priori* crooked but univocal universe.

The beginning of *The Color Out of Space*, with the surveyor traversing a landscape marked by "a touch of the unreal and the grotesque, as if some vital element of perspective or chiaroscuro were awry," introduces this reversal to the foundations of perception.[60] One cannot simply shake the unnaturalness of such a scene but rather begins to ask the question of how normalcy was ever possible in the first place; one is like someone losing the threat of everyday thought, unable to piece it back together, wondering if it was there in the first place. It is the question Kant not only failed to answer but sought to suspend *a priori* through the *a priori*. In other words, such awryness implies the question of a genesis of the common sense and good will of thought on the one hand, and the production of unity in nature on the other.

Alas, however far the "archaeologist of nature" ventures into the remains of the "oldest revolutions," the world is always already captured by the auto-assembling forces of organic at-

---

59   Kant, *Critique of the Power of Judgment*, 261.
60   Lovecraft, "The Colour Out of Space," 341.

tractors, trapping it in perpetual actualism; the earth was never formed, only the world is produced now.[61] From the present, the formative drive extends itself across all of time and space, assimilating them to "propagate itself," warding of the demonical threat of the productive surplus of the real over the possible. Devoid of any will-to-sanity or -health, the thought of transcendental monstrosity penetrates through the covers of societal normalcy and convention, only to be redirected by ethico-teleological diversions: the transcendental illusions of the Idea integrating all of the world by reproducing it in its image — the world, the cosmos, as an organism. Such a limitation is, however, only an auto-immunological reaction to the seemingly destructive forces of the simmering depth, which have not yet been recognized as the continuous genesis of reality, sometimes even wearing the mask of a judgmental God, sometimes subverting Him. While Deleuze and Guattari claim that "[i]f everything is alive, it is not because everything is organic or organized, but, on the contrary, because the organism is a perversion [*détournement*] of life. The life in question is inorganic, germinal and intensive, a powerful life without organs [...] Metal is neither a thing nor an organism, but a *body* without organs [...] matter-flow as pure productivity," how does thinking avoid being itself recalibrated by organic despotism, and reach beyond judgment?[62]

As Heidegger remarks, the Greek *theōrein*, from which "theory" is derived, is an amalgam of *thea*, the visible part of things, and *horān*, meaning "to look at something with attention." The exclusion of the monstrous from Aristotle's *Poetics*, which set in motion a whole philosophical history of stigmatizing the abnormal, is thereby conceivable as a reaction to the complication of the relation of visibility and truth inherent to it. The Latin *monstrum*, meaning "a divine omen or warning," reflected in

---

61 Kant, *Critique of the Power of Judgment*, 419.
62 Gilles Deleuze and Félix Guattari, *A Thousand Plateaus: Capitalism and Schizophrenia*, trans. Robert Hurley and Brian Massumi (Minneapolis: Minnesota University Press, 1987), 411.

the nowadays uncommon use of "monster" in English to mean something that is enormous and threatening, can be short-circuited with the archaic use of "monster" in English, meaning "to demonstrate" or "to exhibit," in order to form a new notion of theory. If the monstrous is characterized by its boundlessness, destroying the concepts determining it due to its excessive magnitude, can thinking be characterized by the same tendency to devour the boundaries that academia, societal discourse, history, or even the given anatomy of the thinking apparatus have erected? Such thinking is what Kant attempted to exclude from philosophy in the *Spirit-Seers*. It is the madness of speculation. The emancipatory value of speculation is therefore most evident in its ability to question and reject any "natural order," that is, to expose it as contingently produced while at the same time enacting a transgression against the conservative economy of thinking every such order would impose. Thinking, as a material reconfiguration of forces, is, if accelerated to an infinite speed, fast enough to avoid the judgment of God; it is an unnatural act. As such, it destroys "nature," understood as given necessity. The animation of the mind is in excess of the organic limits of the living — or, as Brassier writes, "[t]hinking has interests that do not coincide with those of living; indeed, they can and have been pitted against the latter."[63]

Freud's presentation of an energetic model of the nervous system in *Beyond the Pleasure Principle* has been widely discussed in regard to its claims about the compulsion for thanatropic regression, the inevitable dissolution of the organism into inorganic exteriority. Focusing on the organism's desire to return to a state of inanimation conceals the speculative and energetic aspect of the model in the critique of the conservative economic order of the organism, especially revealed in its binding of death. Freud writes:

> If we are to take it as a truth that knows no exception that everything living dies for internal reasons — becomes inor-

---
63 Brassier, *Nihil Unbound*, xi.

ganic once again — then we shall be compelled to say that "the aim of life is death" and, looking backwards, that "inanimate things existed before living ones" [...] For a long time, perhaps, living substance was thus being constantly created afresh and easily dying, till decisive external influences altered in such a way as to oblige the still surviving substance to diverge ever more widely from its original course of life and to make ever more complicated detours before reaching its aim of death.[64]

In Freud's anti-Spinozist twist, while the organic interiority hives off from its inorganic origins in a dynamic interplay of constantly binding death as exteriority, e.g. constant contraction, its dissolution follows an internal "instinct." Since the state towards which the organism is regressing is, at the same, the irretrievable past, older than any organic life, and also the unpredictable future, coming rather than being and hence indifferent to the organism, such a state cannot register as a point in time *for* the organism at all. The traumatic origin of life itself, therefore, is not accessible to transcendental subjectivity, to which it nevertheless gives rise.

In the instinct towards death, thanatropic regression presents itself to the organism as an objective truth which instates itself *a posteriori,* but is nevertheless *a priori* for the organic subject; or, as Levinas put it in regard to the Other, as an "anterior posteriority."[65] Precisely as such an impossible condition, the death-instinct is transcendental, but not determinable by the empirical through analogy or resemblance. Neither transcendental apperception nor the existential "being-towards-death" can assimilate it. Death does not appear as the teleological endpoint of life, but rather life is a temporary anomaly in the order of dysteleological death, or, "[t]he living is only a form of what

---

64 Sigmund Freud, *Beyond the Pleasure Principle*, ed. James Strachey (New York: W.W. Norton & Company, 1961), 32.
65 Emmanuel Levinas, *Totality and Infinity: An Essay on Exteriority,* trans. Alphonso Lingis (Pittsburgh: Duquesne University Press, 1969), 170.

is dead—and a very rare form."⁶⁶ Not beholden to regulative principles, the original state of the inorganic is bound by the organism in that its course of decontraction is guided by the conservative economy of the organism due to it being the medium of dissipation. Rather than the derivative tendency towards economic assimilation of the pleasure principle, or the survivalism of the reality principle which make death appear as an inflection of life, the death instinct reverses this order. In other words, life does not consist in the overcoming or resistance of death, but in its individual modes of binding inorganic exteriority according to the specific economic affordability of the organism by reducing the tendency towards dissolution qualitatively and quantitatively; this is in order that life may die in the way immanent to it. Life is a detour [*Umweg*] towards death and "[d]eath needs time for what it kills to grow in [it]."⁶⁷

In this sense, affordability in the organism as an open system is determined by the incongruity of the exorbitant demand of exteriority and the logic of sustenance as a demand of interiority, or, the projection of life towards ends (interiority) and the destruction of such ends by the very condition of making them in the first place. As such, the death instinct is "monstrous" but also conditioned, since it is only possible through the organic economy. This is the tendency of organisms to exhibit complexity, for example, to temporally postpone such dissolution, but also to ultimately merely represent the detour of this specific dynamic system—and, as could be said with an inversion of August Weismann, such complexity might accelerate the course towards dissipation.⁶⁸ Even if it is supposed that the binding of

---

66 Friedrich Nietzsche, *The Gay Science*, ed. Bernard Williams, trans. Josefine Nauckoff and Adrian Del Caro (Cambridge: Cambridge University Press, 2001), 110.
67 William Burroughs, "Ah Pook the Destroyer," *Dead City Radio* (London: Island, 1990), CD.
68 Weismann poses a challenge to Freud, insofar as he argues that death, from the standpoint of evolutionary life, is a rather late acquisition, questioning its primordial status. Freud however retorts, that "his assertion that death is a late acquisition would apply only to its manifest phenomena and would not make impossible the assumption of processes tending

the inevitable truth of extinction is always unsuccessful, the organism still imposes a "partial" natural order upon the dysteleological tendency of the death drive. Rather than the economic order being shaped by its immanent way of dying, in Freud's model, the latter is determined by the former. The organism is that which rules the economy of dying, or, more precisely, it *is* this conservative tendency. The aim of such a binding of the death drive is to determine the relation between the conservative drives and the seemingly unilateral conditioning of them by inorganic exteriority as ultimately bilateral, resulting in a metaphysical dualism of drives. Freud's death drive is not yet considered transcendental.

In the end of the second chapter of *Difference and Repetition,* Deleuze attempts to retrieve the possible monism abandoned by Freud by unbinding death from the conservative economy of the organism. Taking up the characterization of the death drive as a positive compulsion for repetition operating as a nonempirical principle, it is the latter that Freud ultimately betrays. By presupposing a dialectical model of the drives, characterized by negation, as well as a dialectical model of organic (interiority) and inorganic (exteriority) matter, he repeats the Kantian movement of the tracing of the transcendental from the empirical. The inorganic exteriority is only unanimated if conceived as empirical itself, namely, as the original trauma of the organism it attempts to bind in its immanent way. For Freud, the return to the state before the organism is synonymous with the repetition of a time without life, identifying life with the personal and empirical, binding death. Deleuze's unbinding of death, then, entails thinking it not as a contradiction to personal life. It is not "the limitation imposed by matter upon mortal life, nor the opposition between matter and immortal life, which furnishes death with its prototype. Death is, rather, the last form of the

---

towards it." Freud, *Beyond the Pleasure Principle,* 43. For a philosophical, in-depth discussion of Weismann and Freud, see Keith Ansell-Pearson, *Germinal Life: The Difference and Repetition of Deleuze* (London: Routledge, 1999), 104f.

problematic, the source of all problems and questions, the sign of their persistence over and above every response, the "Where?" and "When?" which designate this (non)-being where every affirmation is nourished."[69]

Transcending any particular life, the "death instinct" in Deleuze capitalizes on the energetic aspect of Freud's model, denoting the energy of an impersonal life. Without being bound to the conservative economy of the organism, matter itself appears as animated.

Deleuze's transcendental empiricism capitalizes on such an opening, flattening the divide between the transcendental and the empirical insofar as the former is remodeled as a genetic process itself immanent to the latter. Although determining the empirical phenomena, the transcendental itself is a synthesis within the empirical field, itself contingently determined by the encounter of forces. There is an immanent logic to the sensible itself, or to the material, which cannot be anticipated or fully governed. On account of this immanence of the transcendental and the empirical, the transcendental is not determined by analogy to the empirical and is therefore not limited to what the limitative judgment of God — His disjunctive syllogism — has determined as possible. In the being of the sensible, as Deleuze remarks, we do not encounter the gods but demons. Such a reversal subverts the retrospective movement of organic thought to integrate what is real into what must have been possible and transmutes reality into a monstrous self-creation. While the notion of matter that Kant proposed was logical, Deleuze's is synthetic and, hence, not yet beholden to the conservative economy of the organic image of thought.

Rather than merely being the intrusion of alterity, that is, inorganic exteriority presenting itself as anterior posteriority, traumatically disrupting the empirical, and retrospectively transcendentalized, natural order, any such order is suspended *a priori*. The death drive does not denaturalize any specific empirical natural order, but transcendentally denaturalizes the

---

[69] Deleuze, *Difference and Repetition*, 112.

naturalization of any order as such. As is evident in Lovecraft, dissolution and destruction are coupled with, or enacted as, an emancipatory practice. This not only subverts the natural order but suspends it. It seems that *we are not condemned to be free but are free because we are condemned.* Without prefigured order, the only thing left is the violence of perception. For Deleuze, this is the "pain of childbirth" as Nietzsche had it, within which thinking ascends towards a "superior empiricism," shedding the conditions of possibility of the human.[70] It is this violence as a new mode of communication that informs the transition from Kant's conditioned to Deleuze's absolute epigenesis: "each faculty communicates to the other only the violence which confronts it with its own difference and its divergence from the other."[71] This discordant accord, revealing the determination of sensation by a super-sensible Idea, "manifests and liberates a depth which remained hidden."[72] The depth-determining sensation, without the determination by a concept, becomes the model for the internal genesis.

This depth of Ideas, however, according to the critique of possibility seen above, must be one which is not preexistent to the experience, but expressed in it. However, since Ideas do not resemble the surface of the sensible, because they are not traced from its outline, they remain conditions irreducible to real experience. Hence, this super-sensible realm of Ideas cannot be actual, but is still real; or, as Deleuze characterizes the virtual, this realm is the ideal part of the real, "real but not actual, ideal but not abstract," since Ideas follow from an encounter with the being of the sensible.[73]

In the strictest sense, such a vital cosmos is a-cosmic, a-theological, and a-personal. The hylemorphic model of thought and determination which Kant employed is replaced in Deleuze

---

[70] Ibid., 69.
[71] Ibid., 146.
[72] Gilles Deleuze, *Kant's Critical Philosophy: The Doctrine of the Faculties*, trans. Hugh Tomlinson and Barbara Habberjam (Minneapolis: Minnesota University Press, 1985), 60.
[73] Deleuze, *Difference and Repetition*, 208.

with a hylozoic model of a material morphogenesis, which may involve the human mind but does not necessarily. Matter determines itself without anything above or beyond it, and it does so as process. Such is the formula of Deleuzian horror. With the failure of the boundaries between the sensible and the intelligible, the madness Kant sought to banish then returns. By subverting the question of the intelligible *de jure* in the *de facto* transcendental genesis of the sensible, one ventures into the infinity of absolute xenogenesis.

5. Creation in the Absence of God

As Nietzsche notes, judgment, since it must force itself upon people, appears first "in the form of the *false judgment* leading to delirium and madness, when man is mistaken about his lot, and in the form of the *judgment of God,* when the form imposes another lot."[74] But now, no such prefigured lots are left. "Nature does not make mistakes" and "nature only makes mistakes" have become synonymous. Instead of stretching the bond between the order of creation and the order of redemption endlessly, it is cut in a Marcionite fashion. The integrity of the body, its boundary to the outside, relied on the judgment of God, which unified it and ascribed every organ its lot. Now, all organs move independently from their corporeal unity. This is the artificial life of the partial objects in Bosch's paintings, which returns in the psychosis of Lacan, or the myriad of autonomous body parts within the horror genre. Such an "organ without a body," an organ which "resists inclusion,"[75] is still created by a compulsion to repeat a state preceding "the dialectic of the prohibitory Law and its transgression" and Oedipal triangulation.[76] This repetition can only register as the experience of a body made up of disjointed pieces if indexed by a subject already constituted by

---

74 Deleuze, "To Have Done with Judgment," 129.
75 Sean McQueen, *Deleuze and Baudrillard: From Cyberpunk to Biopunk* (Edinburgh: Edinburgh University Press, 2017), 159.
76 Slavoj Žižek, *Organs without Bodies: On Deleuze and Consequences* (London: Routledge, 2012), xi.

the symbolic order. Again, judgment is already in place, and we have not reached the continuous flow of desire as *a*subjective — impersonal and energetic flux which constitutes and characterizes the body-without-organs.

The distinction which Aristotle introduces in the *Physics* between *mimeitai,* art's ability to imitate nature, and *epitelei,* its ability to take things further, is instructive for the alchemical lineage of artificial life from the inception of the *aufiric* arts to the creation of *homunculi.* While the manipulation of materials into artworks which resemble nature's products is an imposition upon nature — mere "sophistical transmutations," as Geber declares in the *Summa Perfectionis* — the alchemist's goal is the repetition of creation.[77] *De natura rerum,* written by physician Adam von Bodenstein, posing as the famous alchemist Paracelsus von Hohenheim, describes the process by which a bird can be transmuted into a flask by converting the burned up remains of an ordinary bird into phlegm and heating it up. The bird will not only regenerate, it will be "clarified," that is, it will be better than before, better than natural.[78] The origin of such experiments, including the creation of a homunculus or a basilisk in a flask, while being inspired by Arabic writings on early artificial life, might lie in the tradition of mandragoras (*Alraunen*). Peddlers would carve mandrake roots to resemble human features and sell them, with false promises attached, to superstitious men and women.[79] These minor crimes are harshly condemned by Paracelsus in *Liber de imaginibus.* He proceeds to demonstrate in *De vita longa* the way in which real mandrakes are actually homunculi, created by the sperm or urine of hanged criminals and therefore growing under gallows, hence the name "gallows-man" or "Galgenmann." The superficial resemblance to liveliness is replaced by the non-phenomenal creation of life.

---

77 William Newman, *The Summa Perfectionis of Pseudo-Geber: A Critical Edition, Translation, and Study* (Leiden: Brill 1991), 753.
78 (Pseudo-)Paracelsus, *De natura rerum* (Munich: Oldenbourg, 1922), 312.
79 Cf. Lynn Thorndike, ed., *A History of Magic and Experimental Science* (New York: Columbia University Press, 1958), 8:11.

In Mary Douglas's canonical study, *Purity and Danger*, impurity is categorized by the violation of, and subsequent threat to, the schema ordering cultural categories.[80] The stigmatization of the alchemical lineage of artificial life as heresy points to another kind of fear of a nature ultimately neither controlled nor limited by any external force. This is a horror based on the univocity of all individuated beings via an impersonal genesis. The alchemist does not simulate vitality but rather realizes the genesis of life and therefore moves from human representation to inhuman creation, and maybe even improves upon nature's hitherto implemented methods. While the horror of the noumenal character of life *was* marked by the failure of analogical judgment, hence an *a posteriori* event disrupting the natural order, the transgression of the monstrous generation instates itself *a priori*. As such, alchemy implies a two-fold darkness: of life as materially withdrawn from view by virtue of being a synthetic process of forces necessarily below phenomenality and of the future of life, or of what might become of life. Therefore, alchemy is the proper predecessor to what is now known as chemistry, since "*chemistry* derives from the Egyptian word for "black," which is itself named for the black earth of Egypt."[81] Langton, in his 1987 manifesto on and for artificial life, while conjuring the alchemists of old, already refrains from using "life" as a natural kind, instead proposing: "Only when we are able to view *life-as-we-know-it* in the larger context of *life-as-it-could-be* will we really understand the nature of the beast."[82]

Not bound by prefigured metaphysical laws, monstrous creations exhibit dialethical biologies, being alive and dead, natural and artificial, formed and formless, all at the same time. For

---

80 Mary Douglas, *Purity and Danger: An Analysis of Concept of Pollution and Taboo* (London: Routledge, 1966).
81 Bernadette Bensaude-Vincent, "Lavoisier: Eine wissenschaftliche Revolution," in *Elemente einer Geschichte der Wissenschaften*, ed. Michel Serres (Frankfurt am Main: Suhrkamp, 1994), 13.
82 Chris Langton, "Artificial Life," in *Artificial Life: The Proceedings of an Interdisciplinary Workshop on the Synthesis and Stimulation of Living Systems* (Redwood City: Addison-Wesley, 1989), 33.

the judgment of God, such life appears blasphemous, a "life that should not be living but that is living,"[83] brought about by a fusion of elements deemed incompatible with societal norms, or with the category of the natural, or else brought about by a fission of what is considered inseparable. As the art of generation by transcendental synthesis, alchemy subverts empirical distinctions of naturalness, creating amalgams of: formerly distinct ontological orders (e.g., inorganic materials and flesh, man and animals); spatio-temporal categories (e.g., two souls in one body); genera and species (e.g., mixtures of animals, such as the chimera); or splittings of ontological composites (creatures without souls), spatial wholes (one soul in two bodies, doppelgängers), or temporal continuities (two souls alternating in inhabiting one spatially continuous body).

Transgressing the conceptual category of "natural" that any given culture might champion, monstrous creatures not only pose a threat to an existing scheme, but also to the action of naturalizing any schematization. "Monsters are not only physically threatening; they are cognitively threatening," [84] not because they oppose common knowledge, as Carroll falsely believes, but because they pose a threat to the common sense and good will of thinking, to the conditions of common knowledge as such. Most of Lovecraft's characters, upon looking at the monsters, end up deranged, but their insanity is not an empirical phenomenon. Rather, it is a transcendental madness, or better yet, it is their convergence with the madness that is the transcendental.

The horror of life is not that the category of the "natural" is fragile but that it is laughable.

---

83 Thacker, *In the Dust of this Planet*, 104.
84 Noël Carroll, *The Philosophy of Horror* (New York: Routledge, 1990), 34.

Bibliography

Ansell-Pearson, Keith. *Germinal Life: The Difference and Repetition of Deleuze.* London: Routledge, 1999.

Beaufret, Jean. "Précédé de Hölderlin et Sophocle." In *Remarques sur Oedipe/Remarques sur Antigone,* edited by Jean Beaufret, translated by François Fédier, 1–21. Paris: Union générale éditions, 1965.

Bensaude-Vincent, Bernadette. "Lavoisier: Eine wissenschaftliche Revolution." In *Elemente einer Geschichte der Wissenschaften,* edited by Michel Serres, 645–85. Frankfurt am Main: Suhrkamp, 1994.

Brassier, Ray. *Nihil Unbound: Enlightenment and Extinction.* London: Palgrave Macmillan, 2007.

Brassier, Ray, Iain Hamilton Grant, Graham Harman, Quentin Meillassoux. "Speculative Realism." In *Collapse III: Unknown Deleuze and Symposium on Speculative Realism,* edited by Robin Mackay, 306–449. Falmouth: Urbanomic Press, 2007.

Burroughs, William. "Ah Pook the Destroyer." *Dead City Radio.* London: Island, 1990. CD.

Carroll, Noël. *The Philosophy of Horror.* New York: Routledge, 1990.

David-Ménard, Monique. *La folie dans la raison pure: Kant lecteur de Swedenborg.* Paris: Librairie Philosophique J.Vrin, 1990.

Deleuze, Gilles. *Difference and Repetition.* Translated by Paul Patton. New York: Columbia University Press, 1995.

———. *Kant's Critical Philosophy: The Doctrine of the Faculties.* Translated by Hugh Tomlinson and Barnara Habberjam. Minneapolis: Minnesota University Press, 1985.

———. *Logic of Sense.* Edited by Constantin V. Boundas. Translated by Mark Lester with Charles Stivale. New York: Columbia University Press, 1990.

———. "To Have Done with Judgment." In *Essays Critical and Clinical,* translated by Daniel W. Smith and Michael A.

Greco, 126–35. Minneapolis: University of Minnesota Press, 1997.

Deleuze, Gilles, and Félix Guattari. *Anti-Oedipus: Capitalism and Schizophrenia.* Translated by Robert Hurley, Mark Seem, and Helen R. Lane. Minneapolis: Minnesota University Press, 2000.

———. *A Thousand Plateaus: Capitalism and Schizophrenia.* Translated by Brian Massumi. Minneapolis: Minnesota University Press, 1987.

Derrida, Jacques. "The Parergon." *October* 9 (1979): 3–41.

Douglas, Mary. *Purity and Danger: An Analysis of Concept of Pollution and Taboo.* London: Routledge, 1966.

de Fontenelle, Bernard Le Bovier. *Éloges des académiciens avec l'histoire de l'Académie royale des sciences en* MDCXCIX, Vol. 1. The Hague: Isaac van der Kloot, 1740.

Freud, Sigmund. *Beyond the Pleasure Principle.* Edited by James Strachey. New York: W.W. Norton & Company, 1961.

Grant, Iain Hamilton. "The Chemistry of Darkness." *Pli* 9 (2000): 36–52. https://plijournal.com/papers/iain-hamilton-grant-the-chemistry-of-darkness/.

Hallward, Peter. "Anything Is Possible: A Reading of *After Finitude.*" In *The Speculative Turn: Continental Materialism and Realism,* edited by Levi Bryant, Nick Srnicek, and Graham Harman, 130–41. Melbourne: re.press, 2011.

Harman, Graham. *Weird Realism: Lovecraft and Realism.* Winchester: Zero Books, 2012.

Hegel, G.W.F. *Phenomenology of Spirit.* Translated by A.V. Miller. Oxford: Oxford University Press, 1977.

Houellebecq, Michel. *H.P. Lovecraft: Against the World, Against Life.* San Francisco: McSweeney's Publishing, 2005.

Kant, Immanuel. *Anthropology from the Pragmatic Point of View.* Edited and translated by Robert B. Louden. Cambridge: Cambridge University Press, 2006.

———. "Brief an Moses Mendelssohn, 8. April, 1766." In *Briefwechsel,* 69–71. Berlin: Preußische Akademie der Wissenschaften, 1922.

———. *Critique of Practical Reason*. Translated by Lewis White Beck. New York: Palgrave Macmillan, 1956.
———. *Critique of the Power of Judgment*. Edited by Paul Guyer. Translated by Guyer and Eric Matthews. Cambridge: Cambridge University Press, 2000.
———. *Dreams of a Spirit-Seer*. Edited by Frank Sewall. Translated by Emmanuel F. Goerwitz. London: Swan Sonnenschein & Co, 1900.
———. *Opus Postumum*. Edited by Eckart Förster. Translated by Förster and Michael Rosen. Cambridge: Cambridge University Press, 1995.
Keller, Evelyn Fox. "Booting Up Baby." In *Genesis Redux. Essays in the History and Philosophy of Artificial Life,* edited by Jessica Riskin, 334–44. Chicago: Chicago University Press, 2007.
Kristeva, Julia. *Powers of Horror: An Essay on Abjection*. Translated by Leon S. Roudiez. New York: Columbia University Press, 1982.
Langton, Chris. "Artificial Life." In *Artificial Life: The Proceedings of an Interdisciplinary Workshop on the Synthesis and Simulation of Living Systems,* 1–48. Redwood City: Addison-Wesley Publishers, 1989.
Levinas, Emmanuel. *Existence and Existents*. Translated by Alphonso Lingis. Pittsburgh: Duquesne University Press, 2001.
———. *Totality and Infinity: An Essay on Exteriority*. Translated by Alphonso Lingis. Pittsburgh: Duquesne University Press, 1969.
Ligotti, Thomas. *Conspiracy Against the Human Race: A Contrivance of Horror*. New York: Hippocampus Press, 2010.
Lovecraft, H.P. "The Colour Out of Space." In *Tales,* 340–69. New York: Library of America Literary Classics of the United States, 2005.
Lucretius. *On the Nature of the Universe*. Translated by R.E. Latham. Harmondsworth: Penguin, 1982.
Lyotard, François. "Thought without a Body?" In *The Inhuman: Reflections on Time,* translated by Geoffrey Bennington and

Rachel Bowlby, 8–23. Stanford: Stanford University Press, 1991.

McLaughlin, Peter. *Kant's Critique of Teleology in Biological Explanation: Antinomy and Teleology*. Lewiston: Edwin Mellen Press, 1990.

McQueen, Sean. *Deleuze and Baudrillard: From Cyberpunk to Biopunk*. Edinburgh: Edinburgh University Press, 2017.

Meillassoux, Quentin. *After Finitude: An Essay on the Necessity of Contingency*. Translated by Ray Brassier. London: Continuum, 2008.

Negarestani, Reza. "Bolus Barathuma (Homo Sapiens †)." In *Abyssus Intellectualis: Speculative Horror*, edited by Armen Avanessian and Björn Quiring, 117–24. Berlin: Merve Verlag, 2013.

Newman, William R. *The Summa Perfectionis of Pseudo-Geber: A Critical Edition, Translation, and Study*. Leiden: Brill, 1991.

Nietzsche, Friedrich. *The Gay Science*. Edited by Bernard Williams. Translated by Josefine Nauckhoff and Adrian Del Caro. Cambridge: Cambridge University Press, 2001.

(Pseudo-)Paracelsus. *De natura rerum*. Munich: Oldenbourg, 1922.

Schreel, Louis. "Idea and Animation: A Study of the Immanent Sublime in Deleuze's Metaphysics." Ph.D. Diss., University of Antwerp, 2017. http://hdl.handle.net/1854/LU-8581199.

Stafford, Barbara Maria. *Body Criticism: Imaging the Unseen in Enlightenment Art and Medicine*. Cambridge: MIT Press, 1991.

Stengel, Friedemann. "Kant — 'Zwillingsbruder' Schwedenborgs?" In *Kant und Swedenborg: Zugänge zu Einem Umstrittenen Verhältnis*, edited by Friedemann Stegel, 35–97. Tübingen: May Niemayer, 2008.

Thacker, Eugene. *In the Dust of this Planet: Horror of Philosophy, Volume I*. Winchester: Zero Books, 2001.

Thorndike, Lynn, ed. *A History of Magic and Experimental Science, Vol. 8: Seventeenth Century*. New York: Columbia University Press, 1958.

Vicq d'Azyr, Félix. *Discours sur l'anatomie et de physiologie avec des planches coloriées, representant au naturel les divers organs de l'homme et des animaux.* Paris: l'Imprimerie de France, F.A. Didot l'aîné, 1786.

Wood, Gaby. *Edison's Eve: A Magical History of the Quest for Mechanical Life.* New York: Anchor, 2002.

Žižek, Slavoj. *Organs without Bodies: On Deleuze and Consequences.* London: Routledge, 2012.

8

Survival Strategies for Weird Times

Helen Marshall[1]

Survival Strategies

Barron St. John must have been nearing his seventies by that point. The pictures I'd copied from magazine covers and newspapers charted his rise from a rake-thin tower of a man, nearly six-three, clad in a badly fitting white wool jacket with a thick crop of black hair cut like a bowl around his ears, to his older self: hair grey but still as thick as it had ever been, fine laugh lines etching the curve of that grinning, maniac mouth. In his heyday people had taken to calling him the King of Horror, a real scaremeister — that term always made me laugh — but the man I saw in those later pictures had the look of a grandfather, which I suppose he was, one who could spin a yarn, sure, but not the kid who'd posed with a shotgun for his university paper under the headline "Vote dammit!"

My university had given me a small grant for my research project into St. John's career. I had planned to stay in Hotel 31, the cheapest place Luca and I had agreed we could afford. He

---

[1] Editorial Note: The story "Survival Strategies" originally appeared in *Black Static* 58 (2017). It has been reprinted here and is followed by a commentary, entitled "Survival Strategies for Weird Times," which is published for the first time in this collection.

had wanted me in midtown so I could walk most places. He was a worrier, had never been to New York and the idea of me riding the subway right then made him uneasy.

"It'll be fine," I told him, "nothing will happen. It isn't like that anymore. It hasn't been since the '90s." We both knew that wasn't exactly true. The situation was different now, but scarier in other ways. There were journalists being stopped at the borders, asked invasive questions. Not everyone was allowed in. And Luca, for all his woolly sweetness and soft English manners, had a serious stubborn streak. He was protective, I knew, and didn't like the idea of me traveling on my own, not after I'd reacted so badly to the procedure, and certainly not "abroad" as he called it in that charmingly old-fashioned way of his.

But "abroad" was what I had wanted. Even if it wasn't home for me, which lay four-hundred miles north across the border in Toronto where my sister lived, New York still felt more familiar than the still-drizzly streets of London in the summer. Besides, I suppose there was a part of me that wanted to see how bad things had got.

And St. John was a new obsession of mine, one I'd taken up in my recovery. Luca had been reading his pulpy-looking paperbacks for years, but I'd never touched them. They were too scary, I'd thought, too low brow. I remembered the garish paperbacks though, the ones that showed off his last name in huge embossed letters. They'd been ubiquitous when I was a kid. Each had a plain black cover with a silhouette cutaway so you had to turn the page to get the full effect. *Rosie* was the first I ever saw, his debut, the starting point for his surprising upward trajectory. It featured a small New Hampshire town — eerily similar to the one where I'd grown up, what had once been a small farming community until the petroleum processing plants transformed it. The town was engulfed in a crackling lightning storm. *Gory and horrifying,* read the cover, *you can't put it down!!!*

St. John didn't live in New York, but his former editor did: Lily Argo.

I'd found her e-mail address online. Like St. John she must have been in her seventies but was still working freelance. There were no pictures. The best I could find was a black and white shot of her and St. John at the signing of his fourth book, *What Is Mine,* the last they worked on together. Lily Argo was an inch or two taller than St. John, glorious, an Allison Janney look-alike, which meant the two of them towered over the line of moist-lipped teenage girls who were clustered around the table. That was back in '79.

When I first approached one of my friends — an anthology editor named Dylan Bone (real name or not, I never knew) — about the possibility of an article on the publication of *Rosie,* he told me Argo had died. Dylan had even written up her obituary for *Locus* — but in retrospect he couldn't remember how he'd first found out. She'd been one of the few female editors at Doubleday back then, mostly due to her lucky discovery of St. John. When I mentioned I'd been in contact with her, that she'd agreed to meet me, Dylan had stared at me thoughtfully.

"Just be careful," he said.

"About what?"

He'd just waved his hand. "You know," he said before lurching off to the bar to fetch another round.

◆ ◆ ◆

I didn't have any problems with the border guards. The customs line was tense, but I'd always had that feeling whenever I entered the States. Once I'd swallowed two painkillers before a flight back to London and the random swipe they'd done on my hands had registered a false positive for explosives or drugs. I'd been taken to a small backroom where a dark-haired woman in a uniform demanded to know why I had been in the country. I kept apologizing, I don't know why. She had to search me by hand and the process was brusque and businesslike. She asked me to remove my bra. Then someone else came in, a heavy-set man with a broad forehead. He didn't look at me. Neither of them did. Afterward they let me go but ever since I'd been stopped for "random" checks whenever I boarded a plane. This time though the guard took one look at me and waved me through. I must have looked harmless to him.

◆ ◆ ◆

Hotel 31 was as old as the Overlook, mostly derelict with a walk-in elevator whose grill door you had to close yourself. The room was sparse, but by that point exhaustion had sunk into my skin. I called Luca to tell him I'd arrived and then collapsed under the thin covers.

All night I could hear animal sounds in the walls. The bodies of whatever moved beyond the peeling wallpaper hummed like batteries. Still, I slept. And in the morning I felt better than I had in weeks. Not mended, but stronger.

I was still in that dusky phase of grieving so that sometimes when I slept it felt I had fallen through a hole in the world. Each morning I woke up as a different person, discovered new wrinkles at the corner of my eyes, wires of thick, unrecognizable, grey hair. The doctor warned me of changes in my body, cramping, small clots of blood between my legs. I had expected my breasts to shrink but they'd only gotten larger. I read online the best thing to do was to bind them tightly with a snug towel and apply ice for ten minutes on, twenty minutes off. He hadn't told me how old I would feel after.

I had given myself three days to acclimatize to jetlag before I met up with Lily Argo.

In the meantime, I'd arranged a visit to Doubleday, St. John's first publisher. In the last thirty years Doubleday had joined with Dell and Bantam which in turn joined up with Random House. Size, they had thought, was the best way to survive an uncertain economic climate.

Two weeks ago, I'd contacted an editor at Random House in the hopes he might know if the company had kept some of the records from St. John's days. But after the bag search and the metal detectors, when I was buzzed into the offices, a blonde receptionist told me my meeting had been postponed. She was young, slickly made up in that New York way with manicured fingers and perfect plucked eyebrows. I was wearing a dark blue cardigan which, seeing her, suddenly felt so English, so matronly I almost laughed.

So I waited in the reception for an hour, browsing the display copies of new books by Margaret Atwood and Chimamanda Ngozi Adichie. They too were slickly produced.

After a while I pulled out my beat-up copy of *Strangers and Friends*, a collection of short stories St. John had published in gentlemen's magazines like *Cavalier* and *Penthouse* over the years. The book had never been one of St. John's most popular, but I'd been thumbing my way through it slowly for weeks. On the flight I had started a story called "The Survivalist" in which a doctor finds himself trapped alone in a bunker after a nuclear blast. He lives there for years, decades, devouring canned peaches and Spam until finally he comes to the end of his stashed supplies. He knows he doesn't have many options left. He can open up the door, risk contamination for a sight of the outside world — or he can continue to wait. The doctor stares at the door, wanting desperately to go out, but he can't bring himself to open it. The story ends as, driven half-mad with hunger, he begins to contemplate how long he could survive eating first the flesh of his legs, his thighs, how much he could withstand. He is a doctor after all, and he thinks it could be quite some time…

The story was gross, and it had all the macabre glee you would expect from a St. John chiller. But I didn't feel scared by it. No, what upset me most was its sense of futility. The doctor had given up on hope. He wasn't waiting for rescue. He didn't believe anyone else in the world was alive. He was simply… persisting. If he was the last man on earth, he wanted to last as long as possible. It was grotesque. Why didn't he open the door? That's what Luca would say when I tried to explain the plot him. But then Luca was the kind of man who would have opened the door. He couldn't see another way of living.

Another hour passed. Eventually the receptionist waved me over. Her manicured nails glinted dully in the light. "I'm sorry, ma'am," she said, "but the records from those years haven't been maintained. I didn't even know we were the ones who published Barron St. John." She gave a little laugh.

I asked her what that meant for me.

"No one's free to meet you. We converted to digital years ago," she said, barely sparing me a glance. "Whatever we had, we dumped back then. Besides, who reads that trash anyway?"

◆ ◆ ◆

After that I found myself at loose ends, so I called up a friend of mine, Benny Perry.

Benny and I had gone to grad school together at the University of Toronto, both of us doing doctorates in medieval literature in those early days after the financial crash when we still thought the market would recover enough to give us jobs. I'd kept at it, spinning my work on the scribal culture that produced Chaucer's *Canterbury Tales* into a postdoc in Oxford and then riding that into a full-time position in Publishing Studies of all things at a former polytechnic university. It wasn't glamorous, not like Oxford had been, but I liked the students, I liked my colleagues, and I liked the work itself: imagining how books moved through time and all the people who left their mark on them along the way.

Benny had taken another route. He'd always had a talent with photography and after he dropped out of the program he'd moved to New York and taken a job with *House & Garden* before it closed. It'd paid well enough that he'd stuck with photography, jumping from one magazine to another until he had enough of a portfolio to go freelance. He'd taken one of those famous pictures of Trump, the one where his face seems to be receding into the folds of flesh around his neck. In the past couple of months, I'd seen it on social media from time to time and reprinted in the papers.

"It's made things a bit hard for me," Benny told me as we sat sipping margaritas in The Lantern's Keep, a classy place near Times Square where the cocktails cost four times what they would at home. There had been a teary week before Luca and I made our decision when I'd given up alcohol, and even after we changed our minds I still hadn't felt like touching the stuff. This was the first drink I'd had in eight months.

"How do you mean?"

"Well it's brought me lots of attention, sure, but not the good kind, you know? Trump supporters *hate* that picture. Trump does too, which is why it gets recycled so often."

Benny's face looked strained and he fidgeted with his glass. He wasn't quite how I remembered him. Benny was always a big man, a cornfed, Iowa type whose Baptist parents had taught him to shun dancing and drink. When I'd met him at orientation, he'd been shy, a bit overwhelmed. But after those first awkward weeks he'd just thrown himself into everything. He had this irrepressible love of the new, and he'd taken to those things he'd missed out on most: booze, women — then men, dancing late into the night with this kind of unselfconscious clumsiness which made you want to join in.

He was much thinner now, that kind of thinness that didn't look healthy. "I'm worried about Emmanuel," he said, "worried about ... well. Anyway. People can be absolute shits, can't they?"

I agreed that they could.

"But you're looking good," Benny said, and I caught his eyes skimming over my breasts. Even though it didn't mean anything coming from him I still blushed and pulled at the cardigan. "But not ... I don't know, maybe not entirely good?" he was going on. "Hell. I don't know what I'm trying to say."

I took his hand gently and told him not to worry about it.

As The Lantern's Keep started to fill up eventually we wandered out into the street. It was hot and swampy, that kind of early August weather that makes you feel as if you've been wrapped in a damp blanket and beaten. We headed south toward the West Village by foot so I could see the sights. North was Central Park and Trump Towers, which were all basically off limits now. New York hadn't changed so much, not in terms of that strange and beautiful blend of architecture and anger, but there were bits that alarmed me. Like all the police cars had stickers listing the reward for information on cop-killers with a number you could call.

When I told Benny about the project I was working on, it turned out he'd read St. John as a kid, which surprised me, given his background.

"What I remember about him was that my parents were reading him. They never read *anything* like that otherwise. Murder and cannibalism and demons and all that stuff. But *Faction of Fire,* you know, it was all about faith, wasn't it? In that book there was no getting around it: The Devil was real. And I suppose that's what my parents thought anyway. Good and evil weren't abstract concepts to them. There were good folk and there were bad folk. And it wasn't just that the bad folk made bad decisions. They were... *bad*. It was something more fundamental. Badness worked through them. It was something tangible, real. And St. John, well, his books were all about that, weren't they?"

Benny grinned at me and for a moment I could see his younger self peering out, that kid who'd never touched a drop of liquor in his life before I met him.

"How're your parents doing?" I asked him because that was the kind of thing we were supposed to ask one another now that we weren't kids anymore.

"Mom had a stroke two years ago," Benny said with a shrug. "I go back when I can to help her out. She's lonely, I know, but whenever I do go we just end up fighting."

I didn't ask him about Emmanuel, about whether his parents knew. I figured probably they did. There were enough profiles floating around about Benny's photos so you could only avoid knowing if you really tried.

"How are you and Luca doing?"

"Good."

"He didn't want to come with you?"

"Couldn't get away. You know how it is with these NGOs. Anytime he leaves he feels like he's letting people down."

"It's good what he's doing," Benny told me. "We need more people like him right now." After a moment he stretched, and I heard the joints in his shoulders pop. "It must be hard writing horror stories now, you know? It seems like that's all we've got these days. I can't bear to watch the news anymore."

◆ ◆ ◆

I didn't sleep well that night. When I'd glanced at the papers, they were filled with stories about tensions escalating, something to do with the South China Sea islands and whether the US was being too aggressive. John McCain was trying to dial things back, but you could tell he was getting tired of it. His eyes looked sharp and a little bit scared.

I'd had panic attacks all throughout the October leading up to the election. There'd been Brexit, of course, our own particular mess. At a conference last summer an American colleague had told me, "what we're seeing is radical politics. People stopped believing that they mattered to the system — but all that's different now. It's exciting, isn't it? Anything could happen." Trump had seemed funny back then, dangerous but still avoidable. They called it all a horror show but you could tell there was fascination underneath it all. How close could we come to disaster? But Hillary was ahead in the polls. Some of the Republicans were denouncing Trump, trying to put a little distance between themselves for when the eventual shellacking came on November 8th.

But it didn't come. For weeks after, all throughout the Christmas break, whenever I heard Trump's name it was as if there was a loud gong echoing in my head. My feed was filled with anguish, betrayal, heartbreak. But I had seen all that already. I felt immured, resilient — and besides I still didn't believe, not really, that it would happen. Then eventually the cold hard truth settled in when I watched the inauguration with Luca. As Trump walked to the podium, I burst out laughing, I don't know why, the sheer cognitive dissonance of the whole thing. I felt hysterical. My palms were sweating.

Afterward I learned St. John had written a novel about something similar, *Answering the King,* about a madman who cheats his way to becoming the President of the United States. Eventually it comes down to a fifteen-year-old girl tormented with visions of the past and the future to stop him. The question at the heart of it is: if you could go back in time to stop Hitler, would you? They had made a movie about it with Steve Buscemi. I don't remember who played the girl, only how wide her eyes were, how she captured that world-weariness so well for someone so young. She was a Cassandra. No one would listen to her.

That was the night when the whole thing with Luca happened. Normally we were very careful. I hadn't been in my job for very long, and he'd just moved across the country to live with me. We had talked about having kids one day but... we weren't careful enough. Disaster crept in the way it always does.

◆ ◆ ◆

I called Argo the next day. It was the first time I'd spoken to her and her voice was thin and cagey with a flat, Ohio accent. It sounded as if it were coming from much further away than the Upper East Side.

It felt strange to be listening to her voice and I thought about what Dylan Bone had told me. I'd read the obituary in fact, half as a joke and half because I knew Dylan didn't make mistakes very often. He'd cut his teeth in the eighties horror boom and still made most of his money by convincing writers like St. John and Clive Barker to give him new material. It might sound mercenary, but it isn't, not really: Bone was a believer, a horror fanatic. He loved the stuff and even when the market dropped out of it in the nineties he had kept at it, putting out anthology after anthology with cheesy, hand-drawn skeletons or zombified hands reaching out of the grave. Argo had been part of that, someone who'd made the genre in its heyday.

On the phone Argo was polite and she agreed to meet me for lunch the next day at a cafe. "It'll have to be close to my apartment," she told me, "I can't move very well now."

I told her I understood and could meet her wherever she wanted.

"What's this about then? Really?" Her tone wasn't querulous but wondering. "You know I wrote a chapter about working with St. John for some anthology twenty years ago, *Devilish Discussions* or something like that."

I hesitated because I didn't really have an answer. Yes, I knew the story about how she'd been sent St. John's first manuscript by mistake. It had been meant to go to her boss, but he'd been on vacation. She'd liked it but her boss wouldn't touch it, and she didn't have enough support inside Doubleday to push it through, not then, a low-level assistant. But they'd kept in touch, writing letters when the mood took one or the other. Then when *Rosie* had come along it had been "a day of glory" — so she called it.

I gave her the answer I gave most of my colleagues. St. John had changed the genre, really changed it. For one brief moment horror hadn't been the red-haired stepchild of fiction. Horror had been king. And I wanted to know how that had happened. Part of my answer was true. I'd always been fascinated by the way books were made, the countless decisions that went into them. But if I was really honest it was simply because I'd become a fan, a real fan — maybe not Dylan Bone level — but my admiration for St. John was genuine.

It was more than that though. The real reason was one I couldn't quite put my finger on, but it had something to do with stories of chance — which St. John's certainly was. And that underneath every story is a pivotal moment when things changed. I wanted to know what that looked like. I needed to know if Argo had understood when that manuscript crossed her desk what it would mean, if she'd felt a chill when he opened the envelope. Like someone had walked on her grave.

◆ ◆ ◆

That afternoon Benny took me out to the Cloisters for old time's sake, and it was beautiful, just like he'd promised it would be. The place was a mishmash of architecture taken from a series of medieval abbeys in France, Catalan, and the Occitan, simultaneously peaceful and surreal, liminal, a sliver of another world transplanted into New York.

"I thought you'd like it," Benny told me. We were staring at a tree that had been shaped to fit one of the alcoves in the garden. Its branches curved unnaturally like a menorah to fill the space. I couldn't help but wonder how it had been manipulated, what sort of subtle violence had pressurized the wood to assume the shape it had.

"I do," I told him, shivering despite the mid-day heat.

"So, tomorrow. The editor, what's her name again?" He snapped his fingers. "Argo, right? Lily Argo. You're going to interview her. What about St. John then? Any chance you'll get to speak to him?"

I didn't think so. St. John lived in New Hampshire, and I had no idea what kind of relationship the two of them still had. If they kept in touch. If Argo would even like me.

"Of course she will. You're — well, you're the *makeles quene*, aren't you?" He smiled. "You are without blot."

"Someone back home said she was dead," I told him uneasily. I still didn't like that part of the story. Why would Dylan have thought that?

"Huh," Benny said. "It sounds like the beginning of a ghost story, doesn't it? Like she'll bestow her wisdom on you, settle her unfinished business, and vanish into the night."

"It sounds exactly like that."

"But maybe you're lucky, not seeing St. John."

I asked him what he meant.

"You know. He's bound to be pretty weird, isn't he? I mean he's been writing that stuff for more than forty years now. You can't keep that close to the darkness without some of it sticking to you."

It wasn't the first time I'd heard something like this before. I was used to getting it myself, sometimes at the university. But the horror writers I'd met were among the most well-adjusted people I knew, certainly they were much calmer than the other writers I tended to deal with. Some people said it was because there wasn't much money in horror writing these days. But I thought it was something else: writers were good at channeling their anxieties into something productive. We all have those nasty thoughts, those worries that maybe we don't love our partners as much as we should, or maybe they don't love us. Fears that maybe something awful will happen tomorrow. The phone will ring and it will be the police. An accident somewhere. Or a fight escalated, a button pushed.

"When I studied the Middle Ages," I told him, "it always seemed like it must have been so difficult for those people. I mean, the Black Death wiped out 40% of the population. Imagine whole villages lost, your family — everyone you've ever met — wiped out."

"I know," he said, "I just couldn't take living like that. I'd, I dunno. I'd go crazy, I guess."

I wondered if he really would go crazy. Or if he was going crazy right now, waiting for that call about Emmanuel. Waiting for Trump to finally get around to signing a new Executive Order. I had always liked Benny because he had a sense of outrage, a keen abhorrence of injustice. I knew he had marched in those early protests, and knew that he wasn't marching anymore. He didn't want to draw attention to himself. Benny was strong but he was adaptable. He was finding ways to survive, to keep making his art — but doing it so it didn't hurt Emmanuel.

Luca was the same way. Most nights he didn't come home until close to midnight. There was always more he felt he could be doing. For a while I'd felt really proud of him. And then when things got bad, I'd just felt resentful, angry at him for spending so much time saving other people when what I really wanted was for him to save me.

In the gift shop I chose a postcard for him, a picture of the Flemish tapestry called *The Hunt for the Unicorn*. It showed five young men in aristocratic clothing with their spears and their dogs. If it weren't for the title you wouldn't have been able to tell what they were doing there. I wanted to choose one with the unicorn, but all of them looked too violent or depressing. Something about the unicorn in captivity, collared, in a fence that can barely hold her, reminded me of *Answering the King*, and how the girl had been taken to prison after she shot the president. There had been a coda at the end of the novel, the little girl twenty years later, grown up, in solitary confinement. They had thought she had gone mad because she wouldn't stop hurting herself.

But St. John showed the real reason. The girl had had another vision, one worse than what she'd stopped all those years ago. But this time there was nothing she could do about it.

◆ ◆ ◆

I couldn't get hold of Luca that night. He wasn't answering his e-mail and when I tried him at home — and then at work — the phone just rang and rang. It wasn't that unusual. Sometimes there were emergencies, and Luca would become so totally absorbed in them he would forget everything else.

There were emergencies like that, I knew, one every few days it seemed. So eventually I left a message saying I loved him. I tried the TV but got nothing except static. Eventually I settled down to read. It was another story from *Strangers and Friends* but this one was about a haunted house called "Question the Foundations." It was a twist on the trope: the houses weren't haunted by people so much as the people by houses. In St. John's world each person had a tiny space within them, an impression of the place where they had been born. And it remained there, like a scar, or a memory. And everyone else could see it too, who you were and where you came from. Except there was this young boy who didn't have a place like that. He had nothing. He had come from nowhere. And because he had nothing, he scared people.

I put the book down, confused and unsure of myself. The story bothered me but I didn't know why. It was different from the others, softer, sadder. There was no real horror in the story. It had been about loneliness. How it felt to be hollow, an outsider. Rootless.

Maybe it was just those constellations of images, emptiness and violence. Luca had told me a story once about how his family used to keep chickens. He had lived in the middle of a wood. One day a fox broke into the henhouse and tore open all the chickens. He'd found their bodies, or what was left of them, the next morning. Inside their bodies he had found strings of growing eggs, like pearls.

After he told me that, I couldn't sleep, and it was the same feeling now. I didn't have any regrets. Luca and I had talked, and he had left the decision to me. There had been no pressure, none from him anyway. But I'd been watching the news. And when the first bomb exploded in Paddington Station it had been like a warning sign. Not now. It wasn't safe. Things would settle down soon, they had to. And then we could try again.

I put the book down and touched my stomach gently, tentatively. Beneath my fingers all I could feel was my own thick flesh.

♦ ♦ ♦

Three times I passed the cafe before I finally had the courage to meet Lily Argo. I could see her — at least I thought it was her — sitting in the courtyard with her walker folded up beside her. She had long white hair and a red-and-grey printed dress with long sleeves. I knew her because of how tall she was, even a little stooped over. She still had at least six inches on me.

"Ms. Argo?" I asked her and she nodded politely while I pulled up a seat.

"So you're the one who's come asking about Barron St. John."

"That's right." I tentatively launched into my pitch: an article on St. John's early publication history, documenting her involvement in acquiring and editing his first title. She stopped me with a wave of her hand.

"Sure, honey," she said with a wide, generous smile, "you don't need to go on like that. I'm happy to talk about those days, though I confess they seem a while ago now. You know I got that manuscript by accident, don't you?"

I nodded, and she seemed relieved.

"Good, so we're not starting from scratch. What you want is the story, I take it, of how Bear — that's what I always called him — and I got along in those early days? Where the horror came from?" I nodded again and took out my phone but she eyed it warily. "I'll tell it as best I can and you can make of it whatever you will — but no recordings, okay? You can listen and you can write down what you get from it, but you only get to hear it once."

What was I supposed to say? Already I could feel a kind of strange buzz around her, the magnetic pull of her charisma. I had wanted her story and here she was, ready to give it to me.

◆ ◆ ◆

"I was pretty young in those days," she began, "when I first started working for Doubleday. I'd grown up in Ohio which I never liked very much in part because it didn't seem like I was much use to my parents. I was a reader, even then, but they had wanted me to go to one of the nursing schools, but I knew I'd never be happy with something like that, taking care of people all the time. So when I was seventeen I ran off to New York City.

"Publishing was still very much a gentleman's sport back then and if you were a woman you were either someone's secretary or you were publishing feminist pamphlets and burning your bra. I was the former." She paused and took a delicate sip from her Coke. Her lipstick remained unsmudged though it left a trace of red on her straw. "Most of us at the time wanted to be writers. I suppose I did as much as anyone, and so we'd spend our days editing, and we'd spend our nights writing. What was funny was that we knew all the people we were sending our drivel to, we'd met them at luncheons or for after-hours drinks. I was embarrassed. I was a good editor, and because I was a good editor I knew I wasn't a very good writer. I thought, how on earth will these men take me seriously if they see what I'm coming up with?

"So I did what most women did at the time, or anyone who wasn't Daphne du Maurier anyway, and I made up a name. Mine was Victor Wolf, which today seems so damned fake I don't know why no one thought anything of it. Or maybe they did but they just didn't care. Anyway I may have been writing garbage, but eventually the garbage got better and I started getting some of it published. It was what they called Kooks and Spooks stuff, I suppose, sort of crime fiction but with some other bits thrown in, monsters, sometimes, and ghosts. Possession — or Russian spies using hypnosis to control young American teenagers, that sort of thing. There was a real taste for that sort of thing back then. By the early seventies the papers were going crazy, telling us the irrationalism of our reading was helping the Commies and we had to get back to old-fashioned, American literature. But *Rosemary's Baby* was an absolute hit, and then there was *The Exorcist,* and people just wanted more of it.

"That was when Bear's first manuscript came across my desk. The two of us call it an accident but it wasn't that, not really. See, I was used to reading submissions for Donnie Rogers and when I finished Bear's first one I knew there was magic in it, raw, maybe, but magic nonetheless. And I knew Donnie was slated for laparoscopic gallbladder surgery. He was going to be off for at least a week recovering. That was when I tried to pitch the manuscript.

"Of course, I got laughed out of the offices. No one took me seriously and when Donnie came back he heard what I'd done and he bawled me out in front of the whole crew. Jesus, he took a strip off one side of me and then the other. After that I didn't dare try anything like that for a good long while.

"Still, Bear had appreciated the support. He was poor as a church mouse and he and Mya had a second little one on the way. He tried me with this and that a couple of times, but it never really made it anywhere. I guess it was after a while of him sending me his stuff that I sent him one of mine. God, the nerve I had!" she chuckled, and I couldn't help but chuckle along with her. "Well Bear wrote back and said it was pretty good, and I said it was better than pretty good, that *Playboy* had taken it. Bear had been trying to crack *Playboy* but hadn't managed it by that point.

"For six months Bear went silent after that, and I guess I thought maybe I'd offended him. Men don't like being shown up, not then, not now. That's why there's all the craziness there is today. Women are afraid of violence, but men? Men are afraid of humiliation. Humiliation to them is like dying over and over and over again. And speaking of humiliation, I had just about survived mine. Donnie Rogers had moved over to New American Libraries, and I was covering for him while they looked for a replacement. That was when the next manuscript crossed my desk."

"That was *Rosie*?" I asked her.

"Indeed it was, though it was called *Revenge of the Stars* at the time which was a godawful title, I have to say."

"And this time it stuck?"

"Not right away it didn't. The ending was clunky. It had Rosie transforming into this giant radioactive slug thing and devouring the town that way. Pure St. John, you know. He always loved the EC Comics stuff. People want to say he's got literary chops, and sure he does, but a part of him is pure pulp and is perfectly content to stay that way, thank you very much."

"So what happened?" I wanted to know.

"Oh, that's the easy bit. Some good luck, I suppose. Ira Levin was big, and Bear's book was enough like that for me to pull together an advance for him. Small, you know. The real success came later with the paperback sales, and that wasn't me, not exactly. But I suppose if what you're after is who found Barron St. John then it's me as much as it was anyone."

She paused there to take another long drag of her Coke. While she'd been talking, she seemed so animated, so full of vigor, but as the seconds stretched on I could see how old she was now, how time had etched fine lines around her lips. Her wrists were thin and frail, the skin bunching and slack at the same time.

She moved then, pulled up a black leather handbag and began to dig around in it. Eventually she came up with a Christmas card. "Look at that," she said, her eyes sharp. The paper was old and creased in several places. When I opened it there I found a simple handwritten note. *To Lilian,* it said, *a real wolf in sheep's clothing. We owe you so much. Love, Bear and Mya St. John.*

Lily was smiling slightly as she showed it to me, smiling and watching to see my reaction. I tried to smile back but there was a part of me that felt disappointed. Most of the story was what she had published in that chapter. Little of it really surprised me. It felt rehearsed, the way you keep old memories by telling yourself the story behind them again and again. Whatever I was looking for, it wasn't there.

I was getting restless, and it seemed like she was finished when she cocked her head to the side. "That's not what you wanted to hear, was it?"

I tried to tell her it was great, wonderful stuff. It would certainly make it into the article.

"Sure it will," she said, "but you didn't need any of it. Certainly you didn't need to fly over here from England just to get this story, did you? I could've told you that over the phone. You didn't need to come."

I shrugged.

"What you wanted was him, wasn't it? You wanted Bear."

"Maybe," I told her wearily. The heat was starting to get to me, making me a touch queasy.

"It isn't easy, you know," she said, "to try to tell your story when the best parts are about someone else." She sighed. "You know, I had to give up writing once I found St. John. It wasn't like it had been before. We were so busy all the time. St. John could write like a madman, he was *fast*. There was always another book. And then things got tricky with the contracts. You must know about this?"

I did. Everyone did. St. John had left Doubleday after a series of well-publicized contract disputes. Doubleday had been keeping most of the profits on the paperback sales, and he felt he deserved a bigger cut. Doubleday wouldn't budge and eventually he left.

"There wasn't much I could do for him. They wouldn't give him a better deal and they wouldn't listen when I told them how serious he was about leaving. When he finally did switch publishers all those men at the top said it was my fault. I got parked for a while editing books on what types of music you can play to help your plants grow, that sort of kooky trash. After a year or so they fired me."

I fiddled with my own straw, unsure how to react to any of this.

"Bear didn't take me with him, see. I told him not to. I told him I had enough status in the company — but I was wrong. When you're on top you always think you're going to stay there forever, that there aren't sharks circling beneath. But I guess Barron knew about those sharks. The one thing he knew about was the sharks. He could be one himself when he needed to."

"You didn't want to go back to writing?"

"Nah, I felt I'd spent my chance by that point. I think I had one lucky break in me — and it went to St. John. There wasn't going to be another. I got by after that. I moved over to another house for a little while and convinced St. John to come do a book for us. But by that point things were different. He was a superstar and I felt spent. I had had enough of horror. It was the eighties. Despite everything it still felt as if the world was falling apart. There was the banking crisis, the AIDS epidemic. The people weren't reading the news though. They were reading Bear.

"I did write one more story though. I tried to sell it myself, but no one would buy it. Victor Wolf had been forgotten. Bear liked it though. And he knew I was in danger of losing my mortgage. So he sent it out for me, under his name. When it sold to the New Yorker — his first real literary sale though God knows he deserved others and got them eventually — he gave me the profits." Her smile then was bitter. "I was grateful, you know. At the time he said it was only fair. I had made his name after all. I should get the use of it whenever I wanted.

"And I was grateful at the time. I kept my brownstone, paid it off eventually. When he sold the collection, he gave me the whole advance. For a while I thought about going back to Ohio, but I still couldn't admit to my parents I hadn't been able to last in New York. So instead I stayed."

She stared at me for a moment or two after that, and I could feel the cool ripple of sadness passing over me like a shadow.

"Someone told me you died," I said, just to break the spell of her silence.

"Of the two of us, Barron was always the shark, you see?" she told me wryly, "No, I didn't die. I just learned something he never figured out: how to stay alive when you stop moving."

◆ ◆ ◆

That evening I collected my things from Hotel 31.

Benny offered to drive me to the airport, but I told him he didn't need to do that. I could get a taxi. The university had given me a budget for that. When he said okay it sounded like there was relief in his voice, and I wondered if that meant Emmanuel was home. Or maybe it was just that he didn't want to get so close to the airport. There were regular protests still going on. People were angry about the deportations, but no one knew how to stop them.

"Did you get what you wanted from Lily Argo?" Benny asked me. "She wasn't just a ghost?" I told him I hadn't really known what I wanted but I was certain, despite everything, I had met Lily Argo. But I was probably going to scrap the story. My Head of Department would be pissed but that was how these things went. Sometimes you thought you had something, and you didn't.

What she had told me felt too invasive to write about. What I had wanted, I realized, was not just her story but a glimpse of her secret self. I didn't have a right to it. And that's what had made me want it even more. Maybe we all have a secret self: some of us keep it chained in the basement of our minds while others like St. John learn how to feed it.

"Well," he said, "it was good to see you anyway. Give my love to Luca. You tell him to take proper care of you."

I promised I would.

While I waited for my flight to board, I watched the news. We were all watching the news. We couldn't help it. Tense security officers patrolled the hallways with machine guns at the ready, just in case. There were fewer travelers those days, fewer coming in, fewer getting out. But I felt a kind of solidarity with the others as our eyes were glued to the screens. We were liminal people moving from one reality to another. We were going home.

So we watched the footage of explosions in Yemen. Pleas from refugees who had found themselves trapped in abandoned tenements, living in filth. It was only when I saw the story about the bomb that had gone off on a train along the Victoria Line that I remembered Luca still hadn't called me back.

I was watching them pulling survivors out of the rubble and the blood gelled to ice in my veins. I couldn't move. It had happened then. It had happened. Time seemed to slow. Luca mostly worked from Cambridge, but the NGO had offices in London. He went there from time to time. When had I last heard from him? Who could I call to check? But by that point the attendant was calling me forward. I didn't move. She called me again and the people behind me began to murmur. I must have had a dazed expression on my face, a look they didn't like. The attendant called me a third time as an officer drew near. It was only then I was able to move. I showed them my passport and made my way down the ramp.

Inside the plane most of the seats were empty. The air was canned, stale tasting in my mouth. I wondered if I might have a panic attack but out on the runway I didn't dare check my phone again. The hostesses were murmuring to each other. I could tell they were twitchy. But already a strange calm was taking hold of me — a sense of icy horror. There was something inevitable about what was happening. There was nothing I could do to stop it. Whatever had happened had happened.

And this feeling? It wasn't the same as all those St. John books I had read. There I could find purpose, structure — meaning in all the bad things that had happened. But outside there was only chaos. The unraveling of beautiful things into violence. It signified nothing.

As the plane taxied down the runway I settled back in my chair and tried to sleep.

Survival Strategies for Weird Times

1. Autobiography[2]

> Art sends us information from another place.
> — Timothy Morton, *Hyperobjects*[3]

The short story "Survival Strategies" offers a semi-fictionalized account of a young academic on a research trip to New York to interview the editor of Barron St. John, a bestselling author who came to prominence during the horror boom of the 1970s and eighties. Set against the backdrop of the new Trump administration it uses autobiographical elements to blur the line between fiction and reality. In doing so it asks, where do the boundaries between "true horror" and speculative horror intersect? To what extent can our situatedness in the present moment become a source of the uncanny?

The autobiographical elements of story are important. In the summer of 2016 I began a research project to investigate the publishing history of Stephen King's *Carrie* by the hardback publisher Doubleday in 1974. At the time, I argued that

---

2 I would like to thank Nina Allan whose many conversations on the subject have informed my own developing approach to weird fiction as well as Anglia Ruskin University which funded my research. Thanks also go to Bill Thompson for his generous interview, Bob Jackson for providing copies of a number of crucial documents, and Bev Vincent for his support and guidance on all things King related. Many of the threads discussed in this commentary relate to a series of articles I have written. These include: Helen Marshall, "Introduction," in *The Year's Best Weird Fiction, Vol. 4*, eds. Helen Marshall and Michael Kelly (Toronto: Undertow Publications, 2017), ix–xvii. Also see my discussion of King's work (drafted on this trip) at Helen Marshall, "The Only Lights are Headlights," *Weird Fiction Review*, August 10, 2016, http://weirdfictionreview.com/2016/08/101-weird-writers-43-stephen-king/.

3 I make no claims to be a speculative realist nor a philosopher and so my understanding of Morton's work may be limited. I have responded to his text here as a writer, recognizing a likeness in approach. See Timothy Morton, *Hyperobjects: Philosophy and Ecology after the End of the World* (Minneapolis: University of Minnesota Press, 2013), 47.

the unexpected success of *Carrie* launched "the Stephen King phenomenon,"[4] and was one of several important books inspiring the marketing approach to horror paperbacks from the late seventies to the early nineties. As with the publication of any breakthrough novel, the penning of *Carrie* had taken on its own mythological status. In one of the autobiographical sections of his memoir and guide to the craft, *On Writing* (2000), King opens up about his difficulty in producing a first draft. He managed three single-spaced pages, which he crumpled up and threw away only to have them rescued by his wife, Tabitha.[5] The sense of a historical moment interested me — as I imagine it was intended to. I had recently completed a Ph.D. in medieval literature and was accustomed to working in the archives, aware of how much material had been lost over the centuries. Studying a contemporary novelist was innately appealing: it promised abundance where I had previously encountered dearth. But there was also an extra voyeuristic angle. Here was a writer I admired intensely whose life I might be able to approach in some way through my research. I wanted intimacy.

I was not entirely prepared for what I would find. I contacted Bill Thompson, King's first editor at Doubleday through his editorial freelance website and arranged a meet-up in New York. But in conversation with several horror fans, authors and editors — both in the UK and in the US — I was repeatedly told it would be impossible to meet Thompson because he had passed away years ago. Let me avoid all ambiguity here: as I found when I met him, Thompson was still very much in the land of the living. But my repeated encounter with claims of his apparent death began to evoke that creeping-under-the-skin sensation of the "fantastic" — that moment identified by the Russian structuralist Tzvetan Todorov in which something apparently supernatural is encountered, creating a period of hesitation as

---

[4] Michael R. Collings and Stephen E. Fabian, *The Stephen King Phenomenon* (Mercer Island: Starmont House, 1987), 1.

[5] This story has been recounted in a range of other articles and interviews, but I have found King's sense of the story here to be the fullest in *On Writing: A Memoir of the Craft* (New York: Scribner, 2000), 68.

different possibilities are suggested and discarded.⁶ I did not know how to react. I had been in contact with Bill Thompson, had exchanged e-mails and agreed on a date for meeting, but all that contact had been on-line with no further way of verifying his identity. *I nearly reached the point of believing.* This is the formula Todorov presents to sum up the spirit of the fantastic: "Either total faith or total incredulity would lead us beyond the fantastic: it is hesitation which sustains its life."⁷ I lingered in that period of hesitation. Bill Thompson was alive, of course he was alive, but the sense of the uncanny soaked into my perception of him. The trip came alive with the possibility of the real unreal.

2. The Real Unreal

> The most merciful thing in the world, I think, is the inability of the human mind to correlate all its contents. We live on a placid island of ignorance in the midst of black seas of infinity, and it was not meant that we should voyage far. The sciences, each straining in its own direction, have hitherto harmed us little; but some day the piecing together of dissociated knowledge will open up such terrifying vistas of reality, and of our frightful position therein, that we shall either go mad from the revelation or flee from the deadly light into the peace and safety of a new dark age.
>
> — H.P. Lovecraft, "The Call of Cthulhu"⁸

It was the summer of 2016, and already my world had been destabilized. The Brexit vote had shaken UK politics, threatening my university which was heavily reliant on EU students and EU-

---

6   Todorov's approach to the fantastic has informed my thinking on the nature of my writing although I frequently find myself butting up against the limitations of his definitions. See Tzvetan Todorov, *The Fantastic: A Structural Approach to a Literary Genre,* trans. Richard Howard (Ithaca: Cornell University Press, 1973), 25.
7   Ibid., 31.
8   H.P. Lovecraft, "The Call of Cthulhu," in *The Call of Cthulhu and Other Weird Stories,* ed. S.T. Joshi (New York: Penguin Classics, 2002), 139.

research funds. In New York, the American election was in full swing, already tilting toward Trump. "Be careful," I told friends, "it could happen here." No one took me seriously.

In a 1989 issue of SF Eye, Bruce Sterling described slipstream writing as "a kind of writing which simply makes you feel very strange; the way that living in the twentieth century makes you feel, if you are a person of a certain sensibility."[9] Slipstream writing drew heavily on the fantastic; as Sterling said:

> [I]t is a contemporary kind of writing which has set its face against consensus reality. It is fantastic, surreal sometimes, speculative on occasion, but not rigorously so. It does not aim to provoke a "sense of wonder" or to systematically extrapolate in the manner of classic science fiction.[10]

Where science fiction seemed coherent, the vanguard of a single dominant ideology, slipstream was postmodern, infused with a sense of ironic detachment that seemed to exemplify the natural response to conditions in Anglo-America. But twenty-five years on, how might we describe the contemporary sensibility? In 2016 I was post-postmodern though I had not fully realized it yet. Post-truth, if you like, or rather, pre-post-truth, which is not to say that I was living in a time of truth but rather that we had not recognized its loss. I was locked in a moment of hesitation.

As I write this now, I find Todorov's notion of the fantastic an imperfect vehicle to describe the feeling of that year. He imagines the moment of hesitation as fragile and difficult to sustain, liable to collapse either into "total faith" or "total incredulity." In the years since I have attempted to grapple with this problem. If the twentieth century offered slipstream as its primary mode — ironic and playful — then increasingly it seems as if the twenty-first will be a far *weirder* age. Here, I draw upon the

---

9 Bruce Sterling, "Catscan," SF Eye 5, July 1989, http://indbooks.in/mirror1/?p=311829. The nature of slipstream gets good coverage in James P. Kelly and John Kessel, eds., *Feeling Very Strange: The Slipstream Anthology* (San Francisco: Tachyon Publications, 2006).

10 Ibid.

definition of weird fiction as first proposed by H.P. Lovecraft in his seminal work "Supernatural Horror in Literature" (1927) as writing which exhibits a "malign and particular suspension or defeat of [...] fixed laws of Nature."[11] This mode, discussed by Jeff and Ann VanderMeer, China Miéville, and Roger Luckhurst, among others, to me, plausibly evokes the feeling of living in the twenty-first century: an age thus far characterized by political crises, fake news, and environmental catastrophe.[12] It is an age in which the unreal intrudes upon consensus reality, shattering it with often terrifying consequences.

Of the writing I have encountered on the subject, that of the speculative realist Timothy Morton has most resonated with me. An intimate understanding of the weird infuses his discussion of hyperobjects, real things with discernible impacts which cannot be apprehended in their entirety, but which affect our understanding of what it means to exist. He cites global warming as one significant hyperobject: its effects are massively distributed, so much so that the object itself becomes difficult to grasp, seeming to disappear from our vision or to undulate in our minds and in reality. Morton describes our present moment as the age of asymmetry, a period of hypocrisy in which the ironic detachment characteristic of many postmodern writers is impossible because there is "nowhere to stand outside of things altogether."[13] Hyperobjects engulf us. However much we seek to escape them, we find there is no *away*.

---

11 H.P. Lovecraft, *The Annotated Supernatural Horror in Literature*, ed. S.T. Joshi (New York: Hippocampus Press, 2000), 29.

12 A complete history of the emergence and analysis of weird fiction — with a particular emphasis on the new weird — is beyond the remit of this essay. For reference, I have found the following works particularly useful. Ann VanderMeer and Jeff VanderMeer, eds., *The Weird: A Compendium of Strange and Dark Stories* (New York: Tor Books, 2012); Jeffrey Andrew Weinstock, "The New Weird," in *New Directions in Popular Fiction: Genre, Reproduction, Distribution,* ed. Ken Gelder (Basingstoke: Palgrave Macmillan, 2016): 177–200; Joan Gordon, "Reveling in Genre: An Interview with China Miéville," *Science Fiction Studies* 30 (2003): 91; and Roger Luckhurst, "The Weird: A Dis/orientation," *Textual Practice* 31, no. 6 (2017): 1041–61.

13 Morton, *Hyperobjects,* 12.

This view finds eerie parallels with the primary processes of weird fiction. It evokes the brilliant ghost film *Ju-on: The Grudge*.[14] This was an early foray of mine into horror. I could hardly stand to watch it. The violence seemed senseless and unmotivated. A series of abstract images presented themselves, many of which still haunt me. A ghost clings to the body of a woman, invisible only when she enters a shower and discovers someone else's hand in her hair, as she begins to wash it. Likewise, another woman attempts to escape from the vengeful ghost by crawling into her bed — the psychological source of the greatest safety. But it is too late. She discovers the ghost is already inside, with her. No escape was possible from the ghost of *Ju-on* because no space, however personal, however intimate, was unavailable to it. Likewise, the weird is a profoundly intimate a form of writing, designed to haunt, to project a trace of unreality onto the surface of the real. It creates ruptures, and in doing so, makes briefly visible what lies beneath. We encounter this as an intrusion in most cases, but if it is an intrusion, it is only an intrusion of *some other thing* upon our closed-off perception of the world. Those things were not summoned into being by our perception of them. They already existed, independent of our encounter with them. One of the primary functions of the weird is to remind us how little we see, and how the influence of those things we do not see can still be deadly.

This sensibility flowed into the text of "Survival Strategies" by itself. I did not set out to write a story about Brexit and Trump but the sense of dislocation, the uncanniness of these hyperobjects, permeated multiple aspects of the story, conflating the painfully personal and the public, the story of myself and the story of the world in which I found myself living. To attempt to write about Stephen King as a researcher was to realize that there was no detached, objective position from which I could undertake my research. The story of King was the story of America in the late seventies, and that story is still the story of the present moment:

---

14 Takashi Shimizu, dir., *Ju-on: The Grudge* (Akasaka, Minato, Tokyo: Pioneer LDC, 2003), Blu-ray Disc, 1080p.

one riven with violence and uncertainty, asymmetries in power, wild successes and also devastating failures. It felt profoundly uncomfortable, and it felt uncomfortable in a way that resonated with the experience of Brexit and Trump, the double punch. Taken together they suggested a sort of rising tide of — something. It was not clear to me exactly what. But whatever it was seemed inescapable. It was as if Brexit and Trump were simply "a local manifestation of some vast entity" — Morton's hyperobject.[15] I could not separate myself from it, just as I could not return King to a distance where writing about him seemed easy. The real possibility of encountering King triggered a flight into fiction. The only way to write honestly about the experience was to write myself away from it.

3. Flights

> As the plane taxied down the runway I settled back in my chair and tried to sleep.
> — Helen Marshall, "Survival Strategies"

The narrative voice of "Survival Strategies" is detached and yet the detachment marks a deep emotional engagement. The narrator floats through events, cynical at times, but only as a mask; cynicism deflects, but the narrator absorbs from a distance she seeks to maintain, only to find that no distance is possible. The world intrudes, sometimes violently. In the true fashion of the weird tale, her encounter with Lily Argo demonstrates that the world has *always* dangerously intruded, the world has always *already* dangerously intruded. There is no safe vantage point to observe without becoming immersed. In short, it feels like the end of the world.

Morton has something specific to say about this sense of the ending world in the twenty-first century. He calls into question the notion of *world,* labeling it an "aesthetic effect based on a

---

15   Morton, *Hyperobjects,* 43.

blurriness and aesthetic distance."¹⁶ I cannot help but agree. The act of writing "Survival Strategies" was a simultaneous engagement with and flight from an increasingly inexplicable world. Its world was my world, but not my world — the *unheimlich* home, a home that does not allow one to feel at home. The act of writing was an attempt to create, through aesthetic engagement, a new world. Literally, the act of writing was, for me, an act of worldbuilding.

The process of worldbuilding lies at the heart of speculative fiction and yet it is an area with which I have always struggled, perhaps because my own style is improvisational and intuitive rather than clearly structured along conventional lines. But more than this I find weird fiction a natural fit, because I find the real world — the world as I experience it — to be incoherent and uncanny. It has no respect for genre. My project in writing is not to mask these inconsistencies but to draw them out and highlight their effect. But inconsistency is often considered the sign of poor worldbuilding or a failure of craft. A recent blogpost by the science fiction author Charlie Stross began to clarify my problems with the conventional approach to worldbuilding. Stross candidly discusses his rejection of most contemporary science fiction writing on the basis of flawed worldbuilding:

> The implicit construction of an artificial but plausible world is what distinguishes a work of science fiction from any other form of literature. It's an alternative type of underpinning to actually-existing reality, which is generally more substantial (and less plausible — reality is under no compulsion to make sense).¹⁷

Artificial but plausible — this is a formulation I have since returned to many times in my attempt to grapple with what fiction

---

16 Morton, *Hyperobjects*, 87.
17 Charlie Stross, "Why I Barely Read SF These Days," *Charlie's Diary*, February 6, 2018, http://www.antipope.org/charlie/blog-static/2018/02/why-i-barely-read-sf-these-day.html.

is and what it should do. There is a tension at work in Stross's rejection of science fiction. He seems to seek plausibility from his reading, which in this case coincides with artificiality. This artifice is necessary because, as he says, reality is under no compulsion to make sense. Fiction provides sense. Fiction creates coherence. As a result, the kind of fiction Stross is after — the plausible — is a kind he recognizes as more real than real, one which is therefore inherently *unreal*. Stross's position exemplifies Morton's claims about the aesthetic effects of the notion of the world. Drawing on *Lord of the Rings* as a prime example, Morton alludes to the *Gesamtkunstwerk* (total work of art),[18] a creation in which, as Carl Maria von Weber said in 1816, "partial contributions of the related and collaborating arts blend together, disappear, and, in disappearing, somehow form a new world."[19] The *Gesamtkunstwerk* is the ideal, science fiction story in Stross's formulation, one in which the writer has total control of all aspects. However, for Morton, the *Gesamtkunstwerk* is suspect because the act of worldbuilding extends beyond fiction into the Real, which he also sees as artificial, falsely presented as coherent when in fact it is utterly weird.

Writers of weird fiction do not have the same expectations as writers of science fiction. Their worlds exhibit inconsistency. In fact, the *sine qua non* of the weird writer is that gap in consistency: the extra stair at the bottom of the staircase that makes the reader stumble, the grit in the reader's eye, the living dead. Opposed to Stross's model of the plausibly constructed world is M. John Harrison, an important figure in New Wave science fiction writer who has also contributed to the rise of the New Weird. He says:

> Every moment of a science fiction story must represent the triumph of writing over worldbuilding.

---

18 Morton, *Hyperobjects*, 88.
19 Carl Maria Von Weber, "On the Opera Undine," in *Source Readings in Music History: The Romantic Era*, ed. Oliver Strunk (London: Norton, 1965), 63.

> Worldbuilding is dull. Worldbuilding literalises the urge to invent. Worldbuilding gives an unnecessary permission for acts of writing (indeed, for acts of reading). Worldbuilding numbs the reader's ability to fulfil their part of the bargain, because it believes that it has to do everything around here if anything is going to get done.[20]

Harrison's sensibility speaks to me. His argument is subtle and contentious within the field. He describes the conventional view of worldbuilding as "a bad idea about the world as much as it is a bad idea about fiction."[21] He rejects the notion of the author-God and warns against readers who expect the world of the story to be anything other than a story. For Harrison the invented world has no outward substance. It adheres only in language and in that sense it is purely an aesthetic effect. Stross would not, I think, disagree with this, but the difference between the two lies in the kind of immersion they are seeking. Harrison prefers fiction which acknowledges what it does as "a shell game, a sham,"[22] yet his work is not post-modern in the framework we have been discussing. In fact, he rejects postmodernism with its three impossible claims:

> [F]irstly that we can change the real world into a fully prosthetic environment without loss or effort; secondly that there are no facts, only competing stories about the world; & thirdly that it's possible to meaningfully write the words "a world" outside the domains of imagination or metaphor, a solecism

---

20 This short essay — or collection of notes toward an essay — appears in its full form on *Reddit* though excerpts have been widely shared on the Internet in u/Biomancer (M. John Harrison), "A Short Essay by the Great Sci-Fi Author M. John Harrison about Why Storytelling Must Take Precedence over Worldbuilding," *Reddit,* December 14, 2014. https://www.reddit.com/r/writing/comments/2p8ogc/a_short_essay_by_the_great_sci-fi_author_m_john/.
21 Ibid.
22 Ibid.

> which allows us to feel safely distant from the consequences of our actions.[23]

Reading, according to Harrison, ought to be a ludic act. It offers the possibility of escape, but of a substantially different kind. Escape *into,* not *away from*. Here, escape should not be misread as escapism. Where Stross looks for sense, Harrison's work is profoundly unsettling. It presents fiction as a vehicle for non-sense — the unraveling of sense, the minute exposure of sense-lessness. Crucially, it seems to acknowledge that I may not always know what I mean when I write. Writing is not the attempt to translate coherence of thought from one mind to another. My mind is mischievous. I am not an author-God. There is a need for other sense-makers here.

In Lovecraft's weird tales an encounter with the real leaves three possibilities: death, madness, or flight. In 2016 I found myself struggling to find a new response. If I am honest, I did not find it within "Survival Strategies." The inspiration for the story arrived after a sleepless night following a viewing of *The Invitation* (2015),[24] a claustrophobic film about a man named Will attending a dinner party hosted by his ex-wife, Eden. Eden and her new husband have, it seems, subscribed to the beliefs of a nihilistic, death cult. Before its brutal conclusion, the film shows Will's unease as he is continually encouraged to ignore his growing anxieties through the constant weight of social pressure: surely everything is fine, the film seems to say, and it would be rude to leave, wouldn't it? Will hesitates. He cannot decide how to process the telltale signs of danger he sees around himself. Only one character does, and it is her fate that kept me up that night. Early on in the evening, one of the guests, Claire, unsettled by a game of "I Want" she is forced to play, makes her excuses and is followed out of the house by one of the other guests, David, whose looming presence throughout presages the

---

23 Ibid.
24 Karyn Kusama, dir., *The Invitation* (New York City: Gamechanger Films, 2015), Blu-ray Disc, 1080p.

bloodbath he will later initiate. We never find out what happens to Claire. Does David murder her off-screen, or does she manage to flee to safety, warned by the niggling feeling in the back of her mind that something is wrong? Her fate was important to me, and as the night advanced, I was left wondering: how effective was her strategy? What if our niggling sense of danger is too little, too late? What if we cannot run because what we are fleeing is waiting for us everywhere?

Morton asks another question: "What is left if we aren't the world?" What if — like one of H.P. Lovecraft's hapless intellectuals — our sense of control dissipates as we come to recognize our insignificance in the face of much larger forces? Morton's answer is startling: "Intimacy," he writes, "we have lost the world but gained a soul."[25] If we are not obliterated, we are made more real by the encounter. The narrator of "Survival Strategies" boards the aircraft despite the panic of an ill-described terrorist attack in London. She settles into her seat as the plane launches into the air. Perhaps her husband is dead. Perhaps everything she believed in has fallen apart. She cannot decide. She hesitates. She falls into sleep. The story had no answers for me then, but now I think that was part of the point in writing it. As a story it is not fully coherent. The metaphors do not perfectly unravel into clear meanings. But then a story cannot perfectly digest what it encounters.

The narrator sleeps, but she will wake, flying into, not away from. The world had ended before she ever left London. What is to come is a new kind of intimacy with the real. And wisdom, we can hope — and survival.

---

25   Morton, *Hyperobjects,* 90.

Bibliography

u/Biomancer (Harrison, M. John). "A Short Essay by the Great Sci-Fi Author M. John Harrison About Why Storytelling Must Take Precedence over Worldbuilding." *Reddit,* December 14, 2014. https://www.reddit.com/r/writing/comments/2p8ogc/a_short_essay_by_the_great_scifi_author_m_john/.

Collings, Michael R., and Stephen E. Fabian. *The Stephen King Phenomenon.* Mercer Island: Starmont House, 1987.

Gordon, Joan. "Reveling in Genre: An Interview with China Miéville." *Science Fiction Studies* 30 (2003): 91.

Karyn Kusama, dir. *The Invitation.* New York City, New York: Gamechanger Films, 2015. Blu-ray Disc, 1080p.

Kelly, James P., and John Kessel, eds. *Feeling Very Strange: The Slipstream Anthology.* San Francisco: Tachyon Publications, 2006.

King, Stephen. *On Writing: A Memoir of the Craft.* New York: Scribner, 2000.

Lovecraft, H.P. *The Annotated Supernatural Horror in Literature.* Edited by S.T. Joshi. New York: Hippocampus Press, 2000.

———. "The Call of Cthulhu." In *The Call of Cthulhu and Other Weird Stories,* edited by S.T. Joshi, 139–69. New York: Penguin Classics, 2002.

Luckhurst, Roger. "The Weird: A Dis/orientation." *Textual Practice* 31, no. 6 (2017): 1041–61. DOI: 10.1080/0950236X.2017.1358690.

Marshall, Helen. "Introduction." In *The Year's Best Weird Fiction,* Vol. 4, edited by Helen Marshall and Michael Kelly, ix–xvii. Toronto: Undertow Publications, 2017.

———. "The Only Lights are Headlights." *Weird Fiction Review,* August 10, 2016. http://weirdfictionreview.com/2016/08/101-weird-writers-43-stephen-king/.

Morton, Timothy. *Hyperobjects: Philosophy and Ecology after the End of the World.* Minneapolis: University of Minnesota Press, 2013.

Sterling. Bruce. "Catscan." *SF Eye* 5, July 1989. http://indbooks.in/mirror1/?p=311829.

Stross, Charlie. "Why I Barely Read SF These Days." *Charlie's Diary,* February 6, 2018. http://www.antipope.org/charlie/blog-static/2018/02/why-i-barely-read-sf-these-day.html.

Takashi Shimizu, dir. *Ju-on: The Grudge.* Akasaka, Minato, Tokyo, Japan: Pioneer LDC, 2003. Blu-ray Disc, 1080p HD.

Todorov, Tzvetan. *The Fantastic: A Structural Approach to a Literary Genre.* Translated by Richard Howard. Ithaca, New York: Cornell University Press, 1973.

VanderMeer, Ann, and Jeff VanderMeer, eds. *The Weird: A Compendium of Strange and Dark Stories.* New York: Tor Books, 2012

von Weber, Carl Maria. "On the Opera Undine." In *Source Readings in Music History: The Romantic Era,* edited by Oliver Strunk, 62–67. London: Norton, 1965.

Weinstock, Jeffrey Andrew. "The New Weird." In *New Directions in Popular Fiction: Genre, Reproduction, Distribution,* edited by Ken Gelder, 177–200. Basingstoke: Palgrave Macmillan, 2016.

9

Matrix Pavoris:
Material Dislocation in *House of Leaves*

Luka Bekavac

1. Navidson's Folly

The principal invention of Mark Z. Danielewski's *House of Leaves* is very simple and — twenty years after its publication — fairly well known: a small, featureless spatial dilatation appears in an otherwise ordinary family home. This basic premise goes on to change, expand, and evolve into a more readily recognizable, genre territory, but this inexplicable space, as abstract and benign as it might initially seem, remains scandalous enough to provide momentum for an incredible array of reactions and theories, many of them addressed or staged within the novel itself. It's hard to disentangle one thread from them, but I will try to remain as close as possible to the core of the problem: text as a graphic embodiment of the cognitive inaccessibility of space.

Traditional linguistic representations of spatiality within literary texts (e.g., building fictional objects/environments by recourse to literary tropes) won't suffice to explain the way Danielewski creates his non-correlationist figment, but the idea of "objective space" as a pure abstraction, made legible and available to thought by formalization and mathematization, necessarily misses the mark too. What is at work here is a non-phenomenological notion of space, marked by an inaccessibility to language which cannot be easily pacified by inherited frameworks: a category barely distinguishable from matter — before its configuration into an object — *hulē* that precedes or even terminally escapes articulation, quantification, and cognitive mastery. In this context, literariness could be provisionally redefined as an equivalent of this unintelligibility, and writing as an apprenticeship in dealing with spatiality without subordinating it to purposes of a human viewpoint. Literary work would therefore be a peculiar engagement with materiality rather than an expression of an ideal content or a representation of an anthropocentrically distorted "reality": a non-metaphorical processing of materials that relies precisely on the irreducible exteriority of matter to thought.

To properly follow this line of research, however, we should bear in mind that the story of the Navidson family moving into a house that turns out to be a place of paranormal manifestations is not even remotely equal to *House of Leaves* as a whole: its baroquely elaborated, metafictional structure actually places the story of this "haunting" within the frame of Will Navidson's documentary film, *The Navidson Record*, which in itself exists only in a retelling by the improbably named Zampanò, more precisely in a manuscript posthumously found and ineptly "edited" by the extremely unreliable Johnny Truant, ultimately leaving the final definition of the book to an anonymous group of "Editors."[1]

This is still not the whole story. Within the limits of this text, it would be impossible to describe every narrative or structural nut and bolt of this book; its *horror vacui*, though, working at places against the overall impact of the novel, might be read literally, as a reaction to nothingness at the limits of its fictional universe: a manic struggle to answer the provocation of an in-

---

1   For a detailed analysis of the novel's narrative hierarchy in the perspective of digital mediation, see Mark B.N. Hansen, "The Digital Topography of Mark Z. Danielewski's *House of Leaves*," *Contemporary Literature* 45, no. 4 (2004): 597–636.

different void. Many aspects of Danielewski's work are explicitly readable as horror *topoi* developed precisely through a multileveled involvement with the problem of space: the *haunted house* stereotype, the cliché of home as the ultimate place of *Unheimlichkeit,* the disturbances in spatial relations and the collapse of phenomenology of space, but also the fact that the novel aggressively accentuates its own physicality, mobilizing all typesetting options in order to displace the received modes of reading.

The first necessary step for the adequate presentation of this alien space, with all the varying degrees of its alterity and inaccessibility, is describing its position in regard to the house itself. There is a tendency — both within the novel and its commentaries — to equate the Navidson home on Ash Tree Lane with the opening to this alternate zone by simply using the term "house," while the thing described is obviously something that intersects with the house and is entangled with it in complex ways, but is very sharply differentiated from it. In order to clearly distinguish it from the House, I will call this space the Folly; this is a vaguely archaic term, originally designating any over-expensive edifice, but it gradually came to describe something more enigmatic: an object without apparent purpose, a "useless" structure which might bear the connotations of a "joke" or a "fake," something distinct from home (the House), structurally independent and separate from the House, but still connected to it in some way as a remote element, remaining a part of the same property: perhaps a place of unspecified leisure, a playground of sorts, at once away from home and close to home, a space to while away the time.

This might sound provocative, bearing in mind that this is a place of ultimate emotional, cognitive, and physical annihilation, but even without delving into a psychoanalytical reading, one can accept that — at least on some level — the bizarre, potentially limitless, shapeshifting and absolutely lethal object in the house on Ash Tree Lane is precisely that: a wish fulfillment, an obscure daydream, an excrescence produced by a nobleman's ennui and excesss of energy, the tedium of everyday life and a gnawing need to do or explore something. He devises it for himself (unbeknownst to himself), like a riddle with no hope of solution (that is his secret hope anyway). There is an even more obvious interpretation: this is "a physical incarnation" of pain,[2] the extrafamilial space of emotion generated by guilt, as deep and unstable as a subject can make it, closing only after offering oneself to death.

But the main point, beyond the possibility of reducing a spatiotemporal anomaly to a material consequence of the observer's condition, is the level of cognitive inaccessibility of this foreign object. Early on, Navidson warns: "There's nothing there. Beware."[3] The inability of the mind to adequately conceptualize and represent this "nothing" actually produces all there is: an impossible labyrinth as its first figuration, an ordinary house as its necessary container, a family inhabiting it and, further up the ontological hierarchy, a writer inventing all this, a random, young man who finds the writer's notes, yet another person who might have invented or imagined that man. The entire narrative, with all of its levels, is readable as a traumatized reflex against the unrecountability of pure space ("nothing"), a rewriting of that atemporal exteriority into the language of anthropocentric conveniences (content, causality, chronology, etc.), as negative as it is: a blind man writes a study of a lost or fictional documentary film that tries to capture empty and constantly shifting space in the dark.

"Exploration A" immediately showcases the basic scope of the Folly's capacities: whimsical creation, or opening, of new geometric shapes, as well as elimination of previously existing ones; articulation of space into doors, corridors, rooms, halls; changing orientation and shrinking or extending indefinitely. The building material itself is a mystery: a smooth and highly polished structure (e.g., flat black surfaces, sharp angles) hinting at artificiality rather than natural origin, while remaining

---

2   Mark Z. Danielewski, *House of Leaves* (New York: Pantheon Books, 2000), 21.

3   Ibid., 4.

in constant flux.[4] Nevertheless, the overwhelming impression is one of scarcity of stimuli. There are only a few constant parameters of the Folly and they, ironically, again amount to representations of "nothingness": no light, no sound, no true north, no air streams, constant temperature of zero degrees ("no temperature"), color: all black ("none"). It is closer to a geometric representation of a sculpted space than to a real architectural feat; there is no discernible utility, no historical or contextual reference, no aesthetics in this environment.

This space is all syntax with no semantics: there is no purpose to the Folly, it amounts to an empty frame, restructuring itself permanently and unpredictably with no observable logic. This pure self-referentiality defines the Folly on many levels: in Chapter IX, Zampanò produces unrelenting cascades of text containing nothing but endless lists of names, places, and objects (architects, photographers and cinematographers, documentary filmmakers, film directors, buildings, fixtures, even literary and artistic sources related to the tradition of the "haunted house"), seemingly exhausting the entire field of visibility as articulated by human endeavors, all in order to enumerate everything the Folly does *not* resemble, everything that somehow fails to represent the quality of this space. From pages 135 to 121 (text flowing in reverse), there is a list of architects (Peter Eisenman, Ber-

---

4   It would be interesting to pursue the idea of the Folly as a *filmed* object to its ultimate conclusion: what if it was not merely represented cinematically, as the Unrepresentable itself, darkness unavailable to the lens, but if it existed as a film recording? This is obliquely suggested on the very first page of *The Navidson Record,* invoking other hoaxes (e.g., Billy Meier's UFOs, the Cottingley Fairies, "thoughtography" of Ted Serios, etc.) where the allegedly captured object never existed outside of its photographic inscription. One could read all of Navidson's travails within the Folly as a violent side-effect of editing: sudden interpolations, disappearances, temporal and spatial extensions and contractions, abrupt returns to previously occupied positions, the inability to accurately measure movement and distance, etc. This is being inside of a film, but not in the sense of entertaining ontological switches, common in postmodern narratives, allowing characters to move vertically through embedded fictions: this is existence in the film medium, as one could be moulded in bronze, carved in wood, liquefied, or pulverized.

nard Tschumi, and Zaha Hadid are mentioned on the very first/last page) alongside a "Palladian grammar" seeking to organize building as a rational process with a strict set of rules, but this is just an amusing and ultimately redundant exercise in negativity, since the final verdict, printed in red, suggests: "~~Picture that. In your dreams.~~"[5] We can read this in two significant ways: "There is no way to picture this," or "Dreamscape (with its atemporality, non-causality, non-disjunctive visuality) is the only medium capable of 'representing' this." If the Folly is as close as possible to "nothing," no real and realized architectural "thing" can have anything to do with it.

The Folly is at cross-purposes with reality on many levels. The house itself was apparently built in 1720, but it is subsequently revealed that the a set of stairs was found descending into the earth as early as 1610, this time with no house giving them any rational context. In the aftermath of the events, a fictional architect poses the question of soil bearing capacities needed for an edifice of this type and size (at one point, Navidson calculates the depth of a stairwell he is trapped in as 27,273 miles, exceeding the Earth's equator), and Chapter XVI offers "hard data" about its building materials, allowing for a semblance of an objective description, partially derived form a petrological laboratory where the staff asume they are analyzing meteorite samples. Unfortunately, the better part of the text is damaged by "spilled ink" and looks like this:

XXXXXXXXXXXXXXXXXXXXXXXXXXXXXXXXXX
XXXXXXXXXXXXXXXXXXXXXXXXXXXXXXXXXX
metamorXXXXXXXXXXXXXXXXXXXXXXXXXXXX
XXXXXXXXXXXXXXXXXXXXXXXXXXXXXXXXXX
XXXXXXXXXXXXXXXXXXXXXXXXXXXXXXXXXX
XXXXXXXXXXXXXXXXXXXXXXXXXXXXXXXXXX
XXXXabecedXXXXXXXXXXXXX[6]

---

5   Danielewski, *House of Leaves*, 141.
6   Ibid., 374–75.

Nevertheless, what remains reads like a scientific counterpart to Carl Gustav Jung's "house of the unconscious":[7] samples range from common rock to elements that are extraterrestrial, possibly even interstellar, and most likely older than the Solar System.

We are entering the ancestral realm as described by Quentin Meillassoux: a "reality anterior to the emergence of the human species."[8] The Folly as an arche-fossil (material "indicating the existence of an ancestral reality or event"[9]) would be the only adequate frame for understanding a structure that precedes not only architecture or the accretion of the Earth as a prerequisite of life and consciousness, but perhaps even the constitution of matter and spacetime: an object which annuls the very possibility of manifestation as the crucial site of correlation. This is a "world without thought—a world without the givenness of the world,"[10] indeed, "*the great outdoors; [...] a past where both humanity and life are absent,*"[11] but where no "I" remains to "achieve what modern philosophy has been telling us for the past two centuries is impossibility itself: *to get out of ourselves, to grasp the in-itself, to know what is whether we are or not.*"[12] The world, however we choose to define it, is not sufficient to support the Folly.

---

7   "We have to describe and to explain a building the upper story of which was erected in the nineteenth century; the ground-floor dates from the sixteenth century, and a careful examination of the masonry discloses the fact that it was reconstructed from a dwelling-tower of the eleventh century. In the cellar we discover Roman foundation walls, and under the cellar a filled-in cave, in the floor of which stone tools are found and remnants of glacial fauna in the layers below. That would be a sort of picture of our mental structure." Ibid., 646. Danielewski is quoting from Jung's "Mind and the Earth", in *Contributions to Analytical Psychology*, and it's worth mentioning that Gaston Bachelard quotes the same paragraph in *The Poetics of Space*.
8   Quentin Meillassoux, *After Finitude: An Essay on the Necessity of Contingency*, trans. Ray Brassier (London: Continuum, 2008), 10.
9   Ibid.
10 Ibid., 28.
11 Ibid., 26.
12 Ibid., 27.

There are other possible approaches to this spatial disturbance on Ash Tree Lane. Marc Augé's notion of non-places, sites of utter semantic emptying, solitude and identity loss, "betweenness" inconducive to permanent settling,[13] would help if we imagined them additionally bereft of all possible function. Furthermore, since the disposition and size of the Folly intersects with the house in an "impossible" way, occupying the "same" place in a highly paradoxical simultaneity, Michel Foucault's definition of heterotopia seems tailor-made for it, particularly since it allows for a temporal dislocation as well.[14] Nevertheless, this still wouldn't account for the essential impossibility: the Folly being infinitely larger than the house that contains it. A detour through psychoanalysis, or rather its deconstruction, provides us with the third option: the crypt, a concept developed in Nicolas Abraham's and Maria Torok's studies on the pathology of mourning, a "'false unconscious,' an 'artificial' unconscious lodged like a prothesis, a graft in the heart of an organ, within the *divided self*,"[15] created by trauma or violence as a "fantasmatic, unmediated, instantaneous, magical, sometimes hallucinatory" topos.[16]

The power of a crypt lies is its topography. It forms like a cyst, a self-enclosed "monad" contained within an object, with all the traces of that containment erased, at the same time remaining theoretically infinite because what is "contained" is actually the

---

13 Marc Augé, *Non-Places: Introduction to an Anthropology of Supermodernity,* trans. John Howe (London: Verso, 1995), 75–115.
14 "The heterotopia is capable of juxtaposing in a single real place several spaces, several sites that are in themselves incompatible. [...] Heterotopias are most often linked to slices in time — which is to say that they open onto what might be termed, for the sake of symmetry, heterochronies. The heterotopia begins to function at full capacity when men arrive at a sort of absolute break with their traditional time." Michel Foucault, "Of Other Spaces," trans. Jay Miskowiec, *Diacritics* 16, no. 1 (1986): 25–26.
15 Jacques Derrida, "*Fors*: The Anglish Words of Nicolas Abraham and Maria Torok," trans. Barbara Johnson, in Nicolas Abraham and Maria Torok, *The Wolf Man's Magic Word: A Cryptonymy*. Translated by Nicholas Rand (Minneapolis: The University of Minnesota Press, 1986), xiii.
16 Ibid., xvii.

Outside: it is as if the container-object is unwittingly turned inside-out, so what seems to be its innermost core is actually completely excluded from itself, opening a window to an exteriority larger than itself. This creates a counterintuitive folding vaguely reminiscent of a Moebius strip or a Klein bottle, endlessly confusing our notions of the inside/outside binary, all the while protecting itself with an additional latch: a subject contains this space "without comprehending it, in order to comprehend *nothing* in it."[17]

This is one of the key mysteries of the crypt. What it apparently conserves and locks away is not "something," a privileged object, information or emotion; it is *exteriority* itself. It is *space*. The crypt is not a container but an unnatural entwining of seclusion and exposure without the possibility of synthesis, a specific curvature of space creating an effect of a closed enclave. It is nothing but an empty "envelope," but its very position and orientation makes it disruptive and dangerous. Therefore, the Folly itself is not an object hidden in the house; it is rather as if, to paraphrase Frank Lloyd Wright, the house was suffering from indigestion, keeping a convoluted and sinister network within its walls, channeling and draining the inhabitants' energy into the void.

Even though the "extraterrestriality" (literal ancestrality) of the Folly is scientifically "proven" within the narrative, the idea of Ash Tree Lane being a portal into a different dimension — yet another horror trope — is explicitly dismissed as a product of schizophrenia (a quintessential "disease of the head"?),[18] but it actually seems insufficiently extreme: infinitely more adaptable than our world, far more unstable, but more flexible too, the Folly encompasses everything that physics and matter of our universe can be, but it exceeds all that in unforseeable ways. This line of thought allows for a final inversion of spatiality: the House itself could actually be perceived as a product of the Folly (rather than vice versa), a discrete and ephemeral reduc-

---

17 Ibid., xix.
18 Danielewski, *House of Leaves*, 378.

tion of its building capacities. It's easy to expand the frame of this reversal a step further: our world, including its constituted spatiality, quantifiable physical properties and availability to man, remains nothing but a fraction of the possibilities offered by "real" space/matter, a random combination of its selected properties. The Folly is not a crypt, an impossible enclave of the Other within our universe. This "universe" is an enclave, a limited and isolated "bubble", produced like an unexplained pocket of apparent stability within the formless *tohu wa-bohu* of matter before cognition. Therefore, what Billy Reston describes as the "rape of physics"[19] might mean simply that what is called physics is but one sector of the *phusis* of the real, embodied by the Folly, perhaps incomprehensible and ultimately unavailable to correlation.

The House is undoubtedly too small to contain the Folly, at once inside it and beside it, but a question remains: what does it mean exactly when a rupture occurs, when the walls of the crypt start to leak? The crypt is defined by being non-manifest and non-symbolizable. Therefore, this bleed of one space into another, a drift from the Folly into the House, is the paradoxical interval necessary for anything to occur, for anything to be written or read, finally for the horror to begin, for the story to emerge: the rule of genre allows only for a partial mystery, the total thing remains beyond description, failing to set the narrative in motion.

But there is a routine way of naming this "thing." It is impossible to ascertain, for example, whether the only sound generated within (or by) the Folly is mechanical, organic or otherwise, but the first inkling of the possibility that this space might be unlimited is followed by an intermittent rumbling, soon nicknamed "the growl." This is, of course, a facilitating shortcut: instead of facing the "blank slate" of the Folly, a word is introduced that immediately suggests an entity or an organism — a *monster* — placing *The Navidson Record* back within the recognizable parameters of the horror genre.

---

[19] Ibid., 395.

"Monster" is not a concept, though. It is a traditional placeholder, a lazy xenophobic reduction, a glyph marking the failure of cognition, an archetypal figure of non-knowledge which, as bizarre or unsettling as it might be, offers an illusion of a discrete being, available to description. The trouble with "monsters" is the structure underlying this term and its applications. If the real other is the beyond of cognition, category and naming, formless and unequal to itself to the extent that we can't ascertain if "it" is one or many, an entity or a swarm, if we can't define its ontic limits or even clearly distinguish it as a figure from the ground, then the very fact of subsuming it under one term is just another stratagem of the mind to domesticate the truly alien, a reductive anthropocentric response to the dread of unknowing. Calling it by any name actually annuls the threat and begins the process of domestification, as self-delusional as it is.

The activity of the Folly undermines this small consolation anyway:

> constant refiguration of doorways and walls represents a kind of geological loop in the process of working out all possible forms, most likely *ad infinitum,* but never settling because [...] 'unoccupied space will never cease to change simply because nothing forbids it to do so. The continuous internal alterations only prove that such a house is necessarily uninhabited.'[20]

This could be interpreted alternately as: a) human habitation could stabilize the loops and shifts and reset the space as a "house" — the problem is reducible to a format of "wilderness" to be conquered and tamed; or b) this is not a "house" but simply a spatial vortex of unknown origin and nature, therefore uninhabitable even theoretically, confirmed by the impossibility of leaving a lasting trace within it (the Folly erodes, destroys, or simply erases all signs of human settlement). Between these solutions, a more conservative and genre-friendly option fleet-

---

20 Ibid., 120.

ingly appears: this is not a self-generated set of surfaces, this is indeed a house; therefore, someone or something built it. But what was it built to house (or contain)? The completely ahistorical, artificial, and provisional character of the Folly prompts one character to call it a very "American Monster";[21] nevertheless, in the light of its "impossible" traits (e.g., size, location, orientation, mobility), the very idea of a "house" (instead of a portal, a vessel, a wormhole) leads straight back into the dead end of correlation. Holloway Roberts's claim — "I will not abort this mission"[22] — ultimately leading to murder, is a desperate plight to achieve any kind closure, a willful choice of a convenient "monster" decoy instead of the horror of pure space.

Zampanò's quote from a fictional article, concerning Goethe's equating of architecture with "frozen music," offers a different perspective: the growl is simply the sound of defrosting, the crackling of melting glaciers, spatiality reverting back to time. The changes are not triggered by the mental state of the explorers — a persistent hypothesis — but provoked by their physical, organic presence, perhaps even its bare temporal extension, initiating an ephemeral micro-Anthropocene within the ancestral realm of the Folly. This sound "contains all the harmonies of time and change" and is described as a rustle of wind, amplifying until "finally it's all around you, sweeping over you."[23] Another description is distinctly threatening: "At times it sounded like voices. Hundreds of them. Thousands. Calling after me."[24] The randomness, the apophenic potential, the scale of effect ranging from pleasant and evocative to panic-inducing and physically dangerous: all of this aligns "the growl" with the concept of noise as an atemporal interval contaning every possible syntagmatic occurence, an Aleph of sound where linear time contracts into a "now" without duration, or precisely into an acoustic equivalent of non-duration — *space*.

---

21 Ibid., 357.
22 Ibid., 124.
23 Ibid., 123.
24 Ibid., 322.

The Folly works as a particularly malevolent sensory deprivation tank, the place where one can die of thirst, hunger, cold and fear, but also — one would suspect — of *boredom*. Only hinted at in the novel, boredom could certainly be singled out as a grossly underrepresented index of our contact with alterity (compared with dread, angst, the sublime, *jouissance*, etc.). A microexperience that we suffer daily, it is actually the most easily available and readable parameter of our disconnection from radical exteriority, result of the lack of cognitive traction, absence of template for projection, a pulse of "don't care," "I can't," "nothing there for me," materiality gradually withdrawing from us, our capabilities waning. This drab and unassuming suspension of subjectivity, provoked in the Folly by the absolute lack of visual stimuli, results in an increase of body-sense, in gravitation towards the haptic, recognition of textures instead of shapes.

One step further, what this place actually delivers in the end is an abolition of *any* perceptible spatiality. Even hallways, staircases, and halls are a sideshow, a series of transitional objects on the way to the full appreciation of "nothing." Like a latter-day Descartes, reducing one layer of spatial accessibility after another, Navidson finally reaches a point where nothing remains. There's "no sense of anything other than myself,"[25] everything else is pure void, blank and black space, a materially realized "night" that Merleau-Ponty[26] and Levinas wrote about. Significantly, this complete disappearance of any "something" doesn't result in the impression of utter emptiness, but in an oppressive feeling of diffuse presence, reduced to a field of disembodied forces, "an undetermined menace of space itself disengaged from its function as receptacle for objects, as a means of access

---

25 Ibid., 471.
26 "When, for example, the world of clear and articulate objects is abolished, our perceptual being, cut off from its world, evolves a spatiality without things. This is what happens in the night. Night is not an object before me; it enwraps me and infiltrates through all my senses, stifling my recollections and almost destroying my personal identity." Maurice Merleau-Ponty, *Phenomenology of Perception,* trans. Colin Smith (London: Routledge, 2002), 330.

to beings."[27] But if spatial anchoring is the prerequisite of human existence and "being is synonymous with being situated,"[28] then the collapse of constituted spatiality induces a regression from geometrical articulation of the universe into a pre-reflexive, hyletic materiality, decentered and amorphous, withholding all possibility of thought or dwelling, evacuating a subject into the outside of phenomenology. It is "death."

"This is not for you." The epigraph of *House of Leaves* could therefore be approached in several ways.[29] Both deterring and inviting, it could be an "anti-dedication" to the empirical reader; in terms of typography used to demarcate different narrative and ontological levels, it is clearly attributable to Johnny Truant. But from the vantage point of the Folly, it leaves space for an allegorical reading. Instead of designating "a private matter" (e.g., "the book is not dedicated to you, written for you, meant or appropriate for you"), it spells out: "This exists in itself," unavailable to you, indifferent to you.

2. Towards a Radical Illegibility

The aspect of *House of Leaves* that makes it instantly recognizable is its formal layout, celebrated and reviled for its extravagance. However, it is anything but a self-sufficient "front" for the portion of the plot we have described; the novel's visual composition is both an integral part of its metanarrative structure and the crucial pressure point in a literary rendering of space as the site of alterity and menace.

Danielewski's debut is routinely singled out as an example of ergodic literature, writing where a "nontrivial effort is re-

---

27 Emmanuel Levinas, *Existence and Existents*, trans. Alphonso Lingis (The Hague: Martinus Nijhoff, 1978), 60.
28 Merleau-Ponty, *Phenomenology of Perception*, 294.
29 Alison Gibbons provides an extremely close reading of this sentence in "This Is Not For You," in *Mark Z. Danielewski*, edited by Joe Bray and Alison Gibbons (Manchester: Manchester University Press, 2015), 17–32, elaborated further in her *Multimodality, Cognition, and Experimental Literature* (London: Routledge, 2012), 46–85.

quired to allow the reader to traverse the text,"[30] forcing them to conceptualize the very act of reading in a new way, rather than simply following the story according to the received modes of relating to the fictional content. Its layout certainly presents a considerable material obstruction to smooth idealization of the subject matter, but it would be a mistake to conclude that this radicalism came from nowhere, or that it is related primarily to digitally based interactive narratives. Taking into account only the last century, there is a strong heritage of approaches to writing that completely redefine readability on the material level, with varying degrees of success but in an impressive array of highly individual styles, often conceptually related to non-literary avantgarde codes, breaching the divide between literature and the visual arts: Guillaume Apollinaire's *Calligrammes,* the works of Filippo Tommaso Marinetti (*Zang Tumb Tumb*), and Ardengo Soffici (*BÏF§ZF+18*), Vladimir Mayakovsky and Aleksei Kruchenykh, *lettrisme* and concrete poetry, typewriter art, Raymond Federman's *Double or Nothing,* Christine Brooke-Rose's *Thru,* Claude Ollier's *Fuzzy Sets,* Mirtha Dermisache's asemic writing, Susan Howe's collages, etc.

Nevertheless, none of these influences appear in Danielewski's work as an erudite façade or a self-referential stylistic footnote for the cognoscenti: they always stem directly from the necessities of the plot, or conversely and more creatively, serve to direct and propel the narrative, actively shaping the possibilities of the projected world. In *House of Leaves,* the majority of typographical oddities proceeds from a complex metanarrative layering: different types and sizes of text, pages persistently split into "main text" (actually the object of commentary and analysis) and a sprawling multitude of footnotes, finally the textual acrobatics used in later chapters to illustrate — or immitate, or even *generate*? — the spatial shifts within the Folly. Chapter IX, certainly the most complex and "ergodically" challenging section of the entire book, is the first to include a heavily irregular

---

30 Espen J. Aarseth, *Cybertext: Perspectives on Ergodic Literature* (Baltimore: The Johns Hopkins University Press, 1997), 1.

layout. Beginning in the middle of an unattributed footnote, it branches simultaneously into further footnotes (and their footnotes, etc., sometimes creating closed loops) and "main text" printed in black and red and intermittently crossed out, blacked out, set in multiple columns, different orientations (including inverted blocks and "mirror" sequences, illegible without a reflective surface), in textual "ducts" or "pipelines" (simulating a channel that traverses the pages "vertically"), with odd spacings and blanks, culminating — perhaps most perversely of all — in a very neat bibliography. Chapter XX, on the other hand, presents an attempt to render the final abolition of anthropocentric spatiality in the Folly. After a certain moment, "direction no longer matters"[31] and text, following Navidson's incapability of further spatial constitution or the disoriented and decentered space itself, denying every foothold after page 468, remains distributed across the page unevenly, although not randomly, still pursuing the option of figurative correspondence to the narrated events.

This tendency to adjust writing to the content of a given section creates a conceptual limit to the typography of *House of Leaves*. If the described space is shrinking, the text block is shrinking; if the stairs are stretching and falling, the spacing between the lines is gradually augmented, and so forth. Consequently, there are no formal equivalents of the complete disappearance of all spatial markers in "Exploration #5." This is obviously not a reproach, since the very point of the entire procedure is representation of a certain unrepresentability. Nevertheless, the feeling of material dislocation is most prominent on the pages where disconcerting formal devices, gradually increasing illegibility or unreadability, remain more or less independent from the narrated events. The "damaged" sections, for instance, motivated by intratextual scattering of burning ashes or spilling of ink, manage to produce a quality exclusive to the medium of writing and its non-semantic properties, opening a literary space precisely by ceasing to represent space.

---

31 Danielewski, *House of Leaves*, 433.

This vocabulary has only broadened in Danielewski's subsequent books, along with the wish to control the layout completely, making it an overriding principle, a basic aesthetic grid for the distribution of content, rather than a technical solution for economical and functional ordering of the text. This is perhaps most visible in *Only Revolutions* (2006), an extremely difficult narrative written in verse with fixed parameters for introducing and organizing textual elements on each page.[32] *The Fifty Year Sword* (2005), a more easily approachable take on a "Halloween story," applied careful color coding of quotation marks to differentiate between narrators, exploring simultaneity through the use of illustrations and non-linear distribution of sentence parts on the page. His latest and most ambitious project, *The Familiar* (2015–2017), planned as a sequence of twenty-seven 880-page volumes (at the time of writing, this was temporarily abandoned after the fifth book), attempted to develop a "signiconic" language, a simultaneous engagement of text and visual faculties, aimed at a "third perception" that would give voice to the material world without the interference of mind.[33]

The results managed to resurrect the age-old dirge on "the death of the novel," but it goes without saying that this type of resistance simply points to a considerable *change,* perhaps a new lease on life for a certain art form. It is interesting to note, however, that this always happens when there is a threat of one

---

32 For a detailed formal analysis, see "Only Revolutions, or, The most typical poem in world literature" by Brian McHale and "Mapping time, charting data: the spatial aesthetic of Mark Z. Danielewski's Only Revolutions" by N. Katherine Hayles in *Mark Z. Danielewski,* edited by Joe Bray and Alison Gibbons, 141–58 and 159–77 respectively.

33 It has been noted that various intratextual markers in Danielewski's novels open a legitimate possibility of reading them as a cycle or a series; for instance, *House of Leaves* introduces the name Redwood (possibly Zampanò's killer?) and an elliptically described "VEM™ Corporation," both of which will become extremely important in *The Familiar*. However, an even more interesting criterion for approaching his entire work as an ongoing project would be precisely examining it in its asemic, sensible, material aspects. Instead of thematic links between the books, the connecting thread could be typography and — perhaps before everything else — the use of color.

traditional material substratum or technological support being supplanted by another. The notion of "literature" certainly rests upon a system of material and technological assumptions, invisibly determining forms to be realized, absolutely overshadowing the personal input of a certain author or a "poetics." Much of what Danielewski does, along with scholars reading his work or intense communities at related Internet forums, actually points towards a broad paradigm shift prompted by digital technologies, which is bound to alter the idea of "literary art" as much as it changed in transition from manuscripts to print, or even from oral to written literature.

Consequently, the most lively debate around Danielewski's work revolves around the notion of multimodality, generally contextualized within the evolution of new media, their capability of creating new writing procedures, new concepts of textuality, and new distributions of audiences. The "experimental" strand of the history of world literature takes second place, but one must stress that it has always functioned as the platform of new media to come, systematically suppressing received ideas of writing as expression, imitation, or representation and using text as an open field of research. The common thread running through all of this, as obscure as it might sometimes seem, is actually the strictly materialistic understanding of text, a firm conviction that, in parallel with all of their powers of handling content and reflecting or anticipating a certain "reality," texts are *things*, objects with physical qualities, defined by their link to matter and resistance to easy and complete transfer into comprehension, idea, or pure thought.[34]

All of these themes have been indirectly explored by Jacques Derrida at least since the 1950s. His most widely read works varied between rigorous micrological textual analyses of a wide range of authors, and attempts to assault the logocentric founda-

---

34 "LITERARY EXPERIENCE IS A PHYSICAL MOVEMENT." Gibbons, *Multimodality*, 74. For an early study of *House of Leaves* in the context of non-verbal signifying practices, accentuating the formative power of materiality in inscription, see N. Katherine Hayles, *Writing Machines* (Cambridge: MIT Press, 2002), 108–31.

tions of culture by making philosophers "hear with their eyes."[35] Rather than flippantly allowing for a "free play of the signifier," as some have thought, his provocations in the domain of typography had a specific purpose: "Through the invention or reinvention of formatting devices, primarily the breaking or occupation of the surface, the point was to try to deflect particular typographical norms, *including even paper*."[36] Abandoning the idea of writing as a transcription of the vocal temporal linearity, he "exploited the chances that paper offers to visibility, meaning first of all the simultaneity, synopsis, and synchrony of what will never belong to the same time: thus a number of lines or trajectories of speech can inhabit the same surface."[37] This was thinking "beyond the paper principle," treating paper as a multimedia platform *avant la lettre*.

House of Leaves grants a substantial amount of space to Derrida's 1966 American debut, "Structure, Sign and Play in the Discourse of the Human Sciences,"[38] but its key visual counterpart is *Glas* (1974),[39] a monumental effort in approaching the relation between literature (Jean Genet) and philosophy (G.W.F. Hegel) in a new way. Its prominent place in the construction of this

---

35 Jacques Derrida, "Tympan," in *Margins of Philosophy*, trans. Alan Bass (Chicago: The University of Chicago Press, 1984), xiii.
36 Jacques Derrida, *Paper Machine*, trans. Rachel Bowlby (Stanford: Stanford University Press, 2005), 45.
37 Ibid.
38 Danielewski, *House of Leaves*, 112. The quote in question is introduced as a comment on the decentered nature of labyrinths: the center of a structure is actually not the center, being physically displaced and elevated to a transcendent position from which it continues to govern and program the illusory play of the network. At first glance, this resonates with spatial paradoxes related to crypts, but in fact describes something completely different: a classical metaphysical hierarchy of *arkhē/telos* presiding over everything that plays out between them.
39 It appears twice in *House of Leaves*, but only fleetingly and in the Appendices (pages 545 and 654). "Tympan" (quoted above), a formal prototype for *Glas*, is introduced on page 401. The typographical inspiration for both actually comes from the atypical layout of Jean Genet's "What Remained of a Rembrandt Torn Into Small, Very Regular Squares and Rammed Down the Shithole" (1967).

novel has been noted before,[40] but I will try to explore it beyond the typographical heterodoxy, on the level of unresolvable tension between the sensible and the intelligible within writing. *Glas* is famously divided into two columns of apparently unrelated text in different types and with different spacings, intermittently broken by interpolations in a smaller sans serif type, periodically connected not only by semantic or alliterative "resonances" but by "judas holes," material "windows" within existing blocks of print. This does not begin to describe all that this text does, nor the level of difficulty caused by its graphic layout. Its driving force was Derrida's unrelenting insistence on the fact that this material "superficiality" of writing is the only environment where "philosophy" even exists, as one of its "quotients" or subsets. It generates largely autonomous cultural and political processes outside of texts themselves, but there is a substantial aspect of writing that resists any type of assimilation through reading (e.g., idealization, interiorization, translation), getting lost in traditional approaches to writing as communication or archiving of previously existing content.

This explains the role of sublexical elements within Derrida's work as a whole. These are remnants of language as *vouloir-dire*, a material excess which escapes the dialectics of comprehension precisely through its haptic character, its unreadability and meaninglessness, the resistance of its material.[41] They are a

---

40 Hanjo Berressem, "The Surface of Sense, the Surface of Sensation and the Surface of Reference: Geometry and Topology in the Works of Mark Z. Danielewski," in *Revolutionary Leaves: The Fiction of Mark Z. Danielewski*, ed. Sascha Pöhlmann (Newcastle Upon Tyne: Cambridge Scholars Publishing, 2012), 199–221.

41 Derrida's emphasis on the sublexical layer of language in *Glas*, employed both thematically and performatively, can be read as a "countersignature" to Saussure's obscure and still insufficiently researched manuscripts on anagrams. Far from the rationalist slant of proto-structuralism presented in *Course in General Linguistics*, they convey a vision of language as a spectrum of sound impressions "out of time," chaos of non-semantic particles that produces meaning randomly and independently from an intending consciousness, creating semantic chains as epiphenomena to the asemic core of language.

blunt and surprisingly insurmountable reminder of the physicality of the book as an external object. Too often masked by linear temporality that actually proceeds from the mechanics of our reading, the real temporal modus of all print is *simultaneity*, something we are absolutely unable to deal with outside of our phenomenological tricks and self-indulgences. It's hard to enumerate all of the consequences of our psychophysiological inability to read several things at once, but they share a single source: what blocks the easy idealization of textual content is precisely space.

Significantly, the only thing Danielewski actually quotes from *Glas* is "espaçons": "Let us space."[42] *Espacement,* usually translated as "spacing," described by Derrida as "becoming-space of time"[43] (*devenir-espace du temps*), actually serves as an extreme shorthand for all the processes that render a text unavailable to total comprehension by the reader. One should tread lightly here, since this is the very spot where the most widespread and destructive readings of Derrida are generated: text as an "explosion" of all possible meanings, the inconclusiveness of every interpretation, abandonment of scrupulous methods of reading. What is actually gleaned from Derrida's work is far more radical: a coherent materialistic theory of writing that refuses to concede mastery over the external objects to consciousness, human agency, or the metaphysics of correlation.

The emphasis on the corporeal is derived from investigations into Edmund Husserl's theory of the sign where Derrida closely follows Husserl's own doubts concerning static phenomenology, and accentuates the importance of the reducible, the material, and the passive that precedes all animation by intentional form.[44] Inscription, although empirical and seemingly inferior to the pure and ideal objects, turns out to be necessary for the

---

[42] Jacques Derrida, *Glas,* trans. John P. Leavey, Jr. and Richard Rand (Lincoln: University of Nebraska Press, 1986), 75.

[43] Jacques Derrida, *Of Grammatology,* trans. Gayatri Chakravorty Spivak (Baltimore: Johns Hopkins University Press, 1995), 68.

[44] Derrida's book-length introduction to Husserl's essay "The Origin of Geometry" (1962) probably remains — along with *Voice and Phenomenon*

achievement of their ideality, since the ideal forms gain their objectivity only by passing through the exteriority of writing. These localized and materialized idealities will subsequently have to be reactivated plurally, unpredictably and incalculably (this is what Husserl called "the Crisis"), and their productivity won't be limited to a reproduction of an ideal "stereotype."

This means that the "radical illegibility" is "prior to the book (in the nonchronological sense)," and "is therefore the very possibility of the book."[45] The literary text is a sensible construct, it originates from the formal engraving of a corporeal substratum, without any real existence before and outside of that process. Such material opening of the space of ideality creates a phenomenon that can itself never become purely ideal, or end up fully reconstructed in an author's or any other consciousness. In its aspect of illegibility, the text remains an irreducible element of literary communication, and its materiality keeps it external, unattainable, alien, and somewhat threatening to the reader — this is what accounts for all of the defamations of writing from Plato to Heidegger and beyond.

> The space of writing is thus not an originarily *intelligible* space. It begins however to *become* so from the origin, that is to say from the moment when writing, like all the work of signs, produces repetition and therefore ideality in that space. If one calls reading that moment which comes directly to double the originary writing, one may say that the space of pure reading is always already *intelligible*, that of pure writing always still *sensible*.[46]

Consequently, the literary object, in its allegedly dead materiality, can never simply work as a rough template, waiting to be animated, without any losses, into a *work of art*, a transparent

---

(1967) — the most important work in this series, but all of his writings up to *Glas* form a backdrop for these explorations.

45 Jacques Derrida, *Writing and Difference*, trans. Alan Bass (London: Routledge, 2001), 95.

46 Derrida, *Of Grammatology*, 289.

structure completely available to thought, to commentary, or to theory. That material layer, always partially unintelligible and critically inexhaustible, is a prerequisite of every meaning.

Every inscription, therefore, exists on a scale between the unattainable absolutes of pure sensibility and pure intelligibility, constrained into participating in them both. A sign-structure devoid of matter, pure concept untainted by inscription, wouldn't be a sign at all, it would be an ideal, self-identical thought-content. Equally, an inscription that would be grounded in its materiality to the extent that it becomes a literally singular, unique and unrepeatable event, would cross into pure substance, unavailable to cognition, verging on invisibility.

This is the realm of spacing. The term appears in the programmatic epigraph to Derrida's first book, "le tout sans nouveauté qu'un espacement de la lecture,"[47] a quote from Mallarmé's preface to his own *Un coup de dés jamais n'abolira le hasard* (1897). A monument of modern literature, the proto-text for many ergodic experiments, it is famous for its carefully orchestrated use of typography which thoroughly overwhelms the content, creating an artwork that — while certainly remaining Literature — gains its foremost strength from its material disposition, from the variations of type, size, and blank space, therefore from the sensible layers of print. The materiality of inscription, creating a "hieroglyphic" layer, remains irreducible to content, like an insurmountable barrier to attempts at appropriation and complete *Aufhebung*.[48] This obstinate externality to

---

47 Derrida, *Writing and Difference*, v.
48 Marcel Broodthaers demonstrated the ultimate consequence of this approach. His take on *Un coup de dés* (1969) is a near-exact replica of the original, including different stocks of paper etc., but with the actual lettering blacked out by horizontal stripes of uneven width and length, completely obscuring all content of the poem, retaining, and accentuating, only its visual composition. Significantly, it is commonly treated as an artist's book, and therefore no longer a work of literature, which paradoxically results in a decrease of its radicality and diminishes its capacity for provocation, irreducible if we remain within the scope of "the art of words."

the reader's consciousness firmly places the future of text in its material housing rather than the capabilities of its recipients.

It is quite obvious that this type of approach — treating the book as a spatial object condensed in graphic constructions bordering on unreadability, rather than a container of "meaning" or a "medium" for preserving and conveying information — harmonizes with the effects of *House of Leaves*. What we perceive as the breaking up of natural rhythms of thought actually amounts to our resistance to *temps d'écriture*: the non-linear distribution of time in the graphic medium, rendering it more akin to a visual than musical composition, an icon rather than a song. Everything that accentuates the spatiality of writing, its unreadable or even illegible vectors, is the real and "natural" state of inscription considered outside of its pragmatic aspect, where it remains tied to the limited linearity and causality of cognitive processes. The "time" of writing, once the man is liquidated from the equation, ultimately plays out as a certain type of atemporality or achronia: as space.

Spatiality and writing, taken at all levels of their literal or metaphorical meanings, converge strategically in Danielewski's writing: the insides of the Folly are described as "those inky folds,"[49] and the partial collapse of Navidson's house looks as if "the black ash of below spreads like printer's ink over everything,"[50] the Folly itself dissipating into an asyntactical and sublexical *materia prima* of writing, pure surface noise of ink on paper which ceases to work as a "representation" of an object or event. If words are matter, building blocks of a certain reality, a small step is necessary to reduce the ephemeral effect of meaning and communication from them and examine them in the light of our entire sensorium, favoring all that can be experienced haptically, rather than simply understood, beyond concept and interpretation. A brief glossary to Chapter XV, dedicated to the analysis of samples taken from the Folly, includes only terms from geology and linguistics, hinting at a deeper

---

49 Danielewski, *House of Leaves*, 388.
50 Ibid., 345.

congruence between them, as if they were one united discipline, apart from the others. A book is a medium of negotiation with a thoroughly non-anthropocentric space, but the same could be said about a house and, as Danielewski writes, "why not? Just as stanza means 'verse,' it also means 'room.'"[51]

3. Between *Arkhē* and *Khōra*

A detailed analysis of this link between typographical and architectural spatiality would demand a comprehensive and preferably illustrated book-length study. However, *House of Leaves* was evidently built around other non-metaphorical ideas of space and shaped not only by the invention of the Folly, but also by the work of several architects and philosophers. Danielewski's most obvious prototext appears to have been Bachelard's *The Poetics of Space* (1958), a book that "has everything to do with how our comprehension of space, however confined or expansive, still affords an opportunity to encounter the boundaries of the self just as they are about to give way."[52] Bachelard's "topoanalysis," built on the crossroads of psychology and phenomenology, elevates the house to a basic existential prop: it is described as "a veritable principle of psychological integration," "the topography of our intimate being,"[53] and "our first universe, a real cosmos in every sense of the word":[54] "Without it, man would be a dispersed being."[55]

Nevertheless, the initial philosophical definition of habitation comes from another source, although along apparently similar lines. As I have already mentioned, *House of Leaves* makes no attempt to hide its philosophical or artistic inspirations or predecessors, making them, to the contrary, another

---

51 Mark Z. Danielewski, "Foreword," in Gaston Bachelard, *The Poetics of Space* (New York: Penguin, 2014), ix.
52 Ibid., vii.
53 Gaston Bachelard, *The Poetics of Space,* trans. Maria Jolas (Boston: Beacon Press, 1994), xxxvi.
54 Ibid., 4.
55 Ibid., 7.

tool in defamiliarizing everything that the Folly consists of, so it comes as no surprise when Heidegger is evoked early in the proceedings, interjecting into the narrative in a lengthy block quotation from *Being and Time*. The placement of this interpolation — in terms of its prominence in the development of the story — makes Heidegger the provisional basis of Danielewski's treatment of architecture, an "establishing shot" of the constitutive role of habitation, and various themes in House of Leaves could be traced back to his works.[56]

Focusing on *Unheimlichkeit*, the quote presents dread and anxiety as a peculiar feeling of (being) "nothing and nowhere," and as "everyday familiarity collapses," the nerve of the *Unheimlich* lies in the state of "not-being-at-home"[57] (*das Nicht-zu-hause-sein*) — an evacuation from home or the state of dwelling. Nevertheless, "*the 'not-at-home' must be conceived as the more primordial phenomenon*"[58] than the familiarity of dwelling, so we are witnessing an inversion of the *heimlich*, reduced to a subset or a dissimulation of the uncanny, hiding within metaphysics. "The mask of the familiar is a primitive shelter, a house, or rather a pseudohouse, which veils a fundamental unfamiliarity."[59] At

---

56 "Language is the house of being. In its home human beings dwell." Martin Heidegger, "Letter on 'Humanism,'" in *Pathmarks,* trans. Frank A. Capuzzi (Cambridge: Cambridge University Press, 1998), 239. As hackneyed as this famous dictum might sound today, it's hard to circumvent it in this context. It doesn't appear as such in *House of Leaves,* but read literally, it could pass for an explanation of its very title, the entire activity of the Folly being a realized metaphor of living within language in a severely antihuman key. Multiple correlations of this type could be traced out between certain Heidegger's formulations and events in *The Navidson Record,* which occasionally seem propelled by language or even typography, rather than the other way around: "Language speaks. If we let ourselves fall into the abyss denoted by this sentence, we do not go tumbling into emptiness. We fall upward, to a height." Martin Heidegger, *Poetry, Language, Thought,* trans. Albert Hofstadter (New York: Harper & Row, 1975), 191.
57 Martin Heidegger, *Being and Time,* trans. John Macquarrie and Edward Robinson (Oxford: Basil Blackwell, 1985), 233.
58 Ibid., 234.
59 Mark Wigley, *The Architecture of Deconstruction: Derrida's Haunt* (Cambridge: MIT Press, 1996), 110–11.

Ash Tree Lane, a mock-house is a framing instrument, structuring and sheltering a family, working both as a buffer and an interface to the radical *espacement* of the Folly.

Heidegger pursues the analogy of dwelling and being even more openly elsewhere, but with different overtones. "Building Dwelling Thinking" (1951) states explicitly that "the manner in which we humans *are* on the earth, is *Buan,* dwelling. To be a human being means [...] to dwell,"[60] the fundamental trait of dwelling being "sparing and preserving."[61] This, however, doesn't only mean that being situated in a nurturing space is what enables humans to exist but, far more drastically, that it is the human habitation and use that defines spatiality as such. The example of the bridge, introduced a few pages further, repeats the proceeding already attempted elsewhere:[62] space is a projection of dwelling, rather than a "container" or a preexisting ambiance to be populated by humans. "The location [*der Ort*] is not already there before the bridge is. [...] Thus the bridge does not first come to a location to stand in it; rather, a location comes into existence only by virtue of the bridge."[63] A "location" defined as a spatial index of human dwelling *creates* space as its consequence; in other words, the mathematical formalization of space, reduced to a quantified distance (*Abstand*) or interval (*Zwischenraum*), can never become the true ground of spatiality, and Heidegger dismisses this abstraction of space as an empty name.

---

60 Heidegger, *Poetry, Language, Thought*, 147.
61 Ibid., 149.
62 "The Origin of the Work of Art," in Heidegger, *Poetry Language, Thought*. A Greek temple, "standing there, opens up a world and at the same time sets this world back again on earth, which itself only thus emerges as native ground" (42). This is immediately underscored: humans, animals, plants and the terrain are not an empty "environment" waiting to be completed by a temple. "We shall get closer to what is, rather, if we think of all this in reverse order" (43). It is the temple that provides a ground for everything else to fall in place. "The building produces its site," it "constructs the eye," ultimately making the ground "constituted rather than simply revealed." Wigley, *Architecture of Deconstruction*, 61.
63 Heidegger, *Poetry, Language, Thought*, 154.

The absolute center and foundation of spatiality is man. Space is "opened up" by dwelling, and the only real "locations" are constructed by *building* which is "closer to the nature of spaces and to the origin of the nature of 'space' than any geometry and mathematics."[64] "The nature of building is letting dwell,"[65] and, read from the vantage point of Navidson's occupation of Ash Tree Lane, the final words of the essay — "*Only if we are capable of dwelling, only then can we build*"[66] — sound like a sentence in a juridical sense, a moral judgement or a condemnation. In the eyes of metaphysics, there is no architecture worthy of the name that would be unfit for human habitation. It is the act of dwelling that constitutes a house. But is there a theoretical vocabulary of the uninhabitable, the purely spatial, to the extent that it becomes indistinguishable from matter, defying even the consolation of algebraic abstraction as an immaterial *terra firma* of geometry?

Plato's *Timaeus* offers an enigmatic category to overcome the polarity between the immutable and eternal ideas, and objects exposed to becoming and decay: a *triton genos* that appears to us "as in a dream,"[67] "difficult of explanation and dimly seen,"[68] which "in some mysterious way partakes of the intelligible, and is most incomprehensible," "apprehended without the help of sense, by a kind of spurious reason, and is hardly real."[69] This is *khōra*, the collapse of a fundamental philosophical opposition between the intelligible and the sensible — alternately appearing to be both and neither — and our inability to properly describe it stems from this blind spot in our habitual mechanisms of articulation. Discourse on *khōra* proceeds "from a hybrid, bastard,

---

64 Ibid., 158.
65 Ibid., 160.
66 Ibid.
67 Plato, *Timaeus*, in *The Dialogues of Plato*, trans. Benjamin Jowett (Oxford: Oxford University Press, 1931), 3:472.
68 Ibid., 468.
69 Ibid., 471.

or even corrupted reasoning,"[70] straddling the line between *muthos* and *logos*.

Derrida was writing about similar loci of contamination from the mid-1950s, but at the time of *Khōra*,[71] which leads us directly into the field of architecture and "applied deconstruction," there was a fairly recent and highly influential rescription of the term. Making it a focal point of her idiosyncratic idea of the semiotic, Kristeva developed *khōra*, in *Revolution in Poetic Language* (1974), *Polylogue* (1977), and elsewhere, into a blanket-term for the discourse of the other, heterogeneous to meaning, closely related to rhythmic patterns and "musical" rather than semantic complexes, "anterior to judgement,"[72] a zone of non-linguistic and non-signifying "genotext" and *signifiance* (i.e., interlocking of drives, concepts, and sensible layers of writing) rather than signification, a place of discontinuities and suspended temporality (i.e., nonlinearity, simultaneity), ultimately associating it with *hulē*, formless matter before the thetic phase of establishing discrete objects. It is tempting to treat all this as if it was written about the Folly — a pre-reflexive and vaguely threatening non-symbolizable "no-place" without access for humans, withheld from cognition and quantitative description — and Kristeva's "semanalysis" will certainly remain legible in subsequent linkages of unconscious processes with corporeality and materiality.

Described as "the nurse of all generation"[73] and becoming, "the mother and receptacle of all created and visible and in any way sensible things," *khōra* is repeatedly designated as "invisible and formless."[74] If this third nature is eternal and indestructible, it will have to be devoid of any discernible qualities in order to

---

70 Jacques Derrida, *On the Name*, trans. David Wood, John P. Leavey, Jr., and Ian McLeod (Stanford: Stanford University Press, 1995), 90.
71 This text was originally published in 1987, but Derrida has been working on it as early as 1985. "Plato's Pharmacy" (1968) also briefly deals with Timaeus and *khōra*; see Jacques Derrida, *Dissemination*, trans. Barbara Johnson (Chicago: University of Chicago Press, 1997), 159–61.
72 Julia Kristeva, *Revolution in Poetic Language*, trans. Margaret Waller (New York: Columbia University Press, 1984), 29.
73 Plato, *Timaeus*, 468.
74 Ibid., 471.

accommodate the array of impressions that will enter it from the "outside" and assume an illusory reality only by the grace of its substratum. Consequently, the main analytical challenge will be accepting and guarding this idea of formlessness against the tendency to personify, quantify, or exemplify *khōra* through its "inhabitants." It is the frame of possibility for everything that will ever materially exist, but is nevertheless devoid of agency; and it would be a mistake to confuse its "giving place" with "the gesture of a donor-subject."[75] Reducing it to an *arkhē* would thoroughly misrepresent "the barren, radically anhuman and atheological nature of this 'place.'"[76] Being neither active nor passive, unequal to any specific existent, having no characteristics of a being, it is "'something' without thing".[77]

Furthermore, since pure matter remains inaccessible, the mind being able to recognize only *skhēmata* — imprints ("negatives" of the ideal forms), therefore itself — everything written about *khōra* is bound to remain a transient projection on its diffuse background, a fraction or a quotient of its capacities. *Khōra* "has" (receives, accepts) all interpretations, but "not as its own" and without keeping them permanently. It is a sum of all readings trying to normalize it and give it intelligibility, but it is not their "support," nor can it be exhausted by them or reduced to them. This links it to a specific concept of the "secret" as Derrida described it in *Passions* (1991). Its inaccessible aspect is not a certain content (theoretically accessible via an appropriate code), but the surface, completely out in the open, perfectly reachable, manifest but strictly *material*, physical, corporeal and therefore *uncoded*, non-discursive, unavailable to "translation" or even reading.

In another text, taking care not to allow this persistent negativity to slip into a cryptotheological zone, Derrida writes that *khōra* remains absolutely heterogeneous to both history and re-

---

75 Derrida, *On the Name*, 100.
76 Jacques Derrida, *Psychē: Inventions of the Other*, eds. Peggy Kamuf and Elizabeth Rottenberg, trans. Andrew Benjamin, Kate Linker, Sarah Whiting, et al. (Stanford: Stanford University Press, 2008), 2:174.
77 Derrida, *On the Name*, 80.

ligion. If this "utterly faceless other" is really "nothing (no being, no present),"⁷⁸ "the place of absolute exteriority,"⁷⁹ we are back in the territory of *espacement,* ungovernable by conceptual markers, forcing us to consider the particularity and asemic properties of haptic experience as the only possible area of contact. Unsurprisingly, *khōra* is finally redefined precisely as "the place of inscription of *all that is marked on the world*"⁸⁰ which achronically precedes the discourses of myth and philosophy — that is why philosophy can never coherently describe it. This "antiquity," however, threatening to make it an ancestral prerequisite of all being, has nothing to do with temporal anteriority and reads better as "atemporality," "ageless contemporaneity," or even "a forsaken perpetuity, or the 'Ancient Without Tradition.'"⁸¹ This is a persistent trait of matter as *apeiron* beyond definition, a layer that exists even in the spans where perception has already transcoded it into an object and pacified it through cognition. The "imprint-bearer" is still there, difficult to discern after receiving the form which will obscure it and claim existence only for itself.

The only step that remains is finally naming this amorphous and utter inaccessibility as "chaos," an umbrella term sufficiently durable to guard against any type of cognitive appropriation or facile "objectification," any anthropomorphization and teleologization of exteriority, but Derrida immediately warns against this too: coupled with the "pathos of fright," almost unavoidable in facing "this chasm," "yawning gulf of the abyss,"⁸² *khōra* easily turns into a slightly more abstract effigy of the *monstrous.* As I have already noted, we would be hard pressed to find a more anthropomorphic response to the unknown or inconceivable. This is the point where horror as a possible *Grundstimmung* of

---

78 Jacques Derrida, "Faith and Knowledge: the Two Sources of 'Religion' at the Limits of Reason Alone," trans. Samuel Weber, in *Religion,* eds. Jacques Derrida and Gianni Vattimo (Cambridge: Polity Press, 1998), 21.
79 Ibid., 19.
80 Derrida, *On the Name,* 106.
81 Reza Negarestani, *Cyclonopedia: Complicity with Anonymous Materials* (Melbourne: re.press, 2008), 15.
82 Derrida, *On the Name,* 103.

philosophy, as Harman has suggested via Lovecraft,[83] actually works *against* the probability of our encounter with the exterior, turning into a final mental retraction in the face of the illegible, safeguarding the conceptual status quo. If we are to encounter the unintelligible materiality in any way, it will have to present itself in a more ambiguous guise, it will have to open like a book, it might even resemble a house.

4. Architecture against Itself

A structure built around the thinking of *khōra,* designed to sidestep all of the trappings of anthropocentric architecture as "the last fortress of metaphysics,"[84] was seriously considered and projected by Derrida and Peter Eisenman between 1985 and 1989, to be placed in the network of *follies* in Bernard Tschumi's Parc de la Villette project (1982–1998), "the largest discontinuous building in the world."[85] A significant part of the collaboration revolved around the reading of *Timaeus* and the possibility of its architectural interpretation, and the audacity of this idea logically proceeds from Eisenman's previous work.

His œuvre is often regarded as the ultimate attempt at disengaging architecture not only from the ideas of habitation or utility but from objecthood, location, or even reality.[86] It is a fight against the closure of metaphysics, striving to achieve an architectural equivalent of *différance.* Any careful reader of Derrida knows that deconstruction has little to do with any type of postmodern sentiment and has far more in common with radical modernity.[87] Accordingly, Eisenman's work, although often

---

83 Tom Sparrow, "On the Horrors of Realism: An Interview with Graham Harman," *Pli* 19 (2008): 235.
84 Derrida, *Psyché,* 92.
85 Bernard Tschumi, "Parc de la Villette, Paris," in *Deconstruction: Omnibus Volume,* eds. Andreas Papadakis, Catherine Cooke, and Andrew Benjamin (New York: Rizzoli, 1989), 175.
86 Peter Eisenman, "An *Architectural Design* Interview by Charles Jencks," in *Deconstruction,* eds. Papadakis, Cooke, and Benjamin, 143.
87 Charles Jencks, "Deconstruction: The Pleasures of Absence," in *Deconstruction,* eds. Papadakis, Cooke, and Benjamin, 119.

reviewed in the context of postmodernity, presents a virulent counterattack against postmodern architecture of pseudo-classicist pastiche, ironic metacommentary and contextual games. It is a hermetic "spatial writing," squarely opposing the unavoidably public disposition of architecture with its obstinate illegibility, organized around space as a metaphysical abstraction or a cognitive framework to be disrupted, a "Cartesian grid" to be played upon. Eisenman's attitude towards functionality ranges from simple downplaying to outright hostility, and it is highly indicative that Jencks links his work to Kurt Schwitters and M.C. Escher. "En Terror Firma" advocates the engagement of architecture with the sublime instead of, or against, simply beautiful (as an index of anthropometric scale and aesthetics), with the ultimate aim of restructuring itself according to "the uncertain, the unspeakable, the unnatural, the unpresent, the unphysical."[88] The problem of scale is the key point. Everything is (dis)organized with the purpose of "removing both the architect and the user from any necessary control of the object,"[89] making space for a new autonomy of architecture as the measure of itself.

House VI (1978) exemplifies many of these traits, retrospectively drawing a series of striking parallels with Navidson's Folly. "My work attacks the concept of occupation as given. It is against the traditional notion of how you occupy a house,"[90] because "it is exactly in the home where the unhomely is, where the terror is alive."[91] Jencks describes this project as "supremely Modernist in its rigid exclusion of every contextual fact"; "the building could be upside-down or tilted on its side and it wouldn't make much difference."[92] These dislocations culminate in a disruptive use of empty spaces, the most notorious being a substantial cut in the bedroom floor, severing it in half. An "*absent* column cuts

---

88 Peter Eisenman, "En Terror Firma: In Trails of Grotextes," in *Deconstruction: Omnibus Volume,* eds. Papadakis, Cooke, and Benjamin, 152.
89 Ibid., 153.
90 Eisenman, "An *Architectural Design* Interview," 142.
91 Ibid., 143.
92 Charles Jencks, *The Language of Post-Modern Architecture* (London: Academy Editions, 1987), 121.

through roof, wall and even floor, wreaking its ultimate havoc on domesticity."[93] This hiatus in the heart of a family home, turned into a non-narrative sequence of geometric twists and turns, embodies, for Jencks at least, the purist language of Modernism, coupled with the postmodern lack of semantics: syntax absolved of all context or function. The radicality of this threatens to turn a place of habitation into an overpriced and potentially dangerous "useless object" — a folly.

"It might be worthwhile therefore to abandon any notion of a Post-Modern architecture in favor of a post-humanist architecture."[94] This is not Eisenman's final line of defense, but Tschumi's proposition in a text on Parc de la Villette, in many respects even more directly influenced by Derrida's work. *Folies* are projected as a superimposition of several autonomous systems, out of phase with one another (a similar idea was explored in *Joyce's Garden* of 1976), described like an open sequence of repetitions and distortions with no beginning or end. They seek to abandon the imperative of order and unity by provoking contiguity, undecidability, fragmentation, and "dissociation in space and time," where "relations of conflict are carefully maintained, rejecting synthesis or totality."[95] Attempting to prove that a complex structure can be built without resorting to traditional parameters, Tschumi outlined a radically anticontextual and asymbolic project avoiding any utilitarian "refuge for humanistic thought"[96] and favoring "madness and play over careful management."[97] In its final consequence, this would be "an assault on meaning," "architecture against itself: a disintegration."[98]

Derrida was initially extremely suspicious about the feasibility of an architecture liberated from the ballasts of Presence (it seemed doomed to a double bind of being either unbuildable or metaphysical), but he was ultimately impressed by

---

93 Ibid., 122.
94 Tschumi, "Parc de la Villette," 175.
95 Ibid., 177.
96 Ibid., 181.
97 Ibid., 180.
98 Ibid.

their work as "the most literal and most intense affirmation of deconstruction."[99] This, however, wasn't enough. Eisenman later claimed that he had been "doing *khōra*" before he read Derrida's text and complained that Derrida didn't push him hard enough, keeping to relatively conservative notions of what a house, a park, or a *folie* could be. Derrida's contemporaneous writings initially supported an extreme redefinition of architecture but stubbornly refused to succumb to the lure of the Nihil, the idea of the pure Void, articulated spatiality as a non-metaphysical annihilation of man. Therefore, "No (Point of) Madness — Maintaining Architecture" (1986), "Fifty-two Aphorisms for a Foreword" and "Why Peter Eisenman Writes Such Good Books" (both 1987) at first apparently align with Eisenman's bravest ideas, calling for a non-anthropocentric turn within the very axiomatic of architecture. Very quickly it transpires that this line of disruption moves along the trajectory of "questions to Heidegger," defined by "the genealogy of an ageless contract between architecture and habitation."[100] The underlying teleology of dwelling firmly controls the syntax of architecture from the outside, naturalizing the historically conditioned understanding of its capacities and erasing its singularity. Therefore, the main challenge will be reorienting architecture as a *paleonym,* an "old name" to be crossed out and reinscribed, a "project" directed towards an unmapped and unreadable future. The ancient link between building and meaning will have to be abandoned in favor of "a school still unknown, a style to be defined, [...] an invention of new paradigms,"[101] examining architecture at the very edges of its inhabitability. Tschumi's *Folies,* in that sense, "return architecture, faithfully, to what architecture, since the very eve of its origin, should have signed."[102]

Nevertheless, instead of proclaiming the necessity of erecting uninhabitable artifacts to assert the true and thoroughly inhu-

---

99 Jacques Derrida, *Points... Interviews, 1974–1994,* trans. Peggy Kamuf and Elisabeth Weber (Stanford: Stanford University Press, 1999), 213.
100 Derrida, *Psyché,* 122.
101 Ibid., 118.
102 Ibid., 93.

man essence of architecture, Derrida soon cautiously crosses into more familiar terrain, remote from the "building of the non-anthropocentric future," and searching for a different angle of interpretation, simultaneous breaking down and reconstruction, without utopianism or nostalgia. The basic "wager" would actually be tackling architecture non-destructively: "The without-ground of a 'deconstructive' and affirmative architecture can cause vertigo, but it is not the void, it is not the gaping and chaotic remainder."[103] "Point de folie" repeatedly stresses that wiping the slate clean, annulling all teleology, aesthetics, symbolism, and hierarchy would "lead back to a desert of anarchitecture":[104] instead of liberating us from an old metaphysics and reverting architecture to its self-referential and non-mimetic essence, the ideal of "abstract, neuter, inhuman, useless, uninhabitable, and meaningless volumes"[105] would actually be a covert fulfillment of nihilism-as-metaphysics.

Therefore, what Derrida hoped for in Tschumi's project was a deprogrammed accessibility rather than a rigid and alienating statement of architecture's fundamental alterity. Furthermore, the very idea of an architectural application of deconstruction is finally abandoned as impossible. The vocabulary of the heterogeneous, of non-coincidence, dissociation and destabilization doesn't suffice to actually build something. An invention is required for this dislocating impulse to survive its installation into the material world, and Derrida emphasized a deciding factor in saving this event-to-be from unqualified negativity: it should free the passage towards the *other*'s writing or "countersignature." Alterity is not something we can invent, "faithfully represent," or drag into the present from the future. After the quest for the unattainable sublime, it transpires that the available materials will be both the terrain to be conquered and the tool to be used. "Deconstructions would be weak if they were negative, if they did not construct, and above all if they did not first meas-

---

103 Ibid., 126.
104 Ibid., 93.
105 Ibid.

ure themselves against that which is most solid in institutions, *at the place of their greatest resistance.*"[106] As much as it might sound like a retraction, this raises a challenge. In order to postulate a significantly different architecture, one must clear the path through habitation; in order to open up the full resources of inscription, one must work against the grain of the story.

We are left, then, with compromise formations: constructing a *story* that will, at least partially, be told through the pure and non-semantic materiality of the page; equating building with *writing* instead of dwelling, and opting for a book instead of a construction site. This conclusion appears like a rationalization of failure, but it's a fact that Tschumi, Eisenman, and Derrida always systematically linked architecture and writing, sometimes to the limit of provocation. The figure of "writing" in concrete or steel initially seemed to be a metaphor, but it gradually merged with other types of inscription literally. In Eisenman's and Tschumi's world, "where two writings, the verbal and the architectural, are printed, the one in the other, outside the traditional hierarchies,"[107] and architecture is "nothing that is,"[108] it is certainly not necessary to build. In a way, if the ultimate goal of an architect is to "do *khōra,*" the only natural state of a house would be precisely not having been built. From that perspective, "paper architecture" takes on a different meaning. For Derrida, Tschumi's working papers, drawings, essays, and photographs in *La case vide* (1986) actually are "follies *at work,*"[109] not documents or preparatory notes, temporally disjointed from "the real thing." The physicality of stone, glass or metal has been supplanted by another, "the voluminous text of multiple writings: […] palimpsest grid, supersedimented textuality, bottomless stratigraphy that is mobile, light and abyssal, foliated, foliform."[110]

---

106 Ibid., 98.
107 Ibid., 106.
108 Ibid., 102.
109 Ibid., 96.
110 Ibid., 97.

"Is the Parc de la Villette a built theory or a theoretical building?" Tschumi posed this question, but (although certainly advocating an innovative convergence of architecture and theory) firmly stressed, "La Villette had to be *built*: the intention was never merely to publish books."[111] Eisenman ended up on the different end of the spectrum: "Deconstruction is not ultimately visible. It is about building unbuildable ideas."[112] Perhaps inevitably, Tschumi's *folies* appeared in the end, while Derrida's and Eisenman's project was abandoned. Or was it? The only "real" and tangible result of this collective endeavor turned out to be *Chora L Works* (1997), a book-archive of plans, letters, drawings, essays, and group conversations, perhaps consciously echoing the Socratic dialogue. Maybe this is all it should have been. Such as it is, this volume itself stands as a spectral "no-place" between a past — a document of something that never was — and future — still a "project," although unfinished — with no "now" or presence to found itself upon. If *khōra* really is an interval of becoming between the idea and the object, then a book probably approximates it better than a building. The graphic design elevated it to a new level of haptic disturbance. Plato's *khōra* works like a winnowing machine or a sieve, so the volume is punched through with a grid of holes, interrupting text at random places, brutally equating the content with the physicality of the page. The book itself, then, works as a sieve or a machine for mediating between the chaos of unformed matter and the worlds of correlation: concepts and ideas on one side and objects on the other. Perhaps the machine could work both ways, at least on a conceptual level, producing our "world for us," but also training us for a negotiation with the world without and beyond us. In one direction, a sieve articulates the prime matter into elements. Traversed in another direction, it becomes a metaphysical grinding machine, helping us establish contact with materiality beyond the limits of the readable.

---

111 Tschumi, "Parc de la Villette," 177.
112 Eisenman, "An *Architectural Design* Interview," 149.

5. Transitional Objects

Conclusively, a "book" or a "house" can be perceived as transitional objects *par excellence,* erraticaly balancing material and intelligible layers, the possibility of concretization or habitation and the pressure of corporeal alterity. They both offer a *xenography,* unevenly stratified and mercurial, providing ground for participation and appropriation, all the while directing traffic in the other direction too: from readability and narration *into* a haptic sensibility (because spatiality exceeds the visual); from utility and meaning *into* base matter and irreducibly alien exteriority. *Khōra* is, after all, defined as "non-readable,"[113] and perhaps only a "metaphysics" can opt for one or the other process exclusively. For all existents, this pulsating interval is really the only place left.

Going back to *House of Leaves,* a question remains unresolved: what is the "bottom" of its ontological hierarchy, the narrative structure that pushes the *meta*-factor to extremes? "[E]ach narrative content [...] becomes in its turn the content of a different tale. Each tale is thus the *receptacle* of another. There is nothing but receptacles of narrative receptacles, or narrative receptacles of receptacles."[114] This is Derrida writing on *khōra* again, but it could easily apply to Danielewski's novel; a paranormal space, contained within a documentary film, which is contained within a blind man's recounting, which is contained within a young man's notes and comments, which are contained within a volume (*House of Leaves*), edited by an anonymous group of people. The final spatial disturbance of the inside/outside binarity is the very title, creating a *mise en abyme* of the Alain Robbe-Grillet or Claude Simon variety: a certain *House of Leaves* inexplicably appears in the depth of the Folly, where Navidson eventually burns its pages one by one, in order to keep reading it to the end. Another *House of Leaves* surfaces in Tru-

---

[113] Jacques Derrida and Peter Eisenman, *Chora L Works* (New York: Monacelli, 1997), 36.
[114] Derrida, *On the Name,* 117.

ant's world, published and distributed without his knowing, but including his private notes and addenda.

The majority of theories place the Mother, Pelafina H. Lièvre, as the ultimate holder of these containers: she is not only the author of *The Whalestoe Letters* — containing typographical excesses echoing the ones in *The Navidson Record*, "real-life" persons suspiciously resembling the characters of the novel, a poem previously attributed to Zampanò, etc. — but the "author" of her son (his entire life and torment perhaps being a narrative work of mourning over a child she had lost long ago).[115] Therefore, the entire novel is actually playing out within the "consciousness" of a master-character that never appears as such, giving place to all the stories, resembling all and none of them, remaining permanently unavailable or "dead." "She managed to make you feel as if she had invented you."[116] Many characters explicitly doubt their own ontological persistence, and her presence would be a genre-friendly consolation of sorts: the *mother of horrors* as the "nurse and receptacle" of all that exists. She is the one that "makes them talk," extending her influence all the way to us and all possible interpretations of her work.

This would be the final temptation then: "this strange mother who gives place without engendering,"[117] a "mother" as a creator (not necessarily benevolent) of all that is, an ageless and invisible mother irreducible to her offspring, not there to contain someone in a shelter, but to evict someone, to throw them *out of the house and into space*. But as convenient as this would be — a resolution of all the formal intricacies in a form of subjectivity, a "personality," an intention of a conscious entity — it is only Lièvre's non-manifest nature that tentatively supports this reading. Essentially equal to all the other spectres of this world, she

---

[115] For a sustained examination of the relations between these characters, emphasizing their approaches to language and textuality, see Katharine Cox, "What Has Made Me? Locating Mother in the Textual Labyrinth of Mark Z. Danielewski's *House of Leaves*," *Critical Survey* 18, no. 2 (2006): 4–15.

[116] Mark Z. Danielewski, *The Whalestoe Letters* (New York: Pantheon Books, 2000), xv.

[117] Derrida, *On the Name*, 124.

is simply the outermost point of the same "projection" generated by a deeper — or more superficial? — *khōra,* the matter of writing, and certainly an inappropriate substitute, or another primitive, anthropomorphic *eidolon* for its inhuman, formless, and ultimately indifferent capacities.

This autonomous material doesn't exist in order to give place to something else, to "represent," the mimetic imperative of a backward metapysics. If "it has nothing as its own," and nothing can last or survive in it (the walls being permanently purged of all events, remaining ahistorical and timeless), then everything is there, not only in the pit of the Folly, but in *House of Leaves* and in writing in general, only to lure someone inside, to provide a sufficient amount of cognitive traction enabling a reader to advance toward the "thing itself" of the book, alien to every concept — unreadability, its lack of content misread as emptiness, as "nothing". Readable ephemera can not "belong" to it as *its own* attributes, but in order to approach it at all, in order to open up the full resources of inscription, perhaps a story must be offered, if only to be revoked in the last instance.

Creating everything and keeping no records, like a self-replicating machine or the tree of Yggdrasil — which actually marks the very end of *House of Leaves,* branching out indefinitely, creating and supporting disparate worlds, but stemming out of "nothing" and maintaining itself rootlessly — this material offers the ultimate analogy for the open architecture of Navidson's Folly. It persists, it expands, it evolves with no memory of the changes, it provides room for all that exists, but it is the very reverse of Le Corbusier's *machine à habiter*: the only difficulty left is understanding the human viewpoint within it, perhaps because there is none.

In this type of spatial exploration, every finality would only play into the hands of an old teleology and consolidate our ignorance. What remains is a process that opens itself to habitual uses, but which *continues* to provoke and dislocate. To deal with writing means to establish a perpetually provisional and volatile foothold within it, while the material exteriority, absolutely uninhabitable and inaccessible, is keeping the chasm ajar, maintaining the interruption. The only other option is not to read at all, to go back into ourselves, try and forget, or to simply move on, like the couple in *House of Leaves* who gave up the Folly because they wanted something smaller.

Bibliography

Aarseth, Espen J. *Cybertext: Perspectives on Ergodic Literature.* Baltimore: The Johns Hopkins University Press, 1997.

Augé, Marc. *Non-Places: Introduction to an Anthropology of Supermodernity.* Translated by John Howe. London: Verso, 1995.

Bachelard, Gaston. *The Poetics of Space.* Translated by Maria Jolas. Boston: Beacon Press, 1994.

Berressem, Hanjo. "The Surface of Sense, the Surface of Sensation and the Surface of Reference: Geometry and Topology in the Works of Mark Z. Danielewski." In *Revolutionary Leaves: The Fiction of Mark Z. Danielewski,* edited by Sascha Pöhlmann, 199–221. Newcastle Upon Tyne: Cambridge Scholars Publishing, 2012.

Bray, Joe, and Alison Gibbons, eds. *Mark Z. Danielewski.* Manchester: Manchester University Press, 2015.

Cox, Katharine. "What Has Made Me? Locating Mother in the Textual Labyrinth of Mark Z. Danielewski's *House of Leaves.*" *Critical Survey* 18, no. 2 (2006): 4–15.

Danielewski, Mark Z. "Foreword." In Gaston Bachelard, *The Poetics of Space,* vii–xvi. New York: Penguin, 2014.

———. *House of Leaves.* New York: Pantheon Books, 2000.

———. *The Whalestoe Letters.* New York: Pantheon Books, 2000.

Derrida, Jacques. *Dissemination.* Translated by Barbara Johnson. Chicago: The University of Chicago Press, 1997.

———. "Faith and Knowledge: The Two Sources of 'Religion' at the Limits of Reason Alone." Translated by Samuel Weber. In *Religion,* edited by Jacques Derrida and Gianni Vattimo, 1–78. Cambridge: Polity Press, 1998.

———. "*Fors*: The Anglish Words of Nicolas Abraham and Maria Torok." Translated by Barbara Johnson. In Nicolas Abraham and Maria Torok, *The Wolf Man's Magic Word: A Cryptonymy.* Translated by Nicholas Rand, xi–xlviii. Minneapolis: University of Minnesota Press, 1986.

———. *Glas*. Translated by John P. Leavey, Jr. and Richard Rand. Lincoln: University of Nebraska Press, 1986.

———. *Of Grammatology*. Translated by Gayatri Chakravorty Spivak. Baltimore: Johns Hopkins University Press, 1995.

———. *On the Name*. Translated by David Wood, John P. Leavey, Jr., and Ian McLeod. Stanford: Stanford University Press, 1995.

———. *Paper Machine*. Translated by Rachel Bowlby. Stanford: Stanford University Press, 2005.

———. *Points... Interviews, 1974–1994*. Translated by Peggy Kamuf and Elisabeth Weber. Stanford: Stanford University Press, 1999.

———. *Psychē: Inventions of the Other*, Vol. 2. Edited by Peggy Kamuf and Elisabeth Rottenberg. Translated by Andrew Benjamin, Kate Linker, Sarah Whiting, et al. Stanford: Stanford University Press, 2008.

———. "Tympan." In *Margins of Philosophy*. Translated by Alan Bass, ix–xxix. Chicago: The University of Chicago Press, 1984.

———. *Writing and Difference*. Translated by Alan Bass. London: Routledge, 2001.

Derrida, Jacques, and Peter Eisenman. *Chora L Works*. New York: Monacelli, 1997.

Eisenman, Peter. "An *Architectural Design* Interview by Charles Jencks." In *Deconstruction: Omnibus Volume*, edited by Andreas Papadakis, Catherine Cooke, and Andrew Benjamin, 141–49. New York: Rizzoli, 1989.

———. "En Terror Firma: In Trails of Grotextes." In *Deconstruction: Omnibus Volume*, edited by Andreas Papadakis, Catherine Cooke, and Andrew Benjamin, 152–53. New York: Rizzoli, 1989.

Foucault, Michel. "Of Other Spaces." Translated by Jay Miskowiec. *Diacritics* 16, no. 1 (1986): 22–27. DOI: 10.2307/464648.

Gibbons, Alison. *Multimodality, Cognition, and Experimental Literature*. London: Routledge, 2012.

———. "This Is Not For You." In *Mark Z. Danielewski,* edited by Joe Bray and Alison Gibbons, 17–32. Manchester: Manchester University Press, 2015.
Hansen, Mark B.N. "The Digital Topography of Mark Z. Danielewski's House of Leaves." *Contemporary Literature* 45, no. 4 (2004), 597–636. DOI: 10.2307/3593543.
Hayles, N. Katherine. *Writing Machines.* Cambridge: MIT Press, 2002.
Heidegger, Martin. *Being and Time.* Translated by John Macquarrie and Edward Robinson. Oxford: Basil Blackwell, 1985.
———. "Letter on 'Humanism.'" In *Pathmarks,* translated by Frank A. Capuzzi, 239–76. Cambridge: Cambridge University Press, 1998.
———. *Poetry, Language, Thought.* Translated by Albert Hofstadter. New York: Harper & Row, 1975.
Jencks, Charles. "Deconstruction: The Pleasures of Absence." In *Deconstruction: Omnibus Volume,* edited by Andreas Papadakis, Catherine Cooke, and Andrew Benjamin, 119–31. New York: Rizzoli, 1989.
———. *The Language of Post-Modern Architecture.* London: Academy Editions, 1987.
Kristeva, Julia. *Revolution in Poetic Language.* Translated by Margaret Waller. New York: Columbia University Press, 1984.
Levinas, Emmanuel. *Existence and Existents.* Translated by Alphonso Lingis. The Hague: Martinus Nijhoff, 1978.
Meillassoux, Quentin. *After Finitude: An Essay on the Necessity of Contingency.* Translated by Ray Brassier. London: Continuum, 2008.
Merleau-Ponty, Maurice. *Phenomenology of Perception.* Translated by Colin Smith. London: Routledge, 2002.
Negarestani, Reza. *Cyclonopedia: Complicity with Anonymous Materials.* Melbourne: re.press, 2008.
Plato. *Timaeus.* In *The Dialogues of Plato,* Vol. 3. Translated by Benjamin Jowett. Oxford: Oxford University Press, 1931.

Sparrow, Tom. "On the Horrors of Realism: An Interview with Graham Harman." *Pli* 19 (2008): 218–39.

Tschumi, Bernard. "Parc de la Villette, Paris." In *Deconstruction: Omnibus Volume,* edited by Andreas Papadakis, Catherine Cooke, and Andrew Benjamin, 174–83. New York: Rizzoli, 1989.

Wigley, Mark. *The Architecture of Deconstruction: Derrida's Haunt.* Cambridge: MIT Press, 1996.

10

Encountering Weird Objects: Lovecraft, LARP, and Speculative Philosophy

Chloé Germaine Buckley[1]

Introduction: Philosophy, Play, Props

The speculative and materialist turns of twenty-first century philosophy ask humans to "think about the liveliness of objects."[2] Numerous theorists attempt to overcome what speculative realists call the "correlationist" gap, which abjures the possibility of accessing the "noumenal" realm, and what new materialists frame as idealist and constructivist assumptions, which ignore the importance of bodies, matter, and other nonhuman "actants" in favour of language, discourse, and culture.[3] Of the of-

---

1 I am grateful to Paul Wake and Jonathan Newell for comments on this material.
2 Steven Shaviro, "The Universe of Things," *Theory & Event* 14, no. 3 (2011): 3.
3 For summaries of these critiques see: Levi Bryant, Nick Srnicek, and Graham Harman, "Towards a Speculative Philosophy," in *The Speculative Turn: Continental Materialism and Realism,* eds. Levi Bryant, Nick Srnicek, and Graham Harman (Melbourne: re.press, 2011), 1–18. See also Diana Coole and Samantha Frost, "Introducing the New Materialisms," in *New*

ferings across speculative realism and new materialism, those of interest in this chapter include Graham Harman's object oriented ontology and Jane Bennett's vital materialism.[4] The latter theorist expounds an approach to things that provides a useful mid-point between object-oriented and relational ontologies, both of which offer valid routes beyond correlationism and constructivism. With their very different conceptions of objects, Harman and Bennett negotiate what Steven Shaviro identifies as the "paradoxes of nonhuman actants, of vital matter, and of object independence."[5] Such written speculation on the nature of reality and nonhuman things is well and good but how to make contact with objects such that both the anthropocentrism of Western philosophy and the every-day or common-sense realism it engenders might be disrupted? How to forge an encounter with the "weird reality" Harman suggests lies beyond the gap endemic in Western philosophy?[6] How can humans be jolted out of the hubris that Bennett suggests frames matter as instrumental and results in "earth-destroying consumption?"[7]

This chapter contends that there is at least one human activity alert to the vibrant, strange, and elusive nature of objects: game-playing. In his field-defining analysis of the play-element in culture, Johan Huizinga asserts that gameplay comprises a "temporary abolition of the ordinary world" not merely for the production of a childish fiction but, oftentimes, taking on a ritualistic aspect that "brings about an order of things higher than that in which [we] customarily live," where play, Huizinga suggests, might be a "cosmic happening."[8] The temporary, ritualized

---

  Materialisms: Ontology, Agency, Politics, eds. Diana Coole and Samantha Frost (Durham: Duke University Press, 2010), 1–46.
4 Jane Bennett, *Vibrant Matter: A Political Ecology of Things* (Duke University Press, 2010). See also Graham Harman, *The Quadruple Object* (Winchester: Zero Books, 2011).
5 Shaviro, "The Universe of Things," 3.
6 Graham Harman, *Weird Realism: Lovecraft and Philosophy* (Winchester: Zero Books, 2012), 2.
7 Bennett, *Vibrant Matter,* ix.
8 Johan Huizinga, *Homo Ludens: A Study of the Play-Element in Culture* (Kettering: Angelico Press, 2016), 12, 14.

demarcation of space in play is fundamental in live-action roleplaying (LARP), a niche, gaming activity distinct from table-top roleplaying games and video games. LARPs are physically enacted roleplaying games that require players to enter a specific location — demarcated as "in-game" — as designated "characters." LARPs may last anything from a few hours to a few days, during which time player-characters must respond to dramatic events, puzzles, and crises through an immersive, embodied performance. The resulting improvised narrative interacts with a ludic structure — that is, the rules of the game — comprising gameplay mechanics that govern player-character actions, including some aspects familiar from video and table-top roleplaying games such as health stats and combat skills. LARP is popular in various genres and includes "high" and "low" fantasy games, murder-mystery scenarios, post-apocalyptic and regency-era "polite society" settings to name just a few.

The focus of this chapter is "survival horror" LARP and, specifically, what is often called, by players and organizers, "Cthulhu" LARP, after Lovecraft's fiction and its legacy. Huizinga's phrase defining play as a "cosmic happening" is particularly apposite for "Cthulhu" LARP, which incorporates as theme and content a horrifying encounter with the outside, aiming to produce in players what Lovecraft describes as "cosmic fear."[9] Indeed, "Cthulhu" LARP fits into the category of "dark play," a term that game studies scholars use to describe "dangerous" forms of play that exploit the tension between order and chaos, evoke subversive or otherwise "deviant" themes, and often deceive players such that the boundary between "play" and "not play" becomes very porous.[10] Because it requires constant frame switching as

---

9   H.P. Lovecraft, "Supernatural Horror in Literature," *The H.P. Lovecraft Archive*, http://www.hplovecraft.com/writings/texts/essays/shil.aspx.
10 "Dark Play" is a concept defined by Richard Schechner in *Performance Studies: An Introduction* (London: Routledge, 2002). I synthesize a definition from comments by Miguel Sicart in *Play Matters* (Cambridge: MIT Press, 2014), 19 and Jonas Linderoth and Torill Elvira Mortensen in "Dark Play: The Aesthetics of Controversial Playfulness," in *The Dark Side of Game Play: Controversial Issues in Playful Environments*, eds. Torill Elvira

players negotiate in-game and out-of-game elements simultaneously and a big commitment to the suspension of disbelief that can often create moments of "bleed" between the world of the game and the world beyond, LARP certainly has the potential to disrupt constructed, social reality and provoke psychological stress.[11] However, the Lovecraftian themes also make such play potentially disruptive of players' deeply embedded ontologies, of the common-sense realism that operates in their everyday lives.

Objects and things in the form of game props are central to the success of LARP and key to its potential for metaphysical speculation. Props provide the objects on which ludic mechanics operate, they contribute to the production of a shared narrative, and help transform the space in which the game takes place, specifically, its demarcation from the world of the everyday. Finally, props are central to the production of immersion for the players such that they might feel "cosmic fear" within the game. Props in "Cthulhu" LARP include objects such as an eldritch tome containing information about ancient gods and rituals, fragments of "alien" rock or parts of an ancient "spacecraft," an array of disturbing monster costumes such as a series of "shoggoth tentacles" made from latex and foam, elements of set-dressing such as laboratory equipment, a projected video with ambient sounds used to simulate a shared vision, floodlights and sound-effects to simulate the arrival of a military helicopter. These are a few examples from my own experience. As a LARP designer who also theorizes their practice, I follow Kendall Walton and Chris Bateman in the assertion that props are generative: they prescribe specific imaginings, trigger emotions,

---

Mortensen, Jonas Linderoth, and Ashley M.L. Brown (London: Routledge, 2015), 5.

11 On the disruptive effects of frame switching in LARP, see Chloé Germaine Buckley and Laura Mitchell, "Weird Experience: Transformations of Space/Place in 'Lovecraftian' LARP," *Studies in Gothic Fiction* 7, no. 1 (2020, forthcoming).

and generate the fictional world of the game.¹² Walton's "prop-oriented" view of "make-believe" counters "content-oriented" approaches in that it proposes that objects have independence over and above their role in a story. Indeed, Walton goes as far as to reverse the hierarchy of story and prop, suggesting that props might become the focus of attention such that the act of make-believe is a tool through which we understand the prop. This inverts the view that the prop is a tool through which we understand the story.¹³ This view of props as agentic and generative suggests their affinity with the notion of "object" or "thing" expounded in some speculative realisms and new materialisms. Bennett, for example, suggests that "things" manifest traces of "independence or aliveness, constituting the outside of our own experience."¹⁴ In "Cthulhu" LARP, props explicitly manifest their independence or "outside-ness." Examples from my experience include encountering a strange, meteor-type rock that resisted geological analysis and acted to create some kind of barrier preventing player-characters from escaping a certain location. In another LARP, players uncovered unidentifiable archaeological fragments with strange markings. Together, the fragments comprised a beacon or transmitter that exerted disturbing psychical effects upon player-characters who came into contact with them. The game entirely revolved around putting together the fragments.¹⁵

In addition to their generative function, there is a certain naïveté embodied by props in LARP that accords with the various turns from doubting modes of philosophy explored herein. Indeed, the various (re)turns to materiality and reality represented by speculative realism and new materialism are often

---

12 For an explanation of what Bateman calls "prop theory," see Kendall L. Walton, "Metaphor and Prop Oriented Make-Believe," *European Journal of Philosophy* 1, no. 1 (1993): 39–57 and Chris Bateman, *Imaginary Games* (Winchester: Zero Books, 2011), 100–103.
13 Walton, "Metaphor and Prop Oriented Make-Believe," 39.
14 Bennett, *Vibrant Matter,* xvi.
15 This LARP was "X Marks the Spot," written and organized by Eleanor Black for the UK-based LARP club, *Disturbing Events,* in 2017.

self-consciously naïve, rejecting the skepticism of correlationism and the sophistication of constructivism, both of which equate reality with representation or else do away with it altogether. Harman suggests that naïveté ought to replace radical doubt in philosophical thought and Bennett argues that her notion of "thing-power" is advantageous precisely because it calls to mind "a childhood sense of the world."[16] LARP is likewise a self-consciously naïve activity, a childish game of dress-up and make-believe, which attempts to produce and enact outlandish stories and scenarios using home-made costumes and props. Actual monsters appear and may be fought with latex weapons or replica guns; players pick up mysterious and magical objects made from foam and papier-mâché; and physical space is transformed with theatrical set-dressing, home-made sound effects, and colored lights. It is LARP's playful naïveté that insists on an embodied and oftentimes visceral encounter with materiality.

Material encounters in LARP can produce "Weird" paradoxes, encouraging blurred responses to objects that unsettle both scientific materialism and metaphysical idealism. By way of an example, I offer a prop I made for a "Cthulhu" LARP titled "Professor Lazarus's Emporium of Wonders."[17] This prop, like many others in this genre of LARP, initiated competing and paradoxical encounters for the players. In the game narrative, the prop represented a part magical, part electrical "field generator" that, when switched on, kept a "proto-shoggoth" — a monster we had constructed out of latex, foam, cloth, and an old nylon tent — in an inert state. During the first act of the game, the machine broke, causing the shoggoth to grow out of control and its foam tentacles extended further and further into the game space. Initially, this affected "non-player-characters" who became fused with the creature and attached to one another with grotesque latex umbilical cords. Later, players themselves were subsumed

---

16 Harman, *The Quadruple Object*, 5. See also Bennett, *Vibrant Matter*, 20.
17 "Professor Lazarus' Emporium of Wonders" was written by Chloé Germaine Buckley and Jonathan Buckley for the UK-based LARP club, *The Dark Door*, in 2014.

into the monster. The field generator became an important object for the ludic frame (that is, the frame determining the activity as a game composed of a series of challenges to be solved): players needed to fix the machine to destroy the creature. The object also prescribed several imaginings to produce a fictional narrative. Thus, players encountered the prop through at least two different frames: the fictional narrative demanded their characters imagine its mystical purpose and provenance, while the ludic structure suggested the player approach the object as a puzzle to be solved, drawing on in-game skills and rules that need to be role-played accordingly. These competing "in-character" and "out-of-character" negotiations prescribed by the prop suggest something of its strange nature in the context of play.

The strangeness of the object in this case was also visible in its materiality: it looked very much like a prop. We constructed it from an old carriage clock, to which we affixed colored LEDs, wires, brass knobs, and dials that served no real function. We added an electrical transformer and switch kit, packaged to look like an "old-timey" battery suitable for the 1930s setting. Each of these material components were visible and allowed players to identify the item as a prop within the space of the game. Often, players negotiate between in-game props and items native to the game location, for example, spotting a magical tome on a shelf of otherwise ordinary books. Despite its home-made appearance, the object was treated very much as real and potentially dangerous as players constructed an improvised narrative around it. It had obvious real-world components that could easily have been put back together by anyone with a basic knowledge of electronics, but the players roleplayed having no clue about how the machine worked: they were fumbling about, making guesses in their make-believe pretence of fixing it. Finally, like many props in "Cthulhu" LARP, the field generator worked in both the material dimension and in a seemingly supernatural one. Both the simple electronics and the painted mystical symbols had sensible in-game effects in relation to the monster. The object also prompted quasi-emotional responses from the characters (for example, fear, bewilderment) and real emotional responses in the players (for example, hesitancy). This distinction suggests that props prescribe effects within multiple frames simultaneously, including beyond the world of the game. Some players are often reluctant to interact with an object that could send their character mad or kill them and so end their game experience early. In-game madness is a common feature in "Cthulhu" LARP and it often signifies that props such as the field generator erase separation between normally distinct metaphysical dimensions (the natural and the supernatural, the human and the nonhuman, for example).

In what follows, I will suggest that the ludic interactivity of LARP and its requirement for participants to negotiate multiple and simultaneous frames of experience produces insights about the nature of reality beyond human perception. In short, it has the potential to force its participants to catch a glimpse of a world that is nothing like their common-sense perceptions of it. In line with speculative realist and new materialist philosophies, what encounters with props in LARP may reveal is a curiously unhuman ontology: a world of active, vibrant *things,* to use Bennett's terminology, and independent, mysterious objects, in the sense employed in Harman's schema. My investigation is philosophical and auto-ethnographic. I examine various LARPs I have designed and played, drawing on the intersection between Gothic, horror, and philosophy. I suggest that LARP elucidates some of the speculations in recent philosophy through its affective encounters. That is, horror LARP produces an experiential encounter with the "weirdness" of reality.

LARP, Fakery, and the Gothic Tradition

To explore the disruptive nature of props in "Cthulhu" LARP, I want to make some connections between LARP and the Gothic. The Gothic is a literary mode that informs both the fiction on which LARPs are based (for example, Lovecraft's stories) and the techniques used to gamify those fictions. Horror LARP uses strategies key to the Gothic since the latter's inception in the eighteenth century. One such strategy is the production of performed space, which Emma McEvoy argues is central to Gothic. She calls Horace Walpole's converted dairy, Strawberry Hill, a "dramatized building for which audience response and interaction were essential."[18] Walpole's Strawberry Hill was both a material building and a fictional construct, intimately connected to his novel, *The Castle of Otranto* (1764), which is widely discussed as the first Gothic novel. Just as that novel purported to be a found manuscript but was an invented fiction, Strawberry Hill was not what it appeared to be. In this former and extended dairy building, wooden crenulations masqueraded as stone masonry and pasteboard walls sported fake, Gothic arches. Walpole freely "mixed and matched,"[19] creating stylistic incongruence by assembling a range of artifacts, or "props" that prescribed a variety of imaginings for the buildings' visitors. Such fakery is necessary in LARP, too, to produce a dramatized or performed space in which an immersive game experience can occur. LARP organizers' comparative lack of budget results in a more homemade affair than Strawberry Hill, though, and the Gothic set-dressing is decidedly more Ed Wood than Tod Browning. That said, the production of space in LARP can have very dramatic effects. Elsewhere, I have discussed the experience of seeing an interior wall crumble as a horde of zombies tore its way through. The wall turned out to be a plasterboard fake placed in a venue solely for the game.[20] In another game, organizers bricked up a fireplace in a hired venue just for the weekend so it could be uncovered by players as part of the solution to a ludic puzzle.[21] Such props vary in their levels of authenticity, but all help pro-

---

18 Emma McEvoy, *Gothic Tourism* (Basingstoke: Palgrave Macmillan, 2016), 18.
19 Ibid., 21.
20 See Germaine Buckley and Mitchell, "Weird Experience." The game described was "The Sorrow of Huntingdon Hall," written by Jenny Wilkinson and Lee Wilkinson for *The Dark Door* in 2008.
21 This incident occurred during a game called "God Rest Ye Merry," written and organized by the UK-based organisation, *Crooked House,* in 2015.

duce a performed space that provides narrative effects and ludic challenges in material form.

The production of performed space through fakery (such as pasteboard crenulations or a dummy wall) and incongruence (including the assembling of props from different time periods and contexts) results in the blurring of interpretive frames. Walpole's incongruent stylistic mash-up at Strawberry Hill deliberately muddled distinctions such as that between art and reality, inviting visitors to "walk into a painting" for example.[22] In LARP, such perceptual dissonance often occurs at a ludic level, prompting anxiety over whether something is in-game or not. The fake wall was one extreme example of organizers manipulating performed space to produce a particularly dramatic dissonance, a chaotic moment when "in-character" and "out-of-character" responses blurred as players scrambled to escape. In LARP, such blurrings, what players often call "bleed", can function to problematize players' experience of materiality. In addition, some objects are physical and solid, the home-made field generator, for example, or a skin-bound eldritch tome fashioned from painted latex. Yet, other props are more intangible; they might be part "phys-repped" and part described by a game referee, or they might comprise an image projected onto a screen. Yet, within the game world all such objects occupy the same, objectified reality. LARP discloses that which in everyday experience is unseen or unreal.

The practical difficulties involved in materially manifesting some of the objects described in Lovecraft's fiction calls for an ambiguous and loose definition of the word "prop." In Walton's work, the term prop does not only refer to physical objects but anything that "generates a fictional truth."[23] This broader definition works well for LARP, which incorporates some objects that are very physical and others that might be more intangible, like a video projection. Walton's "props" also accord with Harman's

---

22 McEvoy, *Gothic Tourism*, 29.
23 Walton, "Metaphor and Prop-oriented Make Believe," 59. See also Bateman, *Imaginary Games*, 95.

"objects," which occupy the accessible, "sensual" realm and include "the centaur, Pegasus, unicorn, and hobbit" as well as trees and chairs. Harman also admits "larger emergent entities" like the European Union into his definition of sensual objects.[24] Peter Gratton has suggested that such comments risk "an idealism worse than anything [Harman] critiques" and that Harman's extension of the term "object" to anything and everything suggests a "literal nominalism in which words create things."[25] Gratton's charges suggest serious problems at the heart of Harman's avowedly realist project, but thinking about LARP props as examples of Gothic fakery and as dissonant objects, drawing out some connections with Harman's schematics, allows a more generous assessment of object oriented ontology. Harman himself suggests objects exist in multiple realms (the sensual and the real) and that tensions and torsions between objects and realms produce sensible effects. His analysis of Lovecraft's fiction, in which he elucidates his "weird realism," also suggests a necessary dose of the imaginary in any philosophical endeavour that seeks access, however indirect, to the "outside."[26] Bennett's work echoes this insistence on the importance of an "unrealistic imagination" in accessing the outside.[27] Certainly, "Cthulhu" LARP attempts to manifest indirect access to the outside in the most material form possible (the foam and latex "shoggoth tentacles" I made for "Professor Lazarus' Emporium of Wonders" are a good example), but it also insists upon the suspension of disbelief, demanding immersion in an imaginary narrative (i.e., walking into a Lovecraft story) and on players accepting the "fictional truths" prescribed by props, however home-made they might look. In this sense, LARP continues in a tradition of dramatization inaugurated by Horace Walpole. Thus, in its Gothic fakery,

---

24 Harman, *The Quadruple Object*, 7, 16.
25 Peter Gratton, *Speculative Realism: Problems and Prospects* (London: Bloomsbury, 2014), 99, 102.
26 Harman calls Lovecraft a "great hero to object-oriented thought" because of his explorations of tensions and gaps between real and sensual objects. Harman, *Weird Realism*, 5.
27 Bennett, *Vibrant Matter*, 15.

"Cthulhu" LARP is an exemplary activity in establishing the connections between idealism and materialism that are necessary for any robust realist ontology.

Of course, LARP props might also be so effective that players have no need to roleplay fright or flight responses. Encountering a monster while alone in the subterranean corridors of a crumbling, Northumberland castle prompts an immediate embodied response and a very real, adrenaline injection. In moments where props don't only prescribe "fictional truths" but seem viscerally real, the response of player and character merge and the distinction between game and external reality collapses. Here, LARP most obviously achieves that quintessential Gothic effect described by Chris Baldick as the "sickening descent into disintegration."[28] Lovecraft's stories, too, evoke Baldick's Gothic effect in their depiction of a protagonist increasingly haunted by an eons-dead and long-forgotten truth, drawn to some claustrophobic space (for example, subterranean passages, the strange angle of an attic room, the bell tower of an abandoned church) and that protagonist's eventual descent into madness as they glimpse the terrifying vistas of the cosmos. For all his rejection of clanking chains and skeletons, Lovecraft worked within the Gothic as well as innovating that related mode, the Weird.[29] "Cthulhu" LARP likewise draws on both literary modes but almost always evokes a Gothic structure, wearing away at player-characters' sanity and disintegrating their sense of a stable universe as the game progresses, disclosing or gesturing to something chaotic beyond representation and socially-constructed realities. "Cthulhu" LARP also makes the benign "magic circle," described by Huizinga as central to play, into a claustrophobic trap familiar from Gothic novels. LARP enfolds players in a frenetic twenty-four-hour time-in experience, often ending in their characters' deaths. This kind of LARP does not

---

28 Chris Baldick, "Introduction," in *The Oxford Book of Gothic Tales* (Oxford: Oxford University Press, 1992), xix.

29 For a discussion of Lovecraft's Gothic work, see Xavier Aldana Reyes, ed., *The Gothic Tales of H.P. Lovecraft* (London: The British Library, 2018).

instill the mastery Huizinga and other theorists associate with play culture, but rather produces as the intended outcome the disintegration of a coherent, anchored sense of identity. In this thoroughly "dark play," such disintegrations of selfhood are not simply psychological, but potentially metaphysical.

Finally, "Cthulhu" LARP and the Gothic are both forms that draw attention to surfaces and to the strange disjunctions between presence and absence that manifest on the surface of sensual or perceptual experience. Exploring this surface of experience, which is so heightened in LARP, is the route to speculating about what lies beyond the correlationist gap, as this is where we encounter emerging and withdrawing objects, where we glimpse the vibrancy of things and feel the effects of their agency. The mechanics of LARP and the fakery of the Gothic alike evoke an awareness of the surface. For example, the use of explicit fakery in LARP asks players to be immersed in a narrative but also recognize certain objects as props, an act that would seem to puncture immersion within the game but actually aids it. That is, such puncturing through recognition is necessary for the ludic mechanics: players need to recognize game props as such in order to negotiate the game.[30] This recognition echoes techniques found in the Gothic mode, which habitually draws attention to itself via meta-textuality. Walpole inaugurates such meta-textual playfulness with his first preface to *Otranto,* announcing the novel as a found manuscript.

Eve Sedgwick notes that Gothic's concern with the surface is also seen in its emphasis on tropes and not depths. She argues that Gothic draws attention to the veil rather than the face underneath, for example, evoking "a sense of doubleness where

---

30   Here my arguments echo Janet Murray's comments on immersion and narrative. Murray is often maligned in game studies, but two of her insights are valuable here. First, she suggests that interactivity and immersion reinforce one another. Second, she argues that we must be able to define the boundaries of a narrative before we can become immersed within it. See Janet Murray, *Hamlet on the Holodeck: The Future of Narrative in Cyberspace* (New York: The Free Press, 1997), 114, 129.

singleness should be."[31] Another way of understanding Sedgwick's claim is that Gothic is interested in the objects that manifest on the surface and on their surface effects, and not, as has been most often understood, on treating those objects as ciphers or metaphors that reveal human psychology. Gothic doubleness materialized at a horror LARP I played that was held at an ex-military bunker.[32] The bunker was already populated by items that looked appropriate for the setting of the game. However, the bunker was also a museum, so players were not allowed to touch the native items. Consequently, players needed to differentiate between game items and museum exhibits as they navigated the space. Prop fakery became a signifier of narrative authenticity and, in the process, the bunker became a doubled space. In-game objects formed a layer over the real objects, which receded from the game world into a spectral background that, paradoxically, remained on the surface of experience. Lovecraft's fiction pays attention to such disjunctive surface layers in stories such as "From Beyond." Here, with the help of a machine, the protagonist becomes aware of a second terrifying world of experience that over-layers that of the everyday.

Paradoxical Props: Object Oriented Ontology

Thus far I have suggested some of the technical and thematic ways in which "Cthulhu" LARP props produce paradoxical and disjunctive experiences for players. Reading these experiences alongside Harman's object-oriented ontology suggests how LARP might constitute a disruption of everyday, common-sense conceptions of reality for human perceivers and that it offers its own challenge to correlationist thought that would "debunk objects and deny their autonomy."[33] Harman, contends that materiality is composed of paradoxical objects that are not only fig-

---

31 Eve Kosofsky Sedgwick, *The Coherence of Gothic Conventions* (New York: Methuen, 1986), 13.
32 This game was "The Atlantis Legacy," written and organized by David Garwood for *The Dark Door* in 2014.
33 Harman, *The Quadruple Object*, 6.

ments of the mind of a human perceiver, nor "mere aggregates" of smaller pieces.[34] In his metaphysical schema, objects are autonomous, something more than only their "pieces," and always partly withhold themselves from relations with other entities.[35] Such objects are paradoxical because they both have and do not have the properties they are ascribed in classical metaphysics, that is "accidents, qualities, relations and moment."[36] Harman's object oriented ontology suggests that objects reveal themselves in contact with other objects and that this contact includes but is not limited to human perception. Objects are tricky because they are both noumenal and phenomenological, relational but with an essential kernel that evades all relations; they also possess a surface "eidos" but are comprised of shifting surface qualities that elude totalisation. Much of Harman's work focuses on exploring these tensions. Indeed, Gratton suggests that the term "tension" is key to Harman's metaphysics; it "brings together (fusion) and it drives apart (fission) the object within itself."[37] These tensions become apparent in the way props function in LARP and are central to the form's affective dimension and mechanics of immersion.

LARP props reverse everyday experiences of the material world in which objects tend to withdraw from conscious access. The conception of reality as "withdrawn" is one coordinate of Harman's metaphysics and one of the sources of tension within and between objects.[38] For Heidegger, objects withdraw from conscious access, only coming to notice when they cease to function properly. Harman designates this coming-to-notice as the result of failure, but suggests it can never be addressed since our becoming conscious of things never grasps "the whole of their reality."[39] LARP illuminates the tension of "withdrawal" and "failure" in that it initially reverses the usual conditions in which hu-

---

34 Ibid., 7.
35 Ibid., 19.
36 Ibid.
37 Gratton, *Speculative Realism*, 102.
38 Harman, *The Quadruple Object*, 39.
39 Ibid.

man perception operates, demanding that normally withdrawn objects make themselves known. While in our everyday lives, books on a shelf recede into murky noumena and exist beyond conscious perception; in a LARP, they might contain a vital clue such as a scrap of paper or some journal pages hastily stuffed inside or between them. Thus, the shelf of books must obtrude into the players' experience. Sometimes, the recognition demanded by the ludic frame achieves such obtrusion on its own and players search the seemingly innocent bookshelf because it is likely something could be hidden there. At other times, work is needed to bring withdrawn objects to notice. At one game, a referee placed a magazine we had all been ignoring near an open door, so the wind would ruffle its pages: she was becoming quite frustrated that we had not picked up the magazine or realised that it contained important information! Games are also littered with broken objects that obtrude in unhelpful ways. Broken radios, out-of-order telephones, and generators that have run out of fuel are a few examples of suddenly obtrusive objects that exert agency and work against the players' chances of successfully solving the game scenario. Failure is central to "Cthulhu" LARP, and props are often used in the wrong way, especially if they are of eldritch provenance. Players have many theories about what an object is or how it might be used, but they are always guessing, or only partially understanding the object's provenance and purpose. Even if they manage to put together a partial solution that successfully unlocks one of the object's powers, they will not have grasped the whole of its reality.

Harman's insistence upon "tension" also suggests that objects are not unified, but in strife with their internal qualities. Harman describes this as "fission": "the qualities of the thing break off from the thing as a whole."[40] Another formulation of this tension is that it manifests a gap between the sensual object and its sensual qualities, that is, an object we encounter in the perceptual realm via our senses but that has myriad and shifting qualities. As Harman points out, Lovecraft's writing is re-

---

40 Harman, *Weird Realism*, 242.

plete with such gaps; his "language is overloaded by a gluttonous excess of surfaces and aspects of the thing."[41] The stylistic world of Lovecraft is one in which real objects are in tension with the crippled powers of language and where visible objects "display unbearable seismic torsion with their own qualities."[42] This crippled language suggests a narrator's inability to correlate the multitude of surfaces and qualities they encounter into a unified whole. LARP organizers try to replicate Lovecraft's gluttonous excess of surfaces through the creation of elaborate monster costumes, which aim to evoke an encounter for players in which they are unable to take in the whole of the creature, to fully make sense of its seeming myriad qualities. Practically, this involves layering latex onto foam and adding mixed media materials to produce lumpen, glistening, uneven shapes. Monster costumes made for a single person to wear might include stilts to add height, extra limbs, or protruding tentacles. We might add LED lights, programmed to display random patterns in the darkness. Monsters should never be fully seen, especially not in the daylight. They are most effective when encountered as a series of fragmented and disjointed qualities: strange lights in the darkness beyond the house, a bulky shape in the doorway, an impossibly tall shadow, the swipe of a glistening limb as you try to escape.

Another weird aspect of objects is described by Harman as the "interbreeding between real and sensual realms."[43] This is when the normally inaccessible, "real" object, as opposed to the accessible "sensual" object, slides into the accessible realm, exerting force there. This prompts a form of indirect contact with the real through a tension Harman describes as "fusion": "Instead of the direct sort of contact that we have with sensual objects, there is an allusion to the silent object in the depths that becomes vaguely fused with its legion of sensual qualities."[44]

---

41 Ibid., 25.
42 Ibid., 27.
43 Harman, *The Quadruple Object,* 105.
44 Ibid., 104.

Lovecraft's fiction explores such fusion through its allusion to the existence of inter- or extra-dimensional beings. Cthulhu influences dreamers from his sunken hibernation in the depths of the Pacific in "The Call of Cthulhu," for example, and Crawford Tillinghast is seemingly consumed by some creature that emerges briefly when his "resonance generator" fuses the human sensual realm of the everyday with another, more terrifying realm, in the short story "From Beyond." "Cthulhu" LARP draws on these Lovecraftian scenarios in its themes and plots, of course, but it also produces strange moments of fusion in its attempts to render in physical form interdimensional monsters. Briefly, a "real" object might emerge from a bundle of sensual qualities. Something like this happened to me when I assisted a friend as he prepared an elaborate monster costume, intended to represent a "Hound of Tindalos," a creature invented by Frank Belknap Long. We were in the basement of a dilapidated, Georgian property, away from the players who were immersed in the game a few floors above. I helped my friend attach each separate piece of the costume to his body, which included some comic struggling with awkward stilt-like limbs that attached to his arms. I did not register anything strange about the components, and I was not immersed in the game narrative, only assisting behind the scenes. However, something occurred when my friend donned the last segment of the costume. He hunched over and placed the forearms of the stilt-like limbs on the ground, producing a distinctly unhuman shape and posture. I stepped back to view the effect and felt a moment of horrifying shock, a little rush of adrenaline, the desire to flee the basement. Then, my friend spoke, tightened a fastening, and the effect was dissipated. Whatever horrifying, real object had momentarily emerged, disappeared. The incident recalls Harman's imaginary scenario in which qualities fuse "with an object that we do not normally associate with them. [...] [T]his results in an object that *feels* real simply because it is too difficult to register vividly as a normal sensual object."[45] The Hound of Tindalos costume

---

[45] Ibid., 240.

in its entirety was, however briefly, difficult for me to register as a normal, sensual object: it was genuinely frightening. Here, the many sensual qualities of the monster costume, which I had no trouble accounting for earlier, momentarily fused with a more disturbing whole. Of course, the incident required a human perceiver to disclose the real object. Moreover, the moment of disquietude I felt was the result of an involuntary performance of the man in the costume adjusting his posture to produce an effect something like the emergence of a real object. In this sense, the incident illustrates what Harman calls the "allusive" nature of Lovecraft's writing. Often, his stories present a phenomenon (for example, the appearance of an Old One that cannot be fully described by a narrator) that offers indirect access to the noumenal realm.[46] Such is the difficulty of getting outside the closed circle of correlationism, limiting Lovecraft, and Harman, to an "oblique sort of access to reality" via objects as they appear in the perceptual realm. At the same time "things in themselves must have autonomy from their relation to us, or they are not the things in themselves."[47] What is interesting about the incident I describe, however, is that it occurred outside the narrative frame of the game and so did not only rely on the agency of a human perceiver in the form of a story narrator or player-character. That is, when I was frightened by the Hound of Tindalos I was under no obligation to suspend disbelief because I was not immersed in a story. The encounter was prompted by the object that coalesced from the costume components, suggesting a link between Harman's fusion and Bennett's "thing-power." This latter concept provides another way of getting beyond the correlationist circle, evinced by Bennet's description of stumbling upon a collection of stuff discarded in the street. She describes how the collection of objects "exhibited" its thing-power: "it issued a call even if I did not quite understand what it was saying."[48] The

---

46 Ibid., 25.
47 Harman, *The Quadruple Object*, 53.
48 Bennett, *Vibrant Matter*, 4.

intrusion of thing-power not only points to non-human actants but to the outside of human experience and understanding.

Of course, most affective encounters with props occur within the game and narrative frames of LARP. The in-game narrative of a "Cthulhu" LARP often revolves around an important prop that operates both in the sensual realm and in a realm beyond human perception: the field generator and archaeological fragments discussed above, for example. The fragments turned out to be parts of a damaged beacon from an ancient alien spacecraft that had crashed thousands of years ago. Individually, the fragments exerted physical and psychical effects upon players, making them visibly unwell and affecting their behaviour. Some properties of the fragments could be investigated using in-game medical and scientific skills, but to unlock their more esoteric secrets, players had to find other ways of accessing the object. An in-character, drug-induced trance led to some revelatory visions and began to gesture towards the elusive, real essence of the objects we had uncovered. Although Lovecraft has been characterized as a strict materialist, the monsters and artifacts in his stories are not mere "arrangement[s] of electrons."[49] Harman's objects, too, cannot be reduced to their atoms and electrons. LARP scenarios often draw out this irreducible materiality through props that suggest a reality beyond the measure of the scientific method. The scientist and the medical doctor could only reveal so much: in this game it was the hippy and the philosophy student characters whose visions allowed the players to "fuse" the fragments into a whole, making the beacon function, and allowing the plot to progress.

Non-Separation: LARP and the "Magic Circle"

Although Harman presents his metaphysics in the form of four quadrants, his account of tensions between real and sensual objects implies a dualist ontology, a reality comprised of

---

49 Michel Houellebecq, *H.P. Lovecraft: Against the World, Against Life* (London: Gollancz, 2008), 32.

two realms. At the same time, Harman's concepts of "fusion" and "fission" also suggest non-separation between these realms. Lovecraft's fiction likewise invites a Kantian interpretation wherein the phenomenal realm of human perception gives way to the murky noumena of eldritch beings and unplumbed space, but this separation of noumena and phenomena simplifies the paradoxical maneuver that is a Lovecraftian encounter with the "outside." As Eugene Thacker suggests, horror fiction has long been engaged in confronting the paradoxical proposition that the world is, in reality, a "world-in-itself" beyond the access of human thought. Horror fiction confronts the human-centric concept of the "world-for-us" with a nebulous "world-without-us," a simultaneously "impersonal and horrific" zone between the "for-us" and the "in-itself."[50] This horrific "world-without-us" discloses that the "great outdoors" is not out there, but already within and around us. It is just that we fail to recognize this fact. Thacker suggests that the trope of the magic circle in horror fiction reveals something of this hidden yet omnipresent world-in-itself. Analyzing examples from William Hope Hodgson's Carnacki stories and Lovecraft's "From Beyond," Thacker argues that the magic circle, traditionally held to serve as a protective barrier for the human occultist, becomes a portal to "another dimension," focusing and intensifying the passage between seemingly separate realms. In "From Beyond," the effect of Tillinghast's resonator is to expand the parameters of the magic circle such that the non-separation expands outwards into infinity.[51] In this story, the bounded nature of the experiment dissolves entirely, playing havoc with the Kantian separation of phenomena and noumena.

Magic circles are a common prop in "Cthulhu" LARP. They may provide the means through which players open the passage between what is designated "natural" and "supernatural," or function as a device for summoning or expelling interdimen-

---
50 Eugene Thacker, *In the Dust of This Planet: Horror of Philosophy, Volume I* (Winchester: Zero Books, 2011), 5, 6.
51 Ibid., 62, 72, 77.

sional creatures. Often, the magic circle is a source of in-game entrapment: in one game I designed, we placed a circle of marker stones around the boundaries of a property. These had been activated to provide a circle of protection by a non-player-character, but because our player-characters had been "infected" by a monster's spawn, they were not able to leave the confines of the circle.[52] Beyond the game narrative, however, the magic circle performs a structural and ludic function. Indeed, LARP itself produces a ritually enacted space in which players are bound for the duration of the event. Huizinga draws on the metaphor of the magic circle to describe the ritualistic aspect of play: it suggests play is a temporary sphere of activity with a disposition all its own.[53] Later theorists see this magic circle as constructing a "psychological bubble that allows for a playful mindset" or a "social contract" to manifest in space and time.[54] "Cthulhu" LARP often exploits and emphasizes this ludic structure, marking out the game space in materially distinct ways to emphasize feelings of entrapment. Props such as the boundary marker stones in "Who Do You Think You Are?" merge player and character frames by providing an in-game reason for staying within the game space, otherwise, a sensible character would probably run away, necessitating their player leaving the game, while also creating affect around the themes of isolation and claustrophobia. Thus, LARP transforms the structure of play's "magic circle" into a ludic challenge (find a way to escape) and a source of horror. A form of "dark play," the psychological bubble and social contract of the play space become sources of in-game punishment, stress and fear. The magic circle in "Cthulhu" LARP is not simply a psychological or social device, suggesting that the laws and customs of everyday life no longer count for the duration of play. It is a structure that reveals the usually "hidden" non-separation of different orders of reality. When players enter a "Cthulhu"

---

52 This game was "Who Do You Think You Are?" written and organized by Laura Mitchell and Chloé Germaine Buckley for *Disturbing Events* in 2009.
53 Huizinga, *Homo Ludens*, 8.
54 Linderoth and Mortensen, "Dark Play," 5.

LARP they do not know what will happen to their characters, but they can expect some form of cosmic horror. The bounded nature of LARP (an activity of limited duration that demands immersion, taking place in a relatively constrained space) blurs character and player experience of space, time, and objects in ways that are designed to feel unsafe, challenging, that seek to expose player-characters to the "outside" of human experience. As Thacker states, the magic circle in "From Beyond" reveals the already existing non-separation between natural and supernatural, the "here and now," and the "beyond."[55] In Lovecraft's story, the climax turns upon a magical-scientific prop, Tillinghast's machine, which renders visible a monstrous reality that constitutes the "outside" of human perception. Most horrifying is the revelation that the two worlds are not separate at all, but that the "beyond" is already within and around us. Turning on the machine brings the protagonist into Tillinghast's magic circle, a bounded space, that paradoxically dissolves separation and expands such that the bounded nature of the experiment also dissolves: the protagonist becomes immersed in another realm that was already there. LARP likewise functions to invite players into a magic circle, a discrete space with clear spatial boundaries and temporal limits. Game organizers call "Time In" and "Time Out" to signal the beginning and end of play. They also mark the borders of the play space, indicating, for example, that a particular copse of trees at the boundary of a property is "in game," but the road beyond a fence post is not. Nonetheless, once play begins such boundaries dissolve in the construction of a shared narrative. Almost always, the player-characters encounter a threat "from beyond" that will engulf or consume the game world, a world that extends far beyond a copse of trees or a fence post. Likewise, though player-characters may be trapped within a house, they might experience a terrifying vision of the cosmos or catch a glimpse of an eons-dead world, of vistas of incalculable dimensions, reminiscent of descriptions from Lovecraftian fiction. These "visions" are often narrated by game

---

55 Thacker, *In the Dust of This Planet*, 77.

organizers and such in-game "set-pieces" function to suggest the "cosmic" scale of the game. The initially bounded play space (Huizinga's magic circle) becomes what Thacker describes as a "magic site," no longer a strictly demarked location marked by "human governance" of the borders between apparent and hidden worlds.[56] The magic site is where the hidden world intrudes into the human world; it creeps forth with unhuman entities and independent objects, and threatens expansion beyond its porous edges.

Within the game narrative, a magic circle is also a prop that prescribes an affective encounter with the "outside." Players are often drawn into a dramatic climax whereby they must draw a magic circle to begin a ritual, perhaps to banish a creature to another dimension or close a "portal" that threatens their reality, but once the circle is cast it immediately produces the sense of metaphysical non-separation evoked in "From Beyond," calling forth the very monsters the ritual is designed to expel. Typically, this situation results in a lone player huddled in the middle of a hastily rendered magic circle, fumbling with various crumpled papers containing scrawled translations and half-legible notes, attempting to deliver a ritual the players have devised over the course of the game, while the remaining survivors fend off attack at the edges of the circle from numerous monsters. At the end, most of the defenders are dead and the caster is likely insane. Hopefully, the ritual has done the trick, with a significant human cost, but often it fails and the game ends in total defeat. Here, the magic circle may have represented an attempt at "active human governance of the boundary between the apparent world and the hidden world,"[57] but its failure is built into the narrative and ludic tendencies of "Cthulhu" LARP, which echoes its source material in providing little opportunity for victory. The occult themes in "Cthulhu" LARP also blur distinctions between the natural and the supernatural, and science and magic, with players often having to put together magic rituals with

---

56 Ibid., 82.
57 Ibid.

fragments of in-game knowledge gleaned from folklore, eldritch writings, and scientific or pseudo-scientific theories. One of the most exhausting and terrifying rituals I have enacted in-game took place in a folk horror setting, but combined elements of folk superstition with real-world mathematics and physics. This game, called "The Black Goat,"[58] culminated in a ritual held in the pitch-black woods in an attempt to hold back a nefarious and unseen omnipresent power. We stood in a circle beneath the trees and chanted over and over: "Molecules remain in your natural state and vibrate with consistency and constancy." Thankfully, in this instance, we prevailed, and our molecules remained mercifully unchanged!

Making Monsters: "Thing-Power" in Cthulhu LARP

The vibrating molecules evoked in "The Black Goat" suggest the vibrant or vital materiality expounded by Jane Bennett. While Harman is concerned with orienting ontology around autonomous objects to combat anthropocentric correlationism, Bennett exhorts readers to stop thinking of "matter as passive stuff" and to begin to account for the "active role of nonhuman materials."[59] Harman's recourse to horror literature is explicit: Lovecraft provides an imaginative language of weird monstrosity that allows Harman to elucidate his ontological schema. In contrast, there is nothing necessarily horrifying about Bennett's account of vital materialism, though it accords with some Lovecraftian themes particularly in its insistence on dismantling "fantasies of a human uniqueness [...], escape from materiality, or of mastery of nature."[60] Rather than discrete Newtonian objects extended and moving in a noumenal realm, Bennett describes a paradoxically plural monism, an immanent field composed of "various and variable materialities" that "collude, congeal, morph, evolve, and

---

58 "The Black Goat" was written and organized by Jenny Wilkinson and Lee Wilkinson for *The Dark Door* in 2017.
59 Bennett, *Vibrant Matter*, vii, 2.
60 Ibid., vii.

disintegrate."[61] Bennett is keen to jettison the static term "object" and its implied subject/object binarism, pointing instead to the liveliness of things, to the "strange ability of ordinary, man-made items to exceed their status as objects and to manifest traces of independence or aliveness constituting the outside of our own experience."[62] "Cthulhu" LARP's evocation of Lovecraftian themes — through encounters with strange props, its material manifestation of weird monsters, and its demand for players to immerse themselves in an affective experience of cosmic horror — attempts its own unique evocation of the nonhuman world Bennett describes. While Bennett attempts to use "argument and other rhetorical means to induce in human bodies an aesthetic affective openness to material vitality,"[63] "Cthulhu" LARP encourages its players to experience the strangeness of materiality through the vibrant colors, strange textures, and dissonant sounds used in the production of props.

Although there is a degree of fakery and a DIY aesthetic to many LARP props, they are nonetheless produced to enchant the players, to encourage the suspension of disbelief and immersion in the narrative of the game. Bennett's ontology emphasizes the importance of such enchantment as a form of affect that might cultivate openness to material vitality. In LARP, props must provoke quasi-emotional responses or, perhaps, even genuine emotional responses in moments of "bleed" when real-world and game-world frames collapse such that player and character respond as one. The crumbling wall discussed above is one such example of "bleed" intended by the LARP organizers to prompt real emotional and bodily affect in the players. Not all moments of enchantment are as dramatic as this. It may be that a player sits for several hours, turning over an object, discussing strange markings on its surface, tracing patterns with their fingers. Perhaps they must spend a significant amount of time "in-character" roleplaying a series of scientific tests to determine

---

61   Ibid., xi.
62   Ibid., xvi.
63   Ibid., x.

the composition of the rock or the properties of the strange metal. These activities are common in LARP and suggest the enchanting power of props to promote immersion within the game whilst also evoking a Lovecraftian thematic of mysterious "thing-power": these props offer a glimpse of the outside of human experience and mark the limits of human understanding. Encounters with objects in LARP also evoke the two directions of enchantment that Bennett describes: "the first toward the humans who feel enchanted and whose agentic capacities may be thereby strengthened, and the second toward the agency of the things that produce (helpful, harmful) effects."[64] The ludic frame of LARP produces such two-way encounters with objects. Time spent under the spell of an important prop in the game often confers upon player the knowledge or capability to unlock the next puzzle. For example, after meditating for several hours on the carved fragments uncovered at the archaeological dig in "X Marks the Spot," I was given a vision of how the fragments had come to be buried under the ground and glimpsed their possible provenance and function. There are also less useful moments of enchantment that nonetheless have ludic and narrative effects: a player becomes obsessed with a strange amulet, for example, which exerts a psychical influence driving the character mad over the course of the game. A "mad" character acting under the influence of a strange object is a problem for the other players and threatens their ability to win or survive the game.

Outside of the game, players and organizers devote a lot of time to planning, designing and building props, and developing competencies in various crafts (for example, sewing, painting, working with liquid latex) to improve on props for future games. Often, we are experimenting with mixed media and using what materials we can source cheaply. Sometimes, we are not quite sure what the effects or outcome will be of our efforts. Some prop effects occur by chance, the happy result of how materials congeal or react with one another. I once spent a few weeks covering an old plastic doll in layers of liquid latex, green

---

64 Ibid., xii–xiii.

paint, and synthetic ivy for "Who Do You Think You Are?" I knew I wanted to make a horrid, plant-baby-creature for one of our monsters to carry around, but I wasn't sure what I wanted the "baby" to look like or even if I would use the prop as it wasn't crucial to the narrative. I layered, painted, and sculpted until a "thing" emerged and it turned out to be one of the most terrifying props in the game. On another occasion, an accident with a glue gun, which leaked all over a clay mould, made my "shining trapezohedron" much more horrifyingly effective than in the original design. In both cases material objects (doll, latex, glue gun) and human agency (me as prop-builder) became co-conspiratorial actants in the production of an affective in-game encounter for the player-characters. However, the objects did not become subordinate to a human master: the props that emerged from our encounter were as much the work of the materials as any human intention.

Game organizers work with mixed media to create the effect of hybridity, to produce monsters inspired by Lovecraft's "revolutionary teratology."[65] As China Miéville notes, Lovecraftian monsters are a "radical break with anything from a folkloric tradition. Rather than werewolves, vampires, or ghosts, Lovecraft's monsters are agglomerations of bubbles, barrels, cones, and corpses, patchworked from cephalopods, insects, crustaceans, and other fauna."[66] More than this, monsters in "Cthulhu" LARP attempt to convey category disruptions such that life/matter binaries and hierarchies of life forms imposed by human knowledge on the material world are disrupted. Bennett's vital materialism argues for the same category disruptions, for the recognition of the animate in plants, or the vegetable in animals.[67] For "Who Do You Think You Are," we produced a "Dark Young." This nonhuman, animal-plant hybrid was about seven feet tall. The upper part comprised a "trunk" and "branches"

---

65 China Miéville, "Weird Fiction," in *The Routledge Companion to Science Fiction*, eds. Mark Bould, Andrew M. Butler, Adam Roberts, and Sherryl Vint (London: Routledge, 2009), 512.
66 Ibid.
67 Bennett, *Vibrant Matter*, 8.

made from a plastic and metal frame covered in foam, latex, and paint, to which branch-like tentacles, fake flora, and flashing lights were affixed. We added numerous eyes and mouths rendered in foam and latex. The lower part of the costume was a simple pair of goat-leg trousers made from fake fur and worn over stilts to add height. The inanimate objects (foam, pipe lagging, latex, synthetic fur, and silk plants) produced a seemingly shifting surface of monstrous life and vitality. A similar effect was produced in "X Marks the Spot," for which the organizers constructed monster costumes from cloth garments covered in foam, latex, paint, and flickering LEDs. In the game narrative, these terrifying creatures had been conjured from the mud and branches that littered the copse of trees behind the house. In this example, the "magic site" physically intruded into the human spaces of the game, invading the house and attacking the player-characters.

Though representing the fundamentally unhuman creatures of Lovecraft's stories, LARP monsters are almost always material-human hybrids because the costumes must be worn and manipulated by the game organizers. Their terrifying effects cannot be produced through the materials alone. Rather, inanimate materials and human bodies interact to produce the generative prop. As Bennett argues, agency—defined as a source of action or the power to effect other bodies—is almost always the result of a combination of human and non-human "actants."[68] A recognition that human agency "is itself a kind of thing-power"[69] resonates in "Cthulhu" LARP where game themes often revolve upon player-characters merging with or becoming monstrous. In "Professor Lazarus's Emporium of Wonders" our players were constantly under threat of being absorbed into the shoggoth, becoming part of a monster that comprised all the characters who had died joined together by a network of umbilical cords—made from tangled rope covered in latex and paint—emanating from the body of the shoggoth—a monster

---

68 Ibid., 9.
69 Ibid.

that was itself composed entirely of inanimate materials as described above. "Cthulhu" LARP's themes also bring to the fore the materiality of the human body, what Bennett describes as "the minerality of our bones, or the metal of our blood, or the electricity of our neurons."[70] Bennett notes that we acknowledge this composition but rarely conceive of these materials in themselves as lively and self-organizing.[71] In "Cthulhu" LARP, though, the materials of the human body interact with inanimate props, co-producing a new prop in the course of the game narrative. In such cases, vibrant-material actants congeal with human bodies but do not become subsumed within human agency, retaining something of their thing-power. In "X Marks the Spot," the characters' blood was needed, along with a jolt of electricity, to fuse the separate fragments of the alien beacon into a unified object that could communicate with the creatures threatening human existence. Yet, the object retained something of its alienness, never fully disclosing the reality of the unhuman realm from which it originated. Encounters with monsters and props in "Cthulhu" LARP often constitute this kind of demand: they require a response, a reciprocation from the human characters to become receptive to the "outside," both to the realm of things and to their own thing-power without those material objects becoming wholly subsumed within a world-for-us.

Conclusions

This exploration of the intersection between horror, play, and speculative philosophy suggests the philosophical nature of game playing and the potential of LARP, in particular, to produce embodied and affective experiences that might illuminate both speculative realist and new materialist rhetoric. LARP's prop-oriented framework emphasizes objects and things as lively, autonomous, and agentic. The relationship between the Gothic tradition and LARP also exposes some of the weird spa-

---

70 Bennett, *Vibrant Matter*, 10.
71 Ibid.

tial transformations that props generate during the game. Certainly, Gothic fakery plays a role in the blurring of distinctions between game and reality and thus between materiality and the intangible. LARP props also allow for a generous reading of Harman's object oriented ontology, giving an embodied account of the "tensions" Harman describes between phenomenal and noumenal realms, between the sensual and the real. Moreover, LARP monster costumes and props hybridize the material with the vital, the human with the material, and the plant with the animal, evoking Bennett's "thing-power," itself an effect of the outside of human experience that both speculative realists and new materialists wish to explore. Specifically, "Cthulhu" LARP naïvely attempts to make concrete the processes of allusion present in Lovecraft's writing. Allusion is important to Harman, because it provides access "to something that might be real, but which can never be fully present."[72] LARP concretizes allusive processes, attempting to produce an embodied and affective encounter with a strange and vibrant materiality, a materiality which humans are a part of but which they cannot master.

Perhaps there is also an ethical dimension to the naïveté exemplified in LARP. LARP is a form of game-playing that demands a child-like surrender of disbelief and a commitment to immersion but also a willingness to engage in "dark play," which may deceive or disturb its players. Bennett, whose work is alert to the essential relationship between ethics and ontology, argues that ethics begins with "the recognition of human participation in a shared, vital materiality. […] The ethical task at hand here is to cultivate the ability to discern nonhuman vitality, to become perceptually open to it."[73] The demands LARP makes on its players cultivates this discernment, demanding that they pay close attention to objects' "qualitative moments."[74] LARP is a form of training to perceive the "invisible field that surrounds and infuses the world of objects," but it is a training that requires a

---

72 Harman, *The Quadruple Object*, 68.
73 Bennett, *Vibrant Matter*, 14.
74 Ibid.

willingness to "play the fool," a state Bennett suggests is necessary to correct and "chasten our will to mastery."[75] This ethical-ontological dimension of LARP provides a counter to accounts of play that see it as a fundamentally human activity. Miguel Sicart, for example, suggests that play is a humanist mode, a fundamental part of our moral well-being, of the healthy, mature, and complete human life.[76] Human agency is front and center in this account: humans construct and deconstruct the world through play. In contrast, my reading of LARP suggests the inverse: that such "dark play" forces its players to account for the unhuman nature of reality, to consider that fact that it is the world that makes us.

---

75 Ibid., 15.
76 Sicart, *Play Matters*, 23.

Bibliography

Aldana Reyes, Xavier, ed. *The Gothic Tales of H.P. Lovecraft.* London: The British Library, 2018.

Baldick, Chris, "Introduction." In *The Oxford Book of Gothic Tales,* xi–xxiii. Oxford: Oxford University Press, 1992.

Bateman, Chris. *Imaginary Games.* Winchester: Zero Books, 2011.

Bennett, Jane. *Vibrant Matter: A Political Ecology of Things.* Durham: Duke University Press, 2010.

Bryant, Levi, Nick Srnicek, and Graham Harman. "Towards a Speculative Philosophy." In *The Speculative Turn: Continental Materialism and Realism,* edited by Levi Bryant, Nick Srnicek, and Graham Harman, 1–18. Melbourne: Re-Press, 2011.

Coole, Diana, and Samantha Frost. "Introducing the New Materialisms." In *New Materialisms: Ontology, Agency, Politics,* edited by Diana Coole and Samantha Frost, 1–46. Durham: Duke University Press, 2010.

Germaine Buckley, Chloé, and Laura Mitchell. "Weird Experience: Transformations of Space/Place in 'Lovecraftian' LARP." *Studies in Gothic Fiction* 7, no. 1 (2020, forthcoming).

Gratton, Peter. *Speculative Realism: Problems and Prospects.* London: Bloomsbury, 2014.

Harman, Graham. *The Quadruple Object.* Winchester: Zero Books, 2011.

———. *Weird Realism: Lovecraft and Philosophy.* Winchester: Zero Books, 2012.

Houellebecq, Michel. *H.P. Lovecraft: Against the World, Against Life.* London: Gollancz, 2008.

Huizinga, Johan. *Homo Ludens: A Study of the Play-Element in Culture.* Kettering: Angelico Press, 2016.

Lovecraft, H.P. "Supernatural Horror in Literature." *The H.P. Lovecraft Archive.* http://www.hplovecraft.com/writings/texts/essays/shil.aspx.

Linderoth, Jonas, and Torill Elvira Mortensen. "Dark Play: The Aesthetics of Controversial Playfulness." In *The Dark Side of Game Play: Controversial Issues in Playful Environments,* edited by Torill Elvira Mortensen, Jonas Linderoth, and Ashley M.L. Brown, 3–14. London: Routledge, 2015.

McEvoy, Emma. *Gothic Tourism.* Basingstoke: Palgrave Macmillan, 2016.

Miéville, China. "Weird Fiction." In *The Routledge Companion to Science Fiction,* edited by Mark Bould, Andrew M. Butler, Adam Roberts, and Sherryl Vint, 510–16. London: Routledge, 2009.

Murray, Janet. *Hamlet on the Holodeck: The Future of Narrative in Cyberspace.* New York: The Free Press, 1997.

Schechner, Richard. *Performance Studies: An Introduction.* London: Routledge, 2002.

Sedgwick, Eve Kosofsky. *The Coherence of Gothic Conventions.* New York: Methuen, 1986.

Shaviro, Steven. "The Universe of Things." *Theory & Event* 14, no. 3 (2011): 1–18.

Sicart, Miguel. *Play Matters.* Cambridge: MIT Press, 2014.

Thacker, Eugene. *In the Dust of This Planet: Horror of Philosophy, Volume I.* Winchester: Zero Books, 2011.

Walton, Kendall L. "Metaphor and Prop Oriented Make-Believe." *European Journal of Philosophy* 1, no. 1 (1993): 39–57. DOI: 10.1111/j.1468-0378.1993.tb00023.x.

11

Sublime Horror in the Tales of E.T.A. Hoffmann

Hamad Al-Rayes

> The schizophrene, the cyclothyme,
> Pass from the droll to the sublime.
>
> — Lawrence Durrell[1]

Part 1: The Tales of Hoffmann

Hoffmann Who?
Reading the fantastical tales of E.T.A. Hoffmann (1776–1822) implicates one in a period of immense cultural upheaval. In terms of bearing witness to the bursting forth of a new time, the impact of Hoffmann's cohort in Berlin and Dresden on the self-understanding of modern subjectivity ranks with that of the Greeks in relation to the classical era. In Athens we find a first cohesive and self-aware expression of autonomous "self-institution" — to borrow Cornelius Castoriadis's term[2] — the unprecedented event of a human social formation consciously and

---

1   Lawrence Durrell and James Gifford, *From the Elephant's Back: Collected Essays & Travel Writings* (Edmonton: University of Alberta Press, 2015), 101.
2   Cornelius Castoriadis, *The Imaginary Institution of Society,* trans. Kathleen Blamey (Cambridge: MIT Press, 1998).

deliberately setting forth the law out of itself. A similar drama of self-formation unfolds in the annals of German thought after the French Revolution, precipitating an obsession with questions of *Bildung* or formative cultural education. During these years of early romanticism, political self-institution seemed to coincide with the poetic ideal of giving birth to oneself, the cardinal struggle of the romantic persona,[3] which in the midst of the collapse of a bygone order must reevaluate the underpinnings of its very existence and recreate its values and sensibility anew. With the consolidation of romanticism as an all-embracing cultural tendency, we find the contradictions of political self-institution casting their pall on the intimate caverns of the imagination, undermining the integrity of human experience at its innermost core. Hoffmann's writings find their key context in this historical situation.

It does not detract from Hoffmann's contribution to romantic aesthetics that he was not a philosopher but rather a storyteller and music critic. Although a contemporary of Immanuel Kant and a compatriot of Kant's Königsberg, Hoffmann was not concerned with the problems of transcendental idealism.[4] From his letters, it is fair to assume that he attended some of Kant's local lectures. We know that he'd read Friedrich Wilhelm Joseph von Schelling and was very much impressed by the work of some of Schelling's disciples in the natural sciences.[5] A controversial though somewhat minor figure during his own lifetime, Hoffmann lived to see the commercial success of his own opera, *Undine,* and was in fact embraced by the luminaries of the age. Jean Paul, a doyen of German romantic letters, wrote the preface to Hoffmann's first collection of short stories, which included his pioneering tales of horror and the supernatural. Hoffmann

---

3   Harold Bloom, *Poetry and Repression: Revisionism from Blake to Stevens* (New Haven: Yale University Press, 1976), 28f.
4   Steven Cassedy, "Beethoven the Romantic: How E.T.A. Hoffmann Got It Right," *Journal of the History of Ideas* 71, no. 1 (2009): 1–37.
5   E.T.A. Hoffmann, *E.T.A. Hoffmann's Musical Writings: Kreisleriana, The Poet and the Composer, Musical Criticism,* ed. David Charlton (Cambridge: Cambridge University Press, 2003), 32.

also corresponded affably with Ludwig van Beethoven, otherwise not known for his conviviality. Yet Hoffmann's gravestone puzzlingly lists excellence in his office as Councilor of the Court of Justice as his primary achievement. The next generation of artists, however, came to see Hoffmann with some reverence. Literary France, in particular, embraced the *"fantasticor,"* as Théophile Gautier came to call him.[6] Charles Baudelaire counted him among the "superior artists who have in them the necessary receptivity for absolute ideas," indeed as "the man who until now has apprehended these ideas better than anyone else."[7] Honoré de Balzac named him "the poet of that which seems not to exist yet has life."[8] The reception of Hoffmann in European culture, despite conflicting assessments of the value of his contributions, turns on the otherworldly quality of his tales. The specific streak that distinguishes Hoffmann's accomplishments from, say, the tales of the *Thousand and One Nights,* or even from such trailblazing genre classics as Horace Walpole's 1764 *The Castle of Otranto,* is the preponderance of a sense of horror that accompanies an overpowering experience of sublimity, in a newfound world which sought to distance the supernatural from the circles of good society by consigning it to the playpen of a bygone, adolescent humanity.

The Romantic, the Philistine, the Spirit-Realm
Structurally, Hoffmann's tales of terror typically involve a trinity of basic elements. The reader encounters: (1) a romantic artist attempting to navigate, (2) a philistine middle-class culture without ceding ground on his compulsive obsession with (3) the "spirit-realm," a transcendent world which belies the aesthetic paltriness of everyday existence and which can only be accessed through the pursuit of art. The romantic of Hoffmann's tales is defined less by his artistic skill or success than by his obsessive

---
[6] Christiano Merlo, "Gautier Critique d'Hoffmann," *Études Littéraires* 42, no. 3 (2011): 71.
[7] Hoffmann, *Musical Writings,* 49.
[8] Maximilian Rudwin, "Balzac and the Fantastic," *The Sewanee Review* 33, no. 1 (1925): 10.

longing for a transcendent reality that promises a break with the straitjacket of mundane existence. Carefully documenting their comfortable confusion of romantic fervor for artistic substance, Hoffmann tends to condemn these beautiful souls as dilettantes. The failed romantic artist is depicted by Hoffmann as an essentially ecstatic madman, only capable of recognizing himself on the backdrop of social norms that cannot tolerate his aesthetic worldview. The romantic is only at home in the transcendent spirit-realm, populated by the creations of the imagination. The spirit-realm, in turn, is not any less real than the "real" world surrounding the romantic. On the contrary, the "real" world is simply a thin veneer that conceals the higher "spiritual" order (the German word is "*geistiger,*" which can also be rendered as "spectral" or "ghostly").

In contrast to the dilettante, the picture of the romantic that Hoffmann wants to champion is that of the artist who attempts to transform commonplace existence from within by investing it with the potencies of the romantic spirit-realm, instead of debasing the latter by treating it baldly as a refuge from daily life. Far from berating the artists of his day, Hoffmann chronicles the struggle of producing genuine (read: romantic) art in a culture virtually brought to a standstill by philistinism. The philistine acts as the polar opposite of the genuine romantic artist in Hoffmann's tales. The ubiquity of the figure of the philistine in Hoffmann's tales reflects the birth of this new social class during his own lifetime.[9] The figure of the philistine peeks its head at every turn in Hoffmann's tales, its features closely resembling those of the romantic dilettante. If the genuine romantic is the polar antagonist of the philistine, the romantic dilettante represents, by contrast, the flipside to the philistine's superficiality. A typical example of the philistine is Klara from Hoffmann's most renowned tale of horror, *The Sandman* (1817).[10] Klara ap-

---

9 Peter Bruning, "E.T.A. Hoffmann and the Philistine," *The German Quarterly* 28, no. 2 (1955): 111.
10 E.T.A. Hoffmann, *Tales of E.T.A. Hoffman,* eds. and trans. Leonard Kent and Elizabeth Knight (Chicago: University of Chicago Press, 1969), 93–125.

pears in the novelette as the epitome of healthy common sense. She spares no effort in attempting to convince Nathanael, her fiancé and the main character of the story, that his visions of the fabled Sandman's reappearance in his adult life have no footing in hard reality. For his part, Nathanael, a typically delusional Hoffmannian romantic, is certain that the monstrous folktale creature has already invaded his world, once in childhood in the guise of Coppelius, an old friend of the family, and again with increasing frequency in adulthood, in the guise of the mad peddler Coppola. Nathanael's visions and mystifying interactions with Coppelius-Coppola ignite a series of events, including an unrequited love affair with an automaton named Olympia, that end in Nathanael's succumbing to madness. What is unbearable to the aspiring romantic is not only the ubiquity of philistinism, exemplified by the rationalizations of Klara and her brother Lothar, but the unassailable character of the philistine's pronouncements. The philistine is accused of feeling too much at home in the newly enfranchised middle class. Such comfortable adjustment to the typical demands of modern life (e.g., nuclear family, professional career, fiscal responsibility, etc.) is condemned by the romantic as superficial complacency. Yet in return, the aspiring romantic himself has little to offer beside his mad consumption by a world of imaginary relations. Hoffmann's romantics are lost to a world that has been almost entirely co-opted by the philistine.

In "Der Artushof" or "The Court of Arthur" (1816),[11] Traugott, an aspiring draughtsman, gets distracted from his business duties by copying figures from a mural of King Arthur's fabled court. Traugott repeats Nathanael's tragedy in *The Sandman*. He is set to marry Christina Roos, the Klara-esque character of this tale, who is the daughter of the protagonist's business partner. The figure of the demonic artistic genius also makes an appearance, in the guise of "the old master" Herr Berklinger, himself of dubious footing in the real world (the narrator suggests that

---

11 E.T.A. Hoffmann, *The Serapion Brethren,* trans. Alexander Ewing (London: G. Bell & Sons, 1886), 152–81.

he is a doppelganger of one of the figures in the mural). The mural fulfills its romantic function by revealing itself to be a tunnel into the realm of spirits, seducing Traugott into a theater of fantasies. The setting of the Arthur murals right next to the practical realities of commercial life accentuates the former's fantastical effects. His business partner's nephew urges Traugott against the pursuit of an artistic career. Art's proper function, so the nephew argues, is decorative:

> Amusement — recreation after the serious business of life — is the delightful end and object of all artistic effort; and this is attained exactly in proportion as the productions of art are satisfactory. […] It is only those who practice art on this principle who enjoy that comfort and prosperity which flies away forever from those who, against the true principles of things, look upon art as the primary object and highest aim of life.[12]

Here we have a concise formulation of the philistine aesthetic principle, deliberately articulated as an anti-romanticism. According to the philistine, "living" means "having plenty of money and no debts; eating and drinking of the best, and having a nice wife and children, with no grease spots on their Sunday clothes, etc."[13] This pushes Traugott to reevaluate his romantic inclinations. He dreads the prospect of returning to his office, where "pale faces sit behind shapeless desks, and nothing breaks the gloomy silence, buried in which everybody labors, but the turning of the leaves of big account-books, the jingle of money on the desks, and an occasional unintelligible word or two."[14] Traugott's rejection of the prospect of a life organized around financial security reflects the intensity of his romantic passion. Spurning the aesthetic destitution of clerkdom, Traugott surrenders to the spell of the strange figures that begin to materi-

---

12 Ibid., 159–60.
13 Ibid., 160.
14 Ibid.

alize out of the mural, seeping into the crevices of his psychic life, and allows them to take charge of his artistic development which, unsurprisingly, leads him down a path of madness and dissolution.

In other instances, it seems as though the dreary world of the office is itself responsible for populating the sensitive soul's world with figures conjured up from the spirit-realm. In "The Doubles" (1822),[15] Deodatus encounters his own doppelganger. Despite the widespread belief that society has entered a "completely enlightened" age which has no room for "ruinous superstition,"[16] Deodatus is convinced that the appearance of his doppelganger, Haberland, represents "a marvelous occurrence that his father had prophesied in dark, mysterious words,"[17] with the result that upon meeting Haberland, Deodatus believes himself to be witnessing "a being who had so far been entangled in his life only as in a dream."[18] The typically Hoffmannian theme of the artist's diminishing grip on reality is established, along with the ensuing blurring of the lines that separate the real from the fantastic. As in *The Sandman* and "The Court of Arthur," the protagonist, Deodatus, is consumed by his fear of acting under the spell of dark forces. His doppelganger, Haberland, being a puppeteer, is also an incarnation of his fears. In Deodatus's estimation, Haberland seems to have exerted a kind of supernatural influence from a magical distance, as if circling in on Deodatus's psychic life until their fateful encounter in the forest, where Haberland attempts to slay his double.

The Golden Pot (1814)[19] presents us with yet another variation on the fate of the romantic artist who takes up arms against philistinism. From the beginning, Anselmus, the protagonist, struggles to assimilate to the codes of conduct regulating middle-class life. He stumbles, stutters, and has a hard time keep-

---

15 Hoffmann, *Tales of E.T.A. Hoffman*, 234–79.
16 Ibid., 235.
17 Ibid.
18 Ibid.
19 Ibid., 14–92.

ing himself from rambling incoherently. At the same time, he undergoes a sublime encounter with the romantic realm of spirits via his apprenticeship with the old master, Archivarius Lindhorst. Soon, Anselmus finds himself entangled in an otherworldly battle between the Archivarius, who turns out to be a mythical salamander-king exiled from "primeval times" out of "the fairyland of Atlantis," and his rival, the old witch Liese. Serpentina, one of the Archivarius's three magical salamander-daughters, convinces Anselmus that he is one of the rare youth living "during [the] coarse age" who is able to resonate with the call of the fairyland daughters. His encounter with Serpentina engenders in Anselmus "an anticipatory vision of distant wondrous lands to which he can courageously soar when he has cast away the onerous lot of commonplace life."[20] This story is not without its Klara-figure, who shows up in the guise of Veronica, Anselmus's bride-to-be. An unflinching anti-Bovary, in the style of Hoffmann's female philistines, Veronica hopes for nothing more than to be the wife of a Court Councilor (interestingly, one of Hoffmann's professions in real life).

Anselmus's increasingly frequent encounters with the spirit-realm drive Veronica further away from him until she opts for marrying Herr Heerbrand, the man who succeeds in securing the Court Councilor position originally meant for Anselmus. Faced by the dwindling prospects of a stable middle-class family life, Anselmus plunges deeper into the inverted world of Archivarius Lindhorst which, for all intents and purposes, has swallowed up the real world he used to inhabit. Unlike Nathanael from *The Sandman,* Anselmus willingly surrenders his life to the spirit-realm, "the inexpressible rapture of infinite longing" that had long plagued his romantic soul finally coming to rest in the glow of Serpentina's eyes.[21] From his residence in Atlantis, freshly reconquered by the Archivarius, Anselmus lives entirely in a state of poetic ecstasy, fatally delivered from "the agony of

---

20 Ibid., 66.
21 Ibid., 90.

infinite desire."[22] The novella ends with the Archivarius's proclamation: "Is the bliss of Anselmus [in Atlantis] anything else but life in poetry, poetry where the sacred harmony of all things is revealed as the most profound secret of Nature?"[23] This is an ambivalent statement, as what Anselmus had gained in poetic insight was purchased at the price of mad exile from everyday existence.

Sehnsucht

In a rare moment of self-disclosure, Hoffmann describes himself as "a poet or writer in whom the figures of everyday life are reflected in his inner romantic spirit-realm."[24] Beethoven, according to Hoffmann's vision, embodies the artist who manages to journey into "the romantic spirit-realm" and return, if not unscathed then at least bearing aesthetic riches of unprecedented value. Yet, while Beethoven's achievement may have been exceptional, the condition sparking his creative output was ubiquitous in the German cities of the early-nineteenth century. For Hoffmann, Beethoven only succeeds in exerting artistic control over a paradigmatically modern condition whose effects are felt, one way or another, by the philistine and the romantic dilettante alike. The effort which must be incessantly poured into shaping the work of art is itself spurred by the *Sehnsucht,* or infinite longing, which Hoffmann locates at the heart of romanticism.

In Hoffmann, this longing is often described as reaching out to a "spirit-realm" that remains ineluctably sublime, fundamentally transcending man's grasp. In this sense, the spirit-realm functions as Hoffmann's cipher for the central question that stamps the work of German philosophy from Kant onwards, namely, the question of the thing-in-itself. The connection between the unattainable spirit-realm and the philosophical *Ding*

---

[22] Ibid., 33.
[23] Ibid., 92.
[24] Hoffmann, *E.T.A. Hoffman's Musical Writings,* 78.

an Sich is evident in the musings of one of Hoffmann's characters on the place of music in modern life:

> But now music is expected to step right into everyday life, to come to grips with the world of phenomena [...]. Can one use sublime language to speak of ordinary things? Can music proclaim anything other than the wonders of that region from which it echoes across to us? Let the poet be prepared for daring flights to the distant realm of romanticism, for it is there that he will find the marvelous things that he should bring into our lives.[25]

The contrast is clear in Hoffmann's repeated invocations of a transcendent realm standing against the everyday world of phenomena. The thirst for the sublime, for this is what the transcendent spirit-realm embodies, may be unfulfillable. But it is a thirst that can only be disavowed at the expense of an impoverished existence, which for Hoffmann's romantics consisted in the domesticated, workaday life of the philistine city-dweller.

As Peter Bruning shows,[26] the philistine's dilettantism is not simply the efficient cause that occasions the artist to create in isolation. For Hoffmann, the romantic artist also struggles with the dilettante in himself. Johannes Kreisler, a crypto-autobiographical "character" who haunts the threshold between fact and fiction, is quoted as describing such longing as an "evil demon" which taunts him with an "indescribable restlessness which so often, since my earliest youth, has made me a stranger to myself [...] a wild, crazy longing for something which I seek outside myself in restless activity, although it is hidden within me, a dark mystery, a confused baffling dream of a paradise of the utmost contentment which even the dream cannot name, can only divine, and this idea plagues me with the torments of

---

25 Ibid., 196.
26 Bruning, "Hoffmann and the Philistine," 113.

Tantalus."[27] The torments of Tantalus, let it be remembered, are the wages of unsatisfied desire. Unsatisfied, if not unsatisfiable, desire marks the existential condition of Hoffmann's romantics and goes a long way to illuminate the darker aspects of their behavior.

David Farrell Krell insightfully points out that Schelling chose the word *Sehnsucht* to translate the Latin word *langueo*, which is the precise cognate of the English "languor."[28] Quoting Barthes, with the requisite apologies for the anachronism, Krell shines a light on the intended sense of "languor" at play in the romantic use of "die Sehnsucht": "The Satyr says: I want my desire to be satisfied *immediately*. If I see a sleeping face, parted lips, an open hand, I want to be able *to hurl myself upon them*. This Satyr — figure of the Immediate — is the very contrary of the Languorous. In languor, I merely wait: 'I knew no end to desiring you.'"[29]

Infinite desire determines the romantic *Sehnsucht*. Hoffmann had read Schelling's 1798 *On the World Soul*, coming under the spell of Schelling's ideas of infinite longing and art's superiority to the intellect as a means of communing with the absolute. Gotthilf Heinrich Schubert's groundbreaking 1808 *Ansichten von der Nachtseite der Naturwissenschaften* (*Insights from the Dark Side of Natural Science*), in which Schelling's philosophy of nature is taken up and applied to the observations of a natural scientist, becomes a constant reference during the rest of Hoffmann's career.[30] Schelling's influence shows itself in Schubert's elaborate cosmogony, adapted to the realm of natural phenomena, according to which man's gift of intellectual intuition, the immediate grasp of what is, has been compromised by modernity's lapse into dualistic thinking. Such a gift, however,

---

27 E.T.A. Hoffmann, *The Life and Opinions of the Tomcat Murr,* trans. Jeremy Adler (London: Penguin, 2006), 54–55.
28 David Farrell Krell, *The Tragic Absolute: German Idealism and the Languishing of God* (Bloomington: Indiana University Press, 2005), 86.
29 Roland Barthes, quoted in Krell, *The Tragic Absolute,* 86.
30 Harvey Hewett-Thayer, *Hoffmann: Author of the Tales* (New York: Octagon Books, 1971), 119ff. See also Bruning, "Hoffmann and the Philistine," 114.

may still be found in some artists. The artist's intellectual intuition allows him to restore the lost harmony between nature and spirit, if only aesthetically.

In Hoffmann's *The Golden Pot,* we saw an example of the pernicious path this could have in store for an aspiring romantic, as Anselmus ends up living psychotically in a poetic fairyland. "The Mines of Falun" (1819),[31] drawing directly from resources in Schubert's work, suggests another fate for the romantic. Elis, the protagonist, is jaded with the sea-voyaging he had conducted for years with the East India Company, which, being a trade cartel, stands for the concerns of commercial culture, the same that preoccupy the dreaded philistine. As primarily engaged in the transportation of opium, the East India Company also stands for the ersatz transcendence promised by commercial culture. Elis encounters the spectral figure of a miner who directs him to the untapped depths of the human psyche. The mine, deep in the earth, is contrasted with the East India Company's crisscrossing of the surface of the sea. The depth of artistic truth is pitted against the superficiality of the world of trade.[32] The miner, predictably, leads Elis down a path of ecstatic visions and into a brush with madness, under the swinging axe of a higher truth. The encounter with the miner all but vanquishes Elis's prospects of adjustment to good society. However, he is spared, in the most ambivalent sense of the word, by his engagement to Ulla, the respectable daughter of the man in charge of a local mining company. The reintegration of Elis into the fabric of good society calms Ulla's fears about her betrothed, namely, "her fears that the threatening powers of the subterranean abyss, of which she had often heard the miners speak," would overtake her fiancé.[33] Her sense of relief proves short-lived, as Elis insists on going back to the mines to extract a magical gem for his bride-to-be as a wedding gift. The mine crashes down on

---

31 Hoffmann, *Tales,* 149–72.
32 Cf. Holly Watkins, "From the Mine to the Shrine: The Critical Origins of Musical Depth," *19th-Century Music* 27, no. 3 (2004): 179–207.
33 Hoffmann, *Tales,* 170.

Elis and he never returns. Ulla finally gets to embrace her bridegroom, fifty years later, as his petrified corpse is dragged out from the depths. While *The Golden Pot*'s Anselmus takes refuge from marital bliss in the spirit-realm, Elis is only able to enter it as a dead man.

Part 2: A Brief History of the Sublime

The Power of Imagination
The origin of the tragic course of events suffered by Hoffmann's romantics is tied to the gambit thrown by an imagination that finds itself confined to an aesthetically impoverished existence. The new forms of life that sprouted across European cities during Hoffmann's lifetime, and against which Hoffmann's romantics react, represented the degeneration of the promise of the Enlightenment into the complacency and commonsense pragmatism of middle-class life. In describing the philosophical terrain within which Hoffmann wrote, biographer Hewett-Thayer remarks that it was dominated by a sort of "debased rationalism," where the lofty eighteenth century Enlightenment ideals "in the course of time seemed to degenerate into a drab utilitarianism, a mere recipe for getting on in the world."[34] An overweening confidence in so-called sound common sense eclipsed the rigorously critical commitments of the Age of Enlightenment, such that "the phrase 'a healthy human understanding' became widely current, coupled with the implication that it covered all man needed for success and happiness."[35]

The legitimation of such "debased rationalism" finds its enabling condition in the cultural and political conservative shift which swept through Prussia after the death of Frederick II in 1786.[36] This seismic shift in social relations gave rise to the bureaucrat, who in turn granted the philistine, in one stroke, pro-

---

34 Hewett-Thayer, *Hoffmann*, 113.
35 Ibid.
36 Analyzed at length in Steven Lestition, "Kant and the End of the Enlightenment in Prussia," *Journal of Modern History* 65, no. 1 (March 1993): 57–112.

fessional and social legitimacy. A bureaucratic machine rumbles at the base of Hoffmann's tales. The philistine is only possible in the same "functionally differentiated modernity" which spawns the need for the bureaucrat and in which semi-autonomous systems coexist in an increasingly fragmentary whole.[37] This also yields the problems of art as an increasingly autonomous practice, abstracted from its erstwhile immersion in the religious sphere, problems that troubled the romantics to no end. The romantic raises the banner of art to subdue the philistine's insistence on the subordination of imagination to sound understanding. In championing the romantic imagination, whether defeated or triumphant, deformed or genuine, Hoffmann is drawing on a particular aesthetic tradition, to which we must now turn.

The Sublime at Bay (Burke)
Edmund Burke was the first to isolate the feeling of "delightful horror" as a fundamental element in the experience of the sublime.[38] Exhuming the category from the writings of Longinus, for whom it designated the ecstatic frenzy that a rhetorician could rouse in an audience, for instance by the use of hyperbole, Burke drove home the connection between ecstatic effect and the sense of one's own finitude, limitation, and inevitable demise. Burke does not stray too far from the traditional association of sublimity with astonishment,[39] although he emphasizes another affective element involved in the experience of the sublime. In his 1757 *Philosophical Enquiry into the Origin of our Ideas of the Sublime and Beautiful,* Burke writes:

---

37 Ulrich Schonherr, "Social Differentiation and Romantic Art: E.T.A. Hoffmann's 'The Sanctus' and the Problem of Aesthetic Positioning in Modernity," *New German Critique* 66 (1995): 3.
38 The phrase "delightful horror" is used by Dennis before Burke to describe the effect of the sublime on the imagination; cf. Robert Doran, *The Theory of the Sublime from Longinus to Kant* (Cambridge: Cambridge University Press, 2017), 125.
39 Earl of Shaftesbury (Anthony Ashley Cooper), *Characteristics of Men, Manners, Opinions, Times,* ed. Lawrence Eliot Klein (Cambridge: Cambridge University Press, 2003), 109.

[I]f the pain and terror are so modified as not to be actually noxious; if the pain is not carried to violence, and the terror is not conversant about the present destruction of the person [...] they are capable of producing delight; not pleasure, but a sort of delightful horror, a sort of tranquility tinged with terror; which as it belongs to self-preservation is one of the strongest of all the passions.[40]

The object of this sort of horror, Burke declares, is the sublime.[41] Properly speaking, the sublime designates an aesthetic experience whose distinguishing mark is the terror aroused by the threat of violence. The sublime is that which is capable of occasioning, when at a safe distance, the feeling of horror and the perverse delight that accompanies it. The experience of the sublime is overwhelming because it confronts us with the persistent nearness of our own mortality in the face of overwhelming force or astounding magnitudes. Its capacity to shake us to the core derives from the fact that "the passions belonging to self-preservation," according to Burke, "are the strongest of all the passions."[42] For its part, pleasure is reserved, in line with tradition, for the experience of the beautiful which, Burke writes, "is a name I shall apply to all such qualities in things as induce in us a sense of affection and tenderness, or some other passion the most nearly resembling these."[43] On strength of this principal distinction between pain and pleasure, then, Burke distinguishes the ideas of the beautiful from that of the sublime, two ideas which have been "frequently confounded" and "indiscriminately applied to things greatly differing, and sometimes of natures directly opposite."[44] With this act, Burke opens up the sublime as a genuine field of aesthetic investigation.

---

40 Edmund Burke and James Thompson, *A Philosophical Enquiry into the Origin of Our Ideas of the Sublime and Beautiful* (Notre Dame: University of Notre Dame Press, 2005), 136.
41 Ibid.
42 Ibid., 51.
43 Ibid.
44 Ibid., 1.

Burke treated one's susceptibility to the sublime as something of a disease that must be kept at bay, prescribing exercise as a remedy for the overwhelming feelings it engenders. Surrender to feelings of this sort has long been seen as a sign of inferiority. The Earl of Shaftesbury writes that "astonishment is of all other passions the easiest raised in raw and unexperienced mankind," among whom he counts not only children but "barbaric" peoples such as the "Indians," whose "fine sights" count for him as little more than "enormous figures, various odd and glaring colors and whatever of that sort is amazingly beheld with a kind of horror and consternation."[45] Shaftesbury's low esteem of the sublime betrays the degree to which he is convinced of its dubious philosophical import. For Shaftesbury, a pioneer of aesthetics as an independent field of philosophical research, it is the contemplation of the beautiful that forms the pinnacle of aesthetic experience. Unlike the sublime, the beautiful exhibits "proportion," "unity," and "form," "united all in general in one system" that is capable of igniting the most revealing insights of speculative thought.[46] Burke's precarious flirtation with the sublime is likewise telling. Eager to explain its hold over the mind, he is equally quick to warn against its dangers and prescribe various means of warding it off.

In his reading of Burke's aesthetics, Tom Furniss highlights "the peculiar danger of the threat [of the sublime] in Burke's account," namely, "that it cannot be unambiguously located — that it transgresses the threshold between inner and outer, subject and object, and might therefore be, disturbingly, already at work within the human (or political) body. What most threatens 'the person' [in the experience of the sublime] is not an external danger but 'a dangerous and troublesome incumbrance' already internal to the system."[47]

---

45 Cooper, *Characteristics of Men, Manners, Opinions, Times*, 108–9.
46 Ibid., 274.
47 Tom Furniss, *Edmund Burke's Aesthetic Ideology: Language, Gender, and Political Economy in Revolution* (Cambridge: Cambridge University Press, 2008), 29.

Burke argues that because the sublime affords us an encounter with terror dissociated from the latter's threat, it can engender "a sort of swelling and triumph that is extremely grateful to the human mind," thereby reinforcing the bad habit of "the mind always claiming to itself some part of the dignity and importance of the things which it contemplates."[48] The anti-revolutionary connotations of Burke's view should not be lost on the reader. The self-delusion described here overlaps with John Locke's definition of "enthusiasm," which Burke would later embrace in his tirade against the fanaticism of the French Revolution in the famous 1790 *Reflections on the Revolution in France*, widely considered a fundamental tract of modern conservatism.

Locke writes, "[t]his I take to be properly enthusiasm, which, though founded neither on reason nor divine revelation, but rising from the conceits of a warmed or overweening brain, works yet, where it once gets footing, more powerfully on the persuasions and actions of men, than either of those two, or both together."[49] Furniss isolates the following passage from Longinus as Burke's point of reference: "the Mind is naturally elevated by the true Sublime, and so sensibly affected with its lively Strokes, that it swells in Transport and an inward Pride, as if what was only heard had been the Product of its own Invention." Furniss goes on to draw a connection between such pronouncements on the sublime and Burke's denunciation of the idea of radical autonomy as self-delusion, writing that "the threat [of the sublime object] becomes, or is analogous to, the rhetorical 'terror' instilled in us by 'poets and orators' and therefore enables a fantasy of the creative, originating self."[50] Already in Burke, then, we see the glimmers of a line connecting our delight in sublime horror with the marks of a repetition-compulsion. The latter is the prism through which Freud read *The Sandman*.

---

48 Burke, *Philosophical Enquiry*, 50.
49 John Locke, *An Essay Concerning Human Understanding*, ed. Alexander Campbell Fraser (Oxford: Clarendon Press, 1894), 696.
50 Furniss, *Edmund Burke's Aesthetic Ideology*, 23.

In his 1919 essay on "The Uncanny," which involves an extended analysis of *The Sandman,* Freud reads in Nathanael's infatuation with Olympia, the automaton mistaken for a woman, a sign of "the dominance in the unconscious mind of a 'compulsion to repeat' proceeding from the instinctual impulses and probably inherent in the very nature of the instincts — a compulsion powerful enough to overrule the pleasure principle, lending to certain aspects of the mind their daemonic character."[51] In Olympia, Nathanael is intrigued and terrified by his own unconscious libidinal life. Olympia personifies the repressions necessary for Nathanael's ego to come to its own: "Olympia is, as it were, a dissociated complex of Nathanael's which confronts him as a person, and Nathanael's enslavement to this complex is expressed in his senseless obsessive love for Olympia."[52] Such love, insofar as it is directed at a complex dissociated from one's own self-image, is "narcissistic." All advances motivated by this love are doomed. The automatic, repetitive aspect of the self must be kept at bay to ward off the specter of ego disintegration. Olympia operates as a cipher for the uncontrollable drives which exercise their dominion over the dark caverns of libidinal life, disrupting the noontide of the ego with their incessant encroachments.

Repetition-compulsion is the motor-force behind neurosis, a principal psychopathology of modern life, according to Freud. Throughout *The Sandman,* neurotic Nathanael struggles to fend off the sense that, at bottom, he is "the horrible plaything of dark powers." Yet Nathanael cannot help being drawn to Olympia, the embodiment of heteronomy, by an inexplicable longing which stands behind his restless dissatisfaction with the values of middle-class life, as propounded (with irreproachable good sense) by his fiancée Klara. Ironically, Olympia the automaton

---

51 Sigmund Freud, *The Standard Edition of the Complete Psychological Works of Sigmund Freud, Volume XVII (1917–1919): An Infantile Neurosis and Other Works,* ed. and trans. James Strachey, in collaboration with Anna Freud, and assisted by Alix Strachey, and Alan Tyson (London: The Hogarth Press, 1955), 238.

52 Ibid., 232.

is literally a puppet whose strings are pulled by another. She is Nathanael's nightmarish self-reflection. Nathanael's longing, as is often the case with Hoffmann's romantics, looks toward another reality. The desire for broaching an ecstatic reality, whose glimpses can only be caught through the turbid medium of the imagination (after healthy understanding's conquest of everyday life), could only be achieved at the price of the destruction of the workday self.

Freud writes that "an uncanny effect is [...] produced when the distinction between imagination and reality is effaced, as when something that we have hitherto regarded as imaginary appears before us in reality, or when a symbol takes over the full functions of the thing it symbolizes."[53] Both tropes are Hoffmannian staples, as we have seen. The desire to lose oneself in ecstasy signals a latent death wish, a longing to be enfolded into the libidinal ocean. The theory that Freud proposes in his analysis of *The Sandman* suggests that the feeling of the uncanny is engendered by the unsettling revelation that the self is inherently bound to a repetition-compulsion, such that the daylight of psychic life is contaminated by apparitions familiar yet utterly foreign, embodying Freud's disassociative complexes. Perceptively, Freud links the inaccessible sublime pursued by the romantic with images deriving from a bygone era, possibilities which "we — or our primitive forefathers — once believed [...] were realities, and were convinced that they actually happened."[54] Freud adds that "nowadays we," that is, we Enlightened moderns, "no longer believe in them, we have *surmounted* these modes of thought; but we do not feel quite sure of our new beliefs, and the old ones still exist within us ready to cease upon any confirmation."[55] Contending with such episodes tests the self-certainty of Enlightened understanding. Hoffmann's romantic characters, who dwell on and perversely relish these experiences, are for that reason incurable social misfits. What

---

53 Ibid., 244.
54 Ibid., 247.
55 Ibid.

gets repeated as uncanny is originally, prior to the consolidation of the ego, "something familiar that has been repressed."[56] It belongs, as repressed, to the drives. A drive is emphatically an affair of the body. Even by Freud's admission, a drive represents "an urge inherent in organic life to restore an earlier state of things."[57] Behind the phantasmagoria plaguing Nathanael's existence, the mechanism of the internal compulsion itself is the true sublime object of Nathanael's horror, a vehicle of transcendence and annihilation, desired and feared at once.

It goes without saying that Burke did not resort to a psychoanalytic explanation when accounting for the mind's attraction to the sublime. But he does not even allow himself an empirical explanation either, having repudiated the principle of association in aesthetics.[58] Scandalously, Burke accounted for the feeling of the sublime through a strictly physiological explanation, resorting to a theory of direct physiological causation that jolts the mind with feelings of the beautiful or the sublime, depending on the encounter. This explanation has done more to heap ridicule on its author than to resolve any questions regarding the fixation exerted on us by things perceived as sublime.[59]

The Sublime as Idea (Kant)

The question of the causes underlying the mind's sublime delight in horror was left without a satisfying answer after Burke. Kant contradicted Burke precisely on the point of physiological immediacy. What lies behind sublime terror is, rather, a confused rational idea. The experience of the sublime may begin with the feeling of awe, but it ends with the tranquility of grasping the feared object as nothing but the presentation of an idea of reason.

---

56 Ibid.
57 Sigmund Freud, *The Freud Reader,* ed. Peter Gay (New York: Vintage: 1995), 612.
58 Burke, *Philosophical Enquiry,* 130–31.
59 Timothy Costelloe, *The British Aesthetic Tradition: From Shaftesbury to Wittgenstein* (Cambridge: Cambridge University Press, 2013), 74–76.

One reason why aesthetic judgments were important to Kant lies in their unique ability to assist in determining the legitimacy of attributing moral meaning to the world. We know from the first *Critique* that we are not justified in making theoretical — i.e., "scientific" — claims as to the three major questions that sound the depths of rational inquiry: What can I know, what ought I to do, and what may I hope? The limits of the first question are determined by metaphysics broadly construed: its transcendental critique (as in the *Critique of Pure Reason*) together with its positive claims in a metaphysics of nature (as in the *Metaphysical Foundations of Natural Science*). The second and third questions are answered in a similar two-step by morality and religion. Curiously, questions pertaining to aesthetic judgment do not seem to seamlessly fit within the foregoing division. Aesthetic questions range over the various concerns of philosophy. This is because aesthetic judgments proper, that is, those that are philosophically significant, relate to all the foregoing concerns: the limits of theoretical, moral, and religious knowledge.

The crucible of theoretical, moral, and religious questions is revealed in the very way Kant sets up his aesthetic investigation in the *Critique of the Power of Judgment*. Proper aesthetic judgments are reflective. Unlike "ordinary" attributive judgments, they determine a subjective feeling rather than an objective representation. When Kant is discussing the beautiful, his primary concern is not the determination of some object as beautiful. Such a task would require a sort of empirical tallying of attributes that, when present, would allow us to apply the label "beautiful" to a certain artwork. Such a tallying may not be impossible, but Kant dismisses it as a key to grasping the nature of beauty on account of the contingency of the results it would supply, as well as the fact that it is a deeply socially conditioned practice. *A posteriori* through and through, the procedure neither stems from nor produces necessary cognition. What sets an aesthetic judgment apart from a theoretical one is a difference in kind which requires that in the former we seek to determine a subjective state, while in the latter we are determining an objective representation.

The primary concern of aesthetics for Kant is the extent to which we are justified in associating a purportedly beautiful experience with the feeling of pleasure that is aroused in us at beholding a certain object. We are justified in seeing an aesthetic experience as an experience of beauty when the harmony exhibited between the various elements in a composition triggers a homologous interplay between the cognitive faculties of imagination and understanding. The pleasure evoked by the experience of beauty gives us a glimmer of how things would stand were we living in a world where our purposes as free moral agents were fulfilled. The ensuing harmony of the faculties in such a world would serve as an index of the extent to which rational human desires have been satisfied. The experience of the beautiful thus conceived provides us with a symbol of what it would be like to exist in a morally perfected condition, though no kind of theoretical knowledge may justifiably prescribe what such a condition might look like. Only once we discern that this is the kind of pleasure that we have upon encountering an artwork are we justified in calling the object corresponding to it "beautiful."

Contrast this with the sublime. The feeling of the sublime presents the world as violent, chaotic, and incomprehensible. To this extent, Kant's conception coincides with Burke's. But for Kant, emphatically, no object may be called sublime, whereas we may point to a variety of objects in the world that we deem beautiful. The feeling of the sublime indexes not a property of objects but a confusion of the mind: "We can say no more than that the object is fit for the presentation of a sublimity that can be found in the mind; for what is actually sublime cannot be contained in any sensible form, but concerns only ideas of reason."[60] Those things that we, mistakenly, call sublime, which overwhelm us so and arouse the painful feelings of which Burke had spoken, are

---

60 Immanuel Kant, *Critique of the Power of Judgment,* trans. Paul Guyer (Cambridge: Cambridge University Press, 2000), 245.

inherently formless representations — the limitlessness of the universe, the vastness of the ocean, the dark plunge at the end of a precipice. We describe them as sublime because they defy the figurative capacity of the imagination. Conceptually, Kant notes that these objects represent mathematical (quantitative) or dynamical (having to do with force) exaggerations beyond the limits of human comprehension. They therefore arouse our fear because they present the world as something entirely foreign to our understanding. Such a portrayal undermines the hope of moral perfectibility, intensifying the perceiver's dread. The world now reveals itself as hostile to human purpose, paralyzing ("astonishing," to recall Burke and Shaftesbury's terms) intelligence and repudiating the meaningfulness we assign to human action. But Kant points out that, being the representation of something of infinite proportions or unlimited power, the sublime coincides in its attributes with the ideas of reason (i.e., God, world, and soul) which likewise frustrate theoretical comprehension by constantly leading the mind into aporias. Thus, the true sublime "objects," which truly surpass our comprehension (mathematical) or threaten to obliterate our physical existence (dynamical), are those ideas of reason themselves. On the other hand, the objects we tend to call sublime ("the wide ocean, enraged by storms," is Kant's example) are "provoked and called to mind precisely by this inadequacy,"[61] namely the inadequacy of any sensible form to present an idea of reason. The feeling of the sublime does not point to these objects. Rather, through them, or precisely through their inadequacy to present the sublime, "the mind is incited to abandon sensibility and to occupy itself with ideas that contain a higher purposiveness."[62] Since the first two *Critiques* have shown that the proper grasp of these ideas of ultimate purpose (God, world, and soul) is a moral rather than theoretical task, what occupies the mind in the experience of the sublime, like the beautiful, boils down to a question of moral purposiveness. While beauty puts us in a

---

61 Ibid.
62 Ibid.

mind of how things would stand if moral purpose was fulfillable in the world, the sublime puts us in a mind of how things would look if human purpose existed in a world where it could never be fulfilled, a world altogether impervious to rational ends.

Kant transforms the terrain of aesthetic theory by anchoring questions of the beautiful and the sublime to problems of teleology. The philosophical significance of the sublime for Kant hinges on the capacity of reason to intervene in the experience of sublime horror by showing that what seems to be immeasurable or overwhelming to the imagination is in fact well within the grasp of reason, which knows how to relegate these questions to their proper domain as problems concerning the metaphysics of morals. Reason thus pacifies the shuddering imagination by restoring to the world its sense of meaning and conduciveness to human purpose, if only obliquely.

The Sublime as Demonic (Schiller)
In Kant we behold a "rediscovery of the imagination," to borrow once again from Castoriadis.[63] Kant was able to tie aesthetics to teleology by highlighting how aesthetic reactions are grounded on the interplay between the imagination and the "higher" cognitive faculties — understanding for the beautiful and reason for the sublime. With Kant, the imagination emerges as not merely a faculty that reproduces perceptions without their sensible matter but as a cognitively productive faculty on its own merit, constitutive rather than receptive. Romanticism, broadly construed, understood this. As the capacity to fundamentally give form to representation, the imagination is the actively figurative faculty, a sense preserved in the German *Einbildungskraft*. Eckart Förster writes that the imagination is "an activity without which there could be no combination and consequently no unity of consciousness," since "it takes two elements which are isolated in themselves and *forms* (*Bilden*) something common

---

63 Cornelius Castoriadis, *World in Fragments: Writings on Politics, Society, Psychoanalysis, and the Imagination,* ed. and trans. David Ames (Stanford: Stanford University Press, 1997), 213–45.

which as such can become an object of consciousness."[64] Opting for the verb "to form" instead of "to picture" or "to imagine" as a translation of *bild-* in *Einbildungskraft*, we arrive at the imagination as an en-forming-power (*Ein-bildungs-kraft*), which is the sense tapped into by the romanticism of Schiller.

Schiller's 1795 *On the Aesthetic Education of Man, in a Series of Letters*[65] opens with a survey of the damage inflicted upon man by life in the modern state with its "too intense life of the social instincts," as De Quincey put it.[66] The *Letters* also rehearse the clash between Enlightenment's promise and its reality at the turn of the nineteenth century. Because of their distinct attention to the ways in which the cultivation of aesthetic sensitivity may be brought to bear on the contradictions of modern life, Schiller's observations intersect with Hoffmann's concerns and open a window onto the social dynamics that informed Hoffmann's writings.

Despite the promises of the Enlightenment and the Revolution they inspired, Schiller found European culture torn between a revival of sheer superstition and a crude instrumentalism masquerading as the pinnacle of rationality. The Terror finishes this off for Schiller, the literary aristocrat, with the introduction of barbarism on an unimaginable scale. Surely there was something that the shockwaves of rational Enlightenment and political Revolution had not managed to transform. Premising his observations on the relationship that Kant had established between aesthetics and morality (teleology), Schiller offers the diagnosis that the moral capacities of the very actors who carried forth the work of social change fell tragically short of aspirations. The proper cultivation of man's moral sense begins not with the propagation of moral doctrine but with cultivating

---

64 Eckart Förster, *The Twenty-five Years of Philosophy: A Systematic Reconstruction* (Cambridge: Harvard University Press, 2012), 194.

65 Friedrich Schiller, *On the Aesthetic Education of Man: in a Series of Letters*, trans. Elizabeth Wilkinson and L.A. Willoughby (Oxford: Oxford University Press, 2005).

66 Thomas De Quincey, *De Quincey's Suspiria: I. The Daughter of Lebanon. II. Levana and Our Ladies of Sorrow* (London: De la More Press, 1906).

man's sensitivity to moral ideas. Schiller, in a Kantian frame of mind, understood that the elevation of human sensibility must go through the reform of aesthetic judgment. The problems of the time could begin to find a cure with the cultivation, on a mass scale, of a sense for aesthetic beauty. The experience of beauty for Schiller is inexorably tied to a free-ranging kind of pleasure. This unique brand of aesthetic pleasure Schiller calls "play," a state in which the distinction between work and enjoyment disappears, such that man acts unforced for the sake of his own enjoyment, and his enjoyment is synonymous with his activity as a moral actor in the world. For Schiller, this is precisely the sort of liberty which the French Revolution had promised, or, at any rate, the kind he persistently demanded from it. Leaving aside immediate social and political causes, such a vision was destined not to materialize, because man's desire was not prepared to absorb the full spectrum of its precepts and accept their consequences. Beautiful art can have the morally transformative power of "educating" our desires by orienting them toward the satisfaction of the ideal of freedom as their ultimate end.

Schiller accused the new life of the city dweller of being morally corrupting insofar as it lulls the intellect into a false sense of security. An overconfidence in the rational planning of society also led to the degeneration of the promises of the Enlightenment into banal pragmatism and a superficial faith in the ultimately benevolent end of history. Hoffmann's reasonable characters (Klara et al.) personify this commonsense pragmatism. Cocksure pragmatism and the relapse into superstition, together with the fanaticism that engendered the worst excesses of the Jacobins, can only be checked aesthetically according to Schiller. While cultivating the sensitivity to beauty presents moral ideals to the mind in the form of feeling, the sharpening of the mind's awareness of the sublime is prone to curb moral excess, whether in the form of the pragmatist's complacent faith in rational planning, the superstitious relapse into dogma as the solution to moral problems, or the revolutionary fervor that seeks to put society, once and for all, and by any means necessary, on the right track. Aiming for the absolute cannot come at the expense of disavowing man's inherent limitations. While aiming with every right toward the rational resolution of strife in human history, writes Schiller in "Concerning the Sublime" (1801), one must never at the same time lose sight of "the terrifying and magnificent spectacle of change destroying everything and re-creating it and then destroying it once again, a spectacle of ruin at times eating slowly at things, other times suddenly assaulting them. History," he goes on, "provides ample examples of the pathetic picture of humanity *wrestling* with fate, a picture of the incessant flight of fortune, of confidence betrayed, injustice triumphant, and innocence violated."[67]

As mentioned already, Schiller argues that while the moral purpose of human existence cannot be conceptually articulated (say, in terms of a list of attributes that would specify its character), the mind can develop a sensitivity to the moral task ahead through aesthetic education, that is, by cultivating the mind's sensitivity to beauty. However, in order not to be lost to the world in its own beautiful feelings, this aesthetic sensitivity to beauty must itself be checked. This is achieved by developing the mind's sensitivity to the sublime, beauty's terrible counterpart. In Schiller's wake, the sublime, which Kant located above all in the grandeur of impersonal nature, takes on chillingly historical concreteness. We feel as if the roles were reversed and the sublime images of nature are oblique references to the horrors of history. The sublime expresses "necessity's stern law," symbolized by "the eternal infidelity of everything sensuous" to reason's self-certainty.[68] Schiller remarks that "the capacity for the sublime is one of the most glorious dispositions in human nature, deserving our *respect* due to its origin in the self-sufficient capacity to think and will" — that is, insofar as the sublime forces the capacity to think and will (theoretical and moral reasoning) to reckon with its necessary limitations in practice. Cultivating a

---

[67] Friedrich Schiller, *Essays,* eds., Walter Hinderer and Daniel O. Dahlstrom (New York: Continuum, 1993), 83.
[68] Ibid.

sense of the sublime is thus the necessary counterpart to the cultivation of the sense of the beautiful. "The beautiful renders itself deserving on account of the *humanness* in a human being, the sublime on account of the *purely demonic* in him."[69] The beautiful corresponds to one's "humanness" because its dominion extends over the interplay of the faculties of the human mind. The harmonious interplay it evokes between intellect and sensibility is a symbol of moral freedom. The sublime on the other hand hurls the lot of human faculties into the unknown. Thus, while beauty affords us a pleasurable free play of the cognitive faculties, the sublime only offers us "ecstatic shuddering."[70]

Hoffmann describes the fairyland in which Anselmus is lost in *The Golden Pot* as a region "full of glorious marvels, where both the highest rapture and deepest horror may be evoked."[71] Anselmus, for his part, is overwhelmed by "a feeling he had never before known, one he could not identify as either rapturous or painful."[72] In the novella, Hoffmann describes Anselmus's experience of the sublime in terms that align with the exposition given above: "He felt that an ineffable something was awakening within his inmost soul and provoking that pain of rapture which is the longing that promises man the existence of a more exalted Being."[73] The sublime is expressive of "the *purely demonic*" in us, for Schiller, because it mediates between the profane and the divine, the earthly and the exalted, the mundane and the absolute.

Recall how Kant had argued that the feared object is not what we think is present before us in the experience of the sublime, but rather the speculative idea which the representation calls to mind. With Schiller, the sublime is neither the appearance nor the idea at work behind the appearance, but the fact of human limitation itself. Schiller's characterization of the sublime encounter as demonic allows us to elicit a link between the metaphysics of aesthetic experience and psychoanalysis. The

---

69 Ibid.
70 Ibid., 74.
71 Hoffmann, *Tales of E.T.A. Hoffman*, 32.
72 Ibid., 22.
73 Ibid., 33.

demonic is what haunts the borderline between man and God. Besides representing "the intervening stage between the human and the divine," writes Harold Bloom, "daemonization" acts as a trope of "the principal Freudian defense, repression, the very active defense that produces or accumulates much of what Freud calls the Unconscious."[74] The sublime, repression, and the unconscious are tangled up in one and the same psychodynamic. For Schiller, the demonic which is encountered in the experience of the sublime is emphatically, if paradoxically, a human reality. On this reading, the demonic is not something to be excised or disowned; rather the demonic is the touchstone of which the soul must never lose sight, on pain of losing itself in the comforting reassurances of the beautiful. The demonic marks the human limit this-side of the absolute. Just what exists beyond the sublime threshold, if anything, is a question that cannot be answered in any clear-cut discourse, though an aesthetic symbol may be provided. Far from representing a contamination that must be exorcised, the demonic is an aspect that must be allowed to cohabitate the self. Hoffmann turns our attention to the varying fortunes of those whose destiny it is to embrace the demonic sublime or the "spirit-realm."

Part 3: Hoffmann's Aesthetics

Symptom and Sublime

The Kantian positing of the imagination as a creative and not merely reproductive faculty ushers in a line of thinking that seeks in aesthetics a source of insight into metaphysical truths. Despite Freud's identification of a repetition-compulsion as the force that hurls Nathanael to his fate in *The Sandman*, the reason for Nathanael's condition must be sought in an origin that exceeds the oedipal. Repetition-compulsion undermines linear time through the recurrence of symptoms, reenacting traumas that manage to circle back and dominate the present despite the passage of time. Hoffmann's tales are rife with such instances.

---

74 Bloom, *Poetry and Repression*, 18.

Anselmus has an "entire vision which he had once viewed as if in a heavenly trance" reemerge before his eyes "in the most vivid colors, as if he were looking upon it for the second time."[75] Freud himself points to a host of instances depicting the return of the repressed in his analysis of *The Sandman*. Ursula Lawson notes that while "Nathanael recalls his experiences in chronological order, indicating a normal process of reflection," his manner of relating these experiences to each other departs from the linear sequence of time, resembling rather "the product of a creative, if somewhat morbid, imagination of a highly sensitive child."[76] A symptom bears a symbolic relation to what it signifies. Beneath the symptom there lies the symbol, where the psychodynamic and the speculative overlap. The salient features of Hoffmann's tales speak to the psychological trauma being rooted in a more profound metaphysical malaise, a dissatisfaction with the import of our pronouncements on the ultimate nature of reality. The passage of time, historical time, precipitates this condition.

The earliest glimmers of romanticism, as presented by Friedrich Schlegel, are premised on such a profound consciousness of a transition into a new world-historical era.[77] A historical sequence of events pries open a new time, reshaping the coordinates of subjectivity in the process. The turning point here is the French Revolution. Despite his ambivalence toward the Revolution, Hoffmann intensely lived its philosophical consequences. Having reviewed the dynamics of his tales and situated his work within the aesthetic tradition, we can turn now to Hoffmann's own reflections on aesthetics. These are found chiefly in his musical writings, collected under the title of *Kreisleriana* (1819), in reference to his crypto-autobiographical character, the composer Johannes Kreisler. If Hoffmann had acknowledged the appearance on the historical scene of a new time, which places

---

75 Hoffmann, *Tales of E.T.A. Hoffman*, 33.
76 Ursula Lawson, "Pathological Time in E.T.A. Hoffmann's *Der Sandmann*," *Monatshefte* 60, no. 1 (Spring 1968): 54.
77 Daniel O. Dahlstrom, "Play and Irony: Schiller and Schlegel on the Liberating Prospects of Aesthetics," in *The History of Continental Philosophy*, ed. Alan Schrift (University of Chicago Press, 2011), 1:107–29.

its unique set of demands on the artist, "the romantic" is Hoffmann's hieroglyph of choice for the subject of this new time.

"No idea can arise in us without its hieroglyph," writes the anonymous author of "Johannes Kreisler's Certificate of Apprenticeship."[78] "Idea" here, as in Kant and Schiller, signifies those cognitions which cannot be successfully expressed in discursive propositions. The hieroglyph, while unable to yield a clear and distinct enumeration of properties, provides us with the next best thing, "a vague approximation of what we have distantly heard."[79] Writing alongside Schlegel, who fabricates the romantic as a realm where the novel problems of art may be explored in terms unknown to classical criticism, Hoffmann depicts the plight of the romantic in terms of the acute awareness of a subjectivity grappling with an unprecedented, thus essentially alienating, historical condition.

At the beginning of his literary career, the essence of the romantic was contained for Hoffmann in "absolute" or purely instrumental music.[80] All art tends toward absolute music for the early Hoffmann. Music opens up the gates of the sublime, the higher reality, the spiritual kingdom which is not of this world. What places the crown and scepter in the hands of absolute music is its impermeability to mundane representation. Later in his career, when Hoffmann makes place for other artforms to share the pedestal, we find them still determined by the condition of music. The anonymous author of "Johannes Kreisler's Certificate of Apprenticeship" addresses Kreisler: "What appears to be chiefly necessary has already become part of you. You have sharpened your faculty of hearing to such an extent that now and then you perceive the voice of the poet hidden within you [...] and really cannot believe that it is only you speaking and no one else."[81] Absolute music, like poetry, depends on an art of hearing. The other arts, while no longer subordinated to music,

---

78 Hoffmann, *E.T.A. Hoffman's Musical Writings*, 164.
79 Ibid., 165.
80 Cf. Mark Evan Bonds, *Music as Thought: Listening to the Symphony in the Age of Beethoven* (Princeton: Princeton University Press, 2006).
81 Hoffmann, *E.T.A. Hoffman's Musical Writings*, 160.

nonetheless strive to the condition of absolute music. Neither plastic nor verbal, absolute music surpasses sculpture, painting, and prose by its ability to express itself directly in the medium of sound, described as the medium of an ecstatic experience with its threat of self-dissolution ("you perceive the voice of the poet hidden within you [...] and really cannot believe it is only you speaking and no one else"). In the same text, music is described as channeling "sublime," "gentle spirit-voices."[82] The mature Hoffmann abandons his fanaticism for pure music and begins describing aesthetic experience as hinging on a synesthetic expression of "total effect."[83]

Anachronistically, we may add that by language what Hoffmann had in mind was not simply a system of written and verbal signs but an expansive semiotic edifice, a total signifying system combining sound and sight, tone, figure, and word. The effects of such a synesthetic "language" are described by Hoffmann-Kreisler in "Extremely Random Thoughts" as arising in "a state of delirium" where "the congruity of colors, sounds, and fragrances" is revealed.[84] To Schiller's beautiful artwork, which triggers a harmonious interplay between the mind and the senses, symbolic of the attainment of the moral ideal, Hoffmann seeks to counterpose an ideal of sublimity in art. According to Hoffmann's sublime ideal, genuine romantic art presents us with "the mysterious language of a distant spirit-realm, its wonderful accents resounding in our souls and awakening a higher, intenser awareness" through which "the emotions vie with each other in dazzling array, and then sink back in an inexpressible longing that fills our breast."[85]

In the foregoing passage, a crucial difference transpires between Hoffmann's and Schiller's aesthetics of the sublime. Faithfully Kantian, Schiller's analysis demands a clean distinction between the sublime and the beautiful. The definitive Hoff-

---

82 Ibid., 162, 163.
83 Ibid., 105.
84 Ibid.
85 Ibid., 196.

mannian stance submits that we cannot presume such a distinction to exist. Each instance of beauty turns, of its own accord, into an instance of the sublime.

The wording of the quoted passage is instructive. At first, "all the emotions vie with each other in dazzling array," recalling Schiller's free play of the faculties in the experience of beauty; and then "they sink back in an inexpressible longing that fills our breast." The experience of the beautiful cannot, for Hoffmann, be isolated from the experience of the sublime. What bars beauty from sustaining the free play of the faculties is that, for Hoffmann, beauty can no longer be anchored in any sort of moral certainty. This is why, without denying the moral-teleological possibilities of art, Hoffmann stakes much more on art's capacity to express man's longing for such all-binding absolutes, the *Sehnsucht* for the infinite. Hoffmann's is a world where Kantian aesthetics finds itself unmoored in the absence of a morally binding, universally valid categorical imperative. Sublimity, then, cannot be construed as the other pole of aesthetic experience, at odds with beauty, as the tradition from Burke to Schiller presented it. Rather Hoffmann's sublime is a moment of the beautiful, destined to arrive with irreversible necessity. The romantics of his tales are at first lured by the experience of beauty that ends up spelling their demise. Hoffmann thus throws a different gambit to the romantic artist. While Schiller exhorts artists to fill the world with beautiful creations, Hoffmann foresees the inherently tragic nature of such a mission. If aesthetic education seeks to infuse the ordinary with the sublime, or to diffuse the sublime into the ordinary, the danger, or price, of such a task will be madness, the dissolution of the self. Hoffmann does not disagree with Schiller, or Kant for that matter, insofar as a teleological abyss opens up in Europe after the collapse of the *ancien régime* and the authority of the Church. However, "the magical power of poetic truth" can have a transformative effect,

> for only he [the genuine, romantic artist] can bring before our eyes the wonderful apparitions of the spirit-realm; carried on his wings we soar across the abyss that separates us

from it, and soon at home in that strange land we accept the miracles that are seen to take place as natural consequences of the influence of higher natures on our lives. Then we experience all the powerfully stirring sensations that fill us now with horror and fear, now with utter bliss.[86]

The pursuit of the beautiful is a risky affair. The artist, in his pursuit of beauty, is hounded by the demonic sublime, which threatens ego-death. In the "romantic dimension," on the other hand, "language is raised to a higher power, or rather (since it is part of that distant realm of music) takes the form of song."[87] The key to this transformation of language into a system of synesthetic signification, however, is now tied to an "inner poetic relationship or poetic truth that might kindle music into life."[88] Whether it is poetry that kindles music into life or music which imbues poetry with its inimitable vigor, Hoffmann's stance is unmistakable: whatever the artistic means, the task of genuine (read: romantic) art is to risk the horrors of the spirit-realm and channel the hieroglyphs of the latter into art.

Beethoven
Among the host of feckless romantics that populates Hoffmann's writings, it is two musicians who manage to tower above the distinct misery that only an artistic vocation can deliver. Hoffmann depicts them both as trans-human, demonic figures. We have already encountered some of the fictional Johannes Kreisler's pronouncements on art. As for Beethoven, his success is not merely due to the fact that he boldly trespasses into the transcendent. All of Hoffmann's romantics court the abyss. Rather, Beethoven is emblematic because, like Orpheus, he enters the realm of shadows and manages to come back demonically transfigured, if not altogether triumphant. At the hands of Beethoven, music turns into "the most romantic of all the arts, one might almost

---

86 Ibid., 196.
87 Ibid., 197.
88 Ibid., 200.

say the only really romantic art, for its sole object is the expression of the infinite."[89] Beethoven's role in this transformation of music consists in laying down the bridge between the mundane world and the romantic spirit-world, in the same way that "the lyre of Orpheus opens the doors of Orkus," the underworld.

More than any other work, it is the Fifth Symphony that solidifies Beethoven's quasi-mythical status according to Hoffmann. In his influential 1810 review of Beethoven's Fifth Symphony, republished in 1814 as "Beethoven's Instrumental Music," Hoffmann locates Beethoven's genius in his capacity to compose a genuinely self-originating piece of instrumental music. The review presents the Fifth Symphony as an epoch-defining work of art on account of its portrayal of the drama of self-formation so fundamental to the romantic imaginary. Beethoven's feat, in other words, consists in constructing an elaborate symphonic edifice by working through the inner relationships that tie together the three notes which announce the beginning of the first movement, the so-called, mistakenly, "fate knocking at the door," rather than adhering to the formal prescriptions of symphonic composition in the tradition of Joseph Haydn and Wolfgang Amadeus Mozart. Hoffmann portrays the development of the Fifth Symphony as organically urged on by the natural momentum of its humble beginnings.[90] Invoking the arch-romantic opposition between the mechanical and the organic, Hoffmann writes of how Beethoven "scatters the good old rules in disorder whenever it happens to please him in the momentary excitement of his creative imagination," all the while retaining an "inner, underlying organic structure" that can never be appreciated by "aesthetic mechanicians."

The unity of the symphony, Hoffmann notes, owes less to any formal strictness than to "the inner relationship of the themes with one another which produces that unity which alone is able

---

89 E.T.A. Hoffmann, "Beethoven's Instrumental Music: Translated from E.T.A. Hoffmann's 'Kreisleriana,'" trans. Arthur Ware Locke, *Musical Quarterly* 3, no. 1 (January 1917): 123–33.
90 Cf. Abigail Chantler, *E.T.A. Hoffmann's Musical Aesthetics* (London: Routledge, 2006), 51f.

to hold the listener in one mood." Such unity is revealed, for example, in the "more subtle relationship [that] shows itself merely in the spiritual connection of one theme with another." In Beethoven's music we are exposed to "mysterious premonitions," "magic combinations" from which "a world of visions," even a "circle of mystical visions," may be constructed. These visions and premonitions are subjective, to be sure, but their binding power stems from the fact that, like the phantasmagoria scattered across Hoffmann's tales, they are no less active and indeed at work in the very depths of one's lived reality. These are depths that are destined to remain out of reach were it not for the aesthetic experience, which plumbs them through the "sublime and noble language" of music's hieroglyph. More than anything else, however, it was the holism of Beethoven's music that impressed Hoffmann. The holistic nature of the Fifth was embodied in its self-referential character, its development of its themes out of the four humble notes with which it begins. Indeed, Hoffmann underscores the defining holism of Beethoven's symphony by resorting to the same seed analogy that came to be a staple of romantic self-understanding. The part-whole relationship defining the Fifth Symphony can only be captured by "the deeper glance" which is able to discern in it not a sequence of felicitously arranged accidents but "the beautiful tree with leaves, blossoms, and fruit growing from one germinating seed."[91] Despite its seemingly disorderly veneer, on account of its breaking with tradition, "this very organization of the whole work as well as the constant reappearances of the motives and harmonic effects, following closely on one another, intensify to the highest degree that feeling of inexpressible longing." What holds the work together, rather than a readily discernible formal coherence in line with tradition, is the work's own inner "connecting links," "the constant allusions to the main theme," "the contrapuntal interweavings that bind the work together."[92] The product is a piece of music that gives the illusion of pulling itself

---

91 Hoffmann, "Beethoven's Instrumental Music," 129.
92 Ibid., 130.

up by its own bootstraps, fulfilling the romantic ideal of self-origination.

Feuerkreis
Curiously, in the midst of his Beethoven review, Hoffmann introduces his own fictional-autobiographical character, the Kapellmeister Kreisler, "before whose piano I am now sitting and writing" (!), as the person who "brought it home to me most clearly that we should honor only that which is inspired and that everything else comes from evil."[93] The aesthetic commitments I attempted to trace in Hoffmann's tales and musical writings converge in the figure of Johannes Kreisler. Understanding Kreisler's significance in Hoffmann's work will thus round off my account of the latter's aesthetics.

Hoffmann collected the musical writings of the apocryphal Kreisler in a cycle of essays entitled *Kreisleriana* (1819).[94] The *Kreisleriana* begins with a declaration of the anonymous origins of Johannes Kreisler. The first line reads: "Where is he from? Nobody knows. Who were his parents? It is not known. Whose pupil is he?" and so on. The collection ends, remarkably, with an essay entitled "Johannes Kreisler's Certificate of Apprenticeship," seemingly written anonymously, in the third person, yet signed, unnervingly, with Kreisler's own name. It is as if the "Certificate of Apprenticeship" was awarded by origin-less Kreisler to himself. Taken as a whole, the essay cycle *Kreisleriana* thus bears witness to Kreisler's embodiment of the romantic ideal of self-origination.

The trials and tribulations of Johannes Kreisler, as set forth by Hoffmann, must be read as a hieroglyph of the destiny of the genuine romantic artist as Hoffmann envisioned it. While the *Kreisleriana* introduces us to Kreisler's music criticism, Hoffmann's final novel, whose full title is *The Life and Opinions of the Tomcat Murr, Together with a Fragmentary Biography of Kapellmeister Johannes Kreisler on Random Sheets of Waste Pa-*

---

93 Ibid.
94 Hoffmann, *E.T.A. Hoffmann's Musical Writings*, 23–165.

per (1822), offers us a closer look at the condition of the mad composer. In *Tomcat Murr*, Kreisler gives a different account of his family origins, as he mentions his father's abandoning of his family and his mother's early death,[95] but this account leaves Kreisler's youth and upbringing shrouded in mystery. At the end of the day, it is the symbolism of Kreisler's character that clues us in on Hoffmann's deepest aesthetic commitments. *Tomcat Murr* contains a scene where Kreisler explains his name to his benefactress, Madame Benzon:

> No, there's no getting away from the word Kreis, meaning a circle, and Heaven send that it immediately puts you in mind of those wonderful circles in which our entire existence moves and from which we cannot escape, do what we may. A Kreisler circulates in these circles, and very likely, weary of the leaps and bounds of the St. Vitus's dance[96] he is obliged to perform, and at odds with the dark, inscrutable power which delineated those circles, he often longs to break out more than a stomach constitutionally weak anyway will allow.[97]

Here Kreisler identifies himself, as a romantic artist, with the intimation of a necessity of fate at work in man's lower depths. The longing for the infinite is depicted here as compulsively circular. Honoring such infinite longing constitutes the terrifying pilgrimage to Orkus which the romantic must endure. I have argued that the decision to take up such a fateful vocation as a cartographer of the absolute has little to do with circumstantial biographical details, whether Hoffmann's or Kreisler's, and rather concerns a fundamental metaphysical malaise that gives rise to the infinite, longing characteristic of the romantic mindset. It is the same malaise that compels the romantic to draw

---

95 Hoffmann, *The Life and Opinions of the Tomcat Murr*, 74.
96 A reference to Sydenham's Chorea disease, which used to be known as St. Vitus's Dance, on account of its inducing a dancing mania in children. St. Vitus is the patron saint of dance.
97 Ibid., 49.

nearer to the sublime spirit-realm which threatens the artist's own destruction.

In fact, Hoffmann uses variants of the German *Kreis* (circle), from which Kreisler's name is derived, when describing the destructive trials endured by the romantic protagonists of his tales. Particularly revealing is the repeated mention of a "circle of fire" (*Feuerkreis*) in some of Hoffmann's most influential works. In *The Golden Pot,* a witch attempts to conjure up Anselmus by using her cat to create a "circle of fire" on the ground.[98] In *The Sandman,* Nathanael's delusions are described as a "fiery circle" that never stops turning.[99] In the throes of his fatal collapse at the end of the tale, we find Nathanael "leaping up in the air and shouting, 'Circle of fire! Whirl round, circle of fire! Whirl round!'"[100] Commenting on Hoffmann's usage of "*Feuerkreis*," Neil Hertz notes that "the expression [is] an unusual one in German."[101] Hertz then offers a reading whereby Hoffmann's description of the romantic's repetition-compulsion functions as "what French critics call a *mise en abyme* — a casting into the abyss," which gives "an illusion of infinite regress."[102] The romantic artist aims to "capture and represent the energies figured in the *Feuerkreis* itself,"[103] accounting for the romantic's perverse pursuit of the destructive sublime. "This *mise en abyme,*" Hertz continues, "simulates wildly uncontrollable repetition, and it is just that, I believe, that is imaged [sic] here in the whirling *Feuerkreis,* carrying Nathanael into the black abyss."[104]

The circle of fire is a prime hieroglyph of Hoffmann's aesthetics. So forceful are the equivalences that Hoffmann draws between fire and the effacement of oppositions that Bachelard identifies a "Hoffmann Complex," whereby "[m]adness and in-

---

98 Hoffmann, *Tales of E.T.A. Hoffmann,* 54.
99 Ibid., 109.
100 Ibid., 125.
101 Neil Hertz, *The End of the Line* (Aurora: Davies Group Publishers, 2009), 111.
102 Ibid., 112.
103 Ibid.
104 Ibid.

toxication, reason and enjoyment, are constantly presented in combination."[105] The major opposition effaced by Hoffmann's aesthetics is that of the beautiful and the sublime. In viewing the sublime as a terminal moment of the beautiful, Hoffmann paints the romantic artist as someone who is willing to risk the horrors of madness for the sake of bringing the transcendent fire of the spirit-realm closer to man's impoverished existence.

---

105 Gaston Bachelard, *Psychoanalysis of Fire,* trans. Alan C.M. Ross (Boston: Beacon Press, 1964), 86.

Bibliography

Bachelard, Gaston. *Psychoanalysis of Fire.* Translated by Alan C.M. Ross. Boston: Beacon Press, 1964.

Bloom, Harold. *Poetry and Repression: Revisionism from Blake to Stevens.* New Haven: Yale University Press, 1976.

Bonds, Mark Evan. *Music as Thought: Listening to the Symphony in the Age of Beethoven.* Princeton: Princeton University Press, 2006.

Bruning, Peter. "E.T.A. Hoffmann and the Philistine." *The German Quarterly* 28, no. 2 (1955): 111–21. DOI: 10.2307/401759.

Burke, Edmund, and James Thompson Boulton. *A Philosophical Enquiry into the Origin of Our Ideas of the Sublime and Beautiful.* Notre Dame: University of Notre Dame Press, 2005.

Cassedy, Steven. "Beethoven the Romantic: How E.T.A. Hoffmann Got It Right." *Journal of the History of Ideas* 71, no. 1 (2009): 1–37. DOI: 10.1353/jhi.0.0071.

Castoriadis, Cornelius. *The Imaginary Institution of Society.* Translated by Kathleen Blamey. Cambridge: MIT Press, 1998.

———. *World in Fragments: Writings on Politics, Society, Psychoanalysis, and the Imagination.* Edited and translated by David Ames Curtis. Stanford: Stanford University Press, 1997.

Chantler, Abigail. *E.T.A. Hoffmann's Musical Aesthetics.* London: Routledge, 2006.

Costelloe, Timothy. *The British Aesthetic Tradition: From Shaftesbury to Wittgenstein.* Cambridge: Cambridge University Press, 2013.

Dahlstrom, Daniel O. "Play and Irony: Schiller and Schlegel on the Liberating Prospects of Aesthetics." In *The History of Continental Philosophy,* Vol. 1, edited by Alan Schrift, 107–30. Chicago: University of Chicago Press, 2011.

De Quincey, Thomas. *De Quincey's Suspiria: I. The Daughter of Lebanon. II. Levana and Our Ladies of Sorrow.* London: De La More Press, 1906.

Doran, Robert. *The Theory of the Sublime from Longinus to Kant*. Cambridge: Cambridge University Press, 2017.

Durrell, Lawrence, and James Gifford. *From the Elephant's Back: Collected Essays & Travel Writings*. Edmonton: University of Alberta Press, 2015.

Förster, Eckart. *The Twenty-five Years of Philosophy: A Systematic Reconstruction*. Translated by Brady Bowman. Cambridge: Harvard University Press, 2012.

Freud, Sigmund. *The Freud Reader*. Edited by Peter Gay. New York: W.W. Norton, 1995.

———. *The Standard Edition of the Complete Psychological Works of Sigmund Freud, Volume XVII (1917–1919): An Infantile Neurosis and Other Works*. Edited and translated by James Starchey, in collaboration with Anna Freud, assisted by Alix Starchey and Alan Tyson. London: The Hogarth Press, 1955.

Furniss, Tom. *Edmund Burke's Aesthetic Ideology: Language, Gender, and Political Economy in Revolution*. Cambridge: Cambridge University Press, 2008.

Hertz, Neil. *The End of the Line*. Aurora: Davies Group Publishers, 2009.

Hewett-Thayer, Harvey. *Hoffmann: Author of the Tales*. Princeton: Princeton University Press, 1948.

Hoffmann, E.T.A. "Beethoven's Instrumental Music: Translated from E.T.A. Hoffmann's 'Kreisleriana.'" Translated by Arthur Ware Locke. *Musical Quarterly* 3, no. 1 (January 1917): 123–33. https://www.jstor.org/stable/738009.

———. *E.T.A. Hoffmann's Musical Writings: Kreisleriana, The Poet and the Composer, Musical Criticism*. Edited by David Charlton. Cambridge: Cambridge University Press, 2003.

———. *Tales of E.T.A. Hoffmann*. Edited and translated by Leonard Kent and Elizabeth Knight. Chicago: University of Chicago Press, 1969.

———. *The Life and Opinions of the Tomcat Murr*. Translated by Jeremy Adler. London: Penguin, 2006.

———. *The Serapion Brethren*. Translated by Alexander Ewing. London: G. Bell & Sons, 1886.

Kant, Immanuel. *Critique of the Power of Judgement.* Translated by Paul Guyer. Cambridge: Cambridge University Press, 2000.
Krell, David Farrell. *The Tragic Absolute: German Idealism and the Languishing of God.* Bloomington: Indiana University Press, 2005.
Lawson, Ursula. "Pathological Time in E.T.A. Hoffmann's *Der Sandmann*." *Monatshefte* 60, no. 1 (Spring 1968): 51–61. https://www.jstor.org/stable/30154535.
Lestition, Steven. "Kant and the End of the Enlightenment in Prussia." *Journal of Modern History* 65, no. 1 (March 1993): 57–112. DOI: 10.1086/244608
Locke, John. *An Essay Concerning Human Understanding.* Edited by Alexander Campbell Fraser. Oxford: Clarendon Press, 1894.
Merlo, Christiano. "Gautier Critique D'Hoffmann." *Études Littéraires* 42, no. 3 (2011): 71–82. DOI: 10.7202/1012018ar.
Rudwin, Maximilian. "Balzac and the Fantastic." *The Sewanee Review* 33, no. 1 (1925): 2–24. https://www.jstor.org/stable/27533823.
Schiller, Friedrich. *Essays.* Edited by Walter Hinderer and Daniel O. Dahlstrom. New York: Continuum, 1993.
———. *On the Aesthetic Education of Man: In a Series of Letters.* Translated by Elizabeth Wilkinson and L.A. Willoughby. Oxford: Oxford University Press, 2005.
Schonherr, Ulrich. "Social Differentiation and Romantic Art: E.T.A. Hoffmann's 'The Sanctus' and the Problem of Aesthetic Positioning in Modernity." *New German Critique* 66 (1995): 3–16. DOI: 10.2307/488585.
Shaftesbury, Earl of (Anthony Ashley Cooper). *Characteristics of Men, Manners, Opinions, Times.* Edited by Lawrence Klein. Cambridge: Cambridge University Press, 2003.
Watkins, Holly. "From the Mine to the Shrine: The Critical Origins of Musical Depth." *19th-Century Music* 27, no. 3 (March 2004): 179–207. DOI: 10.1525/ncm.2004.27.3.179.

12

When the Monstrous Object Becomes a Tremendous Non-Event: Rudolf Otto's Monster-Gods, H.P. Lovecraft's Cthulhu, and Graham Harman's Theory of Everything

Eric Wilson

The speculative position: "that the universe is undergirded by a somewhat horrifying power, one which humans can know."
— Fintan Neylan, "The Labour of the Pessimist"[1]

Un-reason: "the ultimate absence of reason […], an absolute ontological property and not the mark of the finitude of our knowledge."
— Quentin Meillassoux, *After Finitude*[2]

Everything Else: "If we look through the aperture which we have opened up onto the absolute, what we see is a rather

---

[1] Fintan Neyland, "The Labour of the Pessimist: Detecting Expiration's Artifice," in *True Detection,* eds. Edia Connole, Paul J. Ennis, and Nicola Masciandaro (San Bernardino: Schism Press, 2014), 85.

[2] Quentin Meillassoux, *After Finitude: An Essay on the Necessity of Contingency,* trans. Ray Brassier (London: Continuum, 2008), 53.

menacing power — something insensible, and capable of destroying both things and worlds, of bringing forth monstrous absurdities, yet also of never doing anything, of realizing every dream, but also every nightmare."

— Meillassoux, *After Finitude*[3]

While explaining the irresistible, sophomoric allure of Friedrich Nietzsche, Tracy Strong once opined that the main drawing power of the coprophagic Anti-Christ was his tectonic plate-shattering capacity to offer a wholly intelligible view of the world (*Weltanschauung*) following the extinction of all human life. Technically, he is incorrect. Arthur Schopenhauer was the first to do so, albeit operating with the caveat that a universe minus a self-aware observer would be indistinguishable from a primordial chaos — real in the sense of actual but un-real in the sense of incoherent, what Eugene Thacker denotes as the "world-without-us."[4] Nonetheless, this image of Nietzsche stuck and the problem remains for all variants of post-Kantian philosophy: is a world without self-awareness truly a "world" in any possible sense of this word?

My chapter will be divided into two parts.[5] The first will revisit in greater detail an issue that I first raised in my monograph *The Republic of Cthulhu: Lovecraft, the Weird Tale and Conspiracy Theory*,[6] namely, that Rudolf Otto's The Idea of the Holy (1917) is a direct but unacknowledged source for H.P. Lovecraft's seminal and semi-confessional work of literary criticism, "Supernatural Horror in Literature" (1927). Otto's work reads like a compendium of Lovecraftian narrative devices. His subjectivist reconstruction of the experience of the Holy as the *mysterium*

---

3 Ibid., 64.
4 Eugene Thacker, *In the Dust of This Planet: Horror of Philosophy, Volume I* (Winchester: Zero Books, 2011).
5 Due to limitations of space, I will omit discussion of three of Harman's favorite topics: the works of Bruno Latour, Manuel DeLanda, and Reza Negarestani.
6 Eric Wilson, *The Republic of Cthulhu: Lovecraft, the Weird Tale and Conspiracy Theory* (Brooklyn: punctum books, 2015).

tremendum enables a direct union of light and dark. All three facets of *mysterium/tremendum* — to be discussed below — are dramatically and discursively central to Lovecraft's magnum opus, the Cthulhu Mythos anchored on the one truly indispensable Lovecraftian text, "The Call of Cthulhu" (1926). The second part will be a systematic re-evaluation of the Ottonian/Lovecraftian aesthetic in terms of the post-neo-phenomenological "object-oriented ontology" (OOO) of Graham Harman. OOO is the branch of speculative realism that I am the most interested in as it directly overlaps with my interests in neo-phenomenology and aesthetics, my own views on these matters are endorsed by Harman himself ("OOO holds that philosophy generally has a closer relationship with aesthetics than with mathematics or natural science"[7]), and my main focus will be upon Harman's shorter text, *The Quadruple Object* (2011), a book that "seeks only to provide a weirder version of Aristotle's theory of substance."[8] My chapter concludes with an atrociously brief comparison of Harman with Quentin Meillassoux, explaining why it is the work of the former and not the latter that offers the preferred interpretation of the seminal work of twentieth-century horror fiction. My conclusion is that Cthulhu represents nothing so much as Harman's concept of the quadruple object.

Lovecraft and Daemonical Dread:
The Case of the Disappeared Cthulhu

> "A catastrophe is the occurrence of an abrupt discontinuity in a system characterized by continuous dynamics."
> — Jean-Pierre Dupuy, *A Short Treatise on the Metaphysics of Tsunamis*[9]

---

7 Graham Harman, *The Quadruple Object* (Winchester: Zero Books, 2011), 9.
8 Ibid., 93.
9 Jean-Pierre Dupuy, *A Short Treatise on the Metaphysics of Tsunamis*, trans. M.B. DeBevoise (East Lansing: Michigan State University Press, 2015), 34.

On reflection, the entirety of the Western tradition of philosophy comes down to this supremely elemental question: is there any essential difference between the death of a human (person) and the death of an insect (non-person)? And, from the perspective of a flat ontology the answer is: absolutely none at all. Admittedly, this is somewhat counter-intuitive. The far more normal response — a possible excrescence of Man's allegedly "eternal quest for meaning" — is to express the inexpressibility of atrocity through a very specific type of moral rhetoric. Jean-Pierre Dupuy's comment on Susan Neiman's treatment of the problem of evil in Western philosophy is most pertinent here.

Her crucial insight, borrowed from Arendt, is that when moral evil attains its height, as at Auschwitz, the categories that we habitually rely on to make moral judgments in ordinary life are shattered. In that case evil can only be accounted for in terms of an attack on the *natural* order of the world[10] [...] this kind of explanation is a piece of metaphysical cunning that makes it possible to do away with some part of the responsibility we would otherwise face, by converting evil into fate, into a secular form of transcendence, as it were.[11]

The problem with any "secular form of transcendence" is that it is ultimately unfeasible: secularity is the domain of finitude, and by extension the relative, while transcendence necessarily signifies the absolute, no matter how metaphysically weak. Hence Gunther Ander's bewilderment concerning the attitude of the survivors of Hiroshima and Nagasaki:

> Their [the survivors of the atomic bombings] steadfast resolve not to speak of those who were to blame, not to say that the event had been caused by human beings; not to harbor

---

10 Hannah Arendt defines "evil" as a fungus: "Evil possesses neither depth nor any demonic dimensions. It can overgrow and lay waste [to] the whole world precisely because it spreads like a fungus on the surface." Cited in Susan Nieman, *Evil in Modern Thought: An Alternative History of Philosophy* (Melbourne: Scribe Publishers, 2002), 301.

11 Jean-Pierre Dupuy, *A Short Treatise on the Metaphysics of Tsunamis*, trans. M.B. DeBevoise (East Lansing: Michigan State University Press, 2015), 13.

the least resentment, even though they were the victims of the greatest crimes — this really is too much for me, it passes all understanding […] They constantly speak of the catastrophe as if it were an earthquake or a tidal wave. They use the Japanese word, tsunami.[12]

On closer inspection this is not a paradox at all: it is a stratagem to obviate any possibility of the collective guilt of the Japanese people for initiating the Pacific War. If the atomic bombings were just like a tsunami, then neither the Americans nor the Japanese are morally to blame. The price of Japanese innocence is the moral absolution of the Americans — the reduction of the Enola Gay to a natural force. What is pertinent in Anders's lament is the implicit reversal that lies within the metaphorical equation of absolute evil with natural disaster: the imaginary of the one can be rendered iterable to the other simply on the basis of scalar considerations. The enormity, or size, of either event, natural or evil, automatically lends itself to a commonality of expression, which in turn leads to a consideration in terms of both religious and aesthetic phenomena. Here is how Dupuy frames the destruction of the World Trade Center: "On 11 September 2001, an apocalyptic event took place on American soil. I use the word 'apocalypse' in its true sense, not with reference to a catastrophe that will put an end to the world, but instead to something that is a bearer of revelation."[13] Now take note of how Anders defines religious phenomena: "What I recognize as being 'religious' in nature is nothing at all positive, but only the horror of human action transcending any human scale, which no god can prevent."[14] What links both passages is an implicit correlation between the event and the sublime: the magnitude of great evil and annihilating destruction triggers an evocation that implicitly conflates the spectacular with the divine. This,

---

12 Gunther Anders, cited in ibid., 63.
13 Ibid., 33.
14 Gunther Anders, cited in Jean-Pierre Dupuy, *The Mark of the Sacred*, trans. M.B. DeBevoise (Stanford: Stanford University Press, 2013), 207.

of course, is in full accordance with Immanuel Kant's classical exposition of the notion of the sublime. Simply put, Kant's entire metaphysical system ultimately serves an end both aesthetic and epistemological: to organize the world in such a way as to make it the grounds for objective understanding and absolute knowledge. In other words, to thoroughly serve "the purposive" — or, in Heideggerian terms, the reduction of both self and object to "correctness."

For Kant, the perception of the world ("the transcendental deduction") requires a synthesis of what appears before us within both time and space. The synthetic project of "pure reason" requires three operational concepts, or "unities of synthesis": apprehension, reproduction, and recognition. Within the Kantian scheme, all knowledge and understanding is ultimately anthropocentric, in that all things must be reduced to units of measure that are compatible with human understanding (*cogito*): "A tree [the height of] which we estimate with reference to the height of a man, at all events gives us a standard for a mountain."[15] The categories of pure reason guaranteeing both the unity of phenomena as well as the ontological unity of the perceiving subject constitutes the transcendental unity of apperception.[16] "In other words, it is not so much that I perceive objects; it is rather my perception that presupposes the [unitary] object-form as one of its conditions."[17] For Kant, "the real (synthetic) formula of the *cogito* is: I think myself, and in thinking myself, I think that the object in general to which I relate is a represented diversity."[18] Therefore, the operations of the a priori categories of synthetic understanding need to be supplemented by the work of an additional faculty, judgment, which is responsible for subordinating

---

15 Immanuel Kant, *The Critique of Judgment,* trans. J.H. Bernard (Amherst: Prometheus Books, 2000), 118.
16 Daniel W. Smith, "Translator's Introduction: Deleuze on Bacon: Three Conceptual Trajectories in The Logic of Sensation" in Gilles Deleuze, *Francis Bacon: The Logic of Sensation,* trans. Daniel W. Smith (Minneapolis: University of Minnesota Press, 2003), vii–xxvii and xvii.
17 Ibid., xvi.
18 Gilles Deleuze, cited in Smith, "Translator's Introduction," xvi.

all of the inherent sensible diversity of spatio-temporal objects to the operational requirements of the synthetic categories of transcendental reason: "The only use which the understanding can make of these [concepts] is to judge by means of them."[19] From this follow two consequences, one phenomenological the other aesthetic. In terms of the former, the human body itself is the final source not only of the units of measurement but of the operational constraints of the synthetic categories of pure reason:

> This primary (subjective, sensory, immediate, living) measure proceeds from the [human] body. And it takes the body as its primary object [...] *It is the body which erects itself as a measure.* It provides the measuring and measured unit of measure: of the smallest and largest possible, of the minimum and the maximum, and likewise of the passage from the one to the other.[20]

In terms of the latter, the lived evaluation of space-time imparts a necessarily aesthetic dimension to judgment, as the operation of perception is inseparable from the appreciation and evaluation of form, which is the domain of the aesthetic properly defined, "[a]ll estimation of the magnitude of objects of nature is in the last resort aesthetic (i.e., subjectively and not objectively determined)."[21] And it is the intrinsically aesthetic nature of judgment that gives rise to one of Kant's seminal concepts — the sublime. Although an aesthetic concept, the sublime is not identical with the beautiful. It is in fact antithetical to it. Whereas the beautiful dwells within the realm of intuition — the natural accordance of the spatio-temporal object with the synthetic categories of the *cogito*[22] — the sublime is better understood as a

---

19 Immanuel Kant, cited in Smith, "Translator's Introduction," xvi.
20 Jacques Derrida, *The Truth in Painting,* trans. Geoff Bennington and Ian McLeod (Chicago: University of Chicago Press, 1987), 140.
21 Immanuel Kant, cited in Smith, "Translator's Introduction," xviii.
22 "Natural beauty [...] brings with it a purposiveness in its form by which the object seems to be, as it were, pre-adapted to our Judgment, and thus

form of sensory trauma, the catastrophic or chaotic sundering of the immediacy of perception from the transcendental unity of apperception.

The sublime, on the other hand, is to be found in a formless object, so far as in it or by occasion of it boundlessness is represented, and yet its totality is also present to thought, that which excites in us, without any reasoning about it, but in the apprehension of it, the feeling of the sublime, may appear as regards its form to violate purpose in respect of the judgment, to be unsuited to our presentative faculty, and as it were to do violence to the Imagination. And yet it is judged to be only the more sublime.[23]

As we should expect, the Kantian sublime is remarkably, almost viscerally, phenomenological in nature — "[n]ature is therefore sublime in those of its phenomena whose intuition brings with it the Idea of its infinity."[24] Essential to the concept of the sublime is not merely the heightening of the *cogito*'s self-awareness of the grounding of perception upon the body, but the abject insult inflicted upon the anthropocentric unit of measurement: "We call that *sublime* which is *absolutely great* [...] *what is great beyond all comparison* [...] *the sublime is that in comparison with which everything else is small.*"[25] Secondly, the subjective experience of the sublime is not the objective perception of the immediately unassimilable sensible diversity of the sublime object but rather the traumatic inducement of a crisis of confidence in the witness' existential faith in the efficacy of judgment.

> [T]rue sublimity must be sought only in the mind of the [subject] judging, not in the natural Object, the judgment upon which occasions this state [...] Consequentially it is the state of mind produced by a certain representation with which the

---

constitutes in itself an object of satisfaction." Kant, *The Critique of Judgment*, 102–3.
23 Ibid., 103.
24 Ibid., 116.
25 Ibid., 106, 109. Emphases added.

reflective Judgment is occupied, and not the Object, that is to be called sublime [...] [*T*]*he sublime is that, the mere ability to think which, shows a faculty of the mind surpassing every standard of sense.*[26]

One of the central artistic paradoxes of supernatural literature, the central topic of this volume, is the manner in which the weird tale combines, not always successfully, elements of both the subversive and the reactionary; subversive because *ratio* is invariably threatened by the narratively necessary presence of the Wholly Other/Monster, reactionary because the subversive presence is, nearly, always successfully challenged and eliminated. "Traditionally, genre horror is concerned with the irruption of dreadful forces into a comforting status quo — one which the protagonists frantically scrabble to preserve."[27] Lovecraft is one of the singular examples of a counter-trend, largely through subliminal interrogation of Heidegger's *alētheia,* or apocalyptic revelation. "By contrast, Lovecraft's horror is not one of intrusion but of realization. The world has always been implacably bleak; the horror lies in our acknowledging that fact."[28] In Lovecraft's own words, "the ultimate reality of space is clearly a complex churning of energy of which the human mind can never form any approximate picture, and which can touch us only through the veil of local apparent manifestations which we call the visible and material universe."[29]

Within "The Call of Cthulhu," the Lovecraftian text that I shall be most concerned with,[30] the conflation of the catastroph-

---

26 Ibid., 110, 117. Emphasis added.
27 China Miéville, "Introduction," in *At the Mountains of Madness: The Definitive Edition* (New York: The Modern Library, 2005), xiii.
28 Ibid.
29 H.P. Lovecraft, cited in Sean Elliot Martin, *H.P. Lovecraft and the Modernist Grotesque* (published by author, 2008), 151.
30 It is interesting to note just how regularly multi-tentacled Cthulhu appears throughout speculative realist writings and associated works. See Steven Shaviro, *The Universe of Things: On Speculative Realism* (Minneapolis: University of Minnesota Press, 2014), 91, 147; see also Timothy Morton, *Hyperobjects: Philosophy and Ecology after the End of the World* (Minne-

ic with the sublime is most clearly on display in the third part of the tale, "The Madness From the Sea."[31] Here, the narrator Thurston recounts his reading of the journal of a recently deceased Norwegian ship captain, Gustaf Johansen, the only survivor of an encounter on March 23, 1925, with a mysterious, uncharted island in the far southern Pacific Ocean (S. Latitude 47°, 9'; W. Longitude 126°, 43'), which turns out to be the prematurely, and only temporarily, re-surfaced sunken city of R'lyeh and a partially awoken Cthulhu, now revealed as the direct source of the concurrent wave of psychic distortions experienced by psychic sensitives throughout the world. Through Johansen we learn that the genocidal arch-priest of the Old Ones is able to leave stasis for a short time because of a localized earthquake that brings part of R'leyh to the surface. In Michel Houellebecq's memorable summary of this cataclysmic event, "Between 4:00 pm and 4:15 pm a breach occurred in the architecture of time. And through the fissure created, a terrifying entity manifested itself on our earth."[32] But oddly, absolutely nothing happens.

Pace Heidegger, Cthulhu, finally, comes into view (*Ereignis*), but it is a total non-event. And it is precisely the un-eventful nature of the event that I wish to discuss here. Where we should expect the end, all that we receive is a deferral; the re-animation of dead/dreaming Cthulhu is reduced to nothing more than a series of aesthetic phenomena, or even "effects," that, while revealing much, alter nothing in terms of the substance of Being, as opposed, of course, to our apperception of it. If, for the sake of academic argument, we were to philosophize seriously about Lovecraft's masterpiece, then I would argue that within the array of formidable speculative realists the concept that is most

---

apolis: University of Minnesota Press, 2013), 64, 175; and see esp. Graham Harman, *Weird Realism: Lovecraft and Philosophy* (Winchester: Zero Books, 2012).

31 H.P. Lovecraft, "The Call of Cthulhu," in Michel Houellebecq, *H.P. Lovecraft: Against the World, Against Life* (London: Weidenfeld & Nicolson, 2006), 145–57.

32 Michel Houellebecq, H.P. Lovecraft: *Against the World, Against Life* (London: Weidenfeld & Nicolson, 2006), 82.

useful for classifying the unclassifiable Ancient Ones is the OOO of Graham Harman, for it is Harman who most incisively manages to separate a "thing" from its "effects." But to understand this more clearly, it is necessary to take a detour through the phenomenological landscape of what is meant by the Holy, for it is there that we discover that at its core lies the horror of the reduction of the self to the pure object — the abject.

Creature Consciousness: From the Holy to the Abject

> The real we have thus far is nothing compared to what we cannot even imagine, precisely because the defining character of the real is that one cannot imagine it.
> — Jacques Lacan, *The Triumph of Religion Preceded by Discourse to Catholics*[33]

Although apparently linked to the supernatural theme in literature, Lovecraft's oeuvre, on closer examination, reveals a metanarrative that is thoroughly modernist in orientation. And this supernaturally-infused modernism, in turn, betrays an almost nostalgic invocation of the notions of both numinousity and transcendence, an atheistic interrogation and re-conceptualization of the Holy that is a central but largely under-appreciated facet of the literary project of modernism. Most germane is the seminal text on the subject of horrific transcendence, Rudolf Otto's *The Idea of the Holy* (1917). Operating from a Wittgensteinian premise — "An object that can thus be thought conceptually may be termed *rational*" — Otto turns dogmatic theology on its head by arguing for the opposite axiom: any object that may be considered real — as in possessing substance — yet lacking "clear and definite *concepts*" must necessarily be considered irrational — that is, an existent that is shapeless or formless.[34] In

---

[33] Jacques Lacan, *The Triumph of Religion Preceded by Discourse to Catholics*, trans. Bruce Fink (Cambridge: Polity Press, 2013), 72.
[34] Rudolf Otto, *The Idea of the Holy: An Inquiry into the Non-Rational Factor in the Idea of the Divine and its Relation to the Rational*, trans. John W. Harvey (Oxford: Oxford University Press, 1958), 1.

theological terms, this anti-formalist insight yields us the category of the numinous which, in existential terms, is subjectively experienced as the Holy or the *mysterium tremendum,* the phenomenological core of religion.[35] A union of light and dark *mysterium* acts as a form of fascination,[36] and *tremendum* as a source of dread.[37] Otto then proceeds to break down the daunting aspect of the Holy into three overlapping components. The first is "awe-fulness" or "daemonical dread," the spectral fear induced by the direct and unmediated encounter with an undefinable and hitherto invisible "Wholly Other."[38]

It first begins to stir in the feeling of "something uncanny," "eerie," or "weird." It is this feeling which, emerging in the mind of primeval man, forms the starting-point for the entire religious development of history. Daemons and gods alike spring from this root, and all the products of "mythological apperception" or "fantasy" are nothing but different modes in which it has been objectified.[39]

The second is alternatively defined as "energy" or "urgency," the raw power of psychic transformation and an annihilating, de-personalizing illumination.[40] Like awe-fulness, energy is both primitive and visceral, best expressed within the Abraham-

---

35 Ibid., 12–13. Not surprisingly, Otto established a clear correlation, or a schematic association in "temporal sequence," between the Kantian sublime and the dualistic nature of the Holy. "Certainly we can tabulate some general 'rational' signs that uniformly recur as soon as we call an object sublime; as, for instance, the bounds of our understanding by some 'dynamic' or 'mathematic' greatness, by potent manifestations of force or magnitude in spatial extent. But these are obviously only conditions of, not the essence of, the impression of sublimity. A thing does not become sublime merely by being great. The concept itself remains unexplicated; it has in it something mysterious, and in this it is like that of the numinous." Otto, *The Idea of the Holy,* 41; see also: ibid., 41–49. In the end, Otto refuses to reduce religious experience to mere aesthetic sensation. Ibid., 45–49.
36 Ibid., 25–40. The signature emotion of *mysterium* is *stupor,* "an astonishment that strikes us dumb, amazement absolute." Ibid., 26.
37 Ibid., 12–24.
38 Ibid., 13–19, 25–30.
39 Ibid., 14–15.
40 Ibid., 23–24.

ic tradition as "the scorching and consuming wrath of God,"[41] a reservoir of supernatural energy that appears devoid of moral qualities. "It is […] 'like a hidden force of nature,' like stored-up electricity, discharging itself upon anyone who comes too near. It is 'incalculable' and 'arbitrary.'"[42] Significantly, in its positive form, it manifests itself as mystic rapture, "the same 'energy'" as "the scorching and consuming wrath of God" but flowing through different channels, ("love", says one of the mystics, "is nothing else than quenched wrath").[43] The third, and the one closest to Lovecraft's own dramatic concerns, is *majestas,* "absolute over-poweringness," or, even better, "creature-consciousness," the "shadow or subjective reflection" of the self's abject dependency upon the Wholly Other.[44]

It is the emotion of a creature submerged and overwhelmed by its own nothingness in contrast to that which is supreme above all creatures. Thus, in contrast to the overpowering of which we are conscious as an object over against the self, there is the feeling of one's own submergence, of being but "dust and ashes and nothingness."[45] And this forms the numinous raw material for the feeling of religious humility.

The "I am naught, Thou art all" is the unique and irreducible core of authentic private religious experience in which the "self-depreciation" of that primordial "element of the *tremendum,* originally apprehended as 'plenitude of power,' becomes transmuted into 'plenitude of being.'"[46] Or, to put it another way, personal religious experience is the phenomenological mapping of the anthropological migration from Monsters to Gods. If the numinous truly stands for that "aspect of deity which transcends or eludes comprehension in rational or ethical terms,"[47] then

---

41 Ibid., 24.
42 Ibid., 18.
43 Ibid., 24.
44 Ibid., 219–23.
45 Ibid., 10, 20.
46 Ibid., 21.
47 John W. Harvey, "Translator's Preface," in Otto, *The Idea of the Holy,* xvi. See also A.S. Herbert cited in Matt Cardin, *Dark Awakenings* (Poplar Bluff:

Otto's great work makes intelligible one of the most repressed truths of the sacred, that the inseparability of religion from horror flows from the primordial "absence of difference" between the Wholly Other and the Monster.

Derived from the Latin noun *monstrum,* which is related to the verbs *monstrare* ("to show" or "to reveal") and *monere* ("to warn" or "to portend"[48]), the coming of the Monster is identical to a revelation of a dangerous truth that is incommensurable with orthodox consensus, both social and epistemological. In its existential dimension, the numinous/monstrous is identical with that unsayable-which-induces-dread, and which therefore lacks a true name. The "nearest that German can get to it is in the expression *das Ungeheuere* (monstrous), while in English 'weird' is perhaps the closest rendering possible."[49] In its anthropological dimension, God-and-Monster signifies both the iterability between Chaos and Order — the eternally recurrent migrations between cosmogony and chaogony — as well as the radically undecidable (anti-schematic) nature of the primal substance of Being.[50] At the risk of simplifying, it may be truthfully said that the greater part of the intellectual edifice of Lovecraft's oeuvre consists of nothing more than an act of translation of what Beal identifies as "the paradox of the monstrous"[51] into the atheistic tropes of Darwinist Biology and Einsteinian Physics. What he yields is an utterly uncanny synthesis of the archaic

---

Mythos Books, 2010), 302, "[t]he word 'holy' is primarily not an ethical term, but one indicating the otherness, the incalculable power, of God, his inaccessibility. He is 'the great stranger in the human world' [...] Holy expressed the mysterious, incalculable, unapproachable quality of the divine in contrast to the human."

48 Timothy J. Beal, *Religion and Its Monsters* (New York: Routledge, 2002), 6–7.
49 Otto, *The Idea of the Holy,* 40.
50 See Beal, *Religion and Its Monsters.* Also see Cardin, "A Horrific Reading of Isaiah," in *Dark Awakenings,* 287–319. Cardin ends his discussion of the Book of Isaiah 24–34 by concluding, "Yahweh, in a very important way, functions as a chaos monster." Ibid., 295; see also ibid., 296, 300, 302.
51 Beal, *Religion and Its Monsters,* 19.

with the super scientific, a monstrous cross-fertilization of the transcendental Wholly Other with the physicalist Alien.

Paradoxically, it is precisely this bleak atheist awe that makes Lovecraft a kind of bad-son heir to a religious visionary tradition, an ecstatic tradition, which, in distinction from the everyday separation of matter and spirit, locates the holy in the everyday. Lovecraft, too, sees the awesome as immanent to the quotidian, but there is little ecstasy [mysterium] here. His is a bad numinous.[52]

Following Otto, we can now see that the central conceit of the Lovecraftian corpus is that his "bad numinous" is *tremendum* with the *mysterium* subtracted out, although it should be noted that Lovecraft does seek a limited re-introduction of fascination, or stupor, in relation to the Wholly Other in some of his last works.[53] Lovecraft himself makes this painfully clear in his semi-confessional work of literary criticism, "Supernatural Horror in Literature" (1927):

> The appeal of the spectrally macabre is generally narrow because it demands from the reader a certain degree of imagination and a capacity of detachment from everyday life [...] There is here involved a psychological pattern or tradition as real and as deeply grounded in mental experience as any other pattern or tradition of mankind; coeval with the religious feeling and closely related to many aspects of it, and too much a part of our inmost biological heritage to lose

---

52 S.T. Joshi, "Introduction," in *The Thing on the Doorstep and Other Weird Stories,* ed. S.T. Joshi (London: Penguin Books, 2001), xiii. Compare Vivian Ralickas on this very point: "In denying humanism and revealing the ostensible unity of the human subject to be a fallacy, I contend that what Lovecraft's work affirms, albeit negatively, is a subjective crisis specific to the modern condition." Vivian Ralickas, "'Cosmic Horror' and the Question of the Sublime in Lovecraft," *Journal of the Fantastic in the Arts* 18, no. 3 (2007), 366, and also 387–88.

53 In particular, "At the Mountains of Madness" and "The Shadow over Innsmouth."

keen potency over a very important, though not numerically great, minority of our species.[54]

Typically, Lovecraft grounds the species' predilection for horror with an atavistic genetic inheritance.[55] "The oldest and strongest emotion of mankind is fear, and the oldest and strongest kind of fear is fear of the unknown"; the artistic merit of "the weirdly horrible tale as a literary form," therefore, is guaranteed not by transcendental notions but by profanely material ones: the ritualistic re-enactment of the primal terror of self-awareness.[56] Against the emotional primacy of horror "are discharged all the shafts of a materialistic sophistication which clings to frequently felt emotions and external events, and of a naively insipid idealism which deprecates the aesthetic motive and calls for a didactic literature to 'uplift' the reader towards a suitable degree of smirking optimism."[57] However, since cosmic horror is the re-

---

54 H.P. Lovecraft, "Supernatural Horror in Literature" in *At the Mountains of Madness: The Definitive Edition* (New York: The Modern Library, 2005), 105.
55 As does Otto. "It may well be possible, it is even probable, that in the first stage of its development the religious consciousness started with only one of its poles — the daunting aspect of the numen — and so at first took shape only as 'daemonic dread.'" Otto, *The Idea of the Holy*, 32.
56 Lovecraft, "Supernatural Horror in Literature," 105. Compare this remarkable passage with Otto on the atavistic relationship between daemonic dread and horror fiction: "This crudely naïve and primordial emotional disturbance, and the fantastic images to which it gives rise, are later overborne and ousted by more highly developed forms of the numinous emotion, with all its mysteriously impelling power. But even when this has long attained its higher and purer mode of expression it is possible for the primitive types of excitation that were formerly a part of it to break out in the soul in all their original naïveté and so to be experienced afresh. That this is so is shown by the potent attraction again and again exercised by the element of horror and 'shudder' in ghost stories, even among persons of high all-round education." Otto, *The Idea of the Holy*, 16, and also 29, where Otto clearly identifies the fear of ghosts as a "degraded offshoot and travesty of the genuine 'numinous' dread or awe." As Stephen King expressed it, in his inestimable EC horror comic book style, horror "invites a physical reaction by showing us something which is physically wrong." Stephen King, *Danse Macabre* (New York: Gallery Books, 2010), 22.
57 Lovecraft, "Supernatural Horror in Literature," 105.

visitation of the (un-)holy, it necessarily follows that the highest form of supernatural literature, or "the weird tale," depends upon the successful narrative deployment of the cultural residue of the theological imaginary:

> The true weird tale has something more than secret murder, bloody bones, or a sheeted form clanking chains according to a rule. A certain atmosphere of breathless and unexplainable dread of outer, unknown forces must be present; and there must be a hint, expressed with a seriousness and portentousness becoming its subject, of that most terrible conception of the human brain — a malign and particular suspension or defeat of those fixed laws of nature which are our only safeguard against the assaults of chaos and the daemons of unplumbed space.[58]

As Lovecraft's greatest critic Maurice Levy points out, the overriding aesthetic impulse of the Lovecraftian text is to induce within the post-theistic reader a sense of that primordial dread that was the hallmark of primitive religious experience, the violent and unmediated encounter with the "Wholly Other."[59] As Lovecraft writes,

> Therefore, we must judge a weird tale not by the author's intent, or by the mere mechanics of the plot, but by the emotional level which it attains at its least mundane point […] The one test of the really weird is simply this — whether or not there be excited in the reader a profound sense of dread, and of contact with unknown spheres and powers; a subtle attitude of awed listening, as if for the beating of black wings or the scratching of outside shapes and entities on the known universe's utmost rim.[60]

---

58 Ibid, 107.
59 See Maurice Levy, *Lovecraft: A Study in the Fantastic*, trans. S.T. Doshi (Detroit: Wayne State University, 1988).
60 Lovecraft, "Supernatural in Horror Literature," 108.

Cosmic horror is a paradoxically anti-therapeutic form of catharsis: curative because of the flooding release of psychic tension that it itself creates but harmful at the same time because of the radical disabuse of human conceit that it involves. As Donald R. Burleson has quite correctly recognized, Lovecraft's aesthetic is essentially post-modern in nature, a "deconstructive gesture of questioning and unsettling metaphysically privileged systems of all kinds." The signature feature of Lovecraft's writing is precisely this ironically self-understood insignificance of being-human, which, given the essentially anthropocentric nature of Western thought, bestows upon the Lovecraftian corpus a status unique within modern literature.[61] "In a society that is becoming each day more and more anesthetized and repressive, the fantastic is at once an evasion and the mobilization of anguish. It restores man's sense of the sacred and the sacrilegious, it above all gives back to him his lost depth."[62] For Levy,

> Lovecraft [...] creates the strange, he excites fear, by *turning the world inside out*. For Lovecraft, writing is the making of the oneiric and wrong side of things appear, substituting the nocturnal for the diurnal, replacing the reassuring image of the Waking World by the alienating ones of the great depths. The world of the surface has in his work no other raison d'être than provisionally and imperfectly to cover up the abyss.[63]

Central to Lovecraft's oeuvre is his highly aestheticized — which is to say, intensely singular — onto-epistemology, a philosophically naïve but dramatically powerful re-presentation of the metaphysics of Schopenhauer: "Life is a hideous thing, and from the background behind what we know of it peer daemonical hints of truth which make it a thousandfold more hideous."[64]

---

61 Donald R. Burleson, *Lovecraft: Disturbing the Universe* (Lexington: University Press of Kentucky, 2009), 158–59.
62 Levy, *Lovecraft*, 120.
63 Ibid.
64 H.P. Lovecraft, "Facts Concerning the Late Arthur Jermyn and His Family," in *The Call of Cthulhu and Other Weird Stories*, ed. S.T. Joshi (London:

In his pioneering deconstruction of the Lovecraftian weird tale, Burleson identifies as the meta-theme of the oeuvre "the ruinous nature of self-knowledge," or, more exactly, "the notion that, when we as humans come to look upon the cosmos as it is, we find our place in it to be soul-crushingly evanescent."[65] The other recursive themes are forbidden knowledge, denied primacy, unwholesome survivals, and, most interesting of all, illusory surface appearances, the general signification that things are not as they appear on the surface, below which deeper and more terrible realities are masked.

All of Lovecraft's plots, in so far as there are any, are occasioned by a traumatic, and traumatizing, cognitive rupturing of the social consensus of reality,[66] culminating in the annihilating revelation of an unspeakable dis-joint between a human(-istic) phenomena and a post-human(-istic) noumena, perfectly suited to the post-theistic aesthetic experience of the weird tale, signified by the obliteration of consciousness and self-awareness, culminating in Lovecraft's trademark literary gimmick, the primordial scream. This scream is the epitome of the Lovecraftian artistic effect, a radically alienating encounter with the annihilating nature of the universe, which in the final instance can only be denoted as the nameless. And as no less an authority than Abdul Alhazred himself declares in his darkly magisterial *Necronomicon,* "Man rules now where They ruled once; They shall soon rule where Man rules now. After summer is winter, and after winter summer. They wait patient and potent, for here shall they reign again."[67]

Penguin Classics, 2011), 14.

65 Burleson, Lovecraft, 158, and also 156–57.

66 "At some point, the text breaks down and reveals something which has not been there. A rupture emerges and, along with it, something new, the unknown. The next step is horror which arises from a threat, not to the narrator but to humanity." Timo Airaksinen, *The Philosophy of H.P. Lovecraft: The Route to Horror* (New York: Peter Lang, 1985), 175.

67 H.P. Lovecraft, "The Dunwich Horror," in *The Thing on the Doorstep and Other Weird Stories,* ed. S.T. Joshi (London: Penguin Classics, 2001), 220.

What we are left with, then, is an unbridgeable dichotomy between reality and sensations: our world remains the same, but we experience it differently. And if we were to follow Eugene Thacker on this point — that the horror tale should be thought of in terms of a philosophical text — then the formal question that Lovecraft's work raises is: how exactly are we to separate an object from its effects? And the answer, for Harman, is to prioritize aesthetics as first philosophy through isolating the substance of an object from the totality of its sensual effects within the world.[68]

The Horror of OOO

> To be is to be perceived.
>
> — George Berkeley[69]

"Instead of beginning with radical doubt, we start from naivete," declares Harman. "My point is not that all objects are equally real [e.g., flying green-eared spaghetti monsters versus major league baseballs], but that they are equally *objects*."[70] Harman, provisionally, solves the problem of absence-of-presence bequeathed to us by Derrida through the re-establishment of the depth of the object as an almost physicalist variation of infinitude, pointing to the underlying inexhaustibility of possible knowledge. Herein, ontology is stabilized via multiplication through space as opposed to correlation with transcendence. Harman espouses what is in essence a variation of flat ontology, the absolute absence of any kind of metaphysical hierarchy among objects ("The human/world relation is just a special

---

68 The "interdisciplinary success of OOO allows us to view it instead as an extremely broad method in the spirit of actor-network theory, but one that rescues the non-relational core of every object, thus paving the way for an aesthetic conception of things." Graham Harman, *Object-Oriented Ontology: A New Theory of Everything* (London: Pelican Books, 2018), 256.
69 George Berkeley, quoted in Harman, *The Quadruple Object*, 11.
70 Ibid, 5.

case of the relation between any two entities whatsoever."[71]) Harman presents himself as the neo-Empedocles of speculative realism, the prophet of a post-modernist (re-)conciliation with the pre-classical Pre-Socratics — the return of philosophy to a natural philosophy of physicalism.[72] The throbbing heart of Harman's philosophical body is his partial synthesis of Edmund Husserl's (1859–1938) eidetic reduction and Martin Heidegger's (1889–1976) tool-being, two of the three, along with Maurice Merleau-Ponty, primary movers of continental phenomenology. Therefore, his oeuvre is founded directly upon the double axes of Husserl and Heidegger, along with their respective treatment of the sensual and the real.

For Harman, reality is divided into two sets of objects: "An object is anything that has a unified reality that is autonomous from its wider context but also from its own pieces."[73] That is, an object's essential characteristic is that it is non-reducible. In turn, each variety of object is divided into two sub-sets. As per Husserl, the dichotomy is between the sensual quality and the sensual object. For Harman, what "makes Husserl so special among idealists is his discovery of objects *within* the phenomenal field."[74] In this way, "Husserl discovers a tension between the object and content *within* the sensual realm — a great fault line that tears phenomena in half from the start."[75]

Although commonly regarded as an idealist, "Husserl's philosophical method is to bracket all considerations of the outside world and focus solely on the phenomena that appears to consciousness" — superficially conservative but latently subversive. Husserl's entire project is not to "restore scientific naturalism to the throne, but to give us the sense of a reality much weirder than

---

71 Graham Harman, cited in Ian Bogost, *Alien Phenomenology, Or What It is Like to Be a Thing* (Minneapolis: University of Minnesota Press, 2012), 6.
72 Graham Harman, *Circus Philosophicus* (Winchester: Zero Books, 2010), 13–26.
73 Graham Harman, *Immaterialism: Objects and Social Theory* (Cambridge: Polity Press, 2016), 116.
74 Harman, *The Quadruple Object*, 30.
75 Ibid., 32.

any that science has known."⁷⁶ The sensual qualities ("SQ"; also known as adumbrations or accidents) of objects are governed by time and are 'observer sensitive,' dependent "on whatever entity encounters them,"⁷⁷ giving rise to what Husserl labels "ideational objects."⁷⁸ Importantly, specifically aesthetic phenomena require the temporal intervention of an actor-observer behaving in a theatrical manner in order to give rise to the ideational object (here, ideational has no bearing on ideology but rather upon the temporal insertion of the perceiving entity into the landscape or field of the sensorium, occupying the ontologically invaluable gap between the subject and its perceivable qualities). By contrast, sensual objects ("SO"; also referred to as *eidos* and subject to what Husserl calls "eidetic reduction") are spatial. Importantly for Harman, the sensual object may be wholly imaginary. The critical point is that they are "only by categorical and not sensuous intuitions, they are never fully present,"⁷⁹ but are in some absolutely basic way always "withdrawn" (not exhausted through categorical perception). Hence, "the accidental properties lie directly before us in experience but the eidetic ones do not."⁸⁰ The true world, therefore, is always, in some sense, withdrawn from us. As Harman writes,

---

76 Ibid., 36.
77 Harman, *Immaterialism*, 41.
78 "Real objects and qualities exist in their own right, while sensual objects and qualities exist only as the correlate of some real object, human or otherwise." Harman, *Object-Oriented Ontology*, 160.
79 Harman, *Immaterialism*, 104.
80 Harman, *The Quadruple Object*, 27. It is tempting to draw a direct comparison here with David Bohm's comments on quantum mechanics. "Quantum theory requires us to give up the idea that the electron, or any other object has, by itself, any intrinsic properties at all. Instead, each object should be regarded as something containing only incompletely defined potentialities that are developed when an object interacts with an appropriate system." Cited in Morton, *Hyperobjects*, 44. What is critical here is the rather old-fashioned notion of anti-essentialism, "there is no essence in what exists." Cited in Morton, *Hyperobjects*, 115. Ergo, every object, as individual or as system, is always "withdrawn" — this as a "pun" on the notion of absence.

eidetic qualities radiate vaguely from the analysed thing, never graspable by the senses [...] In this way we find a second great tension in Husserl's thinking: that between sensual objects and *real* qualities [...]. They hide from every view [i.e., they are non-exhaustive] and are encountered only obliquely [...]. Indeed, [Husserl] often insists that categorical intuition provides *direct* access to reality in a way that the senses do not.[81]

And what we understand as reality, framed as relatively stable in the everyday, is in fact latently unstable and potentially even violent, given the unbridgeable gap between SQ and SO; the phenomenal world, within its totality, "is not just an idealist sanctuary from the blows of harsh reality, but an active seismic [*tsunami*-like] zone where intentional objects grind slowly against their own qualities."[82]

Harman's valiant engagement with Husserl notwithstanding, it is fairly clear that it is the second axis, Heidegger, who is closest to Harman's own heart. Harman encapsulates virtually the entirety of Heidegger's treatment of the object in the grand concept of tool-being: "The key to Heidegger's philosophy is the concept of *Zuhandenheit,* or 'readiness-to-hand,' which I also refer to as 'tool-being.'"[83] *Zuhandenheit* denotes relationality (or temporality[84]): "[r]eadiness-to-hand has everything to do with mode of being of entities, and *nothing* to do with the circumstances under which they were produced."[85] In contrast, *Vorhandenheit* ("presence-at-hand") constitutes a form of essence (a-temporality), signified by the moment when things

---

81 Harman, *Circus Philosophicus*, 60.
82 Harman, *The Quadruple Object*, 26.
83 Graham Harman, *Tool-Being: Heidegger and the Metaphysics of Objects* (Chicago: Open Court, 2002), 4.
84 To the question "what exactly is implied by Heidegger's 'temporality'? My answer [...] is that it implies nothing other than the global reversal between the tool and the broken tool. And these terms cannot be taken as handy human devices, as the correlates of 'know-how,' but must be regarded as the two faces of being themselves." Ibid., 121.
85 Ibid., 4.

go wrong: "the phenomenal reality of things for consciousness does not use up their being. The readiness-to hand of an entity is not exhaustively deployed in its presence-at-hand."[86] In other words, our awareness of the hitherto occluded nature of Being only takes place following a rupture of some kind.

This final point cannot be over-emphasized. For Harman, Heidegger's greatest accomplishment was to hybridize real objects (RO) with the sensual qualities of the object (SQ). Tool-being is nothing less than "the greatest moment in the philosophy of the past century: a thought experiment comparable in power to Plato's myth of the cave."[87] Essentially a crypto-pragmatic revision[88] of Husserlian *eidos* in which the thing-in-itself—the ubiquitous "tool"—is re-presented as the-thing-that-is-*for-something*, "Heidegger's theory of tools had proven that the hammer is irreducible to its effects on any wider system of things, as shown by the surprising breakdown that disrupts its current system of involvements."[89] It must be noted that the broken hammer does not cause the object to cease being a hammer because, if this were true, we would be empowered to re-impose a finality upon the non-exhaustive (withdrawn) essence of the object at hand. Ergo, the four poles of reality (SQ; SO; RQ; RO) are not isolated, but are "always locked in a duel with one another according to various permutations [...] The 'essence (or "reality") of objects never interface, [but] merely their secondary or accidental properties' do."[90]

Both axes are transversed in their entirety by both time and space, resulting in what might be called an ontology of tension (i.e., time, space, essence, *eidos*), yielding a potentially cataclysmic Being-as-Violence eternally threatened by the irruption of

---

86 Harman, *The Quadruple Object*, 39. Ian Bogost usefully expresses the inexhaustibility of the tool as "the hidden density of the unit." Bogost, *Alien Phenomenology*, 58.
87 Harman, *The Quadruple Object*, 37.
88 It should be noted that Harman robustly contests any neo-pragmatic reading of Heidegger. Harman, *Tool-Being*, 114–22.
89 Harman, *Circus Philosophicus*, 33.
90 Harman, *The Quadruple Object*, 123.

chaos.⁹¹ Just as with Lovecraft's metaphysically doomed somnambulists, "conscious awareness makes up only a tiny portion of our lives. For the most part, objects withdraw into a shadowy subterranean realm that supports our conscious activity while seldom erupting into view […]. For all entities tend to reside in a cryptic background rather than appearing before the mind."⁹²

Heideggerian real objects, as opposed to sensual objects, are wholly autonomous (unlike the Husserlian "sensuals" which are always to some degree ontologically dependent upon the presence of an observer⁹³), but, like the eidetic, are always at least partially hidden. We, as the collective bearers of self-awareness, invariably fail to notice — engage directly and authentically with the truth of the Thing — in the absence of the failure of *Zuhandenheit*. Speaking plainly, we take no notice of the hammer until it is broken, causing us to shift our concern from the quality to the essence or meaning of the hammer.⁹⁴

The difference between tool and broken tool is not between unconsciousness and consciousness, but between substance and relation. And if the world has to do with relation, then it is sheer presence-at-hand, no matter how invisible it might be. Heidegger's concept of the world belongs to *Vorhandenheit,* not *Zuhandenheit*.⁹⁵

---

91 Harman, *Immaterialism,* 95, 96, 102.
92 Harman, *The Quadruple Object,* 37. For a solid critique of Harman's neo-substantialism, see Shaviro, *The Universe of Things,* 27–44.
93 Due to the Husserlian requirement of the observer-dependent status of so, "aesthetics gives us a rift between real objects and their sensual qualities, a rift never made explicit in the normal course of everyday experience." Harman, *Object-Oriented Ontology,* 149.
94 Perhaps the absolutely simplest way of expressing this is: so long as we can (practically) use something we do not really think about it in any serious way. The Kantian thing-in-itself has been effectively supplanted by the Heideggerian thing-for-itself. This, of course, is the moment that Dasein — being-aware-of-one's-throwness-into-the-world — becomes wholly active, signified by the hegemony of angst. Harman, *Tool-Being,* 136. According to Morton, "Dasein is the being after the end of the world." Morton, *Hyperobjects,* 200.
95 Harman, *Tool-Being,* 126–27.

Breaking(!) with Husserl, Heidegger asserts that the real — which is at all times as equally inexhaustible or unbounded as the purely sensual — remains fully hidden, impervious to eidetic re-construction. For Heidegger, there is no final transparency, not even Husserl's operational one — of course, other than that of *alētheia* (un-covering), which is the apocalypse, after which nothing matters very much. But the shift from readiness-to-hand to presence-at-hand is erratic, unpredictable and rare. Contra Husserl, "the usual manner of things is not to appear as phenomena [that is, something noticeable and, therefore, in *some* sense transformative], but to withdraw into the unnoticed subterranean realm."[96] It must be noted that only Husserlian sensual qualities actually enter into relations — symbioses — with each other. The Heideggerian essence always remains hidden from view, resisting even the most robust of eidetic re-constructions.[97] Heidegger therefore triumphantly concludes that "the phenomenal reality of things for consciousness does not use up their being. The readiness-to-hand of an entity is not exhaustively deployed in its presence-at-hand."[98] Accordingly,

> Objects need not be natural, simple, or indestructible. Instead, objects will be defined only by their autonomous reality [i.e., those moments in time within which self-awareness remains un-activated]. They must be autonomous in two separate directions: emerging as something over and above their pieces [or constituent atomic parts], while also partly withholding themselves from relations with other entities [due to the incompatible natures of their respective essences].[99]

We can now discern the true post-humanist horror presented by OOO; whereas for classical humanism, the world can only be

---

96 Harman, *The Quadruple Object*, 38.
97 "When objects interact, they do so not from [their] depths but across their surfaces, in their sensual qualities." Bogost, *Alien Phenomenology*, 77.
98 Harman, *The Quadruple Object*, 39.
99 Ibid., 19.

human = human, for OOO, the true equation is objects = objects + people = objects + objects. "OOO uses the term 'object' to refer to any entity that cannot be paraphrased in terms of either its components or its effects,"[100] yielding a radically anti-reductive anti-literalism that makes it metaphysically, and discursively, impossible to privilege the conventionally human in any way.

For Harman, objects have been traditionally either ontologically over- or under-determined. Both the monistic and dualistic approaches implicitly rely upon some kind of variation of the Kantian thing-in-itself resulting in the neologism of *duomining*. Conventional systems of metaphysics engage in undermining ("only what is basic can be real"[101]) which, via reduction, imposes the impossibility of emergence. In contrast, overmining (i.e., essentialism, reification) renders impossible the becoming of the world: "objects are too specific to deserve the name of ultimate reality, and [philosophers] dream up some deeper indeterminable basis from which these specific things arise."[102] Duomining stands for the proposition that no "object can ever be successfully para-phrased [i.e., can never be spoken of literally precisely because each object possesses a surplus exceeding its relations, qualities and actions]."[103] Since any "transient process cannot occur without something [being] withheld from the process," a "truly object oriented ontology [tantamount in every regard to post-humanism] needs to be aware of relations between objects that have no direct involvement with people."[104]

---

100 Harman, *Immaterialism*, 3.
101 Harman, *The Quadruple Object*, 8.
102 Ibid., 10.
103 Harman, *Immaterialism*, 3–4.
104 Ibid., 6. One should take note of the close comparison operating between Harman's notion of the withdrawal of the object and Morton's concept of the hyper-object: "In a strange way every object is a hyperobject […] things that are massively distributed in time and space relative to humans." For both Morton and Harman, the issue is one of the irreducible status of the object: "Hyperobjects provoke irreductionist thinking, that is, they present us with scalar dilemmas in which ontotheological [i.e., teleological] statements about which thing is the most real (ecosystems, world,

The really big problem with all of this, of course, is the lingering presence of (neo-) Kantianism. As we have already seen, Kant managed to both dispense with God and to guarantee ontological, and epistemological, certainty by introducing pure reason through the backdoor in the place of God; the universe must ultimately be truly knowable, for to conclude otherwise would be to nullify the overriding imperative of the anthropocentric restoration. Man needs ultimate ontological certainty to exist as Man (species-being); ergo, finitude/exhaustibility is possible, although perhaps supremely difficult.[105] But, for Harman, OOO manages to circumvent this anthropocentric trap altogether: "[A]n entity qualifies as an object as long as it is irreducible both to its components and its effects: that is to say, as long as the object is not *exhausted* by undermining or overmining methods, though of course these methods often yield fruits of their own."[106] The key here is the irreducible relationality, or symbioses, of all objects, rendering the human wholly inter-exchangeable for the thing. Put in my own terms, I would suggest that what Harman is proposing is nothing other than a wholly horizontal version of what used to be known as the "Great Chain of Being." The "relationality of all objects to both people and (non-human) objects is in itself the true meaning of symbiosis," and all symbioses are either a-symmetrical and/or non-reciprocal.[107] As a result,

> What the model of symbiosis suggests is that both of the usual alternatives [to the problem of objects and attributes] are wrong: entities have neither an eternal character nor a

---

environment, or conversely individual) become impossible." Morton, *Hyperobjects*, 19. Size matters.

[105] "Modern philosophy simply exchanged God for human thought, without giving up the notion that one extra-important type of being was so vastly different from everything else that it deserved to occupy half of ontology. This modern taxonomy continues today in the work of leading European philosophers such as [Slavoj] Žižek, [Alain] Badiou, and [Quentin] Meillassoux." Harman, *Object-Oriented Ontology*, 256.

[106] Harman, *Circus Philosophicus*, 41.

[107] Ibid., 42–45, 120–22.

nominalistic flux of "performative" identities that shift and flicker with the flow of time itself. Instead, we should think of an object as going through several turning-points in its lifespan, but not many.[108]

We are left with an unstable world of both continuous evasion and irreducible uncertainty.

The Call of Quentin: The Sunken City of Correlationism

> The modern age begins with the idea of the infinity of the universe, and if we think that idea through to its end, we come to unreality, for infinity is nothing but a mathematically formulated expression for unreality. If one tries to imagine concretely that the Milky Way consists of more than a billion fixed stars, many of which have a diameter greater than the distance between the earth and the sun, and that the Milky Way does not form a source of tranquility in the cosmos, but is racing somewhere at a speed of 360 miles a second, i.e., about a thousand times as fast as a cannonball, then the assumption that this could have anything to do with reality is reduced to a mere mental game.
> — Hans-Jürgen Syberberg, *Hitler: A Film from Germany*[109]

> Philosophy is the invention of strange forms of argumentation, necessarily bordering on sophistry, which remains its dark structural double.
> — Meillassoux, *After Finitude*[110]

By now, the reader who is hip(?) to speculative realism should be asking herself why I am privileging Harman's notion of the quadruple object over Quentin Meillassoux's apparently more

---

108 Ibid., 47.
109 Hans-Jürgen Syberberg, *Hitler: A Film from Germany*, trans. Joachim Neugroschel (New York: Farrar, Strauss, & Giroux, 1982), 157–58.
110 Meillasoux, *After Finitude*, 76.

relevant notion of anti-correlationism when framing the problem of Cthulhu. Put in criminally brief terms, Meillasoux's *bête noire* is the lingering presence of correlationism,[111] which may be usefully defined in the following way:

> [The] central notion of modern philosophy since Kant seems to be that of correlation. By "correlation" we mean the idea according to which we only ever have access to the correlation between thinking and being, and never to either term considered apart from the other. We will henceforth call *correlationism* any current of thought which maintains the unsurpassable character of correlation so defined. Consequently, it becomes possible to say that every philosophy which disavows naïve realism has become a variant of correlationism.[112]

Meillassoux is able to conclude that, "one could say that up until Kant, one of the principal problems of philosophy was to think substance, while ever since Kant it has consisted in trying to think the correlation."[113]

There is a difficulty with what Meillassoux himself defines as the unresolved struggle between the physicalist Copernican Revolution and the philosophical (humanist?) Ptolemaic Reaction (or what I regard as the Anthropocentric Restoration). Post-Copernican astronomy and physics constitutes the irreversible de-centering of the post-hominids as the primary actors of Creation; the "world" can no longer be exclusively discussed within human terms of reference. Conversely, anti-correlationism — Meillassoux's preferred position — postulates that the thing-in-itself can be rendered knowable only to the

---

[111] "The verdict of modern philosophy since Descartes and Kant, whose ideas entail that we cannot speak of the world without humans or humans without the world, but only of a primordial correlation or rapport between the two." Harman, *Object-Oriented Ontology*, 56.

[112] Quentin Meillassoux, *After Finitude: An Essay on the Necessity of Contingency*, trans. Ray Brassier (London: Continuum, 2008), 5.

[113] Ibid., 6.

degree that it can be translated/expressed within purely mathematical terms: "*all those aspects of the object that can be formulated in mathematical terms can be meaningfully achieved as properties of the object itself.*"[114] Conversely, the Ptolemaic Reaction, which paradoxically historically co-evolved with the Copernican Revolution, perpetuates the (sophistic?) reassertion of humankind via the epistemological double game (bad faith) of correlationism. Any world is meaningful only to the degree that it is given-to-a-living (-or-thinking) being.[115]

Correlationism consists in disqualifying the claim that it is possible to consider the realms of subjectivity and objectivity independently of one another. Not only does it become necessary to insist that we never grasp an object "in itself," in isolation from its relation to the subject, but it is also becomes necessary to maintain that we can never grasp a subject that would not always already be related to an object.[116]

All "those aspects of the object that can give rise to a mathematical thought (to a formula or to digitalization) rather than to a perception or sensation can be meaningfully turned into properties of the thing not only as it is with me, but also as it is without me."[117] The equation of the unknowable with the radically contingent underscores the metaphysical confinement of both the Husserlian *eidos* and the Heideggerian real.

> The thesis that we are defending is two-fold: on the one hand, we acknowledge that the sensible [world] only exists as a subject's [human's] relation to the world; but, on the other hand, we maintain that the mathematizable properties of the object are exempt from the constraint of such a relation, and that they are effectively in [within] the object in the way in which I conceive them, whether I am in relation with the object or not.[118]

---

114 Ibid., 3. Emphasis in the original.
115 Ibid., 5, 112–28, 135–36.
116 Ibid., 5.
117 Ibid., 3.
118 Ibid., 3.

Because only mathematics allows for the true expression of that which exceeds the perceptive (phenomenological) field of the anthropocentric realm, it follows that chaos is the only true thing-in-itself.[119] Being constitutes an irreducible unreason (or, alternatively, a *hyper-Chaos*) by default of the absence of physical necessity — or any other thing that would permit correlationism to operate, which would be any object/event/thing that would be capable of exhaustive definition minus mathematization. What is mathematizable cannot be reduced to a correlation of thought; ergo, "*whatever is mathematically conceivable is absolutely possible.*"[120]

From this it follows, quite incredibly, that "our absolute, in effect, is nothing other than an extreme form of chaos, a hyper-Chaos, for which nothing is or would seem to be impossible, not even the unthinkable."[121] Hence, unreason is nothing other than the absence of necessity within the physical world (of objects). Unreason should not be misunderstood as the principle or thing that guarantees the ontology of reality (conventionally associated with both reason and necessity), but is, rather, itself the (absolute) condition of (absolute) contingent givenness: the de-totalization of the universe as the remainder of an irreducible contingency. Expressed positively, unreason is nothing other than a purely mathematizable post-humanity — "a world that is separable from man"[122] — and is founded upon an unconditional and irreducible contingency within which anything that is mathematically conceivable is physically possible,[123] which effectively demolishes the necessity of the sufficiency of reason. Meillassoux concludes, "[s]o the challenge is therefore the following: to understand how *science can think a world wherein spatio-temporal givenness itself came into being within a time and space which preceded every unity of givenness*"[124] — that is,

---

119 Ibid., 111.
120 Ibid., 117. Emphasis in the original.
121 Ibid., 64.
122 Ibid., 115.
123 Ibid., 111.
124 Ibid., 22.

a world temporally prior to the emergence of a (self-aware) observer.[125]

Contrary to first impressions, the true icon of Meillassoux's anti-correlationism is not Ptolemy or Copernicus, but Charles Darwin (1809–1882), along with the equally revolutionary geologist Charles Lyell (1797–1875). Apart from placing pure randomness at the living heart of the evolution of life, Darwin's most subversive idea was to re-set the biological clock from historical time to geological deep time. Genesis was no longer correlative with the emergence of humans, in radical contrast to Bishop Usher's anthropocentric dating of Genesis to October 22, 4004 BCE, but occurred in a series of eon-length stages: 13.5 billion years for the universe, 4.56 billion years for the accretion of the Earth, 3.5 billion years for the emergence of terrestrial (microbial) life, and a cosmically laughable two million years for the emergence of the very earliest form of humans (*Homo habilis*).[126] Meillassoux tells us,

> Empirical science is today capable of producing statements about events anterior to the advent of life as well as consciousness […] How are we to grasp the meaning of scientific statements bearing explicitly upon a manifestation of the world that is posited as anterior to the emergence of thought and even of life — *posited, that is, as the anterior to every form of human relation to the world?* Or, to put it more precisely: how are we to think the meaning of a discourse which construes the relation to the world — that of thinking and/or living — as a fact inscribed in a temporality within which this

---

125 Emphasis in the original. Dylan Trigg offers an interesting critique of Meillassoux on this point by offering up a neo-phenomenological reading of Schelling's notion of "wild being": the co-existence of Being with a barbaric variant of flesh. In this sense, the universe has never been without an observer of some kind. See Dylan Trigg, *The Thing: A Phenomenology of Horror* (Winchester: Zero Books, 2014), 103–32. The same point can be made in relation to pan-psychism: mind and the universe co-evolved in tandem. Shaviro, *The Universe of Things,* 85–107.

126 Meillassoux, *After Finitude,* 9.

relation is just one event among others, inscribed in an order of succession in which it is merely a stage, rather than an origin? How is science able to think such statements, and in what sense can we eventually ascribe truth to them?[127]

Essence (temporality) precedes existence (biological life). The de-humanizing/de-totalizing quanta of inhuman time undermines correlationism, leaving us with the sole comfort of awareness of the, potential but ultimately exhaustible, mathematization of phenomena. This in turn, yields two of Meillassoux's signature concepts, *ancestrality* and the arche-*fossil*. Ancestrality, or the ancestral, is a "reality anterior to the emergence of the human species,"[128] while the arche-fossil denotes all "materials indicating the existence of an ancestral reality or event; one that is anterior to terrestrial life."[129]

The cosmic payoff, if I can put it like that, is eternal and absolute non-negotiable contingency: "[i]f the ancestral is to be thinkable, then an absolute must be thinkable."[130] The resolution of what is nothing short of a metaphysical crisis following the publications of Lyell's *Principles of Geology* (1830–1833) and Darwin's *The Origin of Species by Natural Selection* (1859) demands nothing less than the unconditional capitulation to post-human mathematical discourse.[131] So the obvious question now becomes: why not Cthulhu as arche-fossil, the master-sign of ancestrality, rather than as the quadruple object?

I have two objections to this maneuver. The second and lengthier one is discussed in the final section below. The first one is concerned with Cthulhu as a specifically aesthetic phenomenon, precisely in the sense of what Harman means by the sensual object. Although clearly "real, Cthulhu always operates as an 'intermediate' object through dreams and globally telepathic apocalyptic visions; his very first manifestation is through the

---

127 Ibid., 10. Emphasis in the original.
128 Ibid.
129 Ibid.
130 Ibid., 51.
131 Ibid., 111.

form of a statue."[132] The "Call" of Cthulhu understood exclusively in terms of an aesthetic phenomenon is directly suggestive of Harman's notion of allure or vicarious causation: "*Allure* means that one object calls to another from a vast distance […] In this indirect and asymmetrical way, Harman says, 'two objects […] touch without touching.'"[133] In other words, the Great Cthulhu constitutes a singular example of what we might call the ineffectual sublime.

"Finally Job cried out": Religion as Horror

> I form the light and create darkness; I make peace and create evil; I the UNNAMEABLE do all these things.
> — 2 Isaiah 45:7[134]

> After He [the unnameable] had spoken to Job, the Lord said to Elipha the Temanite, "I am very angry at you and your two friends, because you have not spoken the truth about me, as my servant Job has."
> — Job 42:7[135]

A flat ontology is one in which "humans are no longer monarchs of being, but are instead *among* beings, *entangled* in beings, and *implicated* in other beings."[136] Strikingly, this is the primary subtext of what is arguably the single most subversive text, at least from the perspective of theodicy, of the Old Testament, the Book of Job. The eponymous hero, having been reduced to the level of the absolutely abject, calls upon God, the Unname-

---

132 Harman, *The Quadruple Object*, 30.
133 Shaviro, *The Universe of Things*, 138.
134 Stephen Mitchell, "Introduction," in *The Book of Job*, trans. Stephen Mitchell (New York: Harper Perennial, 1987), xxiv.
135 Ibid., 91.
136 Levi Bryant, cited in Bogost, *Alien Phenomenology*, 17. Emphases in the original.

able, to un-create a single moment in the seamless "continuum of nature"[137] — the day of his birth.

Finally Job cried out:

> God damn the day I was born
> and the night that forced me from the womb.
> On that day — let there be darkness;
> let it never have been created;
> let it sink back into the void
> [...] let its dawn never arrive.[138]

The theodicy of Job is far more radical than commonly assumed — far more than a mere exercise of a benevolent will "that surpasseth all understanding," God's reply from the whirlwind (*tsunami*) is nothing less than a disquisition upon the impossibility of non-existence. The truly horrific message of the text is that the only real Evil — the absolute un-speakable to the utterly un-nameable — is un-being. The Being of God is identical to the plenary of Creation, a perfect continuum. Herein, any evil is unconditionally superior to non-existence. The problem, of course, is that a radically free (contingent) and wholly omnipotent God may be considered as nothing other than a slightly more developed version of the *mysterium tremendum,* an unbounded and chaotic entity that brings the abject, or creature consciousness, in its wake. The Book of Job contains within it a primitive discussion of the theological problem of radical voluntarism. The goodness of God is identical with the absolute nature of His freedom, the true *summum bonum,* as opposed to the specific moral outcome flowing from the exercise of providential will. Creation itself is the direct result of, and unconditionally dependent upon, God's will-to-create which is unbounded by human criteria. Therefore, the successive states of Job — blessed/cursed — are all equally good because what underlies both of them, and draws them together, is the limitless

---

137 Mitchell, "Introduction," xxiv.
138 Mitchell, trans., *The Book of Job,* 13.

operation of God's will within both. The Unnameable's consent to Job's request for the un-creation of the day of his birth would introduce an unassimilable element of difference into the symbiotic pluriverse of ontological objects, a gross violation of the radical democracy of OOO, and of flat ontology more generally, as "all relations are on exactly the same footing";[139] "the world is jam-packed with entities; there is no room for 'nothingness' in ontology."[140]

The argument that an absolutely free God could be objectively un-just is premised upon a false analogy between the categories of contingency and necessity, which, quite amazingly, corresponds closely to Meillassoux's notion of hyper-Chaos. Both Good and Evil are necessary attributes of Being which is the absolute and, therefore, the true Good — the unmediated emanation of an unlimited God: "we can say that it is possible to *demonstrate the absolute necessity of everything's non-necessity*. In other words, it is possible to establish [...] the absolute necessity of the contingency of everything."[141] His atheism notwithstanding, Meillassoux's language and imaginary are clearly evocative of the *mysterium tremendum* of post-theological Unreason:

> We have succeeded in identifying a primary absolute (Chaos), but contrary to the veracious God, the former would seem to be incapable of guaranteeing the absoluteness of scientific discourse, since, far from guaranteeing order, it guarantees only the possible destruction of every order [...]. We see an omnipotence equal to that of the Cartesian God, and capable of anything, even the inconceivable, but an omnipotence that has become autonomous, without norms, blind,

---

139 Harman, *The Quadruple Object*, 46.
140 Harman, *Tool-Being*, 11.
141 Meillassoux, *After Finitude*, 62. Emphasis in the original. Contra Arendt, to put this in the most powerful manner possible — and, therefore, the most obnoxious manner possible — we would say: every day in Auschwitz was a good day because it was a day. The possibility that the ontological good may be incommensurable with the moral good does not, by itself, signify either a defect or a contradiction in the goodness of God.

devoid of other divine perfections, a power with neither goodness nor wisdom, ill-dispossessed to reassure thought about the veracity of its distinct ideas.[142]

This sounds remarkably Job-like. In terms of a radical theodicy, the absolute necessity of everything's non-necessity is, from the anthropocentric perspective, virtually indistinguishable from the most extreme form of providential voluntarism conceivable: the freedom of God that supersedes the ethical. And this, in turn, paves the way for the return to some form of fideism, to which Meillassoux himself admits:

> So long as we believe that there must be a reason why what is, is the way it is, we will continue to fuel superstition, which is to say, the belief that there is an ineffable reason underlying all things. Since we will never be able to understand such a reason, all we can do is believe in it, or aspire to believe in it. So long as we construe our access to facticity in terms of thought's discovery of its own intrinsic limits and of its inability to uncover the ultimate reason of things, our abolition of metaphysics will only have served to resuscitate religiosity in all its forms, including the most menacing ones. So long as we construe facticity as a limit for thought, we will abandon whatever lies beyond this limit to the rule of piety.[143]

So, to return to my original question, why should I prefer Harman to Meillassoux?

Simply put, the latter is too much of a neo-Cartesian to qualify as a truly apocalyptic thinker. His focus is upon finitude, not *Destruktion*; the exact opposite is the case with Heidegger, whose overriding concern is with *alētheia,* or annihilating revelation. *Zuhandenheit* is a violent and objective rupturing within space-time, whereas the arche-fossil, no matter how metaphysically impressive, remains an artefact of the objective limitations

---

142 Ibid., 64.
143 Ibid., 82.

of consciousness, pursuant to the precepts of anti-correlationism. In contrast, OOO, like Cthulhu itself, is radically inactive: the irreducible inconsequentiality of the revelation/*alētheia* is itself the non-contingent element of contingency. Nothingness never happens. I would go so far as to argue that "The Call of Cthulhu" actually operates as a literary parable of OOO, whose moral is that an anthropocentric universe is one that is ontologically exhausted by readiness-at-hand. Harman counters Meillassoux's arche-fossil with OOO's post-humanistic equation of relationality to object + object. There may not always have been humans but, by definition, objects, of whatever kind, are co-determinate with the universe. Therefore, at no time has reality been superseded by that which can be exhaustively conveyed through the purely mathematical — that is, if two objects interacting with each other is the exact same flat ontological event as two humans interacting with each other, then at no point, in time, has reality not existed. Human/human, human/object, object/human symbioses are merely comparatively recent relationalities of a more primordial state of ancestrality.

As we have already seen, according to Harman, the basic principles of OOO include, but are not restricted to: "All objects must be given equal attention, whether they be human, non-human, natural, cultural, real or fictional"; "[o]bjects are not identical with their properties, but have a tense relationship with those properties, and this very tension is responsible for all of the change that occurs in the world"; "[o]bjects come in just two kinds: *real objects* exist whether or not they currently affect anything else, while *sensual objects* exist only in relation to some real object"; and, vitally, that real objects "cannot relate to one another directly, but only indirectly, by means of a sensual object."[144]

Two things immediately become apparent. First is that Harman's real object uncannily resembles the irrational real of Otto — the formless thing/object that, in its aggregate form, is the sum total of everything yet is itself devoid of properties, ei-

---

144 Harman, *Object-Oriented Ontology*, 9.

ther as attribute or as affect. The efficacy of the real object, in both its phenomenological and non-phenomenological sense(s) is ultimately dependent upon an almost secondary operational plane of sensual objects as mediated by and through aesthetic perception and sensation.

Second, the experience of the real (object) is not only eternally deferred, it is also supersaturated with affectivity. The phenomenological essence of both *mysterium* and *tremendum* is not the Being of the Wholly Other but its affective capacity to instill an aesthetic response of unique and exceptional power within the beholder, or supplicant. Here, the Monster-Gods, or the "Ancient Ones," may best be understood as highly elastic names given to states of altered consciousness rather than as the proper denotation of an actual being. That which we name as God is not the real object that causes *tremendum*; rather, that which causes us to experience *mysterium* is the sensual object that we call God.

By means of the back door of ooo, we return to the dual site of the horrible and the humorous, each incarnated magnificently in Lovecraft's Great Cthulhu: an unapproachable real object that acts in no other way than through the endless multiplication of the aesthetic effects of fascination and dread and whose appearance, and almost immediate withdrawal back into the subterranean/submarine, heralds the non-event of the eternally postponed return of the Ancient Ones, which, in terms of ooo is nothing other than the subsumption of Being (-within-the-World) under the real object, the inarticulable condition of the absolute suspension of the possibility of mediation. In the end, Cthulhu is nothing more than a numinously real object that never actually happens but exists only through an endless series of witness testimonies — an infinite proliferation of narrative Chinese boxes — each a separate tale told by an increasingly unreliable, but wholly fascinated, narrator.

For this very reason, ooo encapsulates, in a manner superior to any other variant of speculative realism, the central aesthetic paradox of the "weird tale": the structural correspondence between horror and the joke — in this case, the practical joke operating on a literally cosmic scale. Horror is always a sublime form of comedy because the signifier of the Wholly Other is invariably shown up as an empty sign — the substitution of a sensual object for a real object. A close comparative reading between Otto and Harman, by way of Lovecraft, becomes a highly fruitful way of conceptualizing an under-appreciated relationship between horror literature and speculative realism.

Since knowledge cannot be metaphorical, for this is the realm of both aesthetics and *philosophia,* it must be literal, which means that it must be a question of articulating the qualities or effects of an object in an overmining/undermining fashion. And since knowledge cannot be truth, which would imply an impossible direct revelation of the world, it needs to have some sort of contact with reality, though not contact of a direct sort, which we have seen to be impossible (incompatible essences). But unlike in aesthetics, the point of knowledge is not to experience the unknowable uniqueness of the real object, but to obtain some sort of partial grasp of the features of a sensual object that is already in our midst. This means that whereas aesthetics brought *real objects* into play, knowledge must somehow bring real qualities into the picture (*Ereignis*).[145]

Cthulhu is nothing other than the allure of the quadruple object. The call is constantly emitted — the sensual object embedded within a potentially infinite expanse of, decidedly asymmetrical, symbioses — yet the substance of the world remains unaltered. The horror of Cthulhu is itself the primacy of the aesthetic nature, and effect, of the world, all of which evidences that we have not truly exited from the *mysterium tremendum.* We have simply substituted a new idol for an old. The horror of Cthulhu is not the aesthetics of horror but the horror of aesthetics.

---

145 Ibid., 170.

Bibliography

Airaksinen, Timo. The *Philosophy of H.P. Lovecraft: The Route to Horror*. New York: Peter Lang, 1985.

Beal, Timothy K. *Religion and Its Monsters*. New York: Routledge, 2002.

Bogost, Ian. *Alien Phenomenology, Or What It's Like to Be a Thing*. Minneapolis: University of Minnesota Press, 2012.

Burleson, Donald R. *Lovecraft: Disturbing the Universe*. Lexington: University Press of Kentucky, 2009.

Cardin, Matt. *Dark Awakenings*. Poplar Bluff: Mythos Books, 2010.

Derrida, Jacques. *The Truth in Painting*. Translated by Geoff Bennington and Ian McLeod. Chicago: University of Chicago Press, 1987.

Dupuy, Jean-Pierre. *The Mark of the Sacred*. Translated by M.B. DeBevoise. Stanford: Stanford University Press, 2013.

———. *A Short Treatise on the Metaphysics of Tsunamis*. Translated M.B. DeBevoise. East Lansing: Michigan State University Press, 2015.

Harman, Graham. *Circus Philosophicus*. Winchester: Zero Books, 2010.

———. *Immaterialism: Objects and Social Theory*. Cambridge: Polity, 2016.

———. *Object-Oriented Ontology: A New Theory of Everything*. London: Pelican Books, 2018.

———. *The Quadruple Object*. Winchester: Zero Books, 2011.

———. *Tool-Being: Heidegger and the Metaphysics of Objects*. Chicago: Open Court, 2002.

———. *Weird Realism: Lovecraft and Philosophy*. Winchester: Zero Books, 2012.

Houellebecq, Michel, *H.P. Lovecraft: Against the World, Against Life*. London: Weidenfeld & Nicolson, 2006.

Joshi, S.T. "Introduction," in *The Thing on the Doorstep and Other Weird Stories*, edited by S.T. Joshi, vii–xvi. London: Penguin Books, 2001.

Kant, Immanuel. *The Critique of Judgment.* Translated by J.H. Bernard. Amherst: Prometheus Books, 2000.

King, Stephen. *Danse Macabre.* New York: Gallery Books, 2010.

Lacan, Jacques. *The Triumph of Religion Preceded by Discourse to Catholics.* Translated by Bruce Fink. Cambridge: Polity Press, 2013.

Levy, Maurice. *Lovecraft: A Study in the Fantastic.* Translated by S.T. Joshi. Detroit: Wayne State University, 1988.

Lovecraft, H.P. "The Call of Cthulhu." In Michel Houellebecq, *H.P. Lovecraft: Against the World, Against Life,* 145–57. London: Weidenfeld & Nicolson, 2006.

———. "The Dunwich Horror." In *The Thing on the Doorstep and Other Weird Stories,* edited by S.T. Joshi, 206–45. London: Penguin Classics, 2001.

———. "Facts Concerning the Late Arthur Jermyn and His Family." In *The Call of Cthulhu and Other Weird Stories,* edited by S.T. Joshi. London: Penguin Classics, 2011.

———. "Supernatural Horror in Literature." In *At The Mountains of Madness: The Definitive Edition,* 103–73. New York: The Modern Library, 2005.

Martin, Sean Elliot. *H.P. Lovecraft and the Modernist Grotesque.* Printed by the author, 2008.

Meillassoux, Quentin. *After Finitude: An Essay on the Necessity of Contingency.* Translated by Ray Brassier. London: Continuum, 2008.

Miéville, China. "Introduction." In *At the Mountains of Madness: The Definitive Edition,* xiii. New York: The Modern Library, 2005.

Mitchell, Stephen. "Introduction." In *The Book of Job,* translated by Stephen Mitchell. New York: Harper Perennial, 1987.

———, trans. *The Book of Job.* New York: Harper Perennial, 1987.

Morton, Timothy. *Hyperobjects: Philosophy and Ecology After the End of the World.* Minneapolis: University of Minnesota Press, 2013.

Nieman, Susan. *Evil in Modern Thought: An Alternative History of Philosophy.* Melbourne: Scribe Publishers, 2002.

Neylan, Fintan. "The Labour of the Pessimist: Detecting Expiration's Artifice." In *True Detection,* edited by Edia Connole, Paul J. Ennis, and Nicola Masciandaro, 76–95. San Bernardino: Schism Press, 2014.

Otto, Rudolf. *The Idea of the Holy: An Inquiry into the Non-Rational Factor in the Idea of the Divine and its Relation to the Rational.* Translated by John W. Harvey. Oxford: Oxford University Press, 1958.

Ralickas, Vivian. "Cosmic Horror: and the Question of the Sublime in Lovecraft." *Journal of the Fantastic in the Arts* 18, no. 3 (2007): 364–98.

Shaviro, Steven. *The Universe of Things: On Speculative Realism.* Minneapolis: University of Minnesota Press, 2014.

Smith, Daniel W. "Translator's Introduction: Deleuze on Bacon: Three Conceptual Trajectories in The Logic of Sensation." In *Francis Bacon: The Logic of Sensation,* translated by Daniel W. Smith, vii–xxvii. Minneapolis: University of Minnesota Press, 2003.

Syberberg, Hans-Jürgen. *Hitler: A Film from Germany.* Translated by Joachim Neugroschel. New York: Farrar, Strauss & Giroux, 1982.

Thacker, Eugene. *In the Dust of This Planet: Horror of Philosophy, Volume I.* Winchester: Zero Books, 2011.

Trigg, Dylan. *The Thing: A Phenomenology of Horror.* Winchester: Zero Books, 2014.

Wilson, Eric. *The Republic of Cthulhu: Lovecraft, the Weird Tale, and Conspiracy Theory.* Earth: punctum books, 2016.

13

Reproducing It: Speculative Horror and the Limits of the Inhuman

John Cunningham

Horror Itself. — As for the sphere of thought, it is horror. Yes, it is horror itself.[1]

Shattered Form. — It is surprising that the fragmentary, those troubled and troubling pieces of the whole, do not dominate the cinematic and literary forms that speculative horror can assume. This is because of the gap that horror establishes between itself and thought, knowledge and representation. The realization and recognition of it ought to shatter form.

Dread Glimpses. — Much genre horror cleaves to classic narratives and easily representable tropes such as anthropomorphic monsters, the old dark house, and other invariants of the horror genre in order to both hint at the unthinkable and resolve it. A less easy resolution is found in what Michel Houellebecq has

---

1 Georges Bataille, *The Unfinished System of Nonknowledge,* ed. Stuart Kendall, trans. Michelle Kendall and Stuart Kendall (Minneapolis: University of Minnesota Press, 2001), 196.

termed the "great texts" of Howard Phillips Lovecraft, inaugurated with The *Call of Cthulhu* in 1926.[2] Lovecraft lays out the form toward the beginning of his account of cosmic horror:

> [T]here came the single glimpse of forbidden aeons which chills me when I think of it and maddens me when I dream of it. That glimpse, like all dread glimpses of truth, flashed out from an accidental piecing together of separated things — in this case an old newspaper item and the notes of a dead professor.[3]

The notes of that particular dead professor include: the ramblings of a decadent aesthete; the report of a police inspector; newspaper clippings documenting suicides and madness; an anecdotal account of a chance encounter with an Eskimo death cult; the notes of a dead Norwegian sailor. Dread truths inhere in the mess of contingent materials. All ultimately cohere for the narrator in the pure contingency of a newspaper scrap found spread beneath mineral specimens in a museum.

Quotidian Cosmos. — The form of the narrative, a montage of fragmented recollections, suggests that "dread glimpses" of cosmic horror lurk in the interstices of quotidian life as much as in the totalized striving of science and philosophy. Knowledge and its limit, "dread glimpses," seep through crumpled newspaper. Lovecraft, in pulp modernist mode, discerns how horror accumulates in formal dispersion, unhinging attempts to collate it into a coherent image or narrative.

Ruined Constellation. — Much theoretical exposition of horror in thought forgets this aspect in favor of an architecture of the concept rather than the ruin of such "dread glimpses."

---

[2] Michel Houellebecq, *H.P. Lovecraft: Against the World, Against Life* (London: Weidenfeld & Nicolson, 2006), 41.

[3] H.P. Lovecraft, "The Call of Cthulhu," *The H.P. Lovecraft Archive*, 1926, http://www.hplovecraft.com/writings/texts/fiction/cc.aspx.

Speculative horror ought to accumulate as the slow explosion of such (in)coherence.

It is often the conjunction of thought and horror aesthetics, or rather, the elision of thought and the horror genre, that blurs the supposedly immutable boundaries between them.

The following is a constellation of fragmentary concepts and images that attempt to sketch some of these possibilities and contradictions, as well as the limits that might cleave to a conjunction of the aesthetics of horror and speculative thought. Or, perhaps, the limits that lie unseen in the formulation of *it* in speculative horror.

The Horror of It. — In Lovecraft's *The Shadow Out of Time,* the central protagonist declaims: "And yet, its realism was so hideous that I sometimes find hope impossible."[4] The awful realism of "it," in this case, dreams of inhuman and utterly alien realities, opens up a vista of hopelessness and dread. The dread of "it" seems best thought of as epistemological, an opening up of the gap between human knowledge and the "real" of the inhuman. Speculative horror dwells in the affective, aesthetic, and conceptual possibilities opened up by this gap, as evidenced through the cosmic terrors of Lovecraft, the eerie mannequins of Thomas Ligotti, the more corporeal terror of apocalyptic zombie cinema. Horror is the inhuman.

Inhuman Negativity (1). — Yet, what is the inhuman? The prefix "in" denotes that which is not, that which is against, but also that which is inside. The negativity of the not human and the against the human is most pertinent to the inextricable intertwining of horror and the inhuman. "It" is then not solely a question of epistemology. The negativity of the not human, the imputed negation of the human, is also virulently active through the in-

---

4 H.P. Lovecraft, "The Shadow Out of Time," *The H.P. Lovecraft Archive,* 1934, http://www.hplovecraft.com/writings/texts/fiction/sot.aspx.

vocation of "it." The inhuman, at least under the aegis of horror, is also anti-human.

Horror Gaze. — Secular hope is an all too human faith reliant upon visions of progress, technical mastery, scientific knowledge, and human agency. Horror, the dissolution of hope, has a gaze that empties all of these categories of meaning, summoning in their place "it" as contingent, violent, hostile, or just indifferent.

This horror gaze is the fictive undoing of anthropocentric knowledge through the emblematic conjuration and exploration of dread through zombies, cosmic terror, and formless monstrosities. The aesthetics of horror is a conjuration with the unthinkable. The collapse of knowledge into worm holes of slithering materiality, abstract nihilism, the sudden apparition of the falsity of the known world. Images that seek to freeze thought and by extension freeze speculation.

Warped Fairground Mirrors. — A fictive undoing of knowledge also pushes horror into the space of speculation. The grotesque, sometimes ridiculous reflection of worldly dread in the warped, fairground mirrors of the horror genre might, as a negative image of knowledge, allow access to a speculative rendering of the aspects of the world that are usually unspoken, unseen. The kaleidoscope of dreadful images, textual or cinematic, that constitute the horror genre can then provide a resource for philosophical speculation.

Kant Zombie Mask. — This could just be a taste for horror, that I share, a way to stylistically mark out a new territory against more polite usages of culture, the mobilization of the bad taste of a genre often dismissed as abject slapstick. Wearing a zombie mask while citing Kant.

Abyssal Thing/Mind. — Trenchant disruption of what Quentin Meillassoux terms the "correlationist" consensus has been central to the exposition of much recent speculative horror. Correlationism is the thesis that an irreducible gap exists between thought and being. The-Thing-In-Itself, Immanuel Kant's intimation of the improbable, inhuman entities and qualities that reside beyond human cognition and knowledge, is never fully graspable, always collapsing back into the abyss between thing and mind. Speculation suggests for Meillassoux, and speculative realist infused thought more broadly, a break with correlationism that can lead thought to the (im)possibilities that swirl beyond the limits of the human. The affinities between this and the "it" of horror are undeniable.[5]

The Wager of "It." — Speculative thought becomes a spiralling of the head in a horror gaze, multiple eyes, inhuman light refracted from innumerable spaces and angles. The wager of such a speculative horror is that, through this distorted prism, conceptual images of the inhuman might emerge. The weirded flatness of phenomenological objects, humanity only one among many; the base materiality of abject substances; the profane mystical nothingness glimpsed through inhuman indifference; the inhuman drives of life, abstraction and cosmic death.

Such conceptual images are the hybrid product of philosophical speculation and the aesthetics of horror.

Inhuman Fidelity. — Epistemological dread is central to the fecund relation between speculative horror and speculative thought drawn to the avatars of "it". While they are not homogenous, what speculative realism, eliminative materialism, and object-oriented thought all share is a fidelity to "it," the inhuman "real." Fidelity is not too strong a term since one of the few binding elements in such speculative thought is the desire to conceptualize the different iterations of "it."

---

5   Quentin Meillassoux, *After Finitude: An Essay on the Necessity of Contingency,* trans. Ray Brassier (London: Continuum, 2008).

Formless Mass. — Inchoate materials bubbling with indifference and occasional (or frequent) malignity to the human. This formless mass would undoubtedly contain Graham Harman's non-anthropocentric ontology of Lovecraftian objects that withdraw and hide from full exposure to cognition and knowledge; the slime ontologies of Ben Woodard dripping with disease; the inhuman bio-horror of life and the subtle, negative mysticism of Eugene Thacker. Perhaps, at the core of the formlessness of "it" are the dark energetics of the death drive itself factored through an eliminative cosmos, as elaborated by Ray Brassier.

Generic Inhuman. — It would be preferable to allow the conceptual images of "it" emergent in speculative horror to retain a certain formlessness. This is not to pursue the Kantian path of relative moderation or to step back from Lovecraftian hopelessness and insanity. It is more that the primacy of "it" as a generic category has more salience than the forms "it" actually manifests.

"It" is as much an aesthetic sensibility active in thought as it is the unveiling of some inhuman truth-content. Horror is the filter through which the inhuman is allowed to take shape as a conceptual image.

Inhuman Negativity (2). — "It" has more facets than an epistemological gap between thought and being or the wonders revealed through a speculative real when affixed to horror. Real horror as an affect and sensation of dread, anxiety, and terror, is something deeply inimical to the human.

"It" — and it is usually an *It* — is what undoes the carefully delimited parameters of the human subject as rational, possessed of autonomy, the owner, so to speak, of certain properties. This visceral, affective, and bodily sense of horror can be traced back to the Latin verb *horrēre,* meaning the moment when the hairs on the body stand on end in response to fear and revulsion.

Rationality evacuated and autonomy replaced by the automatism of life reduced to a shudder. The human dethroned into the shape of a fragile creature through the auspices of "it."

A Negative Sublime. — The mutual infusion of thought with horror and vice versa opens up the temptation and pleasure of what might be termed a negative sublime formulated around the conceptual image of the inhuman. The sublime is one of the prime clichés of aesthetic theory, exhausted but inexhaustible, a phantasmagoria of the immensely epic and the grotesquely dynamic. The sublime, as formulated by Immanuel Kant, is the expression of the inhuman, whether as cosmos, nature, or disaster, whether it takes the mathematical form of ever-increasing magnitude or the dynamic one of incredible force. As such, the sublime is always potentially inimical to humanity, underscoring how "a countless multitude of worlds annihilates, as it were, my importance as an animal creature."[6] It seems that Kant also experienced *horrēre* and was reduced to a less than human state.

Deadly Light. — Horror and its twin, the inhuman, are imbued with the sublime:

The most merciful thing in the world, I think, is the inability of the human mind to correlate all its contents. We live on a placid island of ignorance in the midst of black seas of infinity, and it was not meant that we should voyage far. The sciences, each straining in its own direction, have hitherto harmed us little; but some day the piecing together of dissociated knowledge will open up such terrifying vistas of reality, and of our frightful position therein, that we shall either go mad from the revelation or flee from the deadly light into the peace and safety of a new dark age.[7]

---

6   Immanuel Kant, *Critique of Practical Reason,* trans. Lewis White Beck (New York: Palgrave Macmillan, 1956), 166.
7   Lovecraft, "The Call of Cthulhu."

It is as though this oft quoted opening passage from H.P. Lovecraft's 1926 novella, *The Call of Cthulhu*, is a reply to Kant, though this is a reply that is immersed in the *negative* aspects of the sublime, a reply all too aware of the inhuman correlates that constitute it. Kant, with typical circumspection, emphasises that this sense of being overwhelmed, even horrified, alternates with those sterling qualities that "raise the soul's fortitude above its usual middle range" and the comforting realization that reason and human freedom have more magnitude and dynamism than the sublime phenomena.[8]

Lovecraft, with his own nihilist conviction concerning the inimical aspects of the sublime inhuman, would undoubtedly disagree.

Transcendental Subtraction. — In Kant's formulation, the sublime is an aesthetic category imbricated with both pleasure and fear, intimate to the sudden diminution of humanity and a simultaneous sense of elevation. The sublime in speculative horror shares some of this but often has the added supplement of a subtraction, or even a negation, of the human. Possibly, as with much of the sublime, there is even a pleasure in this.

The negativity of "it" is often formulated through a transcendental sublime. Lovecraft's messy montages resolve into a mythos of cosmic apocalypse. "It" ultimately suggests an indifferent, inhuman, order that cannot be fully understood on anthropocentric terms, let alone opposed or engaged. For all the slime, tentacles, and formlessness, the emblems of speculative horror often retain the quality of being abstracted from the world. It is little wonder "it" attracts philosophers.

The "world-without-us." — What Eugene Thacker succinctly terms the "world-without-us" is "the subtraction of the hu-

---

8   Immanuel Kant, *Critique of Judgement,* trans. Werner S. Pluhar (Indianapolis: Hackett Publishing Company, 1987), 120.

man from the world."[9] "It" is an extinctive, inhuman, indifferent "Planet" that Thacker posits can be apprehended through horror. A conceptual image of dread indifference, the "world-without-us" is imbued with the transcendental form of the negative sublime bequeathed by Lovecraft. The conceptual image of the "Planet" necessarily does away with any mediation for the destruction of humanity, save the indifference of the cosmos. Undoubtedly there is a truth content to this, but it also risks simply *reflecting* the real horrors of the present as catastrophe rather than speculating upon them through horror from tendencies in the present.

Starry Wisdom Cult. — The reproduction of "it" as a conceptual image can on occasion be the repetition of the inhuman as though it were a charm to ward off catastrophe through the *jouissance* the negative sublime provides. The inhuman then becomes fetishized, reified as an idol for acolytes to worship. As frequently beguiling as it is, the negative sublime can become a limit to apprehending certain aspects of the inhuman.

"It" can be valorized in such a way that the reason why it might be salient to invoke the inhuman at this point in time becomes hidden. "It" in thought might operate as *mere* appearance and speculative horror becomes circumscribed and seduced by the jolt of the inhuman. Locked into this, speculative horror would become a charmed (or cursed) circle of its own esoterica.

Abject Slapstick. — It is tempting to invert the transcendence of the negative sublime into the horror immanent to the body, the hilarity of gore. The abject slapstick of cutting your own limb off to rid yourself of the severed and biting but still undead head of a demon, as occurs in *The Evil Dead 2*.

Hack the limb to destroy the head (laughter).

---

9   Eugene Thacker, *The Horror of Philosophy: In the Dust of This Planet, Volume I* (Winchester: Zero Books, 2011), 5.

That overused but useful term "carnivalesque" describes much of the violence in horror cinema, extreme gesture as satirical inversion. The collapse of a certain rationality needs to cut its own limbs, and the human body is less a temple than a receptacle for pain. Rather than the opposite, this is a strange parallel to the sheer terror of knowledge discovered in the cosmic horror experienced by Lovecraft's protagonists. What both share is the unveiling of the insignificance of humanity, the extensive hubris of thinking that humanity can be viewed as central to a universe of screaming, biting heads and/or cosmic indifference (more laughter). Humanity as a *waste* object.

Screaming Winged Ape. — A screaming winged ape or crawling chaotic matter can be just as emblematic as the owl of Minerva at dusk. The crafting and evocation of mood, affect, and concept through the language and imagery of horror is obviously not something to be expelled from thought as though it were an impure addition.

Thought is not only the circumspection of logic, abstract steps, and the feedback loops of reason. Conceptual images are common to thought, as Nietzsche's eternal return or Marx's satire demonstrate. And horror is not only the inevitability of the gap between thought and being. There are other conceptual images within speculative horror and other gaps in the world.

Conflictual Horror. — Might speculative horror provide the conflictual truth of the inhuman in the gap of a certain knowledge? That is, the truth of the inhuman as immanent to capitalism. Generally, "knowledge" would imagine the supposed basis of the "world-for-us" as being founded upon humanity rather than the real and inhuman abstractions that walk among us as commodities, including ourselves, and that constitute "us" through the "it" of capitalist social relations. The inhuman in speculative horror might also, then, be symptomatic of a "real" that bursts through and reveals conflicts and contradictions that ideological knowledge does not acknowledge. A capitalist "real."

Crawling Horizon. — Perhaps, particular forms of the aesthetics of horror emerge into greater visibility at particular times, are illuminated by the structural tendencies that underlie events. Historical trauma often takes weird forms when transmuted into speculative horror. The trauma of the present is capitalism, whether filtered through the banal life of commodities or through climate change. The root of the inhuman, whether abstraction or catastrophic life/death, must also lie nestled in this.

Image Crack. — The cracks in the image of the world can be traced through horror. The world might also break the conceptual image into new fragments, different, less transcendental forms of the inhuman. "It" envelops both the natural and supposedly unnatural, leaving an afterimage of (un)natured dissymmetry.

The Simplicity of a Corpse. — The human can be presented with all of the simplicity of a corpse: internally divided between what Agamben has termed a naked, bare life and subject and cut through with the economic ratio of the value form (Marx).

Further surgical work could be exercised with the mention of unconscious drives as an undoing of the subject (Freud) and the chance and catastrophe of evolution (Darwin). All of this amounts to a definitive displacement of the rational, autonomous human subject as the notional center of the existent, a displacement that has been ongoing, widely acknowledged, and is perhaps primary, the human always already displaced.

So, it goes. The inhuman is not so remarkable in that it surrounds us, and the horror entailed usually labors in the background of life as it is lived, until for some — usually under the duress of class, gender, race — it does not.

The world-not-for-us. — The Thomas Ligotti short story *The Town Manager* is a fable of contemporary capitalism inscribed into horrific allegory. In the events of the story, the new town manager dwells in a ruined hut and communicates in misspelt missives on torn brown paper. Missives such as "GUD […] NXT YUR JBS WULL CHNG" that crumple out of the sky like social media trash talk turned into an occult form of material detritus.[10] The new town manager is as ambient and malign as the capitalist social relation. An abstract, inhuman entity that diffuses through the town it then renames "FUN TOWN," the inhabitants given humiliating service industry roles in newly bizarre neighbourhoods with useless utilities such as a labyrinth of unusable toilets and adult sized play pens. Eventually, "FUN TOWN" is ruined for that most banal inhuman abstraction, the accumulation of money.

Ligotti cannot be claimed for a naïve anti-capitalism. That would run counter to his misanthropy and anti-natalist perspective; life as suffering to the point of desiring death. Yet, in *The Town Manager*, and his other workplace horror fictions, he gestures toward another kind of speculative horror. Rooted in the inhuman while tracing its shapes in the more quotidian forms of the present.

A fable of the *world-not-for-us*.

Horrific Reproduction. — The *world-not-for-us* expresses the gap that exists between much of humanity and the reproduction of the world for the benefit of capitalism. This reproduction of the world also has its double in the way that it is replete with particular forms of horror. This horror of reproduction is consonant with the varied possibilities of a catastrophe of *non-reproduction*, whether on the individual level or through the collapse of socio-economic orders. The dyad of reproduction/non-reproduction is a disjunctive conjunction in that the successful reproduction of one element can scrape away at the reproduction of another, rendering it untenable. "FUN TOWN" ruins its inhabitants.

---

10 Thomas Ligotti, *Teatro Grottesco* (London: Virgin Books, 2008), 31.

Distorted Sublime. — The negative sublime of much contemporary speculative horror undoubtedly refracts some of this horror of (non)reproduction through the distortions of the inhuman. The conflictual truth emerges through dreams of inhuman destruction where everything is erased or where there is, as Reza Negarestani describes it after Lovecraft, a "holocaust of freedom."[11]

Antagonistic Complicity. — Speculative horror has always incorporated this horror of the cyclical, antagonistic complicity between reproduction and non-reproduction. Reliable archetypes of the horror genre such as vampires and zombies are emblematic of the ways that reproduction can merge into its opposite. Marx can claim a similar insight when he writes that "capital is dead labour which, vampire-like, lives only by sucking living labour, and lives the more, the more labour it sucks."[12]

Cult of Cadavers. — Horror is replete with the surplus of destruction, a madness of death, pools of blood uselessly spilled, terror, laughter, corpses, antique occultism, ruins, parasitical zombies, demons, vampires, diseases, deadly materiality revolting against productive use in the most absurd ways. What Georges Bataille termed the heterogeneous, "death and the cult of cadavers," inassimilable to the twin homogeneities of production and systemic philosophy. The evocation of the useless or repugnant does not exist outside of existent capitalist social relations. The heterogeneous is only heterogeneous within a certain system. Waste forms around the *world-not-for-us*.

It Followed Me. — Non-reproduction often takes the form of "it" in speculative horror.

---

[11] Reza Negarestani, "Drafting the Inhuman," in *The Speculative Turn: Continental Materialism and Realism,* eds. Levi Bryant, Graham Harman, and Nick Srnicek (Melbourne: re.press, 2011), 184.
[12] Karl Marx, *Capital,* vol. 1, trans. Samuel Moore and Edward Aveling (Moscow: Progress Publishers, 1965), 163.

The film *It Follows* initially seems to be a fairly standard, if more original, parable about disease, with the traditional horror movie culling of sexually active students thrown in for good measure. *It Follows* revolves around an eponymous "it" that murders those who have sex whether for pleasure or reproduction. The "curse" is mysteriously passed on through having sex. "It," in this case, can only be seen by the prospective victims and is mimetic, adopting the forms of both loved ones and strangers, though always walking with a shuffling gait.

"It" is both embodied and spectral, formless and with a well-defined form, slow violent death in the deracinated suburbs.

Rather than being about disease, *It Follows* could be a parable of the *world-not-for-us,* a parable of non-reproduction. Like capital, "it" drifts through the streets abstractly, reconstituted into whatever flesh might do, ensuring that life cannot go on. An emptied out inhuman form. "It" might well be an emblem of capitalist life as an undead life. A conceptual image of human waste.

"It". — A broken mirror from which might be glimpsed other shapes.

Bibliography

Bataille, Georges. *The Unfinished System of Nonknowledge.* Edited by Stuart Kendall. Translated by Michelle Kendall and Stuart Kendall. Minneapolis: University of Minnesota Press, 2001.

Houellebecq, Michel. *H.P. Lovecraft: Against the World, Against Life.* London: Weidenfeld & Nicolson, 2006.

Kant, Immanuel. *Critique of Judgement.* Translated by Werner S. Pluhar. Indianapolis: Hackett Publishing Company, 1987.

———. *Critique of Practical Reason.* Translated by Lewis White Beck. New York: Palgrave Macmillan, 1956.

Ligotti, Thomas. *Teatro Grottesco.* London: Virgin Books, 2008.

Lovecraft, H.P. "The Call of Cthulhu." *The H.P. Lovecraft Archive,* 1926. http://www.hplovecraft.com/writings/texts/fiction/cc.aspx.

———. "The Shadow Out of Time." *The H.P. Lovecraft Archive,* 1934. https://www.hplovecraft.com/writings/texts/fiction/sot.aspx.

Marx, Karl. *Capital,* Vol. 1. Translated by Samuel Moore and Edward Aveling. Moscow: Progress Publishers, 1965.

Meillassoux, Quentin. *After Finitude: An Essay on the Necessity of Contingency.* Translated by Ray Brassier. London: Continuum, 2008.

Negarestani, Reza. "Drafting the Inhuman." In *The Speculative Turn: Continental Materialism and Realism,* edited by, Levi Bryant, Graham Harman, and Nick Srnicek, 182–901. Melbourne: re.press, 2011.

Thacker, Eugene. *The Horror of Philosophy: In the Dust of This Planet, Volume I.* Winchester: Zero Books, 2011.

13

Horror Uacui
("That Nothing Is What There Is")

Julia Hölzl

[*The following remains a draft, a/s sketch, does not provide answers, nor questions. It is a mere opening toward somewhere else: It is the elsewhere that is of interest here, a/s somewhere or other, but always other; anyway, but never anywhere.*]

I.

> The grounding-attunement of the first beginning is *deep wonder* that beings are, that man himself is extant, extant in that which *he* is *not*. The grounding attunement of the other beginning is *startled dismay*: startled dismay in the abandonment of being [...].
> — Martin Heidegger, *Contributions to Philosophy (From Enowning)*[1]

Oscillating between and before *Er-staunen* (deep wonder), *Er-schrecken* (startled dismay), and *Entsetzen* (freeing dismay), this

---

1   Martin Heidegger, *Contributions to Philosophy (From Enowning)*, trans. Parvis Emad and Kenneth Maly (Bloomington: Indiana University Press, 1999), 32.

essay begins to think, begins by thinking the (non-)relation of being, time, absence, and emptiness via yet another beginning, that is, a/s non-original origin and no/t event.

In this beginning, there is Blanchot's primal scene (*a/s primal scene?*):

> (A primal scene?) *You who live later, close to a heart that beats no more, suppose, suppose this: the child — is he seven years old, or eight perhaps? — standing by the window, drawing the curtain and, through the pane, looking. What he sees: the garden, the wintry trees, the wall of a house. Though he sees, no doubt in a child's way, his play space, he grows weary and slowly looks up toward the ordinary sky, with clouds, grey light — pallid daylight without depth.*
>
> *What happens then: the sky, the* same *sky, suddenly open, absolutelyblack and absolutely empty, revealing (as though the pane had broken) such an absence that all has since always and forevermore been lost therein — so lost that therein is affirmed and dissolved the vertiginous knowledge that nothing is what there is, and first of all nothing beyond. The unexpected aspect of this scene (its interminable feature) is the feeling of happiness that straightaway submerges the child, the ravaging joy to which he can bear witness only by tears, an endless flow of tears. He is thought to suffer a childish sorrow; attempts are made to console him. He says nothing. He will live henceforth in the secret. He will weep no more.*[2]

---

2 Maurice Blanchot, *The Writing of the Disaster*, trans. Ann Smock (Lincoln: University of Nebraska Press, 1995), 72. And this primal scene situates itself of course in relation to Freud: "What is striking is the way in which Freud is animated by a kind of passion for the origin [...]. He thus invites each of us to look back behind ourselves in order to find there the source of every alteration: a primary 'event' that is individual and proper to each history, a scene constituting something important and overwhelming, but also such that the one who experiences it can neither master nor determine it, and with which he has essential relations of insufficiency. On the one hand, it is a matter of going back again to a beginning. [...] It is not a beginning inasmuch as each scene is always ready to open onto a prior scene [...]. It is as though we had access to the various forms of existence only as deprived

Although the term "scene," as Blanchot continues a few pages later, "is ill-chosen, for what it supposedly names is unrepresentable," it "is pertinent in that it allows one at least not to speak as if of an event taking place at a moment in time — A scene: a shadow, a faint gleam, an 'almost' with the characteristics of 'too much.'"[3]

Such an event does not originate, does not eventuate, is no/t event, is no/thing given, but is that which gives. Nothing is given: nothing gives, as we might see.

It is such an almost which makes us wonder — that which gives us to think. What it gives us is this: that nothing is what there is, that such an almost is no(t) beyond — such is not beyond, such is no beyond.

A/s *horror vacui,* (for) such is the horror of beyond. "It is the horror of being where being is without end," as Blanchot writes.[4]

And how, then, to think such an elsewhere, as elsewhere, and always no(t) beyond — an elsewhere to no end; and how to bear such nothing, *nothing beyond,* such absence, such emptiness — *you who live later, close to a heart that beats no more,* how to *affirm and dissolve* this *nothing* that *there is, and first of all nothing beyond?*

But we must, first and foremost, question, call into question, adhere to the question, for it is with/in the answer that "we lose the direct, immediate given, and we lose the opening, the richness of possibility. The answer is the question's misfortune, its

---

of ourselves, and deprived of everything. To be born is, after having had everything, suddenly to lack everything, and first of all being [...]. For the infant, everything is exterior, and he himself is scarcely anything but this exterior: the outside, a radical exteriority without unity, a dispersion without anything dispersing. This absence, which is the absence of nothing, is at first the infant's sole presence. [...] It is always around lack, and through the exigency of this lack, that a presentiment of the infant's history, of what he will be, is formed. But this lack is the 'unconscious': the negation that is not simply a wanting, but a relation to what is wanting — desire." Maurice Blanchot, *The Infinite Conversation,* trans. Susan Hanson (Minneapolis: University of Minnesota Press, 1993), 231–32.

3 Blanchot, *The Writing of the Disaster,* 114, emphasis deleted.
4 Blanchot, *Infinite Conversation,* 120.

adversity."⁵ For "[t]he question places the full affirmation back into the void, and enriches it with this initial void. Through the question we give ourselves the thing and we give ourselves the void that permits us not to have it yet, or to have it as desire. The question is the desire of thought."⁶

And how to think such thought, and from where to affirm its void — perhaps such thinking is to be asked from within the "most profound question," as an earlier Blanchot had named it,

> a question that the question of the whole (dialectical accomplishment), the question that bears everything, does not include. [...] The One, the Same, remain the first and the last words. Why this reference to the One as the ultimate and unique reference? In this sense, the dialectic, ontology, and the critique of ontology have the same postulate: all three deliver themselves over to the One: be it that the One accomplishes itself as everything, be it that it understands being as gathering, light, and unity of being, or be it that, above and beyond being, it affirms itself as the Absolute. With regard to such affirmations, must we not say: "the most profound question" is the question that escapes reference to the One? It is the other question, the question of the Other, but also a question that is always other.⁷

And still, from where are we to ask such a question? From and within absence, a/s moment of presence: such moment might be the instant of affirmation, such moment might be its site of dis-solution.

II.

> Only because the nothing is manifest in the ground of Dasein can the total strangeness of beings overwhelm us. Only when

---

5   Ibid., 13.
6   Ibid., 12.
7   Ibid., 439–40n3.

> the strangeness of beings oppresses us does it arouse and evoke wonder. Only on the ground of wonder — the revelation of the nothing — does the "why?" loom before us. Only because the "why" is possible as such can we in a definite way inquire into grounds, and ground them. […] The question of the nothing puts us, the questioners, in question. It is a metaphysical question.
> — Martin Heidegger, "What Is Metaphysics?"[8]

That nothing is what there is, and first of all nothing beyond, that such nothing *is* (a/s nothing, and first of all nothing beyond); that such nothing might be elsewhere, outside of absence, outside of presence, that it would not situate itself in an and as event, never, but in and as a scene, a/s scenery toward this elsewhere where nothing is revealed. Its mode of presence would be absence, and vice versa.

Following Heidegger, "we shall find in absence — be it what has been or what is to come — a manner of presencing and approaching which by no means coincides with presencing in the sense of the immediate present. Accordingly, we must note: Not every presencing is necessarily the present. A curious matter. But we find such presencing, the approaching that reaches us, in the present, too."[9]

But where does such matter lead us, where is that nothing that there is, where does it reside — what is such nothing, and why to ask this primal question? Why grant nothing a being, why not grant nothing nothing itself?

"The nothing is neither an object nor any being at all," Heidegger reminds us;[10] rather, we ought to re-turn to "the basic question of metaphysics which the nothing itself compels: 'Why are there beings at all, and why not rather nothing?'"[11] A few

---

8   Martin Heidegger, "What Is Metaphysics?" Basic text of Heidegger's inaugural lecture at the University of Freiburg, Freiburg, Germany, 1929, §52.
9   Martin Heidegger, "Time and Being," in *On Time and Being*, trans. Joan Stambaugh (New York: Harper & Row, 1972), 13.
10 Heidegger, *What Is Metaphysics?*, §35.
11 Ibid., §54.

years later, Heidegger would begin his *Introduction to Metaphysics* by asking "Why are there essents rather than nothing?," this "obviously" being "the first of all questions, though not in a chronological sense." [12] This very "question takes in everything, and this means not only everything that is present in the broadest sense but also everything that ever was or will be. The range of this question finds its limit only in nothing, in that which simply is not and never was. Everything that is not nothing is covered by this question, and ultimately even nothing itself; not because it is *something*, since after all we speak of it, but because it *is* nothing. Our question reaches out so far that we can never go further."[13]

But it is not from here where we must move to, toward the void, *absolutely empty,* toward this "nothing is" that there is — and even Heidegger contends — "when we wish to apprehend being, it is always as though we were reaching into the void. The being after which we inquire is almost like nothing, and yet we have always rejected the contention that the essent in its entirety *is not.* But being remains unfindable, almost like nothing, or ultimately *quite* so. Then, in the end, the word 'being' is no more than an empty word. It means nothing real, tangible, material. Its meaning is an unreal vapor."[14]

The emptiness of being ("Can it now surprise us that 'being' should be so empty a word when the very word form is based on an emptying and an apparent stabilization of emptiness?"[15]) reveals its mode of presence, its mode of absence, and we remember, *not every presencing is necessarily the present* — but *such an absence that all has since always and forevermore been lost therein.*

Such a mode of presencing, in turn, reveals the mode of emptiness: in presence and absence, and above all outside both. Emptiness is no/t nothing but might be a silent echo of being.

---

12 Martin Heidegger, *An Introduction to Metaphysics,* trans. Ralph Manheim (New Haven: Yale University Press, 1959), 1.
13 Ibid., 2.
14 Ibid., 35–36.
15 Ibid., 69.

> We take emptiness for "nothingness" in the sense of mere absence of beings and do not experience the reverberation of the still invisible bridge that refers new shores to new shores.[16]

And what does it mean, "to think nothing *as* nothing"? Would such thinking allow for (a) nothing outside the nothing? For Heidegger, "the nothing is nothing, and, if the nothing represents total indistinguishability, no distinction can obtain between the imagined and the 'genuine' nothing. And the 'genuine' nothing itself — isn't this that camouflaged but absurd concept of a nothing that is? For the last time now the objections of the intellect would call a halt to our search, whose legitimacy, however, can be demonstrated only on the basis of a fundamental experience of the nothing."[17]

What does it, then, mean to think nothing — as nothing? Would such thinking lead us to a thinking of being, a thinking from wherein such question can be asked — would it not be from here that being is (to be) thought, that being exists? "Only on the ground of the original revelation of the nothing can human existence approach and penetrate beings. But since existence in its essence relates itself to beings — those which it is not and that which it is — it emerges as such existence in each case from the nothing already revealed. Dasein means: being held out into the nothing."[18]

Nothing *is*. And while for Heidegger "such an attunement, in which man is brought before the nothing itself [...] can and does occur, although rarely enough and only for a moment, in the fundamental mood of anxiety,"[19] that is, "[t]he nothing reveals itself in anxiety — but not as a being," [20] he concludes by questioning: "If Dasein can relate itself to beings only by hold-

---

16 Martin Heidegger, *Mindfulness,* trans. Parvis Emad and Thomas Kalary (New York: Continuum, 2006), 217.
17 Heidegger, *What Is Metaphysics?*, §17.
18 Ibid., §33.
19 Ibid., §21.
20 Ibid., §28.

ing itself out into the nothing and can exist only thus; and if the nothing is originally disclosed only in anxiety; then must we not hover in this anxiety constantly in order to be able to exist at all?"[21]

It is this "being held out into the nothing" that "makes man a place-holder of the nothing. [...] Being held out into the nothing — as Dasein is — on the ground of concealed anxiety is its surpassing of beings as a whole. It is transcendence.[22]

This transcendence points us somewhere else, points us outside such a beyond, points us toward a different attunement, perhaps; beyond transcendence — outside such a beyond — we find an elsewhere — everywhere but nowhere: "Profound boredom, drifting here and there in the abysses of our existence like a muffling fog, removes all things and men and oneself along with it into a remarkable indifference. This boredom reveals beings as a whole."[23]

Boredom, indifferent, always unknown, does not uncover but reveals. It reveals the abyss that Dasein is.

Boredom reveals our fear of the void, and it is for this reason, perhaps, that we must meet it with and by *Gelassenheit*:

> This is what we must first learn: not to resist straightaway but to let resonate. Yet how are we to make room for this initially inessential, ungraspable boredom? Only by not being opposed to it, but letting it approach us and tell us what it wants, what is going on with it. Yet even to do this, it is necessary in the first place that we remove from indeterminacy whatever we thus name and apparently know as boredom. We must do this, however, not in the sense of dissecting some psychological experience, but in such a way that we thereby approach ourselves. Whom? Ourselves — ourselves as a Da-sein. (Ambiguity!)[24]

---

21 Ibid., §36.
22 Ibid., §43.
23 Ibid., §18.
24 Martin Heidegger, *The Fundamental Concepts of Metaphysics: World, Finitude, Solitude,* trans. William McNeill and Nicholas Walker (Bloomington:

Such *Langeweile* (boredom) designates the mood from within which we face the horror of being: boredom opens us to that nothing that there is. *Langeweile* is nothing but the *knowledge that nothing is what there is, and first of all nothing beyond.*

Boredom thus not only reveals the fundamental concepts of metaphysics, world, finitude, and solitude,[25] but is much more fundamental/ist in that it points toward an essence "beyond" essentialism.

Being our time, boredom reveals the essence of nothingness, emptiness, presence, and absence — *an absence that all has since always and forevermore been lost therein — so lost that therein is affirmed and dissolved the vertiginous knowledge that nothing is what there is, and first of all nothing beyond.*

For the time being, "[b]oredom, *Langeweile* — whatever its ultimate essence may be — shows, particularly in our German word, an almost obvious *relation to time,* a way in which we stand with respect to time, a feeling of time. Boredom and the question of boredom thus lead us to the problem of time." [26]

The time of boredom. Boredom gives being its time: "boredom is only possible at all because each thing, as we say, has *its* time. If each thing did not have *its* time, then there would be no boredom."[27]

The time of boredom. Time is given by boredom: "Time for its part stands in a relation of boredom to *us*."[28]

It is thus through and by boredom that time is revealed, and yet, while "[w]e are increasingly tempted to pose the whole problem of boredom simply in terms of the problem of time," "we ought not to give in to this temptation [...]. We must stick with boredom, so that *precisely through its essence we may take a look into the concealed essence of time* and thereby into the connection between the two."[29]

Indiana University Press, 1995), 82.
25 As Heidegger attempts in the eponymous book.
26 Heidegger, *The Fundamental Concepts of Metaphysics,* 80.
27 Ibid., 105.
28 Ibid., 81.
29 Ibid., 99.

It is thus from within boredom and, at the same time, by boredom that we might be able to touch, that we might be able to bear "our horror of emptiness,"[30] for it is here, in and through this long while, that we might be able to encounter, to affirm, to dissolve the "empty intimacy of time."[31]

Such is the time *Langeweile* gives us.

III.

> *We're not bored. — We're not capable of it.*
> — Maurice Blanchot, *The Step Not Beyond*[32]

What does it mean: to be bored?

What does it mean: to be capable of being bored?

What does it mean: to be able to be bored, to bear this nothing that there is?

As is well known, it is in *The Fundamental Concepts of Metaphysics: World, Finitude, Solitude* (1929/30), that Heidegger explores in depth, but not for the first time, this *Grundstimmung*, and where he famously distinguishes three forms of boredom: "Becoming Bored by Something," "Being Bored with Something and the Passing of Time Belonging to It," and the last, deepest one, "Profound Boredom as 'It Is Boring for One.'"

And while, as he writes of and for the first form of boredom, "time has become altogether enigmatic for us," while "[b]ecoming bored and boredom in general are then evidently entirely rooted in this enigmatic essence of time,"[33] the relation of this *muffling fog* to being remains nebulous.

As insinuated above, *Langeweile* gives us (to) time, but what is given by *Langeweile*?

---

30 Blanchot, *Infinite Conversation*, 121.
31 Ibid.
32 Maurice Blanchot, *The Step Not Beyond*, trans. Lycette Nelson (New York: State University of New York Press, 1992), 20.
33 Heidegger, *The Fundamental Concepts of Metaphysics*, 98.

It is the *"being left empty* that is emerging in boredom"[34] that scares us; but "this being left empty cannot mean that in boredom we are transformed in such a way that all things disappear entirely, as it were, so that nothing remains before us or around us. [...] For how can we become bored by *something,* i.e., be left empty by *something,* if nothing at all is at hand? [...] To leave empty does not at all mean: to be absent, not to be present at hand; rather things must be at hand in order to leave us empty."[35]

Outside presence, outside absence, this is where being is in time, this is when being is given.

It is from the analysis of the third form of boredom, Heidegger affirms, that

> we can *give the word boredom, 'Langeweile,' a more essential meaning.* In boredom, *Langeweile,* the *while* [Weile] becomes *long* [lang]. Which while? Any short while? No, but rather that while whilst Dasein is as such, the while that measures out that tarrying awhile [*Verweilen*] which is allotted to Dasein as such, i.e., the while whilst it is to be in the midst of these beings, in confrontation with them and thus with itself. It is this whole while — and yet a short while; and so every Dasein in turn is a short while. [...] With this time what is at issue is not the time of the clock or chronology, but the *lengthening* or *shortening* of *time proper.*[36]

Again, boredom points us to time, time proper, the enigma of time, which reveals the *nothing that there is,* and not least because of this "we cannot possibly treat boredom as an object of

---

34　Ibid., 101.
35　Ibid., 102.
36　Ibid., 152, emphasis in the original. And he summarizes his analysis of profound boredom as follows: "*Boredom is the entrancement of the temporal horizon, an entrancement which lets the moment of vision belonging to temporality vanish. In thus letting it vanish, boredom impels entranced Dasein into the moment of vision as the properly authentic possibility of its existence, an existence only possible in the midst of beings as a whole, and within the horizon of entrancement, their telling refusal of themselves as a whole.*" (Ibid., 153).

psychology. And that is precisely why we cannot draw conclusions with regard to man as a whole from such an object of psychology. We do not even need to draw such conclusions, given that this attunement brings us to ourselves in a far more fundamental and essential way. In attunement we are in such and such a manner. And profound boredom shows us what that means. The Dasein in us manifests itself."[37]

In boredom, Dasein dis-closes itself.

The "essential moments of profound boredom," namely "*being left empty* and *being held in limbo* in the specific concrete form of *our* boredom, *being entranced* and *being drawn into the moment of vision*," "showed us how the utter abyss of Dasein in the midst of Dasein discloses itself in this attunement."[38]

Langeweile points beyond beyond. It points to the abyss of Dasein. It points us to *nothing beyond*. It is in and through *Langeweile* that we might be able to bear *that nothing is what there is*. And it might be within and from another *Stimmung* that boredom reveals, that boredom is revealed:

> Attention waits. It waits without precipitation, leaving empty what is empty and keeping our haste, our impatient desire, and, even more, our horror of emptiness from prematurely filling it in. Attention is the emptiness of thought oriented by a gentle force and maintained in an accord with the empty intimacy of time.[39]

Such thought is to be spoken from a language that does not aim to unveil but that reveals, a Blanchotian "speech such that to speak would no longer be to unveil with light. Which does not imply that we would want to go in search of the joy, or the horror, of the absence of the day: just the contrary; we would want to arrive at a mode of 'manifestation,' but a manifestation that would not be one of unveiling-veiling. Here what reveals

---

37 Ibid., 283.
38 Ibid.
39 Blanchot, *Infinite Conversation*, 121.

itself does not give itself up to sight, just as it does not take refuge in simple invisibility. — This word reveal, I fear, is not quite suitable. To reveal, to remove the veil, to expose directly to view. — Revealing implies, in fact, that something shows that did not show itself. Speech (at least the one we are attempting to approach: writing) lays bare even without unveiling, and sometimes, on the contrary (dangerously), by revealing in a way that neither covers nor uncovers."[40]

— revealing (as though the pane had broken) such an absence that all has since always and forevermore been lost therein —

To reveal, then, is to *affirm and dissolve* this nothing that there is, *and first of all nothing beyond.*
And this is why, following Blanchot, "the ultimate conclusion should be: one must dwell in ignorance, in illusion, and lose oneself in incomprehensible affliction. Certitude, become once again inaccessible and nearly confounded with the emptiness of the sky, might, on this basis, recover its 'reality.'" [41]
Its reality: *the sky,* the same *sky, suddenly open, absolutely black and absolutely empty.*

---

40 Ibid., 29–30.
41 Ibid., 118.

Bibliography

Blanchot, Maurice. *The Step Not Beyond.* Translated by Lycette Nelson. New York: State University of New York Press, 1992.
———. *The Infinite Conversation.* Translated by Susan Hanson. Minneapolis: University of Minnesota Press, 1993.
———. *The Writing of the Disaster.* Translated by Ann Smock. Lincoln: University of Nebraska Press, 1995.
Heidegger, Martin. *An Introduction to Metaphysics.* Translated by Ralph Manheim. New Haven: Yale University Press, 1959.
———. *Contributions to Philosophy (From Enowning).* Translated by Parvis Emad and Kenneth Maly. Bloomington: Indiana University Press, 1999.
———. *Mindfulness.* Translated by Parvis Emad and Thomas Kalary. New York: Continuum, 2006.
———. *The Fundamental Concepts of Metaphysics: World, Finitude, Solitude.* Translated by William McNeill and Nicholas Walker. Bloomington: Indiana University Press, 1995.
———. "Time and Being." In *On Time and Being,* translated by Joan Stambaugh, 1–24. New York: Harper & Row, 1972.
———. "What Is Metaphysics?" Basic text of Heidegger's inaugural lecture at the University of Freiburg, Freiburg, Germany, 1929. http://www.naturalthinker.net/trl/texts/Heidegger,Martin/Heidegger.Martin..What%20Is%20Metaphysics.htm.

Contributors

Hamad Al-Rayes holds a PhD in Philosophy from Stony Brook University and currently teaches philosophy to schoolchildren through Loyola University New Orleans' Philosopher Kids program, where he is also developing a series of philosophy picture-books for children. His current research focuses on the relationship between aesthetics and metaphysics, particularly as it informs the development of modern Arabic poetry. Whenever he has the time, Hamad writes fiction and Arabic poetry. You can find out more and get in touch by visiting https://hamadalrayes.com.

Amanda Beech is an artist and writer living in Los Angeles. Using a range of compelling rhetorical and often dogmatic narratives and texts, Beech's artwork poses questions and propositions for what a realist art can be in today's culture; that is, a work that can articulate a comprehension of reality without the terminal mirror of a human identity that is used to picture it. Beech has shown her artwork and presented her writing at major international venues including: *This Time,* a video commission for the Remai Modern, Canada 2017, *Covenant Transport Move or Die* at The Baltic Center for Contemporary Art 2016, and *Sanity Assassin,* in Neocentric, at Charim Gallery, Vienna, Austria 2016. Other recent work includes her comic strip "Realism and Its Discontents," *Art Margins* 7, no. 1 (February 2018), as well as critical essays for the anthologies *Realism, Materialism, Art* (Sternberg Press, 2015), *Speculative Aesthetics* (Urbanomic, 2015), and catalogue essays for the Irish and Montréal Biennales *Agitationism* and *L'Avenir* (both 2014). She is Dean of Critical Studies, California Institute of the Arts.

Luka Bekavac is Assistant Professor at the Department of Comparative Literature, Faculty of Humanities and Social Sciences, University of Zagreb. His PhD thesis, *Toward Singularity: Derrida and Literary Text*, was published in Croatian in 2015. He is currently working on a book on xenography in contemporary horror fiction (Ligotti, Negarestani, Danielewski).

Chloé Germaine Buckley is a Senior Lecturer at Manchester Metropolitan University. Her publications include *Twenty-First Century Children's Gothic Fiction: From Wanderer to Nomadic Subject* (Edinburgh University Press, 2019), *Telling It Slant: Critical Approaches to Helen Oyeyemi* (Sussex Academic Press, 2020, co-edited with Sarah Ilott), and various articles on different aspects of the gothic. She is a member of the Manchester Centre for Gothic Studies and The Manchester Game Studies Network.

John Cunningham is a writer and researcher based in London. He has worked with *Mute Magazine* as well as other journals, was an editor for the book *Anguish Language: Writing and Crisis* (Archive Books, 2016), and has contributed to other books including *Communization and Its Discontents: Contestation, Critique, and Contemporary Struggles* (Autonomedia, 2011), *On Violence* (Ma Bibliothèque, 2018), and *The Graveside Orations of Carl Einstein* (Ma Bibliothèque, 2019).

Marina Gržinić is a philosopher, theoretician, and artist from Ljubljana, Slovenia. She serves as a professor and research adviser. She works as a researcher at the Institute of Philosophy ZRC SAZU, Ljubljana. Since 2003, she is Professor for Post-Conceptual Art Practices at the Academy of Fine Arts in Vienna,

Austria. She leads the FWF-funded research project "Genealogy of Amnesia" (2018–2021). She publishes extensively, lectures worldwide, and has been involved in video film productions since 1982.

Julia Hölzl holds a PhD in Modern Thought from the University of Aberdeen as well as a PhD in Media and Communications from the European Graduate School, where she is also a Fellow. An independent theorist, "thesis therapist," lecturer, and editor, her work tends to revolve around finitude, transience, and ending/s. Latest publications include "A(s) Step Not Beyond: Blanchot's Écriture Fragmentaire," *Belgrade Journal of Media and Communications* (in print), *On Ending(s)* (Singapore: Delere Press; forthcoming, with Jennifer Hope Davy and Allison Grimaldi-Donahue), and "'A Scandal for Thought': Le neutre" *FKW // Zeitschrift für Geschlechterforschung und visuelle Kultur* 63 (2017).

Eckardt Lindner is a philosopher based in Vienna. He teaches at the University of Vienna, where he is currently completing his PhD on the concept of inorganic life. His philosophical and artistic works are mainly concerned with the history and philosophy of artificial and inorganic life, contemporary (neo-)vitalism and nihilism, as well as the relation between philosophy and non-philosophy.

Helen Marshall is a Senior Lecturer of Creative Writing and Publishing at the University of Queensland. Her first collection of fiction, *Hair Side, Flesh Side* (ChiZine, 2012), which won the Sydney J. Bounds Award in 2013, emerged from her work as a book historian. Her second collection, *Gifts for the One Who Comes After* (ChiZine, 2019), won the World Fantasy Award and the Shirley Jackson Award in 2015. Her debut novel, *The Migration*, was released from Random House Canada and Titan in 2019.

David Peak is the author of *Corpsepaint* (Word Horde, 2018) and *The Spectacle of the Void* (Schism, 2014). He lives in Chicago.

Jovita Pristovšek is a senior lecturer at the Academy of Visual Arts (AVA) Ljubljana, Slovenia, where she teaches practice and theory. She holds an MFA from the Academy of Fine Arts, Ljubljana, and a Ph.D. in philosophy from the Postgraduate School SRC SAZA, Ljubljana, which she completed in 2017 under the supervision of Marina Gržinić Mauhler. Pristovšek's theoretical work focuses on philosophy, aesthetics, theories of contemporary art, epistemology, decolonial theory, and the relationship between the regimes of aesthetics, public and political.

Sara Rich is Assistant Professor of Honors and Interdisciplinary Studies at Coastal Carolina University. Her latest book, *Shipwreck Hauntography: Underwater Ruins and the Uncanny*, is forthcoming from Amsterdam University Press.

Matt Rosen is a metaphysician whose current research focuses on hospitality and perception in moral life; philosophy and literature; and time, death, and chance. Rosen is the author of *Speculative Annihilationism: The Intersection of Archaeology and Extinction* (Zero Books, 2019) and the editor of *Diseases of the Head* (punctum books, 2020). His manuscript, *Speculative Ethics: An Essay on Angst and Abnegation,* has been completed and is forthcoming. He is a Member of New College, Oxford.

Eric Wilson is senior lecturer of public law at Monash University, Melbourne in Australia. He received a Doctorate in History from Cambridge University in 1991 and a Doctorate of Juridical Science from the University of Melbourne in 2005. His publications include *The Savage Republic: De Indis of Hugo Grotius, Republicanism, and Dutch Hegemony in the Early Modern World System (c.1600–1619)* (Martinus Nijhoff, 2008). He is currently editing a series of volumes on critical criminology devoted to the relationships between covert government agency, organized crime, and extra-judicial forms of governance; the first volume in the series, *Government of the Shadows: Parapolitics and Criminal Sovereignty,* was published by Pluto Press in 2009. The second volume, *The Dual State: Parapolitics, Carl Schmitt, and the National Security Complex,* was released by Ashgate Publishing in November 2012. Another volume on parapolitics, *The Spectacle of the False Flag: From JFK to Watergate* was published by punctum books in 2015. His most recent monograph is *The Republic of Cthulhu: Lovecraft, the Weird Tale, and Conspiracy Theory* (punctum books, 2016). His research interests are radical criminology, critical jurisprudence and the application of the work of René Girard to Law and Literature.

Ben Woodard is a post-doctoral researcher at the Institute for Philosophy and Art Theory (IPK) at Leuphana University in Luneburg, Germany. His research focuses on the relationship between naturalism and idealism, especially during the long 19th century. His monograph *Schelling's Naturalism* was recently published by Edinburgh University Press.

www.ingramcontent.com/pod-product-compliance
Lightning Source LLC
Chambersburg PA
CBHW052040220426
43663CB00012B/2386